The Australian
Bed & Breakfast
Book 2003

HOMESTAYS • FARMSTAYS • B&B INNS
• SELF CONTAINED ACCOMMODATION •

Prepared by *Inn Australia*, Brooklyn, New South Wales, Australia

Edited by Carl Southern

Printed in Hong Kong through Bookbuilders

Published by Moonshine Press under licence to *Inn Australia Pty Ltd*
PO Box 1, Brooklyn, New South Wales 2083, Australia.
ABN 38 088 031 109

Cover Photo: Murray House, Echuca

Every effort has been made to ensure that the information in this book is as up to date as possible at the time of going to press. All listing information has been supplied by the hosts. The publishers do not accept responsibility arising from reliance on any contents in the book.

We welcome any feedback, corrections, comments or suggestions for the next edition. You may write to:
The Editor: *The Australian Bed & Breakfast Book*
PO Box 1 Brooklyn, NSW 2083, Australia.

info@bbbook.com.au

ISBN   0-9582149-8-0

Contents

Introduction

Welcome to the 15th edition of *The Australian Bed & Breakfast Book*, the most comprehensive guide to bed and breakfast accommodation in Australia. Inside you will find a wide selection of B & Bs across the continent and in every state from Broome on the spectacular north-west coast of Western Australia to Daintree in the Tropical Rainforest of Northern Queensland and Port Arthur in the historical south coast of Tasmania.

An Australian Experience
The popularity of B & B in Australia has increased each year since we first published *The Australian Bed & Breakfast Book* in 1989. The amazing growth is not only a reflection of changing travel and vacation trends but a response by Australian hosts to open their homes and share their experiences with travellers. Bed & breakfast in Australia means a warm welcome and a unique holiday experience. Most B & B accommodation is in private homes with a sprinkling of guesthouses and small or boutique hotels. A recent trend is the purpose-built B & B or a renovated and refurbished historic home. Each listing in the guide has been written by the host themselves and you will discover their warmth and personality through their writing. *The Australian Bed & Breakfast Book* is not simply a accommodation guide but an introduction to a uniquely Australian holiday experience.

Our definition of Hospitality
Hospitality is defined in the Oxford Dictionary as 'the friendly and generous welcome of friends or strangers', and it is this definition with the emphasis on friendliness and generosity, which we have adopted. Hosts in *The Australian Bed & Breakfast Book* have the justified reputation of being generous with their time, energy and resources.

Great Value
The best holidays are often remembered by the friends one makes. How many of us have loved a country because of one or two memorable individuals we have encountered there? Bed and breakfast offers travellers a special service, quite different to that found in hotels with the opportunity to expereince the real Australia and get to know the people first-hand. You will find Australian hosts generous in their hospitality and offering great value accommodation whether in a simple and welcoming city homestay or on a thousand-acre working cattle station. Quite a few hosts will provide additional services such as an evening meal given sufficient advance notice.

Using *The Australian Bed & Breakfast Book*
B & Bs in each state are listed alphabetically by location, and each is shown on the state or territory map. The index at the back of the book lists all B & Bs by their name. The distance between B & Bs is sometimes quite significant, so we suggest you check travelling times with hosts when you phone ahead to make a reservation.

Styles of Accommodation
Traditional B & B: generally small owner-occupied home accommodation usually with private guest living and dining areas.

Homestay: similar to a traditional B & B where guests may share living and dining areas with their hosts.

Farmstay: country accommodation, usually on a working farm.

Self-contained: separate self-contained accommodation, with kitchen and living/dining room. Breakfast provisions usually provided at least for the first night.

Separate/suite: similar to self-contained but without kitchen facilities. Living/dining facilities may be limited.

Tariffs

B & Bs offer good value accommodation, and room rates cover a broad range reflecting the quality of the accommodation as well as the facilities offered. Tariffs are listed in Australian dollars and where applicable are usually inclusive of a 10% Goods and Service Tax (GST). Rates are subject to change and should always be confirmed with your hosts when booking. Most B & Bs have single occupancy rates as well as for double (one large bed) or twin share (two beds in a room). A few B & Bs have facilities for children or a third adult sharing the same room at an extra cost. Most B & Bs will accept credit cards. Be sure to confirm with your host.

Breakfast

Breakfast is one of the pleasures of a good B&B. Options available include
Continental: cereal, fruit, toast, juice, tea and coffee.
Full: a continental breakfast plus a cooked course.
Special: a wide selection of courses or dishes which are a special treat.

Bathrooms

Most B & Bs offer *ensuite* or *private* bathrooms, which are for your use exclusively. *Share bathroom* means you may share with the hosts or other guests.

Star Ratings and Logos

Properties bearing the stars symbol eg, ★★★ (the "STARS") are independently assessed by AAA Tourism, the national body of the Australian motoring organisations. The STARS are trademarks of AAA Tourism Pty Ltd.

 Accredited Tourism Business

 Independent Access: Accessible to a wheelchair usre travelling independently.

 Access with assistance: Accessible to a wheelchair usre travelling with assistance.

 Access with a maximum of 3 steps.

Smoking

Most of our B&Bs are non-smoking, but smoking is permitted outside. Listings displaying the no smoking logo do not permit smoking anywhere on the property. B & Bs which have a smoking area inside mention this in their text.

Reservations

We recommend you contact your hosts well in advance to be sure of confirming your accommodation. Most hosts require a deposit so make sure you understand their cancellation policy. You may also book accommodation through some travel agents or via specialised B & B reservation services.

Checking In

B & Bs are not rigorous with check-in and check-out times but if guests are leaving the day you arrive you will understand why check-in or check-out times are necessary. Check-in times vary but usually it is around 2.00–3.00 in the afternoon with check-out around 10.00–11.00 in the morning.

'The difference between a hotel and a B&B is that you don't hug the hotel staff when you leave.'

Happy travelling

Carl Southern & Jim Thomas
Moonshine Press

Bed & Breakfast Reservation Services

It's the easy way to book your stay

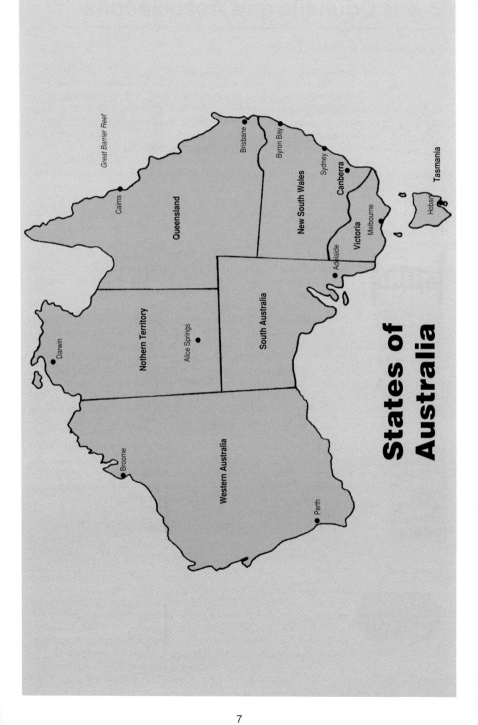

States of
Australia

Great Barrier Reef

Brisbane
Byron Bay
Sydney
Canberra
New South Wales
Cairns
Queensland
Victoria
Melbourne
Adelaide
Tasmania
Hobart

Darwin
Nothern Territory
Alice Springs
South Australia

Broome
Western Australia
Perth

B & B Councils and Associations

The Australian Bed & Breakfast Council

The Australian Bed & Breakfast Council (ABBC) supports the 2003 edition of *The Australian Bed & Breakfast Book* and recommends that when making your bookings you stay in a property which is part of the ABBC network. The Australian Bed and Breakfast Council is made up of the leading State and Territory B&B associations throughout Australia. The Council has a code of standards, which is supported by each of the eight B & B associations. By choosing to stay in a property, which is a member of one of these associations you know you will be staying in a B & B, which has been assessed and then accepted to a nationally recognised organisation. Whether you are travelling for business or pleasure the Australian Bed and Breakfast Council wishes you a truly enjoyable time.

B & B Council of New South Wales

Bed & Breakfast Council of NSW

Bed & Breakfast accommodation is well established in Europe and North America as a way of travelling and seeing the country in which you are visiting. It enables a 'view' of the travellers' world that is not available from big city hotels are even the larger country hotels and motels. Each Bed & Breakfast accommodation is, almost by definition, unique. Each has its own particular interest and point of attraction to guests and each offers its own unique 'spin' on the locality in which it is situated. This is so whether the B&B is located in one of our many fabulous cities, or whether it is in rural Australia on a substantial working farm, in an out of the way rural township, or village, or by the Pacific Ocean. What we do have in common is the traditional B&B warm welcome and our friendly and understanding hospitality not to mention some of the most fabulous breakfasts you could wish for. The B&B Council of NSW represents a growing number of B&Bs throughout the state with more than 275 B&Bs in city and country locations.

Northern Territory B & B Council

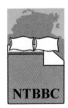

The Northern Territory Bed and Breakfast Council has been established since 1998. Although a small group of only around 20 members, the majority of B & B operators in the NT have joined the association. Territory travellers can choose a variety of B & B accommodation from the Top End (Darwin and rural area), Katherine region and the Centre (Alice Springs). The NTBBC has a commitment to providing quality, hosted accommodation to Territory visitors, and to ensuring that all its members comply with the required regulations and standards. NTBBC, PO Box 41610, Casuarina, 0811.

Queensland B & B Association

The Queensland Bed and Breakfast Association Inc. is a member-based organisation recognised by Tourism Queensland as the peak industry body in the State. We have members state-wide who delight in offering warm hospitality and friendly service. Also rest assured that before being accepted as a member of the QBBA, they are required to meet certain criteria, amongst which is an Approval to Operate from their local council, where applicable, and a willingness to abide by a Code of Conduct. Enjoy your visit to our wonderful state and your B&B accommodation experience. QBBA, PO Box 1242, Capalaba, Qld 4157, email: qbba@bigpond.com.au.

B & B and Farmstay Association of Far North Queensland

A warm welcome awaits you from the members of the B&B and Farmstay Association of Far North Queensland. Our friendly hosts are eager to give special attention to those little details that make your stay extraordinary throughout the Tropical North Queensland region, home to the Great Barrier Reef, World Heritage Rainforests and the Tropical Tablelands. We provide a wide range of accommodation options - from a quiet romantic retreat to a farm holiday with the kids. You will make friends with hosts and fellow travellers as you discover the beauty of Tropical North Queensland. Tel: (07) 40977022. Email: info@bnbnq.com.au.

South Australia B & B and Town & Country Association

The South Australian Bed & Breakfast Association has been promoting quality accommodation in South Australia for 15 years, providing warm hospitality and a very special and often unique holiday experience. The Association began in 1986 with only 20 members; today the Association represents over 200 members offering up to 400 units of accommodation covering all the tourism regions within our state. Destinations and venues may change, but the reception at a South Australian B&B will always be the same ... warm, friendly and welcoming. Tel: (08) 8342 1033. fax: (08) 8342 2033. Email: contact@sabnb.org.au   Website: www.sabnb.org.au

Bed & Breakfast and Boutique Accommodation of Tasmania

"The most comprehensive collection of Tasmania's fine accommodation"

Bed & Breakfast and Boutique Accommodation of Tasmania is a extensive collection of over one hundred bed & breakfast properties from all across Tasmania rated at between three and five stars in standard. They include historical cottages, quaint town houses, large country mansions, penthouse style suites and traditional homely bed & breakfasts. All the properties provide a memorable breakfast and many are in stunning locations. They all offer superb value and a truly memorable stay. If you're staying B&B in Tasmania make sure you choose Bed & Breakfast and Boutique Accommodation of Tasmania.

Bed & Breakfast Council of Victoria

The Bed and Breakfast Council of Victoria is an association of active bed and breakfast operators and businesses relating to the bed and breakfast industry. Launched in 1996, the BBCV provides leadership, advice, membership benefits, marketing services and networking opportunities to its members and actively fosters the growth and professional development of the bed and breakfast industry in Victoria. Recognised by government and the tourism industry as the sector's peak representative body, the BBCV aims to assist B&B operators in their interactions with guests, tourism partners and governments. www.bandbvictoria.com.au

The Western Australia Bed & Breakfast Association

The Western Australia Bed & Breakfast Association (WABBA) represents members who are owners/managers of a varied selection of Bed & Breakfasts (B & Bs) throughout WA. Bed & Breakfast accommodation comes in varying styles, some in private homes, country retreats, or self-contained apartments and cottages. Whatever the style, very high standards and quality are expected of WABBA members. B & B operators are keen to offer their hospitality and properties to travellers who are seeking out accommodation that's "more than just a place to stay".   For more information e-mail: admin@wabnbs.com.au

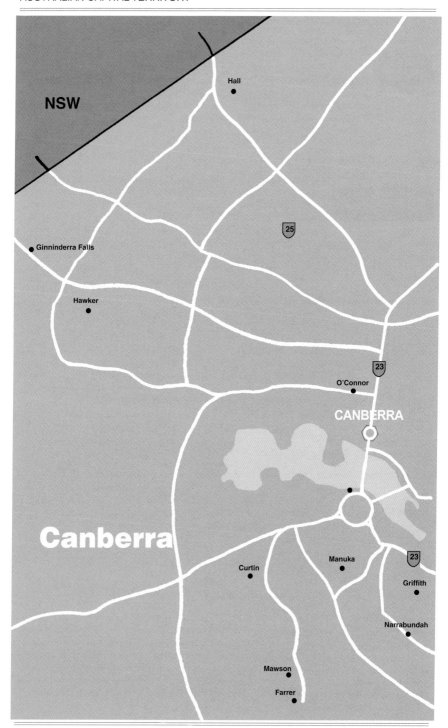

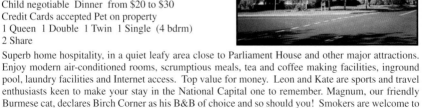

Canberra - Curtin   *Homestay B & B   6 km S of Canberra City*

Birch Corner AAATourism ★★★☆
Leon and Kate Norgate
31 Parker Street, Curtin, ACT 2605

Tel: (02) 6281 4421 Fax: (02) 6260 4641
info@birchbb.com   www.birchbb.com
Double $95-$100 Single $65-$70 (Full Breakfast)
Child negotiable Dinner from $20 to $30
Credit Cards accepted Pet on property
1 Queen 1 Double 1 Twin 1 Single (4 bdrm)
2 Share

A.C.T.

Superb home hospitality, in a quiet leafy area close to Parliament House and other major attractions. Enjoy modern air-conditioned rooms, scrumptious meals, tea and coffee making facilities, inground pool, laundry facilities and Internet access. Top value for money. Leon and Kate are sports and travel enthusiasts keen to make your stay in the National Capital one to remember. Magnum, our friendly Burmese cat, declares Birch Corner as his B&B of choice and so should you! Smokers are welcome to use the verandahs. "True hospitality, sparklingly clean & very comfortable" WG Werribee.

Canberra - Farrer   *Homestay Separate/Suite B & B   15 min S of Parliament House*

Tregilly
Peter & Marie Hoskin
89 Hawkesbury Crescent, Farrer, ACT 2607

Tel: (02) 6286 4022 Fax: (02) 6286 4022
Mobile: 0429 129 727
hoskinpm@ozemail.com.au
www.bbbook.com.au/tregilly.html
Double $95-$130 Single $80-$120 (Full Breakfast)
1 King/Twin 1 Queen 1 Twin (3 bdrm)
1 Ensuite 1 Share

Old brick, cathedral ceilings, pine, Laura Ashley decor, great views. "Tregilly" is set in a large native garden backing onto a beautiful Reserve. Breakfast by a log fire or on the verandah. Cool in a turquoise pool, stroll with kangaroos, play croquet and study wonderful birdlife. Easy sightseeing, restaurants, great days out in the snowfields or at the coast. Book our Beach-house too? Ex-Navy, our interests are Vintage cars, Art exhibitions, Sailing, Golf and welcoming guests to our lovely environment. "Wonderful hosts, scrumptious breakfast, peaceful sleeping!" L.& W.S

Canberra - Ginninderra Falls   *Farmstay B & B   18 km NW of Canberra City*

Ginninderry Homestead B & B
Joe and Sue Sciberras
468 Parkwood Road, Ginninderra Falls, ACT 2615

Tel: (02) 6254 6464 Fax: (02) 6254 1945
Mobile: 0419 547 764   info@ginninderry.com.au
www.ginninderry.com.au
Double $125-$165 (Full Breakfast)
Child $20 (school holidays only)
Credit Cards accepted Pets welcome
3 Queen 1 Double (4 bdrm)4 Ensuite

Country homestead nestled on 70 acres close to Ginninderra Falls, 15 minutes from the centre of Canberra. The ultimate retreat for those who want to escape from it all, but still enjoy the facilities of the city. This spacious Georgian style homestead offers understated elegance and charm, while providing modern comforts. Whether you venture out to explore the scenic countryside, stroll through the gardens or just relax beside the open fires you are sure to go home revitalised.

Canberra - Hall   *B & B   Self Contained*   *25 km N of Canberra*

Ambledown Brook   AAATourism ★★★★
David & Jenny Kilby
198 Brooklands Road, Hall, ACT 2618

Tel: (02) 6230 2280 Fax: (02) 6230 2280
laststopambledownbrook@apex.net.au
www.bbbook.com.au/ambledownbrook.html

Double $110 Single $77 (Full Breakfast)
Child $11 Dinner $25
3 Double 4 Single (4 bdrm)
3 Ensuite

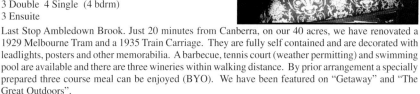

Last Stop Ambledown Brook. Just 20 minutes from Canberra, on our 40 acres, we have renovated a 1929 Melbourne Tram and a 1935 Train Carriage. They are fully self contained and are decorated with leadlights, posters and other memorabilia. A barbecue, tennis court (weather permitting) and swimming pool are available and there are three wineries within walking distance. By prior arrangement a specially prepared three course meal can be enjoyed (BYO). We have been featured on "Getaway" and "The Great Outdoors".

Canberra - Hall   *Farmstay B & B   Self Contained*   *25 km N of Canberra*

Surveyor's Hill Winery and B & B
Leigh Hobba
215 Brooklands Road,
Wallaroo (near Hall), NSW 2618

Tel: (02) 6230 2046 Fax: (02) 6230 2048
Mobile: 0419 404 121   survhill@oalink.com.au
www.bbbook.com.au/surveyorshillbb.html

Double $125 Single $90 (Full Breakfast) Child $20
Dinner $48 Credit Cards accepted Pets welcome
2 Queen 1 Double (2 bdrm)   1 Private

Bed & Breakfast and Farmstay, in a 1930's farmstead surrounded by vineyards and olive groves. Located on a 230 acre property with extensive vineyards, overlooking the Murrumbidgee River and Brindabella Ranges. Easy 20 minute drive to central Canberra. Guests enjoy exclusive use of the cottage, fully private, self contained and separate from the host's residence. Open fire in loungeroom, and heaters in all rooms ensure cosy warmth. Gourmet meals featuring farm and local produce and our own premium wines are provided in the cottage dining room. A fully equipped kitchen enables self catering.

Canberra - Hawker   *B & B*   *1.5 km SW of Hawker*

Betty's Boutique B&B
Betty & Graham Hedgecoe
47 Ambalindum Street, Hawker, ACT 2614

Tel: (02) 6254 2972 hedgecoe1@bigpond.com
www.bbbook.com.au/bettysboutiquebb.html

Double $100 Single $85 (Continental Breakfast)
1 Queen (1 bdrm)
1 Ensuite

Our self-contained cottage is set amidst half an acre of lovely native gardens and sweeping lawns. Property backs onto Canberra Nature Park and has uninterrupted and idyllic views of the Brindabella Mountains and Molonglo River Valley with bush walking tracks at door. Park abounds with kangaroos and bird life. Situated centrally, it's 3 km to Belconnen Town Centre and 10-12 kms from most National Capital attractions, with city-wide bus 100 metres from property. Bikes and helmets are available free of charge. Cottage is tastefully furnished, private and air-conditioned. No smoking indoors and sorry, property is unsuitable for pets and children. Off street parking. Kitchen - no cooking facilities apart from microwave. only.

Canberra - Manuka *B & B* *200m W of Manuka*

Manuka Cottage AAATourism ★★★☆
Tim & Judy Richmond
12 Stokes Street, Manuka, ACT 2603

Tel: (02) 6295 6984 Fax: (02) 6295 6984
trichmon@austarmetro.com.au
www.manukacottage.com.au

Double $145 Single $105 (Full Breakfast)
Credit Cards accepted
1 Double 2 Single (2 bdrm)
1 Private

We offer quality and seclusion in a heritage area close to Parliament House and the National Gallery; only 3 minutes walk to Manuka's many restaurants. Guest accommodation has separate access, off-street parking, exclusive use of two bedrooms, bathroom and a large sitting/dining area. A sunny courtyard and swimming pool are available. Your hosts Tim and Judy know Canberra well. Tim is former Director of the National Botanic Gardens. Judy has a passion for textiles. To ensure your privacy, only one booking at a time is taken.

Canberra - Manuka - Griffith *B & B* *200m SW of Manuka*

La Perouse Bed & Breakfast AAATourism ★★★★
Heather Gaskell
22 La Perouse Street, Griffith, ACT 2603

Tel: (02) 6295 2857 Fax: (02) 6295 2657
Mobile: 0407 952 857   laperousebb@hotmail.com
www.koala-link.net/laperouseb&b

Double $180 Single $120 (Special Breakfast)
Credit Cards accepted Pet on property
1 King 1 Queen 1 Double 1 Single (3 bdrm)
2 Private

A tranquil world of gracious living in the heart of Canberra's heritage homes, a 2 block stroll to the boutique shops and culinary delights of Manuka village with its 49 restaurants and a 3 minute drive to Parliament House and the Nation's Institutions. Elegantly renovated, with Edwardian flair, there are many treasured antiques, chandeliers, fireplaces, fascinating collectables and 2 toy poodles. Homemade soaps, fluffy robes, gourmet cooked breakfast and delicious refreshments add to its charm. The unique Italian inspired rear walled gardens, with salt pool and fountain, offer nooks of seclusion and romance.

Canberra - Mawson *Homestay B & B* *10 km S of Parliament House*

Shackleton B & B AAATourism ★★★★
Wendy & John Whatson
113 Shackleton Circuit, Mawson, ACT 2607

Tel: (02) 6286 2193 Fax: (02) 6286 4720
wendy@shackletonbnb.com.au
www.shackleton.citysearch.com.au

Double $110-$130 Single $88-$100 (Full Breakfast)
Credit Cards accepted
2 Queen 1 Double 1 Twin (2 bdrm)
1 Ensuite 1 Private

Welcome to Shackleton B and B, offering quality accommodation, pleasant hospitality and excellent food. Relax in the large sunny lounge room with your afternoon tea or have drinks and savouries on the balcony and enjoy the beauty of the gardens, the native birds feeding, and the panorama of the legendary Brindabella Mountains. Next morning, a wonderful breakfast awaits you, including seasonal garden produce, home made breads, jams and other delights (vegetarians catered for). We are close to many restaurants and only 10-15 minutes from all major attractions.

Canberra - Narrabundah   *Homestay*   *3 km SE of Parliament House*

Narrabundah B & B
John & Esther
5 Mosman Place, Narrabundah, ACT 2604

Tel: (02) 6295 2837 Fax: (02) 6295 6992
Mobile: 0419 276 231   je@acm.org
www.bbbook.com.au/narrabundahbb.html

Double $90 Single $65 (Continental Breakfast)
Dinner $25pp by arrangement
Credit Cards accepted Pet on property
1 King/Twin (1 bdrm) 1 Ensuite

Comfortable, renovated home in quiet street. Conveniently located in relation to Canberra's main tourist attractions, such as Parliament House, National Gallery and War Memorial. Short drive to restaurants in Manuka. Close to public transport, and to train station and airport. Air-conditioned (heating and cooling). Lounge room and TV shared with hosts. Hosts are semi-retired, and interests include history, genealogy, computing, music, gardening and embroidery. Two small, friendly dogs which can be kept out of your way if you prefer.

Canberra - O'Connor   *Homestay B & B*   *3 km N of Canberra Central*

Pasmore Cottage   **AAATourism ★★★☆**
Alan & Sue Druhan
3 Lilley Street, OConnor, ACT 2602

Tel: (02) 6247 4528 Fax: (02) 6247 4528
pasmore@apex.net.au
www.pasmore.apex.net.au

Double $100-$115 Single $80-$90 (Full Breakfast)
Credit Cards accepted
1 Queen 1 Double 1 Twin (3 bdrm)
1 Ensuite 1 Share

Only 3 km from the city, Pasmore Cottage is located in a quiet street, close to tourist attractions, restaurants, universities and Calvary Hospital, It is an early Canberra Cottage, which has been carefully extended and decorated. Fresh flowers and chocolates compliment the tastefully decorated bedrooms. Guest lounge, TV, stereo tea/coffee and fridge. Ducted heating ensures winter warmth. Afternoon tea served on arrival. Delicious breakfast in sunny dining room overlooking the garden where colourful parrots feed. Washing facilities available. We offer our guests traditional B & B hospitality.

Canberra - O'Connor   *Self Contained*   *3 km N of city centre*

Studio Q   **AAATourism ★★★★☆**
Narelle Wickham
5 Boronia Drive, OConnor, ACT 2602

Tel: (02) 6247 0707 Mobile: 0412 149 755
studio_q@optusnet.com.au
www.studioq.au.com

Double $120 Single $100 (Special Breakfast)
1 Queen (1 bdrm)
1 Ensuite

Studio Q offers you separate studio accommodation designed down to the last detail for absolute comfort. Opened in 2001, features include French door to private deck, extensive use of glass, stainless steel and cedar, quality linen, oversized shower, Victorian ash kitchen, endless hot water, and the best bed! A washing machine, computer port, endless fresh coffee, a range of teas and fantastic breakfast hamper ensure your stay is one you will remember as fantastic. Studio Q is close to everything that matters (city centre, cafes, restaurants and galleries) and your host offers generous hospitality within respectful privacy. Non waged discounts offered.

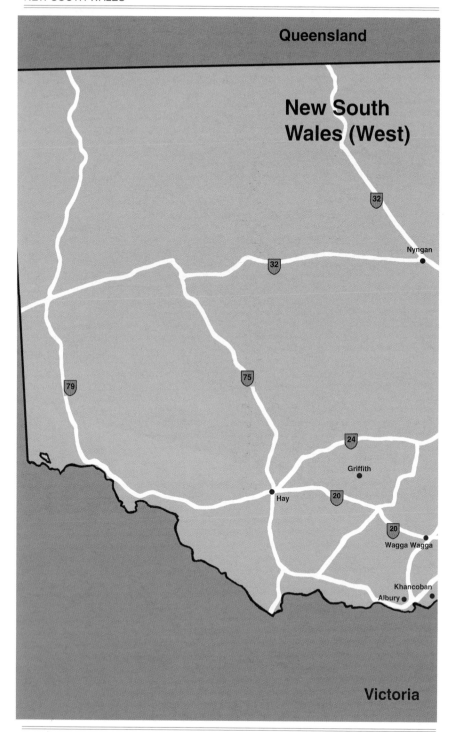

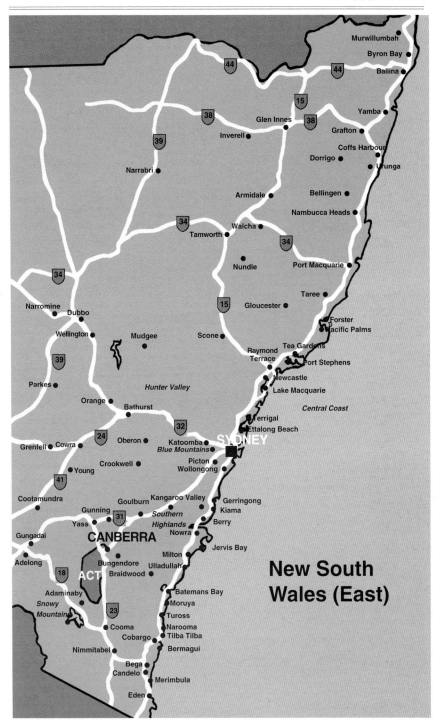

New South
Wales (East)

Murwillumbah
Byron Bay
Ballina
Yamba
Glen Innes
Inverell
Grafton
Coffs Harbour
Dorrigo
Urunga
Narrabri
Armidale
Bellingen
Nambucca Heads
Walcha
Tamworth
Port Macquarie
Nundle
Taree
Narromine
Dubbo
Gloucester
Forster
Pacific Palms
Wellington
Mudgee
Scone
Tea Gardens
Raymond
Terrace
Port Stephens
Parkes
Hunter Valley
Newcastle
Lake Macquarie
Orange
Bathurst
Central Coast
Katoomba
Blue Mountains
Terrigal
Ettalong Beach
SYDNEY
Grenfell
Cowra
Oberon
Picton
Wollongong
Young
Crookwell
Cootamundra
Goulburn
Kangaroo Valley
Gerringong
Kiama
Gunning
Southern
Highlands
Berry
Yass
Nowra
Gungadai
CANBERRA
Jervis Bay
Adelong
ACT
Bungendore
Braidwood
Ulladulla
Milton
Adaminaby
Snowy
Mountains
Batemans Bay
Moruya
Cooma
Cobargo
Tuross
Narooma
Tilba Tilba
Nimmitabel
Bermagui
Bega
Candelo
Merimbula
Eden

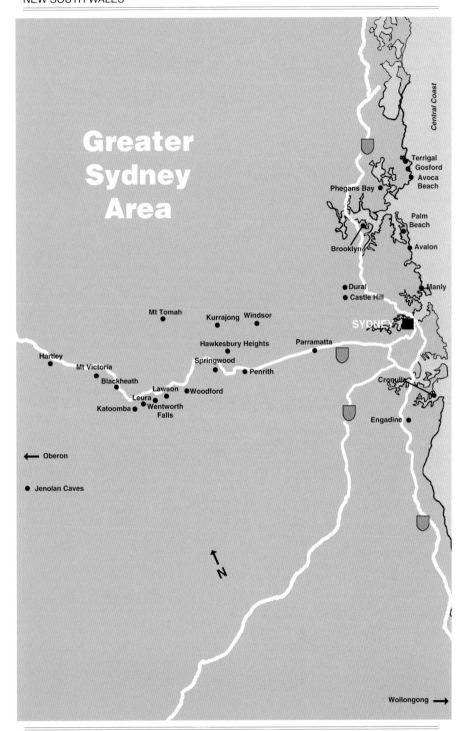

Greater
Sydney
Area

Central Coast

Terrigal
Gosford
Avoca
Beach

Phegans Bay

Palm
Beach

Brooklyn

Avalon

Dural
Castle Hill

Manly

Mt Tomah

Kurrajong Windsor

SYDNEY

Hawkesbury Heights

Parramatta

Hartley

Mt Victoria

Springwood

Penrith

Blackheath

Cronulla

Lawson Woodford

Leura

Katoomba Wentworth
Falls

Engadine

← Oberon

Jenolan Caves

↑
N

Wollongong →

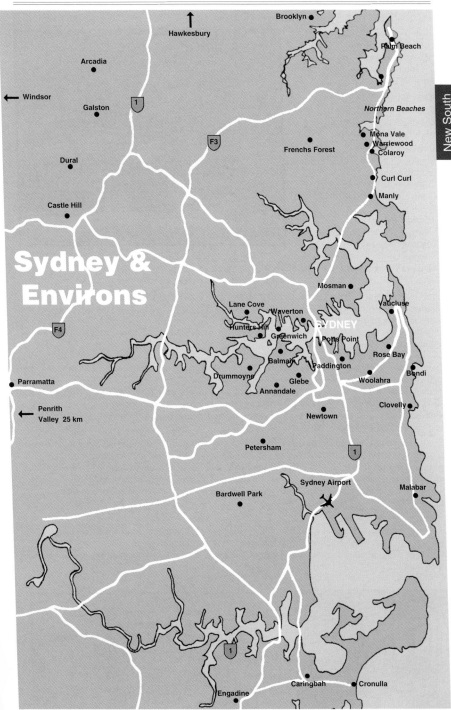

Sydney & Environs

New South Wales

Adelong   *B & B*   *21 km SW of Tumut*

Beaufort Guesthouse
AAATourism ★★★☆
Mike Matthews
77 Tumut Street, Adelong,
NSW 2729

Tel: (02) 6946 2273
Fax: (02) 6946 2553
beaufort@dragnet.com.au
www.beaufort-guesthouse.com.au

Double $95-$135
Single $65.5-$110
(Full Breakfast)
Child $30 Dinner $35
Credit Cards accepted
Pet on property
2 Queen 4 Double
5 Twin 3 Single (14 bdrm)
5 Ensuite 3 Share

ADELONG - BEAUFORT GUESTHOUSE 3 STAR PLUS

"A Romantic Country Retreat." . . . "Like Staying with Friends in The Country."

Half way between Sydney and Melbourne and two hours from Canberra just off the Hume Highway, Heritage listed "Beaufort Guesthouse" offers elegant accommodation with personalised care, attention, hospitality and country-style cuisine.
Situated in the historic Heritage listed, old gold mining town of Adelong NSW, a warm welcome awaits our guests and visitors.
We invite you to enjoy a weekend or longer of pampering.
Sample home made fare in Granny's Kitchen, our coffee shop and take home some of our jams, pickles and chutneys lovingly made by your host Mike.
Dine at night in style by candlelight in our restaurant from our ever changing menu, which includes dishes collected over the years from different countries using fresh local produce.
Our function centre specialises in private lunches and dinner parties, weddings, small seminars, conferences and workshops and coach parties.

Stroll along our tree lined streets and enjoy the country village lifestyle. Visit our museum and craft shops, explore the unique surrounding area of the Adelong Falls Reserve with its rich gold mining past, go fossicking and find gold as they did a hundred years ago. Pick in season fruit at famous Batlow. Tour the surrounding area and visit the "Snowy Mountains - Kosciuszko National Park" or just relax in tranquil surroundings and unwind. Catch up on that good book you promised yourself to read.

Beaufort Guesthouse is also the Adelong Tourist Information Centre with plenty of tours and suggestions to help you enjoy your visit.
If we can be of any assistance with your holiday plans please do not hesitate to contact us.
We are also proud to be members of The Riverina Bed & Breakfast Network.
Your host Mike Matthews assisted by Lesley Clarke look forward to welcoming you to his "Home Away From Home".

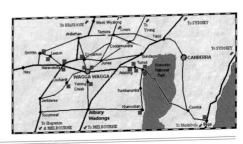

Adelong *Farmstay B & B Self Contained*   *16 km SW of Adelong*

Yavendale Garden Cottage
Susan & Patrick Roche
Yavendale, Adelong, NSW 2729

Tel: (02) 6946 4259 Fax: (02) 6946 4269
www.bbbook.com.au/yavendale.html

Double $90 Single $60
(Full Breakfast) Dinner B/A
1 Double 2 Single (2 bdrm)
1 Private

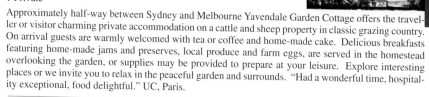

Approximately half-way between Sydney and Melbourne Yavendale Garden Cottage offers the traveller or visitor charming private accommodation on a cattle and sheep property in classic grazing country. On arrival guests are warmly welcomed with tea or coffee and home-made cake. Delicious breakfasts featuring home-made jams and preserves, local produce and farm eggs, are served in the homestead overlooking the garden, or supplies may be provided to prepare at your leisure. Explore interesting places or we invite you to relax in the peaceful garden and surrounds. "Had a wonderful time, hospitality exceptional, food delightful." UC, Paris.

Albury *B & B Self Contained*   *3 km W of Lavington*

Elizabeth's Manor AAATourism ★★★★☆
Larry & Betty Kendall
531 Lyne Street, Lavington, North Albury, NSW 2641

Tel: (02) 6040 4412 Fax: (02) 6040 5166
bookins@elizabethsmanor.com.au
www.elizabethsmanor.com.au

Double $140 Single $115
(Continental & Full Breakfast) Child $20 Dinner $30
$120 Self-contained Cottage Credit Cards accepted
3 Queen (3 bdrm)   3 Ensuite

Elizabeth's Manor would have to be the most luxurious and romantic adults only accommodation in Australia. On arrival guests will be presented with complimentary Champagne and a delicious cheese platter. Breakfast is a true English gourmet delight and can be served in your suite or the Gallery. Although we have a "No Smoking" policy in the house, smoking is permitted anywhere outside. We also have a late check-out, twelve PM. A three course dinner with complimentary wine can be arranged during booking the accommodation.

Albury *B & B Self Contained*   *2 km N of Albury CBD*

810 Albury
Sheila & Robin Manson
810 Burrows Road,
Albury, NSW 2640

Tel: (02) 6025 6122 Fax: (02) 6125 6144
www.bbbook.com.au/810albury.html

Double $120 Discounts for extended stay
Starter Hamper provided Credit Cards accepted
1 Queen 1 Twin (2 bdrm)
1 Private

Wake up to the birds in the gum trees, and open your curtains to view the fairways and parkland of The Albury Golf Course; an ideal place to plan your holiday. The choice is limitless, be it golf in Albury and environs, the Murray River or High Country courses. Visit the Victorian ski fields of Falls Creek, Buffalo or Hotham; the Rutherglen Wineries or the historic towns of NE Vic. Return at night to the comfort of your luxury self-contained apartment. Generous breakfast starter hamper provided. Not suitable for children or pets. Smoking outside only.

Discover paradise situated on a macadamia plantation in the hills above Ballina, just south of Byron Bay

Outdoor BBQ gazebo

Alstonville - Ballina   *B & B*   *8 km S of Alstonville*

Hume's Hovell   AAATourism ★★★★☆
Peter & Suzanne Hume, 333 Dalwood Road, Alstonville, NSW 2477

Tel: (02) 6629 5371 Fax: (02) 6629 5471
Email: stay@humes-hovell.com   **Web:** www.bed-and-breakfast.com.au

Double $165-$231 Single $115-$160 (Full Breakfast) Child $25 Dinner $35
Credit Cards accepted
2 King/Twin 2 King 3 Single (3 bdrm)
3 Ensuite 1 Private

"Hume's Hovell, one of the State's Best Short Break destinations" - NRMA Open Road Magazine review. Located south of Byron Bay, in the rolling green hills above Ballina, Hume's Hovell provides fine boutique accommodation amidst the trees of a Macadamia Plantation. Spacious suites provide maximum privacy with luxurious comfort, featuring King size beds, air-conditioning, cosy lounges, TV/CD/video, guest toiletries, and hand-made soap.

The Plantation Spa Suite is wheelchair friendly.

Pavilion Suite

Enjoy afternoon tea on arrival, plus complementary macadamias, plunger coffee, various teas, and chocolates in your suite. Our rates include sumptuous breakfasts, afternoon tea, and in the evening savouries and pre-dinner drinks. Guests can then choose from dining at local restaurants, by candlelight in your suite or in the Poolside Pavilion (with prior arrangement). BBQ's and Seafood Platters are other delicious popular alternatives.

Enjoy the beautiful beaches and World Heritage Wilderness Areas, stroll the country lanes, play tennis, swim in the salt-water pool, visit local galleries and markets. Do it all - or do nothing.   For a secluded honeymoon, a place to unwind, or simply overnight, Suzanne and Peter will welcome you warmly.

Plantation Suite

Armidale   *Farmstay B & B   6 km S of Armidale*

Poppys Cottage   AAATourism ★★★☆
Jake & Poppy Abbott
Malvern Hill, Dangarsleigh Road Armidale, NSW 2350

Tel: (02) 6775 1277 Fax: (02) 6775 1308
Mobile: 0412 153 819   poppyscottage@bluepin.net.au
http://home.bluepin.net.au/poppyscottage

Double $110 Single $85 (Full Breakfast)
Child $35 Dinner $38 Pet on property Pets welcome
2 Double 2 Single (2 bdrm)   1 Ensuite 1 Private

Poppy's Cottage, Winner 2000 Tourism Award for Excellence in Customer Service, offers an unforgettable, warm and friendly Bed & Breakfast experience in a romantic and cosy atmosphere. Nestled in an enchanting garden with the friendly company of personality farm animals, the cottage allows guests to enjoy peace, tranquillity and privacy. Beautiful Gourmet breakfasts enjoyed beneath the canopy of fruit trees, are a speciality. Option of delicious and intimate candlelit dinner with complimentary wine. The chance to relax and enjoy country hospitality at its best - "warm, friendly and generous". "Gourmet Traveller - this is it! Fantastic food, wonderful host and gorgeous accommodation" K&J, Double Bay.

Armidale   *Homestay B & B   Armidale Central*

Comeytrowe B&B
Cris MacDonald
184 Marsh Street, Armidale, NSW 2350

Tel: (02) 6772 5869 Fax: (02) 6772 5869
www.northnet.com.au/~comeytrowe/comeytrowe

Double $100-$110 Single $85-$90 (Full Breakfast)
extra person $35 Pet on property
2 Queen 2 Single (2 bdrm)
1 Ensuite 1 Private

Comeytrowe (c 1867) has been extensively renovated to create a charming, unique home set among mature elms and a beautiful cottage garden. Our comfortable rooms retain the character of former times but feature the convenience modern travellers require. Privacy is assured. Guests may enjoy a glowing fire or sunny afternoons on the verandahs (with our scandalous cat) or the leafy shade of the courtyard in summer. A private tennis court invites casual play; stroll to the Art Museum or the city-centre in only a few minutes.

Armidale   *Farmstay Self Contained   35 km SE of Armidale*

Wattleton
Lea & Allan Waters
845 Sandon Road, Metz via Armidale, NSW 2350

Tel: (02) 6775 3731 wattleton@bluepin.net.au
www.bluepin.net.au/wattleton

Double $75 Single $65 (Continental Breakfast)
Child $25 Dinner $25 Credit Cards accepted
1 Queen 4 Single (2 bdrm)
1 Private

Wattleton is a sheep and cattle property nestled amongst the scenic and spectacular New England gorges just half an hour east of Armidale. We welcome couples wanting peace and quiet, active people and families wanting to bush walk, bird watch, horse ride, fish, play tennis, spa or swim. Children will also enjoy the many farm animals close to the cottage. The spacious, self-contained cottage has the charm of yesteryear with wood fires along with the modern comforts of today. "Came as guests, left as friends." KF.

Armidale   *B & B   Armidale Central*

Monivea B & B
Carrie Conolly
172 Brown Street,
Armidale, NSW 2350

Tel: (02) 6772 8001
www.bbbook.com.au/moniveabb.html
Double $75 Single $55 (Full Breakfast)
Pet on property
1 Double 2 Single (2 bdrm)
1 Ensuite 1 Share

Monivea is a post federation cottage in Armidale, which lies halfway between Sydney and Brisbane, and is nearly 1000 mts high. It is a pleasantly cool stopover in summer, and is lovely in the cooler months with an occasional fall of snow in winter. Whatever the weather, Carrie and a reasonably civilised Siamese cat called Lucy will welcome you in a relaxed and informal atmosphere, with comfortable bedrooms, a good hot breakfast, a small sitting room with a log fire in winter. Please phone in advance. No smoking.

Armidale   *Farmstay B & B Luxury Self Contained   6 km NE of Armidale*

Beambolong AAAT★★★☆ Denni & Alan McKenzie
Harry McRae Drive, Armidale, NSW 2350

Tel: (02) 6771 2019 Fax: (02) 6771 2019
Mobile: 0428 712 019   denni@beambolong.com.au
www.beambolong.com.au
Double $90-$160 Single $65-$90 (Full Breakfast)
Child $6 - 20 Dinner $20 - $35
Self-Contained $90 - $160 Pets welcome
1 King 1 Queen 2 Double 2 Twin 16 Single (7 bdrm)
2 Ensuite 1 Private 1 Share

Beambolong Retreat features The Chalet - total luxury (min. 2 nights)includes spa, Spin-a-fire, can sleep up to 12; great for reunions, which may also include Candlebark Cottage (sleeps 7). Chalet & Spacious Homestead B&B both have spa baths; verandahs, stunning views, all have wood fires; each completely private. Children's playgrounds in each Cottage; farmyard friends, horses all as friendly as your hosts. Cross-country rides cater for novices to experienced - jumping is an option. We are close to the gorges, golf course, swimming, great shopping, heritage tours, and there's more! Pets welcome to sleep inside.

Armidale   *Farmstay Self Contained   3.5 km W of University*

Glenhope AAATourism ★★★★
Bronwyn and David Mitchell
Red Gum Lane, off Boorolong Road,
Armidale, NSW 2350

Tel: (02) 6772 1940 glenhope@bluepin.net.au
Fax: (02) 6772 0889   www.bbbook.com.au/glenhope.html
Double $105-$115 Single $75-$80
(Continental & Full Breakfast) Child $10
S/C $85 double, $20 extra person Credit Cards accepted
1 Double 2 Single (2 bdrm)   1 Ensuite

Experience the peace and quiet of 'Glenhope', a small, secluded farm surrounded by rolling hills and pastures. We provide country style elegance in s/c accommodation attached to the homestead. Features include a fully equipped kitchenette to prepare your own meals or choose a delicious breakfast of fresh farm produce. Television, books, magazines and games add to your comfort plus central heating to keep you cosy on cold winter nights. Laundry facilities are available. Fall in love with our alpacas and other friendly farm animals including sheep, cattle, chickens and ducks. The university and restaurants are 4km.

Armidale   *Self Contained B & B   2 km E of Armidale*

Creekside
Jane & Ross Stephens
5 Canambe Street, Armidale, NSW 2350

Tel: (02) 6772 2018 Mobile: 0409 904 047
stephens@waterfallway.com.au
www.waterfallway.com.au/creekside
Double $110 Single $85 (Full Breakfast)
Child $5 - $15 S.C. $95 dbl, $77 single
1 Queen 2 Double 6 Single (3 bdrm)
1 Ensuite 1 Private

"Creekside" has two charming self-contained cottages in the garden of a turn of the century homestead on four acres in the heart of Armidale. Enjoy the best of both worlds - country living two minutes from excellent shopping, restaurants and cultural activities. Very private and comfortable, the cottages include electric blankets and heaters, wood fire, TV/video, CD/radio/tape, library and linen. Attractions include: trampoline, cubby and playground; cottage garden and old-fashioned roses; farm animals, vegie garden, orchard; tennis and natural history tours.

Armidale   *Homestay B & B   9.5 km W of Armidale*

Shannon's End
Margaret & Rob Hadfield,   212 Shannon Road,
off Old Inverell Road, Armidale, NSW 2350

Tel: (02) 6775 1177 Fax: (02) 6775 1176
Mobile: 0411 032 625   marghad@yahoo.com
www.home.bluepin.net.au/shannonsend
Double $99 Single $80 (Special Breakfast)
Child $10 - $25 $30 Extra person
Pet on property Pets welcome
2 Queen 2 Double (2 bdrm)   2 Ensuite

Shannon's End, with commanding views towards Mt Duval, offers a quiet and relaxing atmosphere, creating a sense of rest and renewal. The beautiful New England countryside is drawn into your tastefully decorated suite through large windows and doors which open onto pleasant garden areas and a pool. Suites are equipped with TV, microwave, radio/CD player, games, magazines and books. Children will love our friendly dog. Pets by arrangement. "Thanks for the wonderful hospitality, great location and perfect breakfast. Best B&B we have seen and excellent value." N.J. Brisbane.

Armidale - Uralla   *Farmstay Separate/Suite B & B   21 km E of Uralla*

Cruickshanks Farmstay B & B   AAAT★★★★
Anne & Mike Thackway
Tourist Drive 19, Uralla, NSW 2358

Tel: (02) 6778 2148 Fax: (02) 6778 2148
Mobile: 0408 514 428   athack@northnet.com.au
www.home.bluepin.net.au/cruickshanks
Double $83-$115 Single $55-$70 (Full Breakfast)
Child $18 - $30 Dinner $20 - $30 B/A
Credit Cards accepted Pets welcome
1 Queen 1 Double 2 Twin 1 Single (5 bdrm)
1 Ensuite 1 Private 1 Share

The Cottage: - Treat yourselves to a Romantic Interlude in self-contained elegance, or be totally spoilt and have delicious meals delivered.   The Homestead: - True hospitality in three guestrooms, one with ensuite the others share. Simply soak up the tranquillity on a sunny verandah or by a cosy fire. Join in farm activities. Experience a guided 4WD tour over working sheep/cattle property. Birds and kangaroos in wild, Highland cattle, miniature horses. National Parks 30 mins away. Pack expectations of a great holiday and take home wonderful memories!

Avoca Beach *B & B   1 km S of Avoca Beach*

Avoca Treetops
Don & Lynne Cook
18 Baronga Road, Avoca Beach, NSW 2251

Tel: (02) 4382 3867 Mobile: 0416 010 229
avoca70@hotmail.com
www.bbbook.com.au/avocabeachbb.html

Double $130 Single $90 (Full Breakfast)
Credit Cards accepted
2 Queen (2 bdrm)
2 Ensuite

Avoca Treetops is a light and airy cedar home set high amongst tall gum trees. The two private guest rooms both have comfortable queen size beds, spacious ensuites, and their own private entry. Enjoy breakfast on the balcony, relax with a book or just admire the birds. Visitors can go swimming, surfing, canoeing, or visit the famous cinema all within walking distance of Avoca Treetops.

Ballina *Homestay B & B   Ballina East*

Landfall
Gaye & Roger Ibbotson
109 Links Avenue, East Ballina, NSW 2478

Tel: (02) 6686 7555 Fax: (02) 6686 7555
Mobile: 0428 642 077   landfall@spot.com.au
www.bbbook.com.au/landfall.html

Double $85 Single $48 (Full Breakfast)
Credit Cards accepted
1 Double 2 Single (2 bdrm)   1 Share

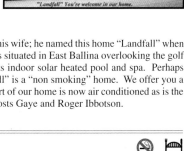

"Landfall" You're welcome in our home.

This home was the residence of Captain Tom Martin and his wife; he named this home "Landfall" when he retired to Ballina after many years at sea. "Landfall" is situated in East Ballina overlooking the golf course. You are invited to relax in our courtyard with its indoor solar heated pool and spa. Perhaps you'd prefer to read in the "chart-room" library. "Landfall" is a "non smoking" home. We offer you a relaxed stay with warm, friendly hospitality. The main part of our home is now air conditioned as is the Double Bedroom for the comfort of our guests.   Your hosts Gaye and Roger Ibbotson.

Ballina *B & B   3 km NE of Ballina*

The Yabsley B & B   AAATourism ★★★★☆
Judee Whittaker and David Clark
5 Yabsley Street, East Ballina, NSW 2478

Tel: (02) 6681 1505 Fax: (02) 6681 1505
Mobile: 0407 811 505
yabsley@bigpond.com
www.tropicalnsw.com.au/yabsley

Double $100-$120 Single $100 (Full Breakfast)
Dinner $30 by arrangement Credit Cards accepted
2 Queen (2 bdrm)   2 Private

The Yabsley is a two minutes walk to Lighthouse Beach, Richmond River and Shaws Bay Lagoon. Also within easy walking distance to a hotel, a resort and three restaurants. The house was recently refurbished and contains private guest suites, guest lounge and delightful courtyards. Watch the whales and dolphins or play tennis and golf. East Ballina gives access to day trips to Byron Bay, the Border Ranges or the Gold Coast. You can negotiate a superb meal of your choice cooked by David who specialises in seafood cuisine. Unfortunately we cannot cater for children.

Ballina   *B & B*   *Centre of Ballina*

Brundah B & B   **AAATourism ★★★★☆**
Ros & Mal Lewis
37 Norton Street, Ballina, NSW 2478

Tel: (02) 6686 8166 Fax: (02) 6686 8164
Mobile: 0414 861 066
brundah@nnsw.quik.com.au
www.babs.com.au/brundah
Double $135-$180 Single $115-$160
(Full Breakfast) Holiday surcharge
2 Queen (2 bdrm)   2 Ensuite

Brundah B & B . . . an elegant National Trust Heritage Home (circa 1908), set on half an acre of peaceful and secluded gardens. Take the time to sip afternoon tea or a cool drink on the wide verandahs or utilise the guest library, lounge or dining rooms all tastefully furnished for your comfort. Get to know the area. A short stroll will take you to the town centre, restaurants, river or beaches. Two Queen rooms both with ensuites. Hosts: Mal & Ros Lewis.

Batemans Bay   *B & B Guest House*   *10 km S of Batemans Bay*

Chalet Swiss Spa   **AAATourism ★★★★☆**
Herbert and Elizabeth Mayer
676 The Ridge Road, Surf Beach,
Batemans Bay, NSW 2536

Tel: (02) 4471 3671   info@surfbeachretreat.com.au
Fax: (02) 4471 1671   www.surfbeachretreat.com.au
Double $110-$275 Single $70-$210 (Full Breakfast)
Child $30 Dinner $42 S.C. Cabin $90 - $190
Credit Cards accepted
2 King 5 Queen 9 Double 3 Twin (18 bdrm)
17 Ensuite 1 Share

Situated on top of "Hero's Hill" above SURF BEACH our 85 ac Retreat & Health Spa offers you - our own mineral spring water, fresh clean air, tranquillity, 180 degree ocean views from our Cafe-verandah, visits by birds and wallabies. Facilities: Indoor heated pool (28 degrees C), Spa, revitalising therapies and massages, rainforest walks, tennis, archery. Guest lounge with large open fireplace, games corner. Welcome drink, afternoon coffees. Delicious full breakfasts with choices. Friendly, widely travelled hosts. A place for you to relax and get pampered.

Bathurst   *Homestay*   *3km NW of Bathurst*

Cherrywood-by-the-River   **AAATourism★★★☆**
Belinda Mansell
238 Eglinton Road, Bathurst, NSW 2795

Tel: (02) 6331 9427 web.ix.net.au/~camxman
Double $90-$120 Single $60-$70
(Full Breakfast) Child $25
Dinner $20 - $25 by arrangement
Pet on property
1 Queen 2 Single (2 bdrm)
1 Share

Our delightful home with a rural garden nestles in two acres. Beyond the ponies paddock, stroll beside the Macquarie River, capture scenic views from our wide verandahs. Large lounge and family rooms have cheerful log fires, TV, coffee and tea making facilities. Gracious dining room, enjoy homemade stylish breakie, recommending my speciality: "Eggs Benedict"! Charming large bedrooms have comfortable beds and electric blankets. Help groom and feed Neffie our Welsh pony, Kiri the shy Burmese cat prefers the fire side. Smokers: verandah please.

Bathurst   *B & B   Self Contained*

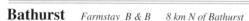

Elm Tree Cottage
Lyn Bosier
270 Keppel Street, Bathurst, NSW 2795

Tel: (02) 6332 4920 Fax: (02) 6331 8566
Mobile: 0407 890 445
elmtree@ix.net.au
www.bathurstheritage.com.au

Double $132-$154 Single $121 (Full Breakfast)
Child $22 - $33 Dinner $44
Additional adults $44 - $55
Credit Cards accepted Pet on property Pets welcome
1 Queen 2 Single (1 bdrm) 1 Ensuite

Quiet and peaceful yet close to town Elm Tree Cottage offers warm country hospitality in the privacy of your own self contained cottage. Set in a beautiful garden, the sun streams in through French windows, Freshly brewed coffee and tea can be enjoyed in the walled garden overlooking the hills while the fountain plays gently in the background.

Bathurst   *Farmstay B & B   8 km N of Bathurst*

Restdown Farm Stay
Audrey and Brian Eccleston
426 Eleven Mile Drive, Bathurst, NSW 2795

Tel: (02) 6337 1220
www.bbbook.com.au/restdown.html

Double $90-$100 Single $60 (Full Breakfast)
Child $15 Dinner $25 Pet on property
2 Twin 1 double 1 single (3 bdrm)
2 Private

Restdown is an Historic Country homestead, elegant and peaceful, with comfortable log fires in dining and lounge areas. There is a private tennis court, farm walks, Angora Goats (breeding these since 1974 and doing shows). Jessie, our sheep dog, displays her expertise with our sheep, for our visitors. Visit local wineries, Abercrombie House, interesting drives which include Heritage properties and villages. Also, have a swing on the golf course. Guests are treated with a sumptuous breakfast. No smoking inside. Pets on property. Children welcome.

Bathurst - Oberon   *B & B   Self Contained   25 km SE of Bathurst*

Bimbadeen
Sue & Tim Arnison
O'Connell, NSW 2795

Tel: (02) 6337 5739 Fax: (02) 6337 5602
arnison381@ozemail.com.au
www.bbbook.com.au/bimbadeen.html

Double $110 Single $75 (Full Breakfast)
Dinner $25 Credit Cards accepted
1 Queen 2 Double 2 Single (4 bdrm)
2 Private

A peaceful comfortable home with views from the verandah across the country/cottage garden, to distant wooded hills, with only an old cat or the lowing of the cattle to disturb you. Mid way between Oberon and Bathurst, 20 minutes each way. Guests are welcome to stroll through the large garden, explore the farm. No smoking please, but there are verandahs where those who must, may. Dinner by arrangement. Breakfast can be taken on the verandah or in the sunny courtyard.

Bega   *Farmstay B & B*   *25 km N of Bega*

Adobe House B & B
Kym Mogridge & Gerri Taylor
624 Warrigal Range Road, Brogo via Bega, NSW 2550

Tel: (02) 6492 7205 Fax: (02) 6492 7131
Mobile: 0427 277 249   info@adobehouse.com.au
www.adobehouse.com.au

Double $120-$140 Single $90-$120
(Special Breakfast) Child $20 in cot
Dinner from $25 extra person $40
Credit Cards accepted Pets welcome
1 Queen 1 Twin (2 bdrm) 1 Private 1 Share

The MUD BRICK B&B. Stay in a hand & soul crafted mudbrick and timber home with character, warmth and a relaxing atmosphere. Quiet location, 6km off the Princes Hwy and 20mins from Bega. Walk in 100 acres of bush with kangaroos, wallabies and echidnas. Watch the eagles soar. Spectacular views, lovely gardens to wander, and a friendly cat. Enjoy a home cooked breakfast with homemade bread and freerange eggs. Attractions include National Parks, beaches, Bega Cheese, winery and local markets & crafts. Pets OK. Children welcome.

Bega   *B & B*   *Bega Central*

The Pickled Pear   AAATourism ★★★★
Wendy and Bob Gornall
60-62 Carp Street, Bega, NSW 2550

Tel: (02) 6492 1393 Fax: (02) 6492 0030
ppear@acr.net.au
www.ausac.com/ppear

Double $95-$150 Single $80-$120
(Special Breakfast) Credit Cards accepted
1 King/Twin 1 Queen 1 Twin (3 bdrm)
3 Ensuite

Special features of our renovated 1870's house include: * scrumptious food * charming ensuites (one with spa) * private suite available * candlelight dinners - (prearranged * weekend markets * old wares * secluded beaches * national parks surround us * the aura of history, tranquillity and warmth * main street location (walk to restaurants, clubs, shops) * read, sleep, walk, fish, paint, golf, or whale watch * no facilities for children * smoking on open verandah * a good stopping off point between Sydney/ Melbourne.

Bega   *B & B Self Contained Cottages*   *27 km N of Bega*

Rock Lily Cottages   AAATourism ★★★★
Delphine Troughear
864 Warrigal Range Road, Brogo, NSW 2550

Tel: (02) 6492 7364 Fax: (02) 6492 7363
Mobile: 0428 514 016   info@rocklily.com.au
www.rocklily.com.au

Double $145-$175 Single $135-$165 (Full Breakfast)
Child $35 Credit Cards accepted Pets welcome
3 Queen 1 Double 2 Single (4 bdrm)
3 Ensuite

Romantic Mountain Hideaways, secluded and private with spectacular views. Two are fully self contained mudbrick cottages facing the mountains on our 100 acre property. They have leadlight windows, cosy wood fire and TV. On a separate 16 acre property is Woodruff Mountain Cabin. It has a four poster bed, old wood stove, old church pews, large deck and panoramic views. You can bush walk, swim, fish or hire a canoe at the Brogo Dam. We have two friendly border collies and 2 horses. Breakfast Hamper included. We accept Dogs too. View more photos on our WEBSITE.

Bellingen   *Homestay B & B Guest House*   *50m E of Bellingen PO*

Rivendell   AAATourism ★★★★
Janet Hosking
10 Hyde Street, Bellingen, NSW 2454

Tel: (02) 6655 0060 Fax: (02) 6655 0060
Mobile: 0403 238 409   rivendell@midcoast.com.au
www.midcoast.com.au/~rivendell

Double $95-$125 Single $85-$125
(Full Breakfast) $125 per night Peak
Credit Cards accepted Pet on property
3 Queen 2 Twin (4 bdrm)   3 Ensuite 1 Private

In the heart of the heritage village of Bellingen, Rivendell is a beautifully decorated Federation style home. Luxurious rooms furnished with antiques, feather & down doonas and fluffy bathrobes, open to shady verandahs and picturesque gardens. Take a refreshing dip in the saltwater pool, or in winter, relax by the log fire. After dinner settle back with complimentary port and chocolates. TV, stereo, books, games, magazines and tea/coffee making is provided in the guest lounge. "A warm & homely ambience in a marvellous old home." T & J, Kotara South.

Bellingen   *Self Contained   2 km E of Bellingen*

Maddefords Cottages
Grahame & Glenys
North Bank Road, Bellingen, NSW 2454

Tel: (02) 6655 9866 Fax: (02) 6655 9866
Mobile: 0413 317 635
madfords@midcoast.com.au
www.bbbook.com.au/maddefordscottages.html

Double $110 (Continental Breakfast)
Credit Cards accepted
2 Queen 2 Double 2 Single   2 Private

Come away to the relaxing riverside retreat of Maddefords Cottages on the banks of the beautiful Bellinger River. Each cottage has privacy, and whilst located in the country is only minutes from town. Dine on the deck or eat in town at one of the many fine restaurants or cafes. * Fully equipped kitchen * TV/VCR and CD Player * All linen and towels provided * Air cond/heated * Canoes, Bikes and BBQ * Close to beaches and rainforests * Christmas holiday surcharge * Discounts for longer stays * Abundant bird life.

Bermagui   *B & B Self Contained Separate/Suite   32 km S of Narooma*

Bimbimbi House   Peter and Beverley Bray
62 Nutleys Creek Road, Bermagui, NSW 2546

Tel: (02) 6493 4456 Fax: (02) 6493 4456
Mobile: 0428 569 803 - 0429 934 456
bimbimbihouse@bigfoot.com.au
www.bbbook.com.au/bimbimbihouse.html

Double $120-$150 Single $100-$120
(Continental & Full Breakfast) Child neg
1 Queen 2 Double 1 Twin 1 Single (4 bdrm)
1 Ensuite 1 Private

Bimbimbi House offers privacy, comfort and tranquillity. Do as international star Billy Connolly did, enjoy the visiting King Parrots and other Australian birds. Experience the serenity of the Bermagui River through spotted gums. Our master guest suite, with private access, has its own kitchen, lounge and laundry. From the garden studio, walk into our Edna Walling inspired garden. Breakfast is provided in your units. Although in a rural setting we are minutes from the picturesque seaside town of Bermagui with restaurants, beaches and sporting activities available.

Berry *B & B   Separate/Suite   8 km E of Berry*

Bimbadeen   AAATourism ★★★★★
Bill & Lily O'Brien, 580 A Tourist Road, Berry, NSW 2577

Tel: (02) 4464 2880 Fax: (02) 4464 3283 Mobile: 0409 642 880
bimbadeen@ozemail.com.au   www.bimbadeen.au.bz

Double $170-$200 Single $150-$180 (Full Breakfast) Credit Cards accepted
1 King 1 Queen (2 bdrm)   2 Ensuite

Set high up on the Berry Mountain escarpment between the mountains and the sea. Each Bimbadeen suite gives guests a remarkable 'birds-eye view' of the world. Bimbadeen (AAA 5-star rated) offers both superior standards of accommodation and superb views.   Within a two-hour scenic drive from Sydney or Canberra, this sophisticated getaway is nestled within 14 hectares of mostly rainforest. Stay here and you feel literally on top of the world as you look down upon the coastal farming land of Shoalhaven and across to Gerroa in the north and Jervis Bay to the south.

Bimbadeen offer exclusive style of accommodation. There are just two guest suites, which shares a separate entrance with under cover parking. Each spacious suite has cathedral timber ceilings. Each has air conditioning, heating, ceiling fan, bar fridge, tea and coffee facilities, TV, VCR, CD player, free video library, full bathroom and private balcony with panoramic views. The Classic Suite has a queen-size bed and a fabulous view from the bathtub, while the Country Suite has a king-size bed and recycled timber furnishings. Both have a sofa and dining setting as well as outdoor furniture on the balcony. Cooked breakfast is served in your room or on your private balcony, where you can have a sumptuous meal while enjoys the magnificent view and crisp mountain air.

Bimbadeen is about nine kilometres from Berry township and twelve kilometres from Kangaroo Valley.

Berry   *B & B   Self Contained   7 km N of Berry*

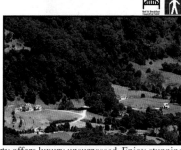

Drawing Rooms of Berry   AAATourism ★★★★☆
Kerry & Adrian Turnbull
21 Wattamolla Road, Berry, NSW 2535

Tel: (02) 4464 3360 Fax: (02) 4464 1741
Mobile: 0411 888 249
info@drawingrooms.com.au
www.drawingrooms.com.au

(Full Breakfast) Credit Cards accepted
7 King/Twin 2 Queen (9 bdrm)
9 Ensuite

Just 2 hrs south of Sydney, this spectacular 15 acre property offers luxury unsurpassed. Enjoy stunning architecture and decor, spa baths, king beds, ribbed towels, CD and DVD players, sumptuous breakfasts and spectacular mountain views. The Drawing Rooms is ideally located within minutes of rainforest walks, pristine beaches, golf courses, wineries and the quaint towns of Berry and Kangaroo Valley. Let us pamper you in our private B&B Guesthouse (3 bedrooms), or unwind in one of our three exclusive 2 bedroom self-contained lodges -The "Rainforest", "Country", or "Palm Tree" Lodges.

Berry   *B & B   1.3 km Berry*

Robynes' of Berry
Robyne & Phillip Macready
146 Kangaroo Valley Road, Berry, NSW 2535

Tel: (02) 4464 2244 Fax: (02) 4464 2250
Mobile: 0417 409 050
robynesofberry@bigpond.com
www.robynesofberry.com

Double $165-$175 Single $135-$145 (Full Breakfast)
Extended stay packages avail.   Credit Cards accepted
3 King (3 bdrm)
2 Ensuite 1 Private

Relax and renew in the peace and comfort awaiting at Robynes' of Berry. Choose your complimentary welcome of either delicious homemade afternoon tea or local wine and cheese, by the fire or in the garden.   Wineries, galleries, country stores and markets are all very Berry pastimes. Or simply do nothing at all! Indulge your own personal pursuit of relaxation, then savour sumptuous breakfast fare served privately off your room in clean, fresh country air.

Berry   *3 self contained cottages   3 km N of Berry*

Figlea Cottages
Pat & Rosemary Sanders
165A Bong Bong Road, Berry, NSW 2535

Tel: (02) 4464 1635 Fax: (02) 4464 1635
figlea@shoal.net.au
figlea.accessit.com.au

Weekend $120 - $180
Midweek $100 - $160
Credit Cards accepted Pets welcome
3 Queen 1 Twin (4bdrm)
2 Ensuite 1 Private

Lovely rural setting abounding with glorious views and walks. Minutes from the charms of Berry - antiques, cafes, craft shops. Range of three self-contained cottages - suiting all needs from a romantic weekend away for 2 to a family stay for a week or more.   Comments - Thank you Pat & Rosemary for creating a little piece of Heaven.

New South Wales

Berry - Jaspers Brush   *B & B*   *5 km S of Berry*

Jaspers Brush B & B
Leonie and Ian Winlaw
465 Strongs Road, Jaspers Brush, NSW 2535

Tel: (02) 4448 6194 Fax: (02) 4448 6254
Mobile: 0418 116 655
iwinlaw@ozemail.com.au
www.bbbook.com.au/jaspersbrushbandb.com.au.html

Double $220 (Full Breakfast)
Credit Cards accepted
2 Queen 2 Single (3 bdrm)
2 Ensuite 1 Private

Come take breakfast overlooking one of nature's most spectacular creations. Our property, located on the Berry escarpment, commands views that stretch from Jervis Bay to Gerringong, taking in the Shoalhaven River, Mt Coolangatta and the lush green pastures of the coastal plain.

The bedrooms, opening onto the wrap around verandah and the view, have private facilities, electric blankets, alpaca fleece doonas, heaters, ceiling fans and fresh flowers from the garden. The house boasts an eclectic art collection and the guest lounge has an open fire with great art, travel, wine and garden books for browsing.

A gourmet breakfast is served in the lounge overlooking the views and our herd of alpacas

Berry - Bolong   *Farmstay B & B   8 km E of Nowra*

Swanlea Farm
Jim & Jan Knapp
RMB 680 Bolong Road,
Bolong via Nowra, NSW 2540

Tel: (02) 4421 7872 Fax: (02) 4421 7872
knapp@shoal.net.au
www.bbbook.com.au/swanleafarm.html
Double $120-$150 Single $85-$100
(Special Breakfast) Credit Cards accepted
1 King/Twin 1 Queen 1 Double (3 bdrm)   3 Ensuite

Located on the Shoalhaven River - close to Berry, Jervis Bay, Kangaroo Valley - Swanlea is a 3rd generation farm and offers a high standard of accommodation in the federation homestead. A guests living area abounds with books, TV and wood fire when the weather is chilly. Relax on the verandahs, wander in the rambling country garden or view this beautiful region from the air in a scenic flight with the host. Experience pure country hospitality and special breakfasts made with fresh farm produce. Annabelle and Tom are the farm cats.

Berry - Jaspers Brush   *B & B Luxurious Accommodation   3 km S of Berry*

Woodbyne Private Hotel
Annette & Jeff Moore
4 O'Keeffes Lane,
Jaspers Brush via Berry, NSW 2535

Tel: 61 2 4448 6200 Fax: 61 2 4448 6211
info@woodbyne.com.au
www.woodbyne.com.au
Double $253-$302.50 Single $150-$275
(Full Breakfast) Child $60 per night
Dinner $70 per person Credit Cards accepted
7 King/Twin (7 bdrm)   7 Ensuite

Woodbyne is in the heart of the rolling hills of South Coast NSW and staying here is truly an experience of luxury and relaxation. The hotel is set in formal gardens filled with century-old trees, carefully tended hedgerows, soothing water features and scented bushes. Our exquisite suites, all with king size beds, Egyptian cotton sheets and ensuite bathrooms, make it the perfect country retreat near the ocean. Our two border collies will assist you in navigating the property.

Blue Mountains - Blackheath   *Self Contained   1km N of Blackheath*

Allendale Cottages
Robert Simmonds
Popes Glen, Blackheath, NSW 2785

Tel: (02) 4787 8270 allendale@pnc.com.au
www.bluemts.com.au/allendale
Double $143-$220 (Continental Breakfast)
Credit Cards accepted
2 Queen (2 bdrm)
2 Ensuite

A secluded hideaway on 9 acres of gardens and forest bordering the Blue Mountains National Park. Nestled in the gardens are two stylish self-contained cottages offering complete privacy. Featuring luxurious glass walled bathrooms with double sunken spa with views over the gardens, forest and colourful birdlife; and a cosy log fireplace adding to the romantic atmosphere. Take a pleasant stroll past the duck pond to the lively village, or into the National Park to some of the best lookouts, waterfalls and walks in the mountains.

Blue Mountains - Blackheath
Homestay   2 km N of Blackheath

Amani B & B
Rosemary & Bill Chapple
31 Days Crescent, Blackheath, NSW 2785

Tel: (02) 4787 8610 Fax: (02) 4787 8894
Mobile: 0411 111 391
www.bbbook.com.au/amanibb.html
Double $110-$130 Single $70
(Full Breakfast) Child $35
1 King/Twin 1 Queen (2 bdrm)
2 Ensuite

Our home is surrounded by lovely gardens on the edge of the National Park, overlooking the spectacular cliffs that tower above the Grose Valley. We enjoy sharing the wonderful views from our home and the many scenic bush walks that begin nearby. Our guest rooms, with private entrance, are upstairs. Two bedrooms, each with an ensuite and a guests lounge. There is central heating, TV, CD, fridge, microwave oven and tea and coffee making facilities. Blackheath is two hours by road or rail from Sydney.

Blue Mountains - Blackheath
Homestay B & B   0.8 km E of Blackheath

Kanangra Lodge
Margaret Howlett
9 Belvidere Avenue, Blackheath, NSW 2785

Tel: (02) 4787 8715 Fax: (02) 4787 8748
Mobile: 0404 472 692   kanlodge@lisp.com.au
www.kanlodge.com.au
Double $185-$225 Single $155-$185
(Full Breakfast) Credit Cards accepted
2 King/Twin 1 King 1 Queen (4 bdrm)
3 Ensuite 1 Private

Set in a classic, tranquil, four season garden, Kanangra Lodge is an elegant country house which offers a scrumptious traditional, silver service bed and breakfast. Cosy, relaxing lounges with open fires, luxurious and private king and queen bedrooms all provide the perfect background for a wonderful Blue Mountains getaway. All just a few minutes walk to antique shops, fine dining, canyon bushwalks and spectacular mountain views. Absolutely relaxing ... As good as ever after six years ... Great relaxing weekend ... A lovely place with ... generous hospitality.

Blue Mountains- Katoomba
B & B   1.5 km S of Katoomba Centre

Edgelinks Bed & Breakfast   AAATourism ★★★★☆
Christine Killinger
138 Narrow Neck Road, Katoomba, NSW 2780

Tel: (02) 4782 3001 Fax: (02) 4782 9902
Mobile: 0410 317 886   edgelinks@hermes.net.au
www.edgelinks.com.au
Double $170-$230 Single $150-$210 (Full Breakfast)
Special rates 3 nights or more
Credit Cards accepted Pet on property
1 King/Twin 2 Queen (3 bdrm) 3 Ensuite

"Edgelinks is a serene island of ease, good taste and tranquillity." Traditional bed & breakfast where comfort and privacy is assured. Set amongst 1° acres of tranquil garden this spacious, elegant, tastefully decorated home offers 3 guest suites containing spa's , TV/VCR, electric blankets, central heating. Guest lounge dinning, with antique furniture has an open fire place adding to the English country house ambience while floor to ceiling glass captures the views. Enjoy superior full cooked sumptuous breakfasts at fireside or on the patio.

Blue Mountains - Katoomba South   *0.5 km S of Katoomba*

B & B   Self Contained

Our Secret Cottage
Helen Rush
47 Waratah Avenue, Katoomba, NSW 2780

Tel: (02) 4567 2071 cjr@acay.com.au
oursecret.cjb.net

Double $140-$160 Single $70-$80
(Continental Breakfast)
2 Queen 1 Single (3 bdrm)
1 Private

This charming, self contained, heritage cottage, surrounded by a private garden, is within 1 1/2 hours drive from Sydney. It is in easy walking distance of the "Three Sisters", numerous spectacular walks, restaurants, cosy cafes, galleries and parks. The cottage is based on the turn-of-the-century local miner's home and now carefully modernised with a care to its quaint character. It is warmly heated and the enclosed verandah provides a sunny retreat on winter days. Smoke-free inside. No pets. Children by negotiation.

Blue Mountains - Kurrajong Heights   *18 km NW of North Richmond*

Self Contained B & B Cabins

Madisons Mountain Retreat   AAATourism ★★★★
Kath & Nathan Lockrey
1880 Bells Line of Road,
Kurrajong Heights, NSW 2758

Tel: (02) 4567 7398 Fax: (02) 4567 7862
Mobile: 0415 404 643   madisons@iprimus.com.au
www.bluemts.com.au/madisons

Double $132-$200 Single $65-$100 (Full Breakfast)
Child $28 - $35 Credit Cards accepted Pets welcome
5 King 3 Queen 8 Double 10 Single (8 bdrm)
8 Private

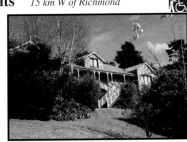

This peaceful bushland retreat is set on 83 acres surrounded by National Park. We have eight spacious cabins accommodating up to five people. Each cabin has a log fire, microwave, stove top, fridge, TV. Other facilities include 18m indoor pool, spa, BBQ areas, wheelchair access, bush walking, close to Zig Zag Railway, Mt Tomah, Mt Wilson, Botanic Gardens, grass skiing. Children and animals welcome.

Blue Mountains - Kurrajong Heights   *15 km W of Richmond*

Separate/Suite B & B

Glenrose Mountain Hideaway
Wendy & Jim Frewin
44 Coach House Place,
Kurrajong Heights, NSW 2758

Tel: (02) 4567 7574 Fax: (02) 4567 7130
Mobile: 0414 677 598   spectrum@hawknet.com.au
www.glenrosehideaway.com.au

Double $135-$165 Single $120-$150 (Full Breakfast)
Child $25 From $30 per extra person
1 Queen 1 Double (2 bdrm) 1 Private

'Glenrose' is located in the Blue Mountains just over 1hr. north-west of Sydney CBD. The tastefully decorated suite has two bedrooms for your family and friends, a beautiful bathroom with claw-foot bath, a large fully equipped lounge with TV, CD, fridge, etc. and is air conditioned for your comfort. The Federation style home is set in a lovely garden with beautiful views. A country style breakfast is served daily. Enjoy walks, antiques, gardens, and lots more. Fine restaurants are close by.

Blue Mountains - Kurrajong Heights - Hawkesbury

B & B Guest House   *Kurrajong Heights*

Trellises Guest House
Teah Callaghan
11 Warks Hill Road, Kurrajong Heights, NSW 2758

Tel: (02) 4567 7313 Fax: (02) 4567 7313
Mobile: 0410 677 313   enquiries@trellises.com.au
www.trellises.com.au
Double $198-$275 (Full Breakfast)
Dinner $22 - $49.50 Pets welcome
Smoking area inside
10 King/Twin (10 bdrm)
10 Ensuite

New South Wales

Boutique guest house surrounded by Sylvan Gardens & Ponds, quiet and secluded. Individually appointed A/C rooms, mini bars. Mini suites also including spas-for-two, fireplaces, CD players. Generous 2 course breakfast served on your verandah. Perfect for schmaltzy getaways or Executive Conferences & Weddings.

Blue Mountains - Lawson *B & B   15 km E of Katoomba*

Araluen   AAATourism ★★★★☆
George & Gai Sprague.
59 Wilson Street, Lawson, NSW 2783

Tel: (02) 4759 1610 Fax: (02) 4759 2554
info@araluen.com   www.araluen.com
Double $135-$220 Single $95-$145
(Special Breakfast) Dinner $55
Credit Cards accepted Pet on property
3 Queen (3 bdrm)   3 Ensuite

"Perfect balance of pampering and privacy". Large, superbly furnished home overlooking Central Blue Mountains golf course (unlimited complimentary green fees). Comfy queen beds, modern ensuites. Sunny living room with romantic log fire, quiet reading room; huge games room (billiards/pool, piano etc). Heating/cooling throughout. Prizewinning gardens. Secluded waterfall walks nearby. Sumptuous breakfasts. (Candlelit dinners/picnic baskets by arrangement.) Close to three BYO eateries. Handy all Blue Mountains attractions. "Ideal getaway for 1, 2, or 3 couples". - Reviewed Sunday Tele 18/2/2001 and "Good Taste" Dec 2001. Sydney Morning Herald "Reader Recommendation" 16/03/02.

Blue Mountains - Leura   *B & B   0.75km E of Leura*

Woodford of Leura   AAATourism ★★★★☆
John & Lesley Kendall
48 Woodford Street, Leura, NSW 2780

Tel: (02) 4784 2240 Fax: (02) 4784 2240
Mobile: 0427 410 625   woodford@leura.com
www.leura.com
Double $130-$190 (Full Breakfast)
Single from $100   Credit Cards accepted
1 King/Twin 2 Queen 1 Double 1 Single (4 bdrm)
4 Ensuite

Elegant guest house located in one of Leura's quietest country lanes, this grand old home offers both suites and standard rooms, all with en-suites, TV and tea making facilities. Promising country hospitality, Woodford is renowned for its sumptuous breakfasts and complimentary afternoon tea on arrival. It also features central heating, indoor heated spa and cosy guest lounge with open log fire. Winner of 2000 Blue Mountains Regional Award for Excellence in Tourism - Hosted Accommodation. "Our 6th annual visit - and still sensational" ..A.S. and friends, St. Ives.

Blue Mountains - Leura *B & B Guest House 2.5 km Katoomba*

The Greens
Rose and Joe
26 Grose Street, Leura, NSW 2780

Tel: (02) 4784 3241 Fax: (02) 4784 3241
greens@hermes.net.au
www.bluemts.com.au/greens

Double $110-$165 Single $85-$95
(Full Breakfast) Credit Cards accepted
4 Queen 1 Twin (5 bdrm)
3 Ensuite 2 Share

The Greens built in the early 1920's was originally a pair of semi-detached cottages, now converted into a B&B adults retreat. The literary theme is throughout our home focusing on poets and writers inspired by their love of romance and nature. High ceilings, chandeliers, marble fireplace, library (with secret door), full size billiard table and heritage style bedrooms create an ambience of cosy comfort. Only 150 metres to Leura Village Mall, restaurants and cafes. - Central heating - non smoking indoors - sorry, no pets - 4 poster beds.

Blue Mountains - Leura *Homestay B & B 300m W of Leura*

White Gables AAATourism ★★★★
Libby & Robert Sayers
63 Railway Parade, Leura, NSW 2780

Tel: (02) 4784 1008 Mobile: 0411 095 350
whitegables@optusnet.com.au
www.whitegables.com.au

Double $110-$175 Single $95-$160 (Full Breakfast)
Extra person in suite $40 Credit Cards accepted
Pet on property
2 Queen 1 Single (3 bdrm) 1 Ensuite 1 Private

White Gables offers all the size, comfort and graciousness you would expect in a home built for a wealthy jeweller in 1924. This timber and slate home features stained glass entrance, wood panelling, and picture windows in every room. Gourmet breakfasts, central heating and log fires, beautiful bathrooms and bedrooms, spectacular views - yet just 300 metres to Leura village and station. Set in one acre of secluded gardens, what more could you wish for? Robert, Libby and Candy the Labrador look forward to welcoming you.

Blue Mountains - Leura *B & B 400m S of Leura*

Broomelea
Bryan & Denise Keith
273 Leura Mall, Leura, NSW 2780

Tel: (02) 4784 2940 Fax: (02) 4784 2611
Mobile: 0419 478 400   info@broomelea.com.au
www.broomelea.com.au

Double $154-$215 Single $130-$190 (Full Breakfast)
Cottage $154 - $190 Credit Cards accepted
3 Queen 2 Twin (4 bdrm)
4 Ensuite

Built in 1909, Broomelea is a wonderfully appointed Victorian home, perfect for a luxurious stay in the World Heritage listed Blue Mountains. The spacious rooms each have their own ensuite, fire place, four poster bed, TV and video. We are located just a short stroll from the restaurants and galleries of Leura Village and famous cliff top walks. Broomelea - the right balance between detailed attention and respectful privacy.

Blue Mountains - Leura   *B & B*   *800 m NW of Leura*

Bethany Manor Bed & Breakfast   AAAT★★★★☆
Greg & Jill Haigh
8 East View Avenue, Leura, NSW 2780

Tel: (02) 4782 9215 Fax: (02) 4782 1962
Mobile: 0402 068 208   bmanor@optusnet.com.au
www.bethanymanor.com.au

Double $120-$190 Single $100-$170 (Full Breakfast)
Credit Cards accepted
2 Queen 1 Double (3 bdrm)
3 Ensuite

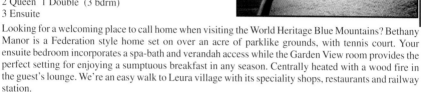

Looking for a welcoming place to call home when visiting the World Heritage Blue Mountains? Bethany Manor is a Federation style home set on over an acre of parklike grounds, with tennis court. Your ensuite bedroom incorporates a spa-bath and verandah access while the Garden View room provides the perfect setting for enjoying a sumptuous breakfast in any season. Centrally heated with a wood fire in the guest's lounge. We're an easy walk to Leura village with its speciality shops, restaurants and railway station.

Blue Mountains - Leura - Katoomba   *B & B*   *0.5 km E of Katoomba*

Leura Falls Bed & Breakfast
Ian Clare
56 Merriwa Street, Katoomba, NSW 2780

Tel: (02) 4782 9660 Fax: (02) 4782 9660
Mobile: 0414 934 822
leurafal@pnc.com.au
www.leurafalls.com

Double $130-$150 Single $120-$130 (Full Breakfast)
Credit Cards accepted
2 Queen (2 bdrm)   2 Private

Built early 1900's and situated in a peaceful bush location within the World Heritage Blue Mountains National Park. Short walk to shops and restaurants, with spectacular Jamison Valley Lookouts and bush-tracks only 100 metres away. (see website for our location). This romantic cottage has separate guest quarters with 2 bedrooms, own bathrooms, one with spa bath. Guest lounge and dining room with combustion fires. Electric blankets, TVs, coffee and tea. Enjoy a full hot breakfast in front of the fire or out in the terraced gardens.

Blue Mountains - Little Hartley - Mt Victoria   *15 km W of Mt. Victoria*

B & B   Separate/Suite Private Cabins
Karawatha Cabins
Inara and Ted Hawley
43 Megalong Place, Little Hartley, NSW 2790

Tel: (02) 6355 2330 Fax: (02) 6355 2407
info@karawathacabins.com.au
www.karawathacabins.com.au

Double $200-$250 (Full Breakfast)
Credit Cards accepted Pet on property
1 King (1 bdrm)   1 Ensuite

We specialise in luxury retreat style accommodation for couples. We offer a cozy warm atmosphere with timber lined cottages, fabulous views over Kanimbla Valley, open gas fireplace, bubbling spa, king size bed, double shower, the latest in entertainment systems, fully equipped kitchen and BBQ. Breakfast provisions, linen, towels and hairdryer are provided. Built on 30 acres, the cabins are private from the main house and each other. All you have to do when you arrive is immerse yourself in peaceful relaxation. We are unable to accommodate pets or children.

Blue Mountains - Mount Tomah - Bells Line of Road

B & B   14 km W of Bilpin

Tomah Mountain Lodge   AAATourism ★★★★☆
Bill & Gai Johns
Skyline Road, Mount Tomah via Bilpin, NSW 2758

Tel: (02) 4567 2111 Mobile: 0419 908 724
tomahlodge@ozemail.com.au
www.tomahmountainlodge.com.au

Double $180-$190 Single $165 (Full Breakfast)
Dinner $45 each Credit Cards accepted
3 Queen (3 bdrm)   3 Ensuite

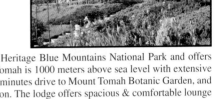

Tomah Mountain Lodge is situated in the World Heritage Blue Mountains National Park and offers prestige executive style accommodation. Mount Tomah is 1000 meters above sea level with extensive mountain views. This secluded setting is only two minutes drive to Mount Tomah Botanic Garden, and a short drive to the historic gardens at Mount Wilson. The lodge offers spacious & comfortable lounge rooms with log fires, you will often find Ben the kelpie enjoying the fire also. Gourmet three course candlelit dinners are a speciality.

Blue Mountains - Oberon - Jenolan Caves   *25 km E of Oberon*

B & B   Self Contained

Duckmaloi Farm   AAATourism ★★★★
S & R Paterson
54 Karawina Drive, Duckmaloi, NSW 2787

Tel: (02) 6336 1375 Fax: (02) 6336 1560
Mobile: 0414 445 018   paterson@lisp.com.au
www.bluemts.com.au/duckmaloi

Double $110-$145 (Full Breakfast) Dinner B/A
Cottages $110 - $145 Credit Cards accepted
2 King/Twin 1 Queen (2 bdrm)   1 Ensuite 1 Private

Award winning self care two bedroom cottages with two person spa, wood fire, full kitchen, TV/CD/ VCR etc, including linen and starter pack. Also two B & B rooms - a Queen bed with ensuite or two king singles and adjacent own bathroom, plus private guest lounge featuring open log fire, TV etc, board games & library, and quick snack cooking facilities. 100 acres of farmland with 4 acres of established gardens, tennis court, BBQ facilities, spectacular views and walks, 25 minutes from Jenolan Caves. Breakfast is provided in the B & B - the cottages are self catering. Children welcome in cottages.

Blue Mountains - Springwood   *Separate/Suite B & B   Springwood*

Southall
Helena & Greg Crumpton
353 Great Western Highway,
Springwood, NSW 2777

Tel: (02) 4751 8212 Fax: (02) 4751 8212
Mobile: 0415 119 019
southallretreat@bigpond.com
www.bbbook.com.au/southall.html

Double $200 Single $120-$150 (Full Breakfast)
2 Queen 1 Single (2 bdrm)
2 Ensuite

Escape to the magnificent Blue Mountains. Southall c1886 - Formerly The Old Vicarage. Built by Charles Moore former Lord Mayor of Sydney (Moore Park). This grand old sandstone home will capture your heart. Offering totally separate accommodation in quaint old romantic guest residence. Southall is so full of history and romance. An experience you'll treasure. - A yearning for yesterday. A promise for tomorrow -

Blue Mountains - Wentworth Falls

B & B Country House and Self Contained Cottages   8 km E of Katoomba

Whispering Pines by the Falls   AAATourism ★★★★☆
Maria & Bill McCabe
178 Falls Road, Wentworth Falls, NSW 2782

Tel: (02) 4757 1449 Fax: (02) 4757 1219 Mobile: 0412 144 917
wpines@bigpond.com
www.whisperingpines.com.au

Double $165-$250 Single $120-$250 (Continental Breakfast) (Full Breakfast) Cottage $165 - $440
Credit Cards accepted
3 Queen 1 Double 2 Twin (4 bdrm)
3 Ensuite 1 Private

Whispering Pines (c.1898) is a heritage-listed retreat on 4 acres at the head of the most spectacular waterfall in the beautiful Blue Mountains. Our home is perched right on the escarpment and we border the National Park with over 600,000 acres of unspoilt wilderness on our doorstep for you to explore. Birds are abundant - rosellas, king parrots, gang-gangs, and on a quiet night (when the pines aren't whispering) you can hear the falls tumbling into the valley. Our bedrooms are warm and spacious with feather doonas, electric blankets and luxury appointments. They have views down the peaceful Jamison Valley to Mt Solitary and the valleys beyond - a wondrous outlook especially at sunset. Our guests have use of a large lounge with open fire, sunny breakfast room (tea & coffee available at all times) and barbecue facilities.

We also have a self-contained accommodation available with all necessities supplied for couples and groups.

For information on these cottages follow the links on our web page. Non smoking, no pets or children. Directions: Please phone first - Complimentary pick up from station available.

Home Page: www.whisperingpines.com.au

"The character, attention to detail and remarkable setting all make this an unforgettable experience" - Australian Country Style

Blue Mountains - Wentworth Falls
400m S of Wentworth Falls

B& B   Self Contained

Moniques B & B
Jann & John Small
31 Falls Road, Wentworth Falls, NSW 2782

Tel: (02) 4757 1646 Fax: (02) 4757 2498
jjsmall@bigpond.com   www.moniques.com.au

Double $80-$150 (Full Breakfast)
Whole Cottage $240 - $390 Credit Cards accepted
1 King 1 Queen 1 Double 1 Single (3 bdrm)
3 Ensuite

Guests stay in the private, self-contained cottage. There are three bedrooms (king, queen/twin, double), each with ensuite, a large comfortable lounge/dining room with enclosed log fire, TV/video, a fully-equipped kitchen and a sunny terrace. The French Provincial style house and cottage are set in a quiet, mature garden. Features include: * generous self-catered breakfast * suitable for couples, groups of friends, families * walking distance to village shops and cafes * log fire, heating, electric blankets * close to famous bushwalks * attractive longer-stay rates.

Blue Mountains - Woodford   *B & B   18 km E of Katoomba*

Braeside
Robyn Wilkinson & Rex Fardon
97 Bedford Road, Woodford, NSW 2778

Tel: (02) 4758 6279 Fax: (02) 4758 8210
Mobile: 0414 542 860   Braeside.BandB@bigpond.com
www.bbbook.com.au/braeside.html

Double $100-$125 Single $70-$80 (Full Breakfast)
Child by arrangement Dinner by arrangement
Credit Cards accepted
1 King/Twin 1 Queen 1 Double (3 bdrm)
2 Ensuite 1 Private

Situated in the heart of the mountains Braeside offers a quiet escape as well as being central to all the attractions of the upper mountains. Bedrooms include one king/twin room with a private bathroom; a queensized room with ensuite; and a double room with ensuite and small sitting room with direct access to the garden. Bedrooms have heaters and electric blankets and the guests lounge has an open log fire for colder weather. No smoking indoors. Dinner, including BBQ's, available with notice.

Braidwood   *B & B   90 km SE of Canberra*

The Snow Lion
Margaret A Fair
58 Wilson Street, Braidwood, NSW 2622

Tel: (02) 4842 2023 Mobile: 0407 922 306
snowlion@ozemail.com.au
www.bbbook.com.au/snowlion.html

Double $100-$130 Single $75-$100 (Full Breakfast)
Credit Cards accepted Pet on property
2 Queen 1 Double 1 Single (3 bdrm)
2 Private 1 Share

Stay in a beautiful two storey Colonial terrace, refurbished with a unique eastern flavour. Relax in our comfortable sun rooms or wander quietly in the spacious garden. Situated in middle of town adjacent the park and local swimming pool, we enjoy a secluded but central location. Browse amongst the antique shops and galleries, or venture out to the local swimming holes, picnic areas and tourist destinations. The friendly patrons at "The Snow Lion" look forward to showing you where we live.

Bungendore   *B & B   30 km E of Canberra*

The Old Stone House
Geoff and Carolyn Banbury
41 Molonglo Street, Bungendore, NSW 2621

Tel: (02) 6238 1888 Fax: (02) 6238 1888
stnhsebb@tpg.com.au
www.bbbook.com.au/theoldstonehouse.html
Double $165 Single $110 (Full Breakfast)
Dinner by arrangement Credit Cards accepted
2 Queen 2 Double 1 Single (4 bdrm)
3 Ensuite 1 Private

The Old Stone House has attracted admiration since 1867. Now charmingly extended and furnished with fine antiques, guests can relax by firelight with "Tiggy" the dog. Behind the gate lies an acre of delightful garden. Down the steps to Giverny-inspired rose arches, discover the reflective pool, kitchen garden and wisteria walk. Leave the car and stroll to village attractions or drive to spring-time gardens and wineries close by. Retreat from the Nation's Capital half an hour away to life in a country village. Small celebrations/functions. No smoking please.

Bungendore   *Homestay B & B   30 km E of Canberra*

Birchfield
Gary & Kathy Royal
34 Turallo Terrace,
Bungendore, NSW 2621

Tel: (02) 6238 0607 Fax: (02) 6238 0607
Mobile: 0418 620 571   kroyal@ozemail.com.au
www.bbbook.com.au/birchfield.html
Double $130 Single $90 (Full Breakfast)
1 Double 1 Single (2 bdrm)
1 Ensuite 1 Private

Romantic and peaceful attic accommodation in historic "Birchfield". Double attic bedroom, sitting room, bathroom with spa and private entrance. Breakfast is served in the delightful cottage garden in the warm weather or by cosy wood fire in winter. "Birchfield" is a Victorian Gothic-style house built in the 1880's by Father Patrick Birch. Recently operated as "Birchfield Herbs". Restored to its former beauty, complimented by the fragrant, rambling cottage gardens. Located in Bungendore, a friendly, historic rural village, on the Kings Highway, just 30 minutes drive to Canberra. On Sydney to Canberra rail line.

Byron Bay   *B & B Guest House   Byron Bay Central*

Sandals B & B   AAATourism ★★★☆
Sue & David Shearer
1/11 Carlyle Street, Byron Bay, NSW 2481

Tel: (02) 6685 8025 Fax: (02) 6685 8599
Mobile: 0414 658 025
baysand@linknet.com.au
www.byron-bay.com/sandals
Double $90 Single $75 (Continental Breakfast)
Credit Cards accepted
1 King 1 Queen 2 Twin 1 Single (5 bdrm)
2 Ensuite 2 Share

Nestled in a quiet cul-de-sac in the heart of Byron, close to the many attractions, Sandals is a short stroll past the many and varied high quality shops and restaurants to the town centre and Main Beach. Sandals is more than just another Bed & Breakfast - it is a home away from home.....a place to unwind, soak in the sunlight, put your feet up and enjoy our complimentary tea, coffee and home-made biscuits any time of the day. To your charming hosts, your comfort, relaxation and every need is their only priority.

Byron Bay   *Homestay B & B   400m E of town*

Baystay
John Witham
30 Marvell Street, Byron Bay, NSW 2481

Tel: (02) 6685 7509 Fax: (02) 6685 7609
Mobile: 0418 857 509
baystay@nor.com.au
www.bbbook.com.au/baystay.html

Double $88-$98 Single $48-$58 (Special Breakfast)
Apartment $98 Credit Cards accepted Pet on property
1 Queen 3 Double 1 Twin 1 Single (6 bdrm)
2 Ensuite 2 Private 2 Share

Quiet, yet only a short stroll to beach and town. Set in a lush native garden, Baystay is a lovely modern beach house offering great value and great breakfasts. With delightful and comfortable guestrooms, spa, sauna, BBQ, bikes, a beautiful black Labrador and an amusing Gizmo, your stay will be relaxing and enjoyable. Your host, John, has lived in the area for over 18 years and can guide you on wonderful bush tours in and around town or just assist you to relax.

Byron Bay   *B & B   6 km W of Byron Bay*

Victoria's at Ewingsdale & Victoria's at Watego's
AAAT★★★★★   Victoria McEwen
Top of McGettigans Lane, Byron Bay, NSW 2481

Tel: (02) 6684 7047 Fax: (02) 6684 7687
Mobile: 0428 847 047   indulge@victorias.net.au
www.victorias.net.au

Double $295-$595 (Full Breakfast) Child POA
Credit Cards accepted
1 King 2 Queen 2 Double (5 bdrm)
5 Ensuite

Only minutes from Byron Bay, is the multi-award winning "Victoria's At Ewingsdale" (formerly "Ewingsdale Country Guest House"). This stately country manor is situated on 3 acres of landscaped gardens, and features panoramic ocean, mountain and rural views. "Victoria's at Wategos", is a stunning Tuscan style guest house, nestled in an exclusive ocean front valley at beautiful Wategos beach, just under the famous Cape Byron lighthouse, Experience personalised service in our small and exclusive boutique retreats, dedicated to providing the best in first class hospitality, quality and style.

Byron Bay   *Homestay B & B   2.5 km W of Byron Bay*

Planula B&B Retreat
Tim Hochgrebe
Lot 1 Melaleuca Drive, Byron Bay, NSW 2481

Tel: (02) 6680 9134 Fax: on request
Mobile: 0403 357 969   relax@planula.com.au
www.planula.com.au

Double $80-$140 Single $70-$120
(Continental Breakfast) Child over 7 y/o
Credit Cards accepted
3 Queen 2 Twin (5 bdrm)
1 Ensuite 4 Share

PLANULA offers modern B&B style accommodation just outside the town centre of Byron Bay. Spacious and beautiful and set on 2.5 acres amongst tropical gardens and ponds, PLANULA is close to everything but feels like a remote relaxed oasis. Features include large lounge room under cathedral ceiling, upstairs library and an extensive shady outdoor deck area with hammock and BBQ. Tariffs include extensive continental breakfast. Relax, indulge, enjoy - please book early to avoid disappointment.

Byron Bay   *B & B   0.5 km W of Centre of Town*

Byron Bay Balinese Guest House
Donnatella Ehrenberg
70 Kingsley Street,
Byron Bay, NSW 2481

Tel: (02) 6680 8886 Mobile: 0414 862 684
sleepme@bigpond.com
www.byronbayguesthouse.com.au

Double $120-$200 (Continental Breakfast)
Credit Cards accepted Pets welcome
1 King/Twin 1 King 2 Queen 1 Double (3 bdrm)
3 Ensuite

The Byron Bay Guest House combines a unique blend of Balinese style living with federation style charm. Our rooms are spacious and have polished timber floors. Some rooms have ensuites and we have a private courtyard. Ideally situated at the top end of Kingsley Street which is a short walk to Clarks Beach and a short stroll to the beach and town. Rates based on a 2 night stay. Surcharge applies Easter & Christmas. 10% discount if you mention the *The B & B Book* when booking.

Byron Bay - Kingsclift   *B & B   15 km W of Kingscliff*

Wangaree Homestead   AAATourism ★★★★☆
Nanette & Gerry O'Connell
Lot 1 Hattons Road, Durambah, NSW 2487

Tel: (02) 6677 7496   gerry.nanette@wangaree.com.au
Fax: (02) 6677 7492   Mobile: 0413 059 869
www.bbbook.com.au/wangaree.html

Double $140-$160 Single $130-$150
(Special Breakfast) Dinner $50 double
Credit Cards accepted
1 King/Twin 2 Queen (3 bdrm)   3 Ensuite

Secluded on 35 acres in the beautiful Tweed Valley, only 15 minutes to Gold Coast airport, incredible beaches, gourmet restaurants, championship golf courses, and close to Heritage rainforests, Mt. Warning and Byron Bay is Wangaree Homestead an Historic "Queenslander" 1885 filled with collectables and antiques. Luxury accommodation with TV in each bedroom, & open fire in the lounge room. Enjoy breakfast from local produce on the verandah overlooking the hoop pines and landscaped gardens, guest BBQ and swimming pool. Dinner by arrangement. Refresh your spirit here with us at Wangaree.

Candelo   *B & B   20 km SW of Bega*

Olivers of Candelo
Jeniffer & Robert Scowen
31 Kameruka Street, Candelo, NSW 2550

Tel: (02) 6493 2322 Fax: (02) 6493 2323
www.oliversofcandelo.com.au

Double $100-$130 Single $80-$100
Dinner $20-30 Picnic hampers $15-25
Credit Cards accepted Pet on property
2 Queen 1 Twin (3 bdrm)
1 Ensuite 2 Private

Do as the Wagoners of old, and stop and rest awhile in the picturesque village of Candelo. Relaxation our speciality. Olivers is a charming home built in 1888 and furnished in character. Take in the views, relax and listen to the birds from the wide verandahs. The high ceilings and open fires make for comfortable living all year. Rob restores old and antique furniture in the Coach house. We grow our own produce for the table and hampers. We look forward to meeting you and making your stay at Olivers a memorable one by catering to your every need. . .

Candelo - Bega Valley *Farmstay B & B   Self Contained   20 km SW of Bega*

Bumblebrook Farm   AAATourism ★★★☆
Rick & Ann Patten
Kemps Lane, Candelo, NSW 2550

Tel: (02) 6493 2238 Fax: (02) 6493 2299
bumblebrook@acr.net.au
www.bbbook.com.au/bumblebrook.html

Double $90-$105 Single $75-$90 (Full Breakfast)
Child under 13 free Dinner $40 Weekly from $440
Credit Cards accepted Pet on property Pets welcome
1 King/Twin 1 Queen 3 Double 4 Single (4 bdrm)
4 Ensuite

A 100 acre beef property on top of a hill with magnificent views and lovely bush walks, fronting Tantawangalo Creek. We have four well equipped self-contained units. Breakfast is a "cook-your-own" from our fresh farm ingredients. Children are welcome and can often help feed the farm animals. With prior notice guests are welcome to a friendly, candlelit, family dinner in the homestead. BBQ's are provided by the creek and in the rustic playground near the units. Beaches and National Parks nearby. Pets welcome with prior arrangement.

Central Coast - Blue Bay - Towoon Bay *0.5 km S of Toowoon Bay*

Homestay B & B   Self Contained

Shells at Blue Bay   Dawn Strauss
15 Yethonga Avenue, Blue Bay, NSW 2261

Tel: (02) 9534 2236 Fax: (02) 9534 2236
Mobile: 0419 223 090
www.bbbook.com.au/shellsatbluebay.html

Double $135-$280 Single $120-$210
(Continental & Full Breakfast)
Child $30 - $50 Dinner $30 pp B/A
4 Queen (4 bdrm) 1 Ensuite 1 Private

Shells at Blue Bay is a luxurious 4 bedroom air conditioned home with outdoor jacuzzi, beautifully decorated in 'By the sea style'. Short walk to the beach and a stroll to shops and restaurants. Offering Bed & Breakfast or self catering accommodation to suit couples or small groups, we provide VCRs, DVD and Foxtel entertainment, whilst tea/coffee, chocolates and biscuits are at hand. Located in a very quiet street offering privacy with a nautical/tropical ambience throughout. Security parking available. Children 12 yrs and over.

All our B&Bs are non-smoking
unless stated otherwise in the text.

Central Coast - East Gosford   *Homestay B & B   1 km S of Gosford*

Bliss Bed & Breakfast
Judy & George Kliendienst
8 Spears Street, Point Frederick, 2250

Tel: (02) 4325 4754 Fax: (02) 4325 4754
Mobile: 0411 220 147   gjail@tpg.com.au
www.bbbook.com.au/blissbb.html

Double $130 Single $80
(Continental & Full Breakfast) Credit Cards accepted
2 Queen (2 bdrm)
2 Ensuite

New South Wales

Just over an hours drive north of Sydney you can sit back and enjoy the blissful sounds of water lapping on the shore, the tinkling of masts in the breeze, everchanging waterviews and magnificent sunsets. Judy and George welcome you to "Bliss B & B" with three QS bedrooms each with ensuite and access to the heated pool and spa (and Sauna). Yummy breakfasts can be served in your own room, on your private terrace or create your own in the kitchenette.

Central Coast - Green Point   *B & B   7 km E of Gosford*

Binawee Bed & Breakfast   AAATourism ★★★★☆
Kevin & Patricia O'Donnell
295 Avoca Drive, Green Point, NSW 2251

Tel: (02) 4369 0981 Fax: (02) 4369 0997
Mobile: 0418 203 671   Binawee.@bigpond.com
www.bbbook.com.au/binawee.html

Double $135-$175 Single $75
(Continental & Full Breakfast) Dinner B/A
Credit Cards accepted
1 King/Twin 2 Queen (3 bdrm) 1 Ensuite 2 Private

Luxury accommodation featuring three theme rooms Titanic, Barrier Reef & Lighthouse. Hosts Kevin & Patricia greet guests with aperitifs and welcoming drinks whilst overlooking extensive water views. Guests can wander in the gardens, relax by the solar pool or indulge in the therapeutic spa. In winter enjoy the open fire and sunroom where we offer full video, CD, DVD and Foxtel. Binawee offers Gourmet Breakfasts, barbeque and tea making trolley. We are close to Terrigal, Erina, arts, cinemas, restaurants, beaches, Bushwalking, Reptile Park, Old Sydney Town. Free pickup from Rail, Bus or Ferry.

Central Coast - Hardys Bay   *B & B   12 km SE of Woy Woy*

McGregors by the Bay
Dawn & John McGregor
100A Araluen Drive, Hardys Bay, NSW 2257

Tel: (02) 4360 2631 Fax: (02) 4360 1004
sjdobbs@bigpond.com.au
www.bbbook.com.au/mcgregors.html

Double $150 Single $110 (Full Breakfast)
Credit Cards accepted
2 King/Twin 1 King 2 Queen (4 bdrm)
4 Ensuite

We are situated 1 1/2 hours north of Sydney via Woy Woy overlooking the tranquil Hardys Bay. Our home is brand new and has been designed to ensure all guest rooms have views of the scenic surroundings. Luxury rooms with ensuites are standard. A country styled full breakfast overlooking the Bay is a relaxing way to start the day. We are surrounded by Bouddi National Park and have excellent restaurants within walking distance. We regret children and pets are not catered for. Come watch the sunset over the bay.

Central Coast - Phegans Bay   *B & B   Self Contained   6 km W of Woy Woy*

Minervas Garden Cottage
Barbara & Brian Goodey
60 Phegans Bay Road, Phegans Bay, NSW 2256

Tel: (02) 4341 4295 Mobile: 0402 482 170
minervasgarden@yahoo.com.au
www.bbbook.com.au/minervasgardencottage.html

Double $85-$95 Single $70-$80 (Full Breakfast)
Dinner $20 B/A extra persons $35 - $40
1 King/Twin (1 bdrm)
1 Ensuite

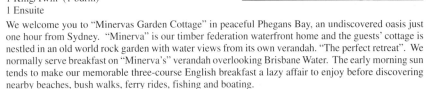

We welcome you to "Minervas Garden Cottage" in peaceful Phegans Bay, an undiscovered oasis just one hour from Sydney. "Minerva" is our timber federation waterfront home and the guests' cottage is nestled in an old world rock garden with water views from its own verandah. "The perfect retreat". We normally serve breakfast on "Minerva's" verandah overlooking Brisbane Water. The early morning sun tends to make our memorable three-course English breakfast a lazy affair to enjoy before discovering nearby beaches, bush walks, ferry rides, fishing and boating.

Central Coast - Terrigal - Avoca   *Homestay B & B   4 km E of Terrigal*

Figtree Cottage B&B   AAATourism ★★★★
Margaret & David Killen
247 Avoca Drive, Kincumber, NSW 2251

Tel: (02) 4368 3056 Fax: (02) 4365 2749
Mobile: 0410 683 056   ftcottage@ozemail.com.au
www.bbbook.com.au/figtreecottagebb.html

Double $120-$130 Single $80
(Continental & Full Breakfast) Credit Cards accepted
2 Double (2 bdrm)
1 Ensuite 1 Private

Nestled beneath an enormous fig tree, five minutes from Terrigal and Avoca beaches lies Figtree Cottage. Two double rooms available, guests are assured privacy, peace and quietness. One of the oldest properties in the region. Your hosts have created an atmosphere of warmth and comfort in beautiful surroundings and offer good old fashioned hospitality. Guests can enjoy an open fire in their own private lounge, stroll around the beautiful 2.5 acres of garden, relax by the pool and spa. Free limousine service to a beautiful restaurant.

Central Coast - Terrigal - Avoca   *B & B   2 km SW of Terrigal*

Fairbanks Lodge   AAATourism ★★★★☆
Sue Collett
250 Scenic Highway, Terrigal

Tel: (02) 4384 1752 Fax: (02) 4384 1573
deer@fairbankslodge.com.au
www.fairbankslodge.com.au

Double $165-$195 Single $95-$165
(Full Breakfast) Credit Cards accepted
3 Queen 1 Double (4 bdrm)
4 Ensuite

Fairbanks Lodge is a boutique Bed and Breakfast designed for couples, situated in a rural setting, minutes from the magnificent beaches of Terrigal and Avoca, boutique shopping, cafes and restaurants. The property, located on the Central Coast of New South Wales (90 minutes north of Sydney) has sweeping views across bush to the water, daily deer feeding, bushwalking tracks on property and full country breakfast.

Cobargo   *Homestay   500m W of Cobargo*

Old Cobargo Convent
Bob & Dianne Saunders
Wandella Road, Cobargo, NSW 2550

Tel: (02) 6493 6419 Fax: (02) 6493 6419
Mobile: 0413 362 812   oldconvent@asitis.net.au
www.babs.com.au/oldconvent

Double $100-$120 Single $65 (Full Breakfast)
Dinner $20 Credit Cards accepted
1 Queen 1 Double 2 Single (3 bdrm)
1 Ensuite 1 Share

Experience the ambience of yesteryear in historic Old Cobargo Convent. Comfortably restored, French doors lead onto the verandahs, for endless cups of tea or coffee and homemade treats. Enjoy magnificent, unspoilt rural views. We offer accommodation with warm, friendly, personalised service. A short stroll to historic working village of Cobargo which has preserved much of its fine original architecture. Centrally located, a short drive to village of Tilba, fishing and swimming at Narooma or Bermagui. We enjoy the company of guests and look forward to meeting you. We have a friendly cat and dog.

Cobargo   *Homestay   8 km W of Cobargo*

Eilancroft Country Retreat   AAATourism★★★★
Margaret and George Law
County Boundary Road, Cobargo, NSW 2550

Tel: (02) 6493 7362 Mobile: 0421 659 696
eilancroft@acr.net.au
www.bbbook.com.au/eilancroftbb.html

Double $95-$110 Single $80 (Full Breakfast)
Dinner $25 - $35 Credit Cards accepted
2 Queen (2 bdrm)
2 Ensuite

Welcome to our lovely 100 year old home, located amidst spectacular mountain scenery, overlooking the historic village of Cobargo. Our rooms have comfortable Queen beds, electric blankets, ensuites and private verandahs. We have a guest lounge/dining room with wood fire, tea & coffee making facilities. We serve delicious dinners by arrangement and have a smoke free interior. Nearby, beautiful Bermagui and Narooma beaches, historic Tilba, cheese factories and wineries. We look forward to meeting you and sharing our love of this beautiful area with you.

Coffs Harbour   *B & B   Self Contained   9 km N of Coffs Harbour*

Santa Fe Luxury Bed & Breakfast   AAAT★★★★☆
Sharon Howell
235 Gaudrons Road, Coffs Harbour, NSW 2450

Tel: (02) 6653 7700 Fax: (02) 6653 7050
santa_fe@bigpond.com.au
www.santafe.net.au

Double $165 Single $125 (Full Breakfast)
Credit Cards accepted
1 King 2 Queen 1 Twin (3 bdrm)
3 Ensuite

'SANTA FE' is not only the romance of Santa Fe but the irresistible appeal of it's lifestyle . . .a casual elegance. Tucked away in a secluded valley just 10 minutes nth of Coffs Harbour & 2min to Beautiful Sapphire Beach. Discover 6 acres of total luxury . . . adobe walls, vibrant colours, hammocks, textures & fragrances. Guest suites are each a haven, lavishly & romantically furnished with gorgeous ensuites, TV/video, plunger coffee, toiletries, hair dryers & pool towels.   All have private entrances & decks with table & chairs. 'Navajo' suite has a covered outdoor spa overlooking the lagoon & valley.

Coffs Harbour   *B & B Boutique Resort*   *15 km N of Coffs Harbour*

The Waterside   AAATourism ★★★★★
Christof & Gabrielle Meyer
80 Tiki Road, Coffs Harbour, NSW 2450

Tel: (02) 6653 7388 Fax: (02) 6653 7300
holidays@waterside.com.au
www.waterside.com.au
Double $199-$304 Single $125.5-$236.5
(Special Breakfast) Dinner From $39.50
Credit Cards accepted
1 King/Twin 3 Queen (4 bdrm)   4 Ensuite

This 5 star guesthouse is situated on 10 acres of tropical gardens, flanked by an estuary with a pristine beach only a short walk away through neighbouring National Park. The emphasis here is on personalised service, glorious food and matured wines in a luxurious yet relaxed and informal manner. Ideally suited to couples, the individually crafted guestrooms offer all facilities and comfort. The property includes a walk-in wine cellar, guest library, a tropical swimming pool, flood-lit half-tennis court, canoe and bikes. Bookings are essential.

Coffs Harbour Hinterland   *17 km NW of Coffs Harbour*

Farmstay B & B   Self Contained
Laurel Park Stud
Rosalind & John Hurst
38 Priors Road, Coramba, NSW 2450

Tel: (02) 6654 4230 Fax: (02) 6652 4824
Mobile: 0421 904 429   rozhurst@ozemail.com.au
www.laurelparkstud.com.au
Double $100 (Full Breakfast)
Child $25 (2-14 yrs) Credit Cards accepted
1 Queen (1 bdrm)   1 Private

Self-contained guest house including bedroom with queen sized bed and double sofa-bed, 3-way bathroom, sunroom/dining room, kitchenette, TV and video. Verandah with own BBQ. Set in 100 acres of lush rural setting on a working miniature horse stud. Enjoy new season's foals up close as well as an "Enthusiastic" Dalmatian and a well behaved Kelpie. Located in the beautiful Orara Valley just 17km NW of Coffs Harbour. Many attractions nearby. Dinner by arrangement. Pets not permitted. Outdoor spa available summer 2002-3. Your hosts are Rosalind and John Hurst.

Coffs Harbour - Sawtell   *B & B*   *8 Km S of Coffs Harbour*

Woodlands Beach House B & B
AAATourism ★★★★
Ron & Judy Woodlands
4 Boronia Street, Sawtell, NSW 2452

Tel: (02) 6658 9177 Fax: (02) 6658 9177
Mobile: 0410 543 824   juron727@ecopost.com.au
www.woodlandsbeachouse.com.au.htm
Double $100-$150 Single $70-$100
(Full Breakfast) Credit Cards accepted
2 Queen (2 bdrm)   2 Ensuite

We are situated near the southern headland of Sawtell with beautiful views of the ocean, creek estuary and Bongil Bongil National Park. The surf beach, rock pool and lookout are nearby. Sawtell is an unspoilt seaside village, containing popular restaurants, heritage cinema, shops and clubs. Activities available include surfing, fishing, boating and golf. Coffs Harbour and its attractions are only 10 minutes away. We have two rooms, both tastefully decorated and with private ensuites. One has ocean views. Airport, rail or coach transfers are available.

Coffs Harbour - Sawtell   *B & B   S of Sawtell*

Alamanda Lodge Sawtell   AAATourism ★★★★☆
Sue & Wal Midgley
59 Boronia Street, Sawtell, NSW 2452

Tel: (02) 6658 9099 Fax: (02) 6658 9098
alamanda@ozemail.com.au
ozemail.com.au/~alamanda

Double $85-$150 Single $77-$121
(Continental Breakfast) Credit Cards accepted
4 Queen (4 bdrm)
4 Ensuite

New South Wales

Alamanda Lodge is 4 1/2 star accommodation situated within 5 minutes of Sawtell Beach, BYO restaurants and unique cinema. A stylish B&B purpose built for couples. Four queen rooms with private bathrooms and balconies. Whether it's a short getaway, a relaxing holiday, or a stopover our "rather special place" provides our guests with an atmosphere in which to spoil themselves. Breakfast included in tariff is buffet style with a selection of fresh fruits, cereals, eggs, toasts and spreads. A full cooked breakfast is an optional extra.

Cooma   *Farmstay B & B   15 km S of Cooma*

Springwell B & B
Patrick & Stephanie Litchfield
Springwell, Cooma, NSW 2630

Tel: (02) 6453 5545 Fax: (02) 6453 5539
Mobile: 0429 993 660
springwell@snowy.net.au
www.bbbook.com.au/springwellbb.html

Double $100 Single $55 (Full Breakfast)
Child $25 inc GST Dinner $25 - $35
3 Double 1 Twin (3 bdrm)   3 Private

Enjoy an Historic Country Homestead on a working property. Available is a tennis court, large verandahs, spacious garden and farm walks on the Monaro Treeless plains with views to the Snowy Mountains. Trout fishing and horse riding can be arranged. The unique Snowy Mountains Hydro Scheme, the Snowfields and the "Sapphire South Coast" can all be reached in just over an hour. Sumptuous Australian "country" dinners are available by arrangement and the cooked breakfasts are renowned. Contact for direction. Children welcome, no pets.

Cooma - Snowy Mountains - Nimmitabel

Nimmitabel Central   B & B Guest House

Royal Arms   AAATourism ★★★☆
Jack, Rhondda & Heidi Garside
Snowy Mountains Highway, Nimmitabel, NSW 2631

Tel: (02) 6454 6422 Fax: (02) 6454 6433
stay@royalarms.com.au   www.royalarms.com.au

Double $93 Single $52 (Full Breakfast)
Dinner $28 4 suites from $130
Credit Cards accepted Pets welcome b/a
4 Double 3 Twin (9 bdrm)   2 Ensuite 3 Share

Historic Royal Arms in pioneering village of Nimmitabel, restored featuring modern facilities whilst retaining its olde world charm with antique furnishings. Since 1989, family-staff have provided weary travellers with a friendly atmosphere plus hearty country meals (a tradition that began back in the 1850's when it played host to horse drawn carriages), picnic baskets on request. Our delightful building boasts of a friendly ghost, used as the hotel in 1960' film "The Sundowners". Central, trout fishing, bird watching, bush walks, wineries, ski fields, only 1 1/2 hours Canberra. Come on home to the Royal Arms.

Cootamundra - Young   *Self Contained Farmstay   3 km N of Wallendbeen*

Old Nubba Schoolhouse
Fred & Genine Clark
Wallendbeen, NSW 2588

Tel: (02) 6943 2513 Fax: (02) 6943 2590
Mobile: 0438 432 513   nubba@dragnet.com.au
www.bbbook.com.au/oldnubbaschoolhouse.html

Double $95 Single $75 (Full Breakfast) Dinner $30
Pet on property Pets welcome
1 Queen 4 Double 8 Single (6 bdrm)
3 Private

Old Nubba is a sheep/grain farm midway between Cootamumdra and Young, 3 1/2 hours SW of Sydney, 1 1/2 hours west of Canberra. The Schoolhouse, Killarney Cottage and Peppertree Cottage are all fully self-contained and have heating, cooling, electric blankets and linen provided. They sleep 4-8. Children will love the chickens, ducks, geese, dogs and pet lambs and will be able to help with farm activities. Other farm attractions include peace and quiet, bush walks, birdlife, bike riding, fishing and olive picking (in season). Pets under control are welcome.

Cowra   *Farmstay B & B   24 km S of Cowra*

Oakleigh
Shirley Webster
Cowra, NSW 2794

Tel: (02) 6345 4226 Fax: (02) 6342 1430
www.bbbook.com.au/oakleigh.html

Double $110 Single $70
(Continental & Full Breakfast)
Child $30 - $45 Dinner $25
4 Double 4 Single (4 bdrm)
1 Ensuite 1 Private 1 Share

Oakleigh a third generation merino sheep property of 2500 acres. It is not a hobby farm but a real piece of Australia. You can help or watch mustering sheep or cattle - chase a few rabbits or find kangaroos. You will experience home cooked meals, swimming and tennis with the family, who are all keen sportsmen and good hosts. Four beautifully decorated bedrooms overlook large garden with tennis court and swimming pool enclosed. Attractions: Japanese gardens, vineyards, Wyangala Dam. The Webster family welcome you to Oakleigh. Aussie Host.

Cowra   *B & B   30km N of Cowra*

Conargo B & B Woodstock
Barbara & Peter Carne
Conargo, 286 Nargong Road, Woodstock, NSW 2793

Tel: (02) 6345 0365 Fax: (02) 6345 0004
Mobile: 0429 848 232
conargo_woodstock@hotmail.com
www.bbbook.com.au/conargobb.html

Double $121 Single $88 (Full Breakfast)
Dinner $30 Credit Cards accepted
1 King/Twin 1 Queen (2 bdrm)
2 Ensuite

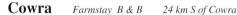

A quiet friendly stylish Bed & Breakfast where our guests enjoy comfort and privacy of this purpose-built cottage on a fine wool Merino property on sealed road - between Blayney and Cowra (30km from Cowra) in the beautiful clean air of the Central Tablelands. Bedrooms have ensuites and all rooms open onto a wide verandahs with spectacular views of rolling hills, trees and pastures. Birds and wildlife abound. Delicious breakfasts served or self-cater if preferred. Dinners are a speciality on request.

Crookwell   *Farmstay Homestay B & B*   *15 km SE of Crookwell*

Minnamurra Farmstay   AAATourism ★★★☆
Tony & Mary Prell
Minnamurra, Crookwell, NSW 2583

Tel: (02) 4848 1226 Fax: (02) 4848 1288
mprell@tpg.com.au
www.bbbook.com.au/minnamurrafarmstay.html

Double $140-$165 Single $70 (Special Breakfast)
Child $35, 5 - 12yrs Dinner B/A
1 Double 2 Twin 1 Single (4 bdrm)
1 Ensuite 1 Share

Award winning Minnamurra Farmstay is a 1080 hectare farm just 3 hours from Sydney, running 9000 sheep. Our home is warm, friendly and comfortable with fresh flowers in every room and tender loving care always on hand. Special breakfast - other meals by arrangement. Good homestyle country cooking. Laundry facilities available. Smoke-free and quiet - no children under 5 and no pets in the house. Undulating and picturesque country. Tennis. Trout fishing. Farm activities at certain times. Fresh air and blue skies. Rest and Relaxation. Gracious Living. AussieHost accredited. Winner of Awards for Excellence in Tourism.

Crookwell   *Farmstay Homestay B & B*   *30 km NW of Goulburn*

Gundowringa   AAATourism ★★★☆
Jess & Jeff Prell
Crookwell, NSW 2583

Tel: (02) 4848 1212 Fax: (02) 4848 1212
Gundowringa@ozemail.com.au
www.bbbook.com.au/gundowringa.html

Double $140 Single $70 (Full Breakfast)
Child $35t Pets welcome
2 Double 1 Twin 4 Single (4 bdrm) 2 Share

Gundowringa is a Heritage listed Federation homestead, built in 1905 by Charles E Prell OBE. Gundowringa homestead is surrounded by a large award winning garden. Spectacular views of the paddocks and picturesque undulating countryside are had from many vantage points. This gracious homestead has central heating and an open log fire in the sitting room. All beds have electric blankets and bed lights. Three large rooms have handbasins. Guests share two bathrooms. A tennis court, trout fishing and swimming pool are available for guests to enjoy. We welcome children inside and pets outside. Smoke free.

Crookwell   *B & B*   *Self Contained*   *40 km NW of Crookwell*

Markdale Homestead
Geoff & Mary Ashton
Mulgowrie Road, Binda, NSW 2583

Tel: (02) 4835 3146 Fax: (02) 4835 3160
gashton@compuserve.com
www.markdale.com

Double $120-$200 Single $60-$100 (Full Breakfast)
Dinner $30 - $40 Credit Cards accepted Pets welcome
2 Queen 1 Double 6 Twin (6 bdrm)
1 Ensuite 2 Private

Food for the soul and your Country Estate. A beautiful landscape stretching over 8000 acres, trout stocked streams, solar heated pool and all weather tennis. The Markdale Homestead and Garden is the only example combining the talents of two Australia Icons; Edna Walling, the famous garden designer, and Professor Wilkinson, architect for the Homestead. Live in two adjoining, self contained, beautifully renovated, 1850s stone houses. Both have central heating, open fire, sitting room, kitchen including microwave, laundry, TV, and CD player.

Dorrigo   *B & B   Rural   6 km W of Dorrigo*

Fernbrook Lodge   AAATourism ★★★★
Ross & Sue Erickson
4705 Waterfall Way, Dorrigo, NSW 2453

Tel: (02) 6657 2573 Fax: (02) 6657 2573
fernbrooklodge@midcoast.com.au
www.midcoast.com.au/~fernbrooklodge

Double $90-$105 Single $60 (Full Breakfast)
Child $25 Dinner $25 - $30
2 Queen 1 Double 2 Single (4 bdrm)
4 Ensuite

If you would enjoy quality comfort, warm consideration of your needs, fresh mountain air, fresh flowers, books, cushions and comfy chairs, magnificent views to the sea, a peaceful old garden of sighing pines, tree ferns, great birdlife and afternoon tea on arrival we would be delighted to welcome you. Dinner by arrangement features local produce. Dietary needs thoughtfully catered. Two verandah rooms garden access. 10 minutes Dorrigo Rainforest, Dangar Falls, excellent craft & art. One hour drive four National Parks, surf beaches, rivers, Ebor Falls, Wollomombi Gorge, trout fishing. Aussie Host Gold.

Dubbo   *Farmstay   22 km Dubbo*

Immarna B & B
Michele McFarland
12R Coolbaggie Road, Dubbo, NSW 2830

Tel: (02) 6887 3131 Mobile: 0419 012 494
russ@hwy.com.au
www.bbbook.com.au/immarnabb.html

Double $85 Single $60 (Full Breakfast)
Child $10 Dinner $10 - $22
Cottage $100 Credit Cards accepted Pets welcome
3 Queen 1 Double 1 Single (5 bdrm) 1 Share

Immarna has to be the perfect setting for time out from your busy lifestyle. Enjoy country hospitality with in-house chef's French/Italian cuisine amongst the tranquil surroundings of Immarna's 720 acres. Immarna was built in 1912 and is the oldest historic B&B in Dubbo. We accommodate up to 10 guests including a separate cottage, all located in expansive gardens. At Immarna you can crayfish, take a Kangaroo tour, view the Angus cattle and Polwarth sheep studs, play croquet or simply relax and soak up the fresh country air. Children welcome.

Eden   *Self Contained Homestay B & B   Eden Central*

Gibsons by the Beach   AAATourism ★★★★
Allan and Ruth Gibson
10 Bay Street,
Eden, NSW 2551

Tel: (02) 6496 1414 gibsons@asitis.net.au
www.bbbook.com.au/gibsons.html

Double $120-$160 Single $95-$120
(Full Breakfast) Child $15 - $35
2 Queen 3 Single (2 bdrm)
1 Ensuite 1 Private

Nature Lover's Paradise. Self-contained garden apartment (sleeps up to 5), including spa bath. Also available Q-bed room with ensuite. 2 minute bush walk to protected Cocora Beach Come and explore the magnificent beauty of Twofold Bay, beaches and surrounding National Parks. Excellent Bay Cruises or fishing trips with whale watching Oct/Nov. Enjoy bushwalking, golf, fishing, swimming, snorkelling, diving or just relaxing, here or at the wharves. Great restaurants. Children are welcome.

Eden   B & B   *Eden Central*

Crown & Anchor Inn B & B   AAATourism ★★★★
Eric and Jennifer Shuwalow
239 Imlay Street, Eden, NSW 2551

Tel: (02) 6496 1017 Fax: (02) 6496 3878
crownanchor@acr.net.au
www.acr.net.au/~crownanchor
Double $150-$170 Single $130-$150 (Full Breakfast)
Dinner B/A   Credit Cards accepted
4 Double (4 bdrm)
4 Ensuite

Step back in time and experience romantic early Australian charm in an original 1840's Inn. Spectacular ocean and bay views, ensuite bathrooms, antique furnishings, open fires and complementary champagne. The generous breakfast is old-fashioned country style complemented by freshly squeezed fruit juice, fine coffees and teas to be enjoyed overlooking Twofold Bay. Watch whales from the veranda during October and November. Central to Eden and wonderfully quiet; walk to restaurants, beaches and working wharf. As seen on Getaway. Not suitable for children. Smoking outside.

Eden   *Centre of Eden*

Cocora Cottage   AAATourism ★★★★
Gail and David Ward
2 Cocora Street, Eden, NSW 2551

Tel: (02) 6496 1241 Fax: (02) 6496 1137
Mobile: 0427 218 859
wardg@acr.net.au
www.cocoracottage.com
Double $125-$135 Single $110
2 Queen (2 bdrm)
2 Ensuite

Heritage listed Cocora Cottage was the original Police Station in Eden. It is centrally located in a quiet area close to Eden's famous Killer Whale Museum, the Wharf and Eden's fine restaurants. Breakfast is served upstairs with spectacular views down to the Wharf and across Twofold Bay to the foothills of Mt Imlay. Both bedrooms have a Queen sized bed, a television and an ensuite with a spa. The front bedroom features the original open fireplace while the back bedroom offers bay views.

Ettalong Beach   B & B   *1 km S of Ettalong*

Ettalong Beach House B & B   AAATourism ★★★★
Pam & Sueann
129 The Esplanade, Ettalong Beach, NSW 2257

Tel: (02) 4343 1895 Fax: (02) 4343 1894
enquiries@centralcoast-b-and-b.com.au
www.centralcoast-b-and-b.com.au
Double $120-$155 Single $100-$135
(Full Breakfast) Credit Cards accepted
4 King/Twin 4 King (4 bdrm)
4 Ensuite

Mediterranean in design, this idyllic seaside retreat is situated on Ettalong Beach, only 1 hour north of Sydney on the scenic Central Coast. Beautiful waterways surrounded by national parks offers much to see and do. Enjoy a leisurely breakfast served on the Ocean View Deck with panoramic views out over Broken Bay, Lion Is. with Pittwater in the background. Imagine being lulled to sleep by the sound of waves. Pristine beaches to stroll, sparkling blue waters to swim or just sit back and relax over a good bottle of wine.

Forster - Black Head Beach

Homestay B & B   20 km N of Forster / Tuncurry

Waves on High St   AAATourism ★★★★
Glenda & Vince Arnold

36 High Street, Black Head Beach, Hallidays Point, NSW   2430
Tel: (02) 6559 3600 Fax: (02) 6559 3263   Mobile: 0428 36 00 36
wavesonhighst@ceinternet.net.au www.wavesonhighst.com.au

Double $135-$150   Single $120-$135
(Full Breakfast)   Visa/MC/BC accepted
Beds: 3 Queen (3 bdrm)   Bath: 3 Ensuite

Treat yourself to an idyllic break in a captivating, picturesque seaside village.
Commanding panoramic ocean views from every room await. Our spacious beachside retreat is perfect for that impromptu escape or short getaway. Soak up this unique, tranquil setting with its spectacular coastline and rolling countryside.

The luxurious bedrooms are large, bright and sunny, each decorated with individual seaside themes and of course all enjoying a sensational ocean view. Comfortable queen sized beds, fluffy towels, quality linen and outstanding fittings are provided. Let the ocean lull you to sleep or just gaze at the myriad of stars.

Our coastal hideaway is 3 hours north of Sydney - a traditional B&B with refreshments on arrival and a chat with friendly hosts. As well as the gourmet breakfasts, we offer fresh orange juice, homemade breads and seasonal fruits. Complete the breakfast experience with locally produced preserves, and freshly brewed coffee and tea.

Local attractions include swimming with dolphins, pristine beaches, a beautiful ocean pool, great golf courses, rainforest walks or a stroll through the village streets. Alternatively select a cosy armchair in one of the comfy living rooms and read a book or watch cable TV.   The perfect setting for a casual, relaxed break - enjoy a home away from home.

Forster - Green Point   *Homestay B & B*   *5 km S of Forster*

New South Wales

Lakeside Escape B & B   **AAATourism ★★★★**
Denise & Rob Dunsterville
85 Green Point Drive, Green Point, Forster, NSW 2428

Tel: (02) 6557 6400 Fax: (02) 6557 6401
Mobile: 0412 314 426   lakesideescapebnb@tsn.cc
www.bbbook.com.au/lakesideescape.com.au.html

Double $140-$150 Single $110-$125
(Special Breakfast) Dinner $25 - $45pp
Extra person $50 Credit Cards accepted
1 King/Twin 2 Queen (3 bdrm)   3 Ensuite

Indulge in tranquillity and luxury at our purpose-built, bush-setting, waterfront home. Choose from undisturbed intimacy or harmony with your hosts. Unwind in the outdoor heated spa among the trees or around the cosy fire. Close, stunning water views of Wallis Lake from every room. Observe the changing moods and colours of the lake and awesome sunsets. See our website for special packages. Five minutes to cafes, restaurants, shops, safe beaches and a huge variety of sport, recreational and relaxing activities to suit all requirements.

Forster - Tuncurry - Hallidays Point   *B & B*   *15 km N of Forster*

Blackhead Beach B & B   **AAATourism ★★★★**
Richard & Margaret Flint
23 Woodlands Drive, Hallidays Point, NSW

Tel: (02) 6559 2143 Fax: (02) 6559 2104
Mobile: 0412 325 675
flintsbnb@blackheadbeachbnb.com.au
www.blackheadbeachbnb.com.au

Double $120-$135 Single $120 (Special Breakfast)
Dinner $27.50 Credit Cards accepted
Pet on property Pets welcome
2 Queen 1 Twin (3 bdrm)   1 Ensuite 1 Share

We have luxury 4 Star Bed & Breakfast accommodation only 12 mins north of Forster, and three hours from Sydney. There are three beautiful beaches only six minutes drive from our large home, which includes two hectares of gardens, native birds and wildlife. You are welcomed with a country afternoon tea. Dinner is available with notice. Breakfast is THE meal of the day with gourmet a la carte dishes and home made bread, jams and yoghurt. Well-behaved pets are welcome, as are teenage children.

Gerringong   *Homestay B & B*   *50m E of Gerringong*

Tumblegum Inn   **AAATourism ★★★★**
Heather Williams
141C Belinda Street, Gerringong, NSW 2534

Tel: (02) 4234 3555 Fax: (02) 4234 3888
Mobile: 0419 469 099
tumbleguminn@hotmail.com
www.tumbleguminn.com.au

Double $100-$120 Single $90-$110
(Full Breakfast) Credit Cards accepted
2 Queen 1 Twin (3 bdrm)   3 Ensuite

With rolling green hills that lap to pristine beaches, Gerringong reminds visitors of Ireland. Tumblegum Inn is a newly-built Federation style home featuring antique furnishings and warm hospitality. Two queen and one twin share bedrooms each contain ensuites, electric blankets, fans, clock radios and remote TV. Separate guest lounge has fridge, tea and coffee facilities, and home baked goodies. Only 1 1/2 hour south of Sydney, local attractions include beach side golf course, saltwater pools, boutique wineries, Minnamurra Rainforest and Kiama blowhole. Sorry no children or pets.

Glen Innes   *B & B   Glen Innes Central*

Glen Innes Bed & Breakfast
Bill & Joyce Stringer
95 Church Street, Glen Innes
P.O. Box 683, Glen Innes, NSW 2370

Tel: (02) 6732 4226 Fax: (02) 6732 6578
Mobile: 0421 310 900   gibandb@bigpond.com.au
www.bbbook.com.au/gleninnesbedbreakfast.html

Double $85 Single $50
(Continental & Full Breakfast)
Child $25 Dinner by arrangement
2 Queen 2 Single (3 bdrm)   1 Share

This quaint two storey Cape Cod cottage is set in half an acre of gardens and has all the old fashion comforts and genuine hospitality you could wish for. We are located on the New England highway just a short leisurely stroll to the historic main street, the majority of buildings being heritage listed, the remaining legacy of our past colonial charm. Picturesque Glen Innes is Australia's Celtic capital nestled in the Northern Tablelands of the delightful New England district. A perfect place to rest while travelling.

Glen Innes - Ben Lomond   *32 km N of Guyra*

Farmstay Homestay B & B   Self Contained
Silent Grove Farmstay   AAATourism ★★★☆
John & Dorothy Every
Silent Grove, Ben Lomond, NSW 2365

Tel: (02) 6733 2117 Fax: (02) 6733 2117
Mobile: 0427 936 799   silentgr@northnet.com.au
http://home.bluepin.net.au/silentgrove

Double $75 Single $40 (Full Breakfast) Child $15
Dinner $18 SC $80 per night Credit Cards accepted
1 Queen 1 Double 2 Single (3 bdrm)   2 Share

Enjoy country hospitality in a peaceful rural setting, short detour by sealed road from the New England Highway. Top of the Tablelands. Working sheep and cattle property. Farm activities. 4WD tour through property to see Kangaroos & Birdlife (fee applies). Panoramic views, scenic walks, yabbying (seasonal), tennis court, trout fishing, occasional snow fall. Easy access to new England, Gibraltar Range, Washpool National Parks. Glen Innes Australian Stones. Smoking outdoors. Have a cat. Winner of 2001 Big Sky Regional Tourism Hosted Accommodation. Campervans welcome.

Gloucester   *Homestay B & B   109 km N of Newcastle*

Arrowee House B & B
Kay Wright
Barrington Road,
Gloucester, NSW 2422

Tel: (02) 6558 2050 Mobile: 0417 417 673
www.bbbook.com.au/arroweehousebb.html

Double $100 Single $50 (Full Breakfast)
Child $20 Dinner $20 Credit Cards accepted
4 Queen 10 Single (7 bdrm)
5 Ensuite 1 Share

Gloucester - Barrington Tops. Delightful rural setting of cosy Arrowee House. Large brick home, surrounded by verandahs and open scenic views of rolling hills and mountains. Inviting wood heater for winter and cool air conditioning for summer. Homely spacious lounge dining area to return to, after bush walking, canoeing, horse riding, scenic drives, golfing or using local sporting complex. After a days activity a sumptuous 3 course dinner with a complimentary wine and port optional. A satisfying cooked breakfast with home baked bread to start another day.

Gloucester - Barrington Tops   *Homestay B & B   Gloucester Central*

Gloucester Cottage B & B   AAATourism ★★★☆
Keith & Betty Anido
61 Denison Street, Gloucester, NSW 2422

Tel: (02) 6558 2658 Fax: (02) 6558 2658
anido@tpg.com.au
www.barringtons.com.au/gloucestercottage
Double $90 Single $60 (Full Breakfast)
Child $15 - $30 Dinner $20 - $25
3 Queen 4 Single (4 bdrm)
3 Share

Come, visit our delightful Federation timber home in picturesque Gloucester, "Basecamp of the Barringtons". Discover why guests wrote "World's Best B&B"! Visit our website and view our high-ceilinged bedrooms with their hand-painted friezes. Relax by a crackling log fire, or be cooled by the breezes on our spacious verandahs. Eat delicious country breakfasts in our friendly breakfast room, and by arrangement, family-style dinners or takeaway picnics. Courtesy XPT train pickup. (Hear Keith's world famous Kookaburra call!)

Gloucester - Barrington Tops - Dungog   *30 km S of Gloucester*   🚶

Self Contained Farmstay B & B
Valley View Homestead B & B
AAATourism ★★★★   John & Denise Glew
1783 Bucketts Way, Wards River, NSW 2422

Tel: (02) 4994 7066 Fax: (02) 4994 7066
Mobile: 0417 409 729   www.valleyviewbnb.com
Double $100-$110 Single $60 (Full Breakfast)
Child $5 under 3 yrs Credit Cards accepted
Cottage $120 double, extra persons $20 Pet on property
1 King/Twin 2 Queen (3 bdrm) 1 Ensuite 2 Share

Enjoy the relaxed atmosphere at this tranquil retreat set in 30 acres at the foothills of The Barrington Tops. Included in your accommodation is our sumptuous full country breakfast. Listen to the sounds of the native birdlife while you relax around the pool or have a BBQ and just sit back and enjoy the magnificent views. The Barrington area caters for many varied activities - horseriding, 4x4 driving. Sightseeing around historic Stroud and Gloucester. Bushwalking. Golf. Mountain biking. Canoeing and Kayaking. We also have the self-contained Bower Bird cottage where children and pets are most welcome.

Grafton   *Farmstay Homestay B & B   10 km Grafton*   🧗

Seeview Farm   AAATourism ★★☆
Mona Ibbott
440 Rogans Bridge Road,
Seelands Grafton, NSW 2460

Tel: (02) 6644 9270 Fax: (02) 6644 9270
Mobile: 0429 004 872
www.bbbook.com.au/seeviewfarm.html
Double $90-$110 Single $70-$80
(Continental & Full Breakfast) Child $17.50
Dinner $20 Pet on property Pets welcome
1 Queen 2 Single (2 bdrm) 1 Private 1 Share

Seaview Farm is a pretty cattle property on the banks of the Clarence River which is noted for river boat and water skiing. Grafton is famous for its Jacaranda Festival and its historical buildings. Close to beaches and mountains. Enjoy peaceful countryside - many overseas students have visited the farm, where pets are welcome. Kangaroos and bird life to watch. Good stopover from Sydney or Brisbane. Relaxing and friendly. Children are welcome.

Grenfell   *Farmstay Homestay B & B*   *15 km N of Grenfell*

Garrawilla
Pip & Colin Wood
Grenfell, NSW 2810

Tel: (02) 6343 3218 Fax: (02) 6343 3218
pippacol@hotmail.com
www.bbbook.com.au/garrawilla.html

Double $75 Single $40
(Continental & Full Breakfast)
Child per year of age Dinner $15 Pets welcome
1 Twin 2 Single (2 bdrm)
1 Ensuite 1 Private

Garrawilla is a farming and grazing property in Central West NSW - the sheepdogs are friendly, the garden is large and the guest room has its own door onto the verandah and garden. It is a twin room with ensuite, TV, electric blankets, heater, fan and garage. A warm welcome with tea, coffee and home-made goodies awaits your arrival, plus a wholesome meal if needed.   Grenfell is a small country town in a farming district. Henry Lawson Festival of Arts, Ben Hall bushranger, Weddin Mountain National Park.

Griffith   *B & B Self Contained   15 km E of Griffith*

Ingleden Park Cottages
Gerardine & Trevor Hill
Coghlan Road, Griffith, NSW 2680

Tel: (02) 6963 6527 Fax: (02) 6963 6527
Mobile: 0429 042 979
ingleden@webfront.net.au
www.bbbook.com.au/ingleden.html

Double $88 Single $66 (Continental Breakfast)
Child $10 $10 per extra adult/child Pet on property
2 Queen 3 Twin (5 bdrm)
2 Private

Ingleden Park is just 15 minutes from Griffith. Guests are welcome to look in on farming activities or relax and enjoy the country atmosphere in a cottage garden. Crops grown: rice, azuki beans, pumpkins, wheat, faba beans and Canola. Livestock included: crossbred herd of cattle and prime lambs.   The renovated cottage includes all the comforts of home - linen, electric blankets, wood heater, air conditioning, tv, video and washing machine.

Gundagai   *Farmstay B & B   14 km NW of Gundagai*

Gundagai Farmstay B & B
Des and Carol Manton
1420 Burra Road, Gundagai, NSW 2722

Tel: (02) 6944 8242 Mobile: 0407 217 616
mantons@dragnet.com.au
www.bbbook.com.au/gundagaibb.html

(Full Breakfast) Cottage $99 - $120
Credit Cards accepted
2 Queen 4 Single (2 bdrm)
2 Private

We offer you a choice of 2 self contained cottages in a quiet rural setting. Breakfast supplies to prepare at your leisure, which may include any fruit available from our garden. Bird watching, bush walking, fishing the dam for crayfish or a native bream, or just space and privacy to relax in your own way. Explore our historic town and sample its culinary delights. True blue Aussie country hospitality. Stay overnight, or as long as you like.

Gunning   *Guest House   45 km W of Goulburn*

Frankfield Guesthouse
Susan Hansen-Smith
1-3 Warrataw Street, Gunning, NSW 2581

Tel: (02) 4845 1200 Fax: (02) 4845 1490
Frankfield.House@GunningPostOffice.net
www.bbbook.com.au/frankfield.html
Double $90-$145 Single $55-$95 (Full Breakfast)
Child B/A Dinner $25 - $35
Weekend package $175 - $235 Credit Cards accepted
10 Double (10 bdrm)   2 Ensuite 3 Share

Built in 1870 as the Frankfield Inn and now a charming guest house. Each bedroom is fitted out with antique furniture, brass beds and four posters. Relax in front of an open fire, or outside in award winning gardens. Enjoy a gourmet meal in our period dining room. 2 1/2 hours from Sydney, 50 mins from Canberra, Gunning is only minutes from the new Highway. Visit cold climate vineyards and historic townships all within half hours drive. Local facilities include golf, tennis and swimming. You may meet our children, cats, dogs and chooks in our extensive gardens.

Gunning   *B & B Guesthouse   69 km N of Canberra*

Do Duck Inn Guesthouse and Cafe   AAAT★★★★
Maureen & Peter Quinn
22 Old Hume Highway, Gunning, NSW 2581

Tel: (02) 4845 1207 Fax: (02) 4845 1207
doduckin@webone.com.au
www.bbbook.com.au/doduckinn.html
Double $125-$135 Single $110 (Full Breakfast)
Dinner Bed & Breakfast from $198 double
Credit Cards accepted
2 Queen 5 Double 1 Single (6 bdrm)   6 Ensuite

Do Duck Inn Guesthouse was built in 1890 as a Cobb & Co stopover. Today this beautiful renovated homestead offers air-conditioned ensuite accommodation for Hume Highway travellers, a base for Canberra visitors or just an indulgent romantic getaway. Within this lovely landscaped property lies the 'Bentley on Hume Licensed Cafe', offering the perfect venue for couples and groups wishing to celebrate any occasion. Our formal dining room is a delight for evening dinner and breakfast.

Hawkesbury   *Self Contained Farmstay Homestay B & B*

Hawkesbury Hideaways

Tel: (02) 4575 5149
www.hawkesburyhideaways.com.au
(Continental, Full & Special Breakfast)
Pets welcome

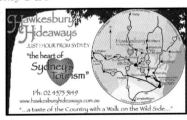

Hawkesbury Hideaways "the heart of Sydney;s Tourism" . . . taste of the Country with a Walk on the Wild Side. Enjoy romantic guest houses and bed 'n' breakfasts in an historic area that's more than three-quarters wilderness. Marvel at the beautiful sandstone gorges of Australia's majestic Hawkesbury River system, visit historic townships, wineries, restaurants and pubs, take invigorating bushwalks or just relax and be pampered at one or our many fine hideaways. . .

Hawkesbury *B & B   Self Contained*   *12 km E of Richmond*

Hidden Valley Retreat Cottages   Lesley Wood
168 Cabbage Tree Road, Grose Vale, NSW 2753

Tel: (02) 4572 1474 Fax: (02) 4572 2476
Mobile: 0419 609 476   hiddenvalley@mbox.com
www.hiddenvalleyretreat.com.au

Double $165-$220 (Special Breakfast) Child $50
Credit Cards accepted Pet on property
Pets welcome Smoking area inside
1 King/Twin 1 Queen 2 Single (1 bdrm)
1 Ensuite 1 Private

Private, romantic self-contained accommodation in solid slab settler's cottages on 40 acres isolated natural bush surrounded by reserve. Full kitchen, gas BBQ, double spa and open fire with complimentary Champagne, toiletries, bubble bath and oils, stereo, candlelight. Guests can enjoy bushwalking, tennis court and pool at main homestead or imply relax on couch or hammock on verandah listening to birdsong, trickling creeks or the silence of the bush. Featured on the best of 'Getaway'. Map and directions supplied on booking.

Hawkesbury - Bilpin   *Self Contained B & B*   *30 km W of Richmond*

Blue Wren Cottage
Joe & Ria Stokman
Lot 2 Powells Road, Bilpin, NSW 2758

Tel: (02) 4567 2163 Fax: (02) 4567 2141
Mobile: 0407 674 599   jstokman@hawknet.com.au

Double $165 (Special Breakfast)
Additional persons $44 Pets welcome
Smoking area inside
1 Queen 3 Single (2 bdrm)
1 Private

Just 90 minutes from Sydney you will find Blue Wren Gardens flower farm and deer park run by Dutchman Jo Stokman and his jovial wife Ria. Guests are accommodated in their own iron bark log cabin. The cabin sleeps 4 comfortably, comes with ensuite, fully equipped kitchen, TV, CD and washing machine and features an old wood fireplace. Guests can enjoy the collection of over 150 varieties of trees and shrubs and deer park in a beautiful lakeside and parkland setting. A quiet retreat without formality, hustle or bustle.

Hawkesbury - Colo   *B & B Self Contained*   *26 km NE of Windsor*

Ossian Hall
Diane & Jim Swaisland
1928 Singleton Road, Colo, NSW 2756

Tel: (02) 4575 5250 Fax: (02) 4575 5250
Mobile: 0428 640 435   info@ossianhall.com.au
www.ossianhall.com.au

Double $135-$160 Single $110-$135
(Full Breakfast) Child $25
Credit Cards accepted
2 Queen 2 Twin (2 bdrm)
1 Ensuite 1 Private

Ossian Hall is located on 86 acres in a secluded valley fronting the Colo River. We breed horses, sheep, goats and have 2 friendly dogs and 1 cat, a selection of free range chooks which supply our eggs & turkeys. Our guests in our cottages can relax by their own log fire or in their private 2 person spa. Our pool is sola heated we also have a 4 person hot tub spa available to all guests. A leisurely row down the river or a spot of fishing maybe your choice or sip on a quiet glass of wine & watch the river go by.

Hawkesbury - Kurrajong   *Self Contained   13 km N of Wilberforce*

Kurrajong Trails & Cottages
Steve & Lee Finnane
Blaxlands Ridge Road,
East Kurrajong, NSW 2758

Tel: (02) 4576 1617 kurra@zip.com.au
www.hawkesburyhideaways.com.au
$385 midweek (4 nights) or weekend (2 nights)
for 6 persons   Pet on property
1 bedroom loft, sleeps 6
1 Private

Hundreds of acres of fabulous views surrounded by Wollemi National Park. 4 self contained solar cottages each comfortably sleeping 6 guests. Lawns and gardens blend in with native bush and picturesque Wheeney Creek runs through the valley below. Enjoy bush walking, fishing, swimming, canoeing and huge entertainment shed with open fire. Wood burning heaters and barbecues. Ideal for groups.

Hawkesbury - Kurrajong Heights   *B & B   Kurrajong Heights*

Wynella Gardens
Noelle & Alan McPhee
1318 Bells Line of Road,
Kurrajong Heights, NSW 2758

Tel: (02) 4567 7546
www.bbbook.com.au/wynellagardens.html
Double $140-$160 Single $100 (Special Breakfast)
Dinner $45 B/A   Credit Cards accepted
Specials available from $60 per person
1 King/Twin 3 Queen 2 Single (3 bdrm)
2 Private 1 Share

Come stay, come play high on a mountain top at a place where you can opt out from your cares and enjoy being taken care of.   Sit by the fire or on the terrace, enjoy foods like soufflés, pastries, sponges and home made bread fresh from the Aga Cooker.   delectable Romantic Dinners can be arranged. Only 75 minutes from the Sydney CBD and yet a world away. All here at Kurrajong Heights the Gateway to the World Heritage Listed Blue Mountains.

Hawkesbury - Oakville   *Self Contained Farmstay B & B   10km E of Windsor*

Oakville B & B
Annette and Ken Ferris
62 Midson Road, Oakville, NSW 2765

Tel: (02) 4573 6788 Fax: (02) 4573 6898
Mobile: 0414 557 275
b&b@disabilityhire.com.au
www.wheelchairs.com.au/oakvilleb&b.html
Double $80-$100 Single $50-$80 (Full Breakfast)
Child 15 Dinner TBA Credit Cards accepted
Pet on property Pets welcome
2 Double 2 Single (2 bdrm)
1 Private 1 Share

Five acres at the gateway to the Hawkesbury. Choice of self-contained private unit, or traditional style B&B. Adjacent to Scheyville National Park. Dog, Horse n Kidz friendly. Wheelchair accessible, personal care assistance & mobility equipment available. Wheelchair accessible van, minibus & car hire. Airport pickup a/v. 60 min to CBD.

Hawkesbury - St Albans   B & B Self Contained   20 km N of Wisemans Ferry

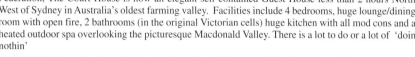

The Court House Retreat   AAATourism★★★☆
Estelle Ehmann
19 Upper MacDonald Road,
St Albans, NSW 2755

Tel: (02) 4568 2042
Fax: (02) 4568 2042
www.courthousestalbans.com.au

From $145 Credit Cards accepted
1 Queen 2 Double 1 Twin (4 bdrm)
2 Private

"Exclusively yours whether it is just you (Mid week) or your party of eight (Week ends)" Built before Federation, The Court House is now an elegant self contained Guest House less than 2 hours North West of Sydney in Australia's oldest farming valley. Facilities include 4 bedrooms, huge lounge/dining room with open fire, 2 bathrooms (in the original Victorian cells) huge kitchen with all mod cons and a heated outdoor spa overlooking the picturesque Macdonald Valley. There is a lot to do or a lot of 'doin nothin'

Hawkesbury - Windsor   B & B Self Contained   10 km N of Windsor

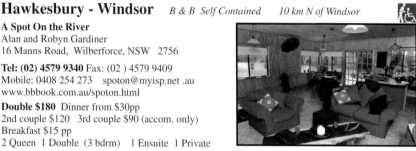

A Spot On the River
Alan and Robyn Gardiner
16 Manns Road, Wilberforce, NSW   2756

Tel: (02) 4579 9340 Fax: (02) 4579 9409
Mobile: 0408 254 273   spoton@myisp.net .au
www.bbbook.com.au/spoton.html

Double $180 Dinner from $30pp
2nd couple $120   3rd couple $90 (accom. only)
Breakfast $15 pp
2 Queen 1 Double (3 bdrm)   1 Ensuite 1 Private

Watching the morning mist dance across the water soothes the soul. The Hawkesbury River is your front door. With private boat ramp and pontoon, this is a water paradise. Your luxury self-contained cabin has river views from every window. Perfect for a romantic rendezvous, or catch up with some 'ol' friends. The cabin caters for 3 couples. The undercover entertainment area has a bar and a gas BBQ. Toast complimentary marshmallows by a campfire. Sink into a hammock and soak up the atmosphere of river life.

Hawkesbury - Windsor   B & B Self Contained   Windsor

Rivers Edge   AAATourism ★★★★
Maureen Mansfield
39 George Street, Windsor, NSW 2756

Tel: (02) 4577 3149
Fax: (02) 4577 2684
Mobile: 0414 579 892
rarnett@acay.com.au
www.riversedge.home.dhs.org

Double $120 (Special Breakfast) Extra couple $80
Weekly from $600 Credit Cards accepted
1 Queen 1 Double (2 bdrm)   1 Private

Perfect for both a romantic weekend away or a break from hectic city life. Situated on the banks of the beautiful Hawkesbury River, the house overlooks the Hawkesbury Plains with majestic views of the Blue Mountains. Barely 2 mins walk from antique shops & restaurants. Rivers Edge provides a fully self catered living space sleeping up to six comfortably. • First floor access • Separate dining room overlooking beautiful gardens, river and mountains • Lounge (sofa bed) • TV/video • Kitchen •Undercover parking • Air Conditioned

Hawkesbury - Wisemans Ferry - Windsor   *20 km NE of Windsor*
Self Contained B & B

Two Rivers Retreat   AAATourism ★★★★
Coral & Valentine Jones751 River Road,
Junction Hawkesbury & Colo Rivers, Lower Portland

Tel: (02) 4575 5372 Fax: (02) 4575 5272
Mobile: 0427 840 399   2riversretreat@boxtek.com.au
www.tworiversretreat.com.au

Double $100-$200 (Special Breakfast)
Dinner $30 - $60 Credit Cards accepted
Pet on property Pets welcome
1 King/Twin 3 Queen (3 bdrm)   2 Ensuite 1 Private

Our 4 star lovers hideaway is romantic & luxurious accommodation nestled in a beautiful valley overlooking the junction of the Colo & Hawkesbury Rivers. Romantic spa baths, chandeliers, log fires, air conditioning, BBQ, mini pools, fairy-lit waterfall gardens. Ghost and history tours, wineries/ Fishing/ golfing/river cruises/ Farm gate trail/ massage/ Foxtel TV/mountain bikes. Central to Sydney, Blue mts/ 70 min. Hunter Valley, Central Coast, Southern Highlands/100 min. Packages from $100 per couple.

Hay   *B & B   Hay Central*

Bank Bed & Breakfast
Sally Smith
86 Lachlan Street,
Hay, NSW 2711

Tel: (02) 6993 1730 Fax: (02) 6993 3440
ttsk@tpg.com.au
www.bbbook.com.au/bankbb.html
Double $100 Single $70 (Full Breakfast)
1 King 1 Twin (2 bdrm)
1 Private

This National Trust classified mansion was built in 1891 to house the London Chartered Bank, one of the historic buildings restored to its original condition in Lachlan Street. The residence consists of a large dining room complete with period furniture and decor. The cedar staircase leads to the guest suite of two bedrooms and a fully modernised bathroom (complete with spa). The guest sitting room opens onto the balcony overlooking the main street. We look forward to you experiencing the hospitality of Hay with us.

Hunter Valley - Broke   *B & B   7.5 km N of Broke*

Green Gables Lodge   AAATourism ★★★★★
Helen & Geoff Sharrock
558 Milbrodale Road, Broke, NSW 2330

Tel: (02) 6579 1258 Fax: (02) 6579 1258
Mobile: 0427 671 878 www.greengableslodge.com.au
greengableslodge@bigpond.com

Double $185-$225 Single $110-$135
(Continental & Full Breakfast)
Credit Cards accepted Pet on property
1 King/Twin 2 Queen (3 bdrm)   2 Ensuite 1 Private

Relax at this intimate five star bed & breakfast. Green Gables Lodge is set on a rising landscape of 43 acres with the glorious mountains of Yengo National Park immediately behind. Two spacious suites upstairs with large ensuite bathrooms and private balconies offering stunning views over vineyards and olive groves. One downstairs bedroom with its own bathroom. Continental or full breakfast. Fully air conditioned. Therapeutic garden spa with great views. Guest barbecue. Refreshments on arrival. Two hours drive from Sydney. Fifteen minutes from Pokolbin.

Hunter Valley - Cessnock   *B & B*   *500m S of PO*

Cessnock Heritage Inn   **AAATourism ★★★★**
Linda Fulton
167 Vincent Street, Cessnock, NSW 2325

Tel: (02) 4991 2744 Fax: (02) 4991 2720
Mobile: 0410 680 450   fultonlinda@hotmail.com
www.hunterweb.com.au/heritageinn.html
Double $90-$120 Single $70-$100 (Full Breakfast)
Child On application Dinner On application
Credit Cards accepted
9 Queen 4 Double 7 Single (13 bdrm)
13 Ensuite

We are a comfortable and friendly B&B in the heart of Cessnock, just a leisurely stroll from clubs, pubs, restaurants, shops and cinema. Only a few minutes away are the famous Hunter Valley vineyards and a host of attractions that Hunter Valley Wine Country offers. Guests enjoy a delicious breakfast in the dining room, while our spacious lounge is ideal for relaxing with friends old and new. Our Inn has character and charm that keeps guest coming back time and again.

Hunter Valley - Lochinvar   *3 km W of Lochinvar (turn off Hwy Kaludah Ck)*

Farmstay B & B
Lochinvar House
Don & Elena Maxwell
1204 New England Highway, Lochinvar, NSW 2321

Tel: (02) 4930 7873 Fax: (02) 4930 7798
www.bbbook.com.au/lochinvarhouse.html
Double $100-$150 Single $80-$130 (Full Breakfast)
Dinner B/A Credit Cards accepted
5 Queen (5 bdrm)
2 Share

A gracious historic Georgian-Victorian country homestead circa 1840 set on an 88 acre grazing estate on the Hunter River. With grand entrance and dining room, luxuriously appointed rooms featuring 13 foot ceilings and antique furnishings, Lochinvar House overlooks beautiful Loch Katrine on the estate. A large solar heated swimming pool and spa with BBQ area are available. Situated 1 km north of the New England Highway, close to Wyndham Estate vineyards, equestrian centre, historic Maitland and Cessnock. Kennels available.

Hunter Valley - Lovedale   *Homestay B & B*   *12 km N of Cessnock*

Bluebush Estate   **AAATourism ★★★★**
David & Robyn McGain
Wilderness Road, Lovedale, NSW 2321

Tel: (02) 4930 7177 Fax: (02) 4930 7666
Mobile: 0418 768 023
sleep@bluebush.com.au
www.bluebush.com.au
(Full Breakfast) Dinner B/A $110 - $175
Credit Cards accepted Pet on property
3 King/Twin 1 Queen (4 bdrm)
4 Ensuite

Bluebush is located amongst the boutique vineyards of Lovedale in The Hunter Valley wine region 2 hours north of Sydney. Enjoy afternoon tea on arrival and dinner can be served by prior arrangement. All rooms have R/C air conditioning, open fire in the lounge and the estate has a tennis court and swimming pool. Robyn, a textile artist and David can guide you to galleries, antiques, wineries, restaurants and historical towns or organise golf or ballooning. Connie, the Cocker Spaniel will welcome you.

Hunter Valley - Lovedale - Pokolbin

Farmstay B & B Guest House Self Contained   17 km N of Cessnock

Hill Top Country Guest House
81 Talga Road,
Rothbury, NSW 2320

Tel: (02) 4930 7111 Fax: (02) 4930 9048
stay@hilltopguesthouse.com.au
www.hilltopguesthouse.com.au

Double $88-$240 Single $85-$230 (Continental Breakfast) (Full Breakfast)
full breakfast extra charge Credit Cards accepted
2 King/Twin 1 King 3 Queen (6 bdrm)
4 Ensuite 2 Private

The picturesque 300 acres abounds with wildlife. The 4WD Night Wildlife Tour lets you be with kangaroos, wombats, possums feeding in their natural environment.

Horse riding is a favourite activity capturing spectacular views of wine country below. Ride mountain bikes to wineries, walk scenic bush trails, explore the river by canoe.

The luxury accommodation offers spa suites, wood fires, Queen, King and single beds. 10' billiard table, grand piano, delicious meals. In-house massage, pool, reverse-cycle air-conditioning.

Awards for excellence, 1998, 1999 and 2000. Selected by leading international tourist guides.

Hunter Valley - Pokolbin   *Guesthouse*   *23 km NW of Cessnock*

Catersfield House   AAATourism ★★★★
Rosemary & Alec Cater
96 Mistletoe Lane, Pokolbin, NSW 2320

Tel: (02) 4998 7220 Fax: (02) 4998 7558
Mobile: 0417 448 136   catersfield@catersfield.com.au
www.catersfield.com.au

Double $140-$225 (Full Breakfast)
Child $35 Dinner $40
Weekend packages $410 Credit Cards accepted
7 King 1 Queen 1 Double 14 Twin (9 bdrm) 9 Ensuite

A Boutique Country Resort situated amongst the vineyards of Pokolbin with spectacular views of the Brokenback Ranges. Six luxurious bedrooms with king-size or twin beds, two with two-person spas, a special French room with a traditional four poster bed, a separate Summerhouse also with a two person spa and a Terrace Room with a log fire. Rooms have reverse cycle A/C, TV's, VCR's, fridges, tea/coffee facilities, irons/boards and hairdryers. There is a log fire in the Guests lounge, a salt-water swimming pool, table tennis, petanque, fishing and BBQ facilities.

Hunter Valley - Pokolbin   *B & B Motel Style Units*   *5 km W of Cessnock*

Elfin Hill   AAATourism ★★★
Marie & Mark Blackmore
Marrowbone Road, Pokolbin, NSW 2320

Tel: (02) 4998 7543 Fax: (02) 4998 7817
Mobile: 0412 199 373   elfinhill@hunterlink.net.au
www.hunterweb.com.au/elfinhille

Double $98-$159 (Continental Breakfast)
Child $16.50 Extra adult $25 Credit Cards accepted
Pet on property
6 Queen 5 Single (6 bdrm)   6 Ensuite

Serenely nestled atop a foothill of Brokenback Range, Elfin Hill has breathtaking views to McWilliam's and Lindeman's Wineries. Delightfully enhanced by the birdlife in tall Spotted Gum trees, as befits our new Wildlife Corridor Status. Rooms are freshly refurbished in log cabin style rooms, with covered barbecue area right beside the salt water swimming pool. Simple delicious breakfasts, plenty of car free walking tracks and the nearby State Forest compliment the renowned Wine Tasting and Fantastic Cuisine! All the advantages of a B & B with the benefit of private rooms.

New South Wales

Hunter Valley - Wine Country - Wollombi

B & B Country Guest House & S/C Cottage   29km SW of Cessnock
Capers Guesthouse & Cottage   AAATourism ★★★★★
Anne & John Kelly
Wollombi Road, Wollombi, NSW 2325

Tel: (02) 4998 3211 Fax: (02) 4998 3458 Mobile: 0407 624 939
capers@hunterlink.net.au
www.capersguesthouse.com.au

Double $196-$275 Single $180-$250 (Full Breakfast) Dinner From $55 Cottage $160
Credit Cards accepted
1 King 5 Queen 2 Double 1 Twin (8 bdrm)
8 Ensuite

The Hunter's finest luxury Sandstone Guest House in Wine Country. This beautiful and unique 1850's convict hewn sandstone house was transported from Macquarie Street, Sydney and re-built in Wollombi.

Magnificent views, elegant dining, fabulous breakfasts and attention to detail have become the hallmark of Capers. All suites have been individually designed for maximum comfort and have ensuites, some with spa baths. French doors lead from each bedroom to wide stone paved verandahs with stunning views. All are air conditioned, centrally heated and have tea coffee facilities, mini bar and in-house licence.

Enjoy the romance of candlelit dinners on the terrace beneath a million stars, or in the chilly winter months in front of a roaring fire, and wake to a gourmet breakfast served on the terrace which in winter is heated for your comfort.

Wollombi is perfectly situated in the Wine Region of the Hunter Valley. Only 90 minutes from Sydney and minutes to world famous wineries. Anne and John can arrange wine tours, 4 wheel drive experiences in the Mt Yengo National Park and the Barrington Tops, tennis, horse riding at the local stables, numerous bush walks, and for the more adventurous - sky diving and hot air ballooning.

We also have a delightful 3 bedroom luxury cottage for families and small groups.

Our website is extensive so please take a visit and whet your appetite

Inverell   *B & B*   *6 km W of Inverell*

Blair Athol
Kathy & Jeff Muddiman
Blair Athol Warialda Road,
Inverell, NSW 2360

Tel: (02) 6722 4912 Fax: (02) 6722 4912
www.bbbook.com.au/blairathol.html

Double $105-$140 Single $85 (Continental Breakfast)
Dinner $40 Credit Cards accepted
2 Queen 2 Double 1 Single (5 bdrm)
4 Ensuite

Experience old world charm at a turn of the century country manor. Set amidst 5 acres of botanical type gardens with trees dating back to 1850. 50 acres of peace, tranquillity and spectacular birdlife. Situated 6 km west of Inverell on the Warialda Road. * Delightful 4 course dinners, BYO wine. * Open log fires, invigorating fresh air. * Featured in June 2001 Country Style Magazine. * Children not accommodated. * Dogs by arrangement.

Jervis Bay - Callala Bay   *Self Contained B & B*   *21 km E of Nowra*

Pa's Corner
Dawn & Greg Stores
26 Fleet Way,
Callala Bay, NSW 2540

Tel: (02) 4446 5640 pascnr@tpg.com.au
www.bbbook.com.au/pascorner.html

Double $65-$90 Single $45-$70
(Full Breakfast) Child $15
1 Double 2 Single (1 bdrm)
1 Private

Tucked away from the hustle and bustle, Pa's Corner is a private, ground floor, self-contained unit minutes from the beach. The fully equipped kitchenette/dining area opens on to a screened, outdoor sitting and BBQ area overlooking the garden. Callala Bay is on the Northern side of beautiful Jervis Bay which is renowned for its safe, sandy beaches and dolphin pods. Charter a catamaran, fish, snorkel, swim and wind-surf in the crystal clear water, or play golf, tennis or bowls close by. Restaurants and licensed clubs in close proximity. Brochure available.

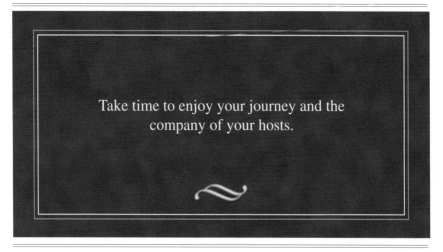

Take time to enjoy your journey and the company of your hosts.

New South Wales

Jervis Bay - Huskisson
B & B Guest House   0.5 km SE of Huskisson

Jervis Bay Guesthouse   AAATourism ★★★★☆
Bill Rogers, 1 Beach Street, Huskisson, NSW 2540

Tel: (02) 4441 7658 Fax: (02) 4441 7659 info@jervisbayguesthouse.com.au
www.jervisbayguesthouse.com.au

Double $130-$220 Single $115-$205 (Full Breakfast) Credit Cards accepted Pet on property
3 Queen 1 Twin (4 bdrm)   4 Ensuite

Experience the beauty of Jervis Bay and it's pleasant coastal climate at our multi-award winning guesthouse, just 50 metres from the incredible white sand beaches of Jervis Bay. Sydney and Canberra are just 2.5-3 hrs away, and we're walking distance from Huskisson's shops and restaurants. It's the perfect place for a weekend-away or a mid-week break, and also as the first or last stop for overseas travellers visiting NSW.

There are four beautiful guest rooms, all with Queen-size beds and ensuites (one with a spa bath). French doors lead from the rooms onto the verandah, where there are spectacular views of the bay, and

you can hear the sound of the waves on the beach.

Come and listen to the Kookaburras laugh, have a swim before breakfast in summer, or curl up in front of the wood heater in the guest lounge in winter. Walk on the beach and look for dolphins playing in the surf... go fishing, swimming or diving... go for a dolphin-watch cruise (year round) or a whale-watch cruise (June-July, September-October)... be dazzled by the whitest sand in the world... play golf on scenic courses... or hire bikes and explore the bike trails. One of the must-see places is Booderee National Park, where you can go walking, visit the amazing ruined

lighthouse, picnic in the botanical gardens, see kangaroos and marvel at the many beautiful parrots. There's a lot to see, so try to allow at least two days.

Everyone knows Jervis Bay's a great place to visit in Spring and Summer, but the big secret is that it's wonderful in Autumn and Winter too. To celebrate this fact we offer a free lunch at Hyams Beach Cafe and free entrance to the Lady Denman Heritage Centre for two-night midweek stays from March-November (except school holidays).

Jervis Bay - Vincentia *B & B*   *30km S of Nowra*

Bay View
Val & Ian Fielder
306 Elizabeth Street, Vincentia, NSW 2540

Tel: (02) 4441 5805
www.bbbook.com.au/bayview.html

Double $95-$105 Single $50-$55
(Continental Breakfast) Child $15
Extra person $25
1 Queen 1 Double (2 bdrm)
2 Ensuite

We welcome you to enjoy the privacy of our home on Jervis Bay. Queen size suite is upstairs with large windows to capture view, also sun-deck. Double suite has tranquil view of water which can be reached via our steps. Both areas have private dining, equipped with microwave, refrigerator, television and tea making facilities. Ideal for walking around beaches and National Park. Aquatic playground for dolphins and penguins. Close to clubs and restaurants. Children by arrangement. Hosts Val and Ian Fielder.

Jervis Bay - Vincentia *B & B*   *30 km S of Nowra*

Nelson Beach Lodge
Robyn Pash
404 Elizabeth Drive, Vincentia, NSW 2540

Tel: (02) 4441 6006 Fax: (02) 4441 6006
Mobile: 0402 263 997   rbrown303@hotmail.com
www.bbbook.com.au/nelsonbeachlodge.html

Double $75-$130 Single $55-$95
(Special Breakfast) Child 1/2 price Dinner $20
Full breakfast add $5 Credit Cards accepted
3 Queen 2 Twin (4 bdrm) 1 Ensuite 2 Share

Enjoy a relaxing weekend or stopover at Nelson Beach Lodge. Ideally situated 2 1/2 hours from Sydney and Canberra. A cozy comfortable home, with guest lounge and balcony overlooking Jervis Bay and secluded garden. Just two minutes walk from white sands, red cliffs and crystal clear waters of Nelson Beach. Baywatch cruises see the dolphins, seals and penguins. Also diving, fishing, swimming, sailing, golf, bike riding and bush walking tracks around the waterfront and many picnic spots in local National and Marine Park, Botanic Gardens, Winery, and historic towns nearby. Aussie Host Business.

Kangaroo Valley *B & B*   *Kangaroo Valley*

River Oak Lodge
John Payne
149A Moss Vale Road, Kangaroo Valley, NSW 2577

Tel: (02) 4465 2123 Fax: (02) 4465 2123
Mobile: 0414 718 586
riveroak@optusnet.com.au
www.kangaroovalley.net

Double $125-$160 Single $75-$85
(Special Breakfast) Credit Cards accepted
1 King/Twin 3 Queen (4 bdrm) 4 Ensuite

River Oak Lodge, set on five acres is situated in the heart of the beautiful Kangaroo Valley. All bedrooms have ensuite facilities with own external entrance and verandah. For your comfort they are fully air conditioned. Your television lounge/dining room, with spectacular views of Barrengarry and Cambewarra Mountains, has tea and coffee making facilities plus a fridge/freezer and microwave oven. Floors throughout are allergy free polished timber. Your choice of tariff includes a self-service continental or the full breakfast (taken at 'Cafe Bella' 80m from the Lodge). River Oak Lodge has access to Kangaroo River.

Kiama   *B & B   1.5 km S of Kiama*

Saddleback House
Pauline and Harry Best
41 Saddleback Mountain Road, Kiama, NSW 2533

Tel: (02) 4232 2528 Fax: (02) 4232 2528
sbhouse@ihug.com.au
www@1earth.net/~sbhouse

Double $100-$110 Single $80-$90
(Continental & Full Breakfast) Extra person $50
1 King/Twin 2 Queen (3 bdrm)
3 Ensuite

Welcome to our home set on a hillside in beautiful Kiama. The spacious rooms have reverse-cycle air conditioning, ensuites, TV, tea and coffee making facilities and private balconies with lovely coastal and rural views. A full breakfast can be enjoyed in the dining room or a continental breakfast served in your room. Free transport locally if required. Limited facilities for children. No smoking indoors. Sorry we cannot accommodate pets. "Simply the best, 11 out of 10. Thank you. Tim & Margaret, Cornwall, England.

Kiama   *Self Contained Homestay B & B Cottage   2.5 km W of Kiama*

Kiama Bed & Breakfast   AAATourism ★★★★★
Tony and Marian van Zanen
15 Riversdale Road, Kiama, NSW 2533

Tel: (02) 4232 2844 Fax: (02) 4232 2868
kiamabnb@kbb.com.au   www.kbb.com.au

Double $150-$220 (Full Breakfast) Child $33
Dinner $50 pp Credit Cards accepted
2 King/Twin 2 Queen 1 Double 4 Single (4 bdrm)
4 Ensuite

Award-winning Kiama Bed & Breakfast offers 5-star air conditioned comfort, luxury furnishings, huge private living areas, spectacular views, sunny verandahs, landscaped gardens and scrumptious breakfasts in either the bed and breakfast guest rooms or the cottage B&B suites. Four distinctively different rooms catering for couples, families, groups and singles on tranquil acreage and just two minutes drive to town and surf. Families welcome. Decadence assured. Winner in the 2001 Illawarra Awards for Business Excellence in Tourism and 2001 Finalist in NSW Awards. 90 minutes drive south coast of Sydney

---

Kiama   *Separate/Suite B & B   2 km W of Kiama*

Bed and Views Kiama   AAATourism ★★★★☆
Sabine & Rudi Dux
69 Riversdale Road, Kiama, NSW 2533

Tel: (02) 4232 3662 Fax: (02) 4232 3662
bedandviewskiama@bigpond.com
www.bedandviewskiama.com.au

Double $110-$150 Single $80-$100
(Special Breakfast) Suite from $160
Credit Cards accepted
1 King/Twin 2 King 1 Queen (4 bdrm)   4 Ensuite

Enjoy crystal clear waters at various beaches, see the world famous "Blow Hole", walk the nearby Rainforest or simply relax in our garden with views from the mountains to the sea. Only 2 min. away from the seaside town Kiama the Guesthouse offers modern king-bed rooms with ensuite, some with spa, all air-conditioned (cool/heat). Relax in the private "Blue Ocean" guest lounge or find your favourite spot outside to watch the sunset. Welcoming European hospitality. Day-tour ideas are provided. "Thank you for sharing a bit of paradise." A. & L.G., Dallas Texas

Kiama   *B & B   Self Contained   Cottages*   *2.7 km W of Kiama*

Spring Creek Retreat Country House & Cottages AAATourism ★★★★★
Sue & Jack Stoertz, 41 Jerrara Road, Kiama, NSW 2533

Tel: (02) 4232 2700 Fax: (02) 4232 2600 springcreekret@bigpond.com
www.innaustralia.com.au/springcreek

Double $175-$435 (Full Breakfast) Self contained cottages from $165/nt, $320 - $435/2 nts
Credit Cards accepted Pet on property Pets welcome
Country House: 5 suites: 1 king twin, 1 triple, 3 Queen
Cottages: 2x2bedroom, 1x1 bedroom   8 Ensuite

A country retreat by the sea offering 5 King/Queen bedroom Bed & Breakfast and 3 one/two bedroom
Cottages   Tranquil 20 acre rural retreat in rolling green hills on a ridge overlooking Kiama and the
Pacific Ocean, in magnificent landscaped grounds bounded by dry-stone walls.

Walks, a swimming hole in the creek and private picnic spots on the property make it very easy to drive
in the gate, park the car and throw away the key.

All of this can be combined with either:

• The five star luxury of the guest house, which has five exquisite suites (3 with spas), satellite TV, CD
players, bathrobes, complimentary Port and chocolates, and gourmet breakfast in the French quarter
dining room OR

• 3 self-contained cottages, (two with spas in the bathroom), featuring lounge/dining room, full kitchens
and large verandah with barbecues. Air conditioning and ceiling fans cool summer days and nights.

Honeymooners and small group functions of up to 10 couples catered for.   Winners of the 2001
Innovation Award in the Illawarra Tourism Awards for Business Excellence and finalists in the 2001
NSW Tourism Awards. Winners Tourism & Hospitality 2001 SIBTA. For lovers young and old, Spring
Creek sets the scene for special experiences.

Kiama   *Self Contained   Kiama*

Sea Mist Cottage
Marilyn Richardson
37 Tingira Crecent,
Kiama, NSW 2533

Tel: (02) 4232 2116
www.bbbook.com.au/seamist.html
(Continental Breakfast) Cottage $135 -$200
Weekly rates available Credit Cards accepted
1 Queen 3 Single (3 bdrm)
1 Ensuite 1 Private

New South Wales

Waterfront Cottage close to the Little Blowhole. Panoramic ocean views from the spacious living areas. Relax and unwind on the patio or take a short stroll along the Coastal Walk to the beach. Self-cater facilities include a light continental breakfast hamper (on night of arrival) modern kitchen, microwave, dishwasher. Internal laundry.TV/VCR/BBQ. Sleeps 2 -6. 90 minutes South of Sydney, 2∏ hours to Canberra. Phone for bookings or brochure: 02 4233 2116.

Lake Macquarie - Rathmines   *Self Contained B & B   6 km S of Toronto*

Overnight Reflections Luxury B & B
AAATourism ★★★★   Narelle & Bill Drain
113 Fishing Point Road, Fishing Point, NSW 2283

Tel: (02) 4975 1430 Fax: (02) 4954 8484
overnight_refl@hotmail.com
www.bbbook.com.au/reflections.html

Double $120-$160 Single $70 (Full Breakfast)
Child $25 Credit Cards accepted
3 Queen 1 Double 1 Single (4 bdrm)   4 Ensuite

Imagine yourself waking to the sounds of lapping water and sunrises you will never forget (if your awake) all this and more you will receive at Overnight Reflections. Situated on absolute waterfrontage on Lake Macquarie only 1.5 hours from the start of the freeway, Overnight Reflections is that perfect getaway. Hosts Narelle & Bill provide one of the finest B & Bs on Lake Macquarie, with freshly baked bread, homemade jams and fresh poached fruit, and those scrambled eggs! Operating 7 years Overnight Reflections offers luxury comfort in our boat Cottage accommodating 2 persons, B & B in house offers 3 queen rooms with ensuites, and our Lakeview House accommodates 6 persons. Our guest book tells it all.

Merimbula   *B & B   25km S of Bega*

Bellbird Bed & Breakfast - Merimbula
AAATourism ★★★★   K & B Campbell
28 Tantawanglo Street, Merimbula, NSW 2548

Tel: (02) 6495 3536 Fax: (02) 6495 3536
Mobile: 0403 013 536
bellbirdbandb@yahoo.com.au
www.bellbirdbandb.ozvisits.com

Double $130-$140 Single $90-$100
(Continental & Full Breakfast) Credit Cards accepted
2 Queen 1 Single (2 bdrm)   2 Ensuite

Experience peace and tranquillity at Bellbird Bed and Breakfast, Merimbula. Enjoy the lake and wetlands via the boardwalk - only minutes to town. Both rooms have own ensuites. The private suite has a large, separate lounge providing TV, video, music, activities and cosy wood heating. Guests may breakfast on the deck overlooking the bush and lake or in privacy. At Bellbird the relaxed atmosphere, calm and peaceful setting and the unobtrusive hospitality of Kath and Bryan all contribute to a memorable stay. Bookings recommended. AAA ****

Merimbula   *B & B   Self Contained   2 km N of Merimbula*

Robyn's Nest Guest House   AAATourism ★★★★☆
Robyn and Michael Britten
188 Merimbula Drive, Merimbula, NSW 2548

Tel: (02) 6495 4956 Fax: (02) 6495 2426
Mobile: 0428 954 956
enquiries@robynsnest.com.au
www.robynsnest.com.au
Double $165-$210 Single $150 (Full Breakfast)
Credit Cards accepted
1 King 11 Queen 2 Twin (14 bdrm)
14 Ensuite

Robyns Nest is award winning luxury Guest House set amid 100 acres of natural bushland with 25 acres of absolute lake frontage halfway between Sydney and Melbourne on the coastal route. Facilities include a solar heated pool, tennis court, spas and sauna. The tranquillity of this mini resort is just 5 minutes from the town centre that has 20 restaurants, pristine beaches, whale watching, bush walking and fishing. Regional Award Winning B & B, plus accommodation to 5*. 6 FSC units available - 1 & 2 B/R.

Merimbula   *B & B   Town Centre*

Bella Vista
Judy Hori
16 Main Street,
Merimbula, NSW 2548

Tel: (02) 6495 1373
Fax: (02) 6495 2344
www.bbbook.com.au/bellavista.html
(Full Breakfast) $135 - $185
2 King/Twin (2 bdrm)
2 Ensuite

Quite like the Riviera but a little closer to home. Spacious Mediterranean Villa style accommodation with waterfront deck overlooking sparkling Merimbula lake. Minutes walk to town centre, restaurants, clubs and beaches. 5 minutes drive to airport and 15 hole golf course. Bella Vista is a place to relax. Peace with everything at your finger tips. Guest comment: "The perfect environment"; "A class act!" F.G. Albury

Milton - Ulladulla   *B & B   3 km S of Milton*

Meadowlake Lodge   AAATourism ★★★★☆
Diana & Peter Falloon
318 Wilfords Lane, Milton, NSW 2538

Tel: (02) 4455 7722 Fax: (02) 4455 7733
meadowlake@bigpond.com
www.meadowlakelodge.com.au
Double $180-$220 Single $140-$180 (Full Breakfast)
Dinner B/A Credit Cards accepted
1 King/Twin 2 Queen (3 bdrm)
3 Ensuite

Meadowlake Lodge is a modern country house set on 100 acres of tranquil rolling countryside overlooking lakes and wetlands which have prolific seasonal birdlife. * Only 3 hours from Sydney and Canberra * 3km from historic Milton * Close to beaches at Mollymook and bush walks in the Budawangs * Spacious and elegant rooms * Ensuites with baths * Fine country cooking a speciality * Peaceful and relaxing surroundings. The ideal adult rural retreat.

Milton - Ulladulla - Mollymook   *B & B*   *2 km N of Ulladulla*

Fairmont Ridge   AAATourism ★★★★
Peter & Jan Humphries
13B Bishop Drive, Mollymook, NSW 2538

Tel: (02) 4455 1563 Fax: (02) 4455 1563
Mobile: 0438 551 563
www.bbbook.com.au/fairmontridge.html
Double $150-$170 Single $130
(Full Breakfast) Credit Cards accepted
1 King/Twin 3 Queen (4 bdrm)
4 Ensuite

Welcome to Fairmont Ridge. Situated 3 hours from Sydney and Canberra. Set on 6 picturesque acres. Minutes fom beaches, shops, restaurants and clubs. A short stroll to Mollymook's famous Championship golf course. Guests' bedrooms open onto the wide verandah and are spacious, comfortable and luxuriously appointed. Wake up to a full country cooked breakfast. Relax in front of the cosy log fire in the lounge or enjoy a complimentary drink in the entertainment room. Nellie and Bindy are the friendly outside dogs. Adults only retreat.

Moruya   *B & B*   *500m Moruya PO*

Post & Telegraph Bed & Breakfast
Wayne & Jennifer Thors
Cnr Page & Campbell Streets, Moruya, NSW 2537

Tel: (02) 4474 5745 Fax: (02) 4472 8866
Mobile: 0412 421 914
pandt@sci.net.au
www.southcoast.com.au/postandtel
Double $110-$135 Single $90
(Full Breakfast) Credit Cards accepted
3 Queen 1 Single (3 bdrm)
1 Ensuite 1 Share

The Post & Telegraph Bed & Breakfast invites you to partake in the pleasures of this beautifully restored, heritage building which offers luxury accommodation in a warm and friendly atmosphere. * Cosy sitting room with open fire and teamaking * Sunny verandahs * Wholesome cooked breakfast served in dining room * Easy walk to river, shops and restaurants   * Close to beaches, National Parks * 2Π hours drive from Canberra.

Moruya   *B & B*   *Guest House*   *12 km S of Moruya*

Apple Gums Cottage Guest House
Bill & Joan Newton
47 Berriman Drive,
Congo, NSW 2537

Tel: (02) 4474 3686 Fax: (02) 4474 3686
applegums@ozemail.com.au
www.bbbook.com.au/applegums.html
Double $120-$100 Single $100-$80 (Full Breakfast)
3 Queen (3 bdrm)
1 Ensuite 2 Share

Situated among the beautiful rural landscape of the South Coast. Enjoy a freshly brewed cup of coffee or maybe a glass of wine while relaxing on the wide verandah enjoying the views of the spectacular mountain ranges. Experience the peace and tranquility of this special place. Take a leisurely walk through the Eurobodalla National Park to the beautiful unspoilt beaches at Congo.

Moruya   *B & B*   *25 km S of Batemans Bay*

Braemar House Bed & Breakfast
Graham & Noelene Cowdroy
97 South Heads Road, Moruya, NSW 2537

Tel: (02) 4474 2469 Fax: (02) 4474 2469
Mobile: 0407 190 950
gcowdroy@ozemail.com.au
www.southcoast.com.au/braemar

Double $110-$120 (Full Breakfast)
1 Queen 3 Double (4 bdrm)
1 Ensuite 1 Share

Braemar House, set on a 22 acre property, boasts magnificent mountain, river and rural views. It is 5 minutes to Moruya township and the beautiful beaches at Moruya Heads and 10 minutes to Moruya airport. Braemar House provides a relaxing atmosphere in which you can unwind in the comfortable lounge/sitting room, enjoy the extensive facilities (pool, tennis court, bushwalking, etc.) or discover the many attractions in the local region. There are three double rooms with a shared bathroom and another double ensuite bedroom.

Moruya   *B & B*   *3 km S of Moruya PO*

Bryn Glas   AAATourism ★★★★☆
Sandra & John Spencer
19 Valley View Lane, Moruya, NSW 2537

Tel: (02) 4474 0826 Fax: (02) 4474 3439
Mobile: 0409 428 355
brynglas@bigpond.com
www.users.bigpond.com/brynglas

Double $110-$130 Single $90-$110 (Full Breakfast)
Dinner $12 - $25 B/A Credit Cards accepted
2 Queen (2 bdrm) 2 Ensuite

Bryn Glas is a modern homestead style residence situated on 5 rural acres. Within a short driving distance are Batemans Bay, Mogo, Tuross and Narooma, wonderful beaches and National Parks, fishing and boating.   Bryn Glas is rated 4 Star plus, has Air Conditioned ensuite bedrooms with TV, guest sitting/dining room, wide verandas with magnificent mountain views and country side.   Stroll round and see our young calves, chickens, and friendly dog. 300 lavender plants in our developing gardens give a wonderful show.

Mudgee   *B & B*   *7 km S of Mudgee*

Old Wallinga Country House   AAAT
65 Wallinga Lane, Mudgee, NSW 2850

Tel: (02) 6372 3129 Fax: (02) 6372 3129
oldwallinga@winsoft.net.au
www.bbbook.com.au/oldwallinga.html

Double $165 Single $90 (Full Breakfast)
Child $40 Dinner $50 B/A
Credit Cards accepted Pet on property
2 King/Twin 2 Queen 4 Single (4 bdrm)
4 Ensuite

Old Wallinga Country House is an 1865 homestead with views of gentle rolling hills, vineyards and grazing cattle. Relax in our guest sitting room before an open fire, amongst books and antique furniture. A courtyard leads to barbecue facilities, swimming pool and tennis court. Two guest rooms in the homestead have underfloor heating. Two suites in the old stables nearby have combustion fires, queen beds and a spiral staircase leading to the loft with two single beds. Dinner by arrangement. Children and pets welcome.

Mudgee   *B & B   Mudgee*

Evanslea (formerly Lynchs at the Stables)
Val and Derek Evans
146 Market Street, Mudgee, NSW 2850

Tel: (02) 6372 4116 Fax: (02) 6372 7925
Mobile: 0414 262 795
evanslea@hwy.com.au
www.evanslea.com
Double $132-$154 Single $132
(Full Breakfast) Credit Cards accepted
3 Queen (3 bdrm)   2 Ensuite 1 Private

Charming accommodation, expansive rural views, just a short walk to town centre. Privacy is assured whether you choose to stay in the shaded garden room, spacious loft or in the beautifully renovated stables (c.1860). All rooms are air conditioned with own bathrooms, tea and coffee making facilities, and complimentary port. Award-winning gardens surround the swimming pool with vine covered pergolas and shady lawn areas opening into a new olive grove leading to the river. Accommodation limited to just 3 couples ensures a relaxing stay.

Mudgee   *B & B   17 km SE of Mudgee*

Riverlea B & B
Pauline & Robert Betts
63 Riverlea Road, Apple Tree Flat,
via Mudgee, NSW 2850

Tel: (02) 6373 1386 Fax: (02) 6373 1387
riverlea@hwy.com.au
www.riverlea-bnb.com.au
Double $120-$160 (Full Breakfast)
Dinner By arrangement Pet on property
3 Queen (3 bdrm)
3 Ensuite

Riverlea is an intimate and luxurious boutique B&B famous for its comfort, hospitality and sumptuous country breakfasts. Riverlea's 3 double bedrooms (each with ensuites and queen-size beds) are complemented by spacious dining, lounge and courtyard areas for the exclusive use of guests. Set on 16 tranquil acres in the scenic Cudgegong Valley, Riverlea is only a 12-minute drive from Mudgee. It is an ideal weekend getaway location for three couples.

Murwillumbah   *Self Contained Farmstay B & B   2 km SE of Murwillumbah*

Torokina Cottage   AAATourism ★★★★☆
Nicola and Bill Stainlay
PO Box 5121, South Murwillumbah, NSW 2484

Tel: (02) 6672 1218 Fax: (02) 6672 6672
Mobile: 0412 317 522   torokina@norex.com.au
www.bbbook.com.au/torokina.html
Double $150-$160 (Continental & Full Breakfast)
$30 - $35 per extra person per day
Credit Cards accepted
1 Queen 4 Single (3 bdrm)   2 Private

Exclusively yours! Whether self-catering or having B&B, this 1904 workers cottage, set in lovely park-like grounds on a sugar cane farm, is the perfect base from which to explore the beautiful Tweed Valley and north-eastern NSW. With its fully equipped kitchen and laundry, wide verandas, barbecues, ceiling fans, open fire, electric blankets, 2 garages, use of the owners' Synpave floodlit tennis court and glorious views, the Cottage is your 365-day-a-year weekender. Because the garden's unfenced, the Cottage is unsuitable for young children and pets.

Murwillumbah - Crystal Creek *B & B*   *12 km NW of Murwillumbah*

Hillcrest Bed & Breakfast   **AAATourism ★★★★☆**
Clive and Tracy Parker
Upper Crystal Creek Road,
Crystal Creek via Murwillumbah, NSW 2484

Tel: (02) 6679 1023 Mobile: 0408 791 023
info@hillcrestbb.com   hillcrestbb.com

Double $120-$140 Single $105 (Full Breakfast)
Dinner from $40pp Credit Cards accepted
2 Queen 1 Double (3 bdrm)
1 Ensuite 1 Private

Peace, privacy, spectacular views from Mt Warning to the Border Ranges, solar heated pool, jolly good food and only 12 minutes from town. Separate guest lounge with stereo and stocked fridge opens to central atrium with decorative fishpond. Both guest rooms have tv/video and huge fluffy towels in ensuite/private bathrooms. Regional Tourism Award winners 2000/2001.   "One of the best bed & breakfasts we ever found! We leave Australia relaxed and happy. We would give you a 5th star!" - H. & A. Stemmler, Switzerland

Murwillumbah - Crystal Creek   *14 km SE of Murwillumbah*
Farmstay B & B

Lodon Lodge   Donald McHenry
303 Upper Crystal Creek Road,
Crystal Creek via Murwillumbah, NSW 2484

Tel: (02) 6679 1518 Fax: (02) 6679 1510
Mobile: 0427 310 408   lodon@norex.com.au
www.bigvolcano.com.au/custom/lodon

Double $110 Single $55 (Full Breakfast) Dinner $33
Child $27.50 Credit Cards accepted Pets welcome
1 Queen 1 Double 2 Twin (3 bdrm)   1 Private

Lodon Lodge 14km North of Murwillumbah, 35km South of Gold Coast and approx 2hrs from Brisbane. Located in beautiful Tweed Valley with spectacular views of Mt.Warning, Border Ranges and Springbrook World Heritage Listed National Parks, our multi award winning Farmstay provides a total B&B experience. Enjoy a farm 4X4 tour(weather permitting),go fishing in our stocked springfed lake, bushwalks or relax in our peaceful gardens. Tariff includes full farm style breakfast, complimentary morning/afternoon teas with homemade cookies. Our friendly pets, Cappa the cat and Red the dog will also make you welcome.

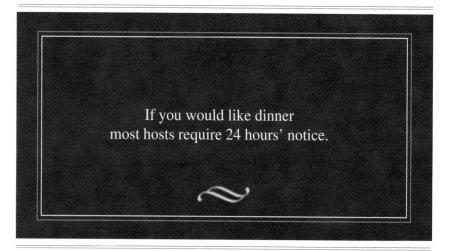

If you would like dinner
most hosts require 24 hours' notice.

Nambucca Heads   *B & B   Guest House*   *900m E of Nambucca Heads*

Beilbys Beach House   AAATourism ★★★★
Eric Mayer & MaÔta van Stockum
1 Ocean Street, Nambucca Heads, NSW 2448

Tel: (02) 6568 6466
beilbys@midcoast.com.au
www.beilbys.com.au

Double $60-$85 Single $50-$70 (Special Breakfast)
Suite $77 - $105 Credit Cards accepted
1 King/Twin 2 Queen 2 Double (5 bdrm)
3 Ensuite 2 Private

You will feel relaxed and comfortable at idyllic Beilbys Beach House, in its quiet, traffic-free hideaway location surrounded by tropical gardens. A 4-minute stroll through the bushland walkway to the warm golden sands of Nambucca's famous beaches, 900 meters to town, restaurants in walking distance. Comfortable rooms, all with verandah, TV, c/fan, heating, polished floors. Sumptuous buffet breakfast, fully equipped guest kitchen and dining room, large swimming pool, covered barbecue area, Internet facilities, laundry. Off-street parking, 2 lock-up garages. Three-night specials.

Nambucca Heads - Macksville   *B & B   Guest House*   *3 km W of Macksville*

Jacaranda Country Lodge   AAATourism ★★★★
Jude Rhoades
PO Box 364, Macksville, NSW 2447

Tel: (02) 6568 2737 Fax: (02) 6568 2769
jacaranda@midcoast.com.au   www.jaclodge.com.au

Double $100-$120 Single $80-$100
(Continental Breakfast) Child $10 Dinner $25
Credit Cards accepted
5 Queen 2 Double 5 Twin (12 bdrm)
12 Ensuite

Country club facilities with B & B hospitality. Gracious accommodation set amidst pastures, wetlands and lily-filled ponds. Savour home baking and local fruit on our breakfast buffet. Relax in the lounge with its over-stuffed sofas, TV, billiard table and fireplace. Enjoy the pool, sauna, spa, tennis court, or fish from our Nambucca River jetty. Be entertained by the resident band of thoroughbreds and the prolific bird life. An idyllic place for a quiet night's rest or a base for exploring the scenic delights of the Nambucca Valley.

Nambucca Heads - Valla   *B & B*   *3 km N of Nambucca Heads*

Cedar Creek Bed & Breakfast
Janine Gatcum
1 Foxs Road, Valla, NSW 2448

Tel: (02) 6568 9888 Fax: (02) 6569 4164
Mobile: 0438 370 379   cedarcreekbnb.com
bookings@cedarcreekbnb.com

Double $70-$80 Single $52-$60
(Full Breakfast) Queen $85-$100
1 Queen 2 Double 1 Twin (4 bdrm)
1 Ensuite 1 Share

Surrounded by National Forests and set on 4 acres, our Tudor home awaits you for a relaxing holiday. Walk amongst the landscaped gardens overlooking Cedar Creek and relax to the sounds and sights of the area. Alternatively, explore Nambucca Heads just 3kms away. Guests have their own lounge room & dining room where you start your day with a home-cooked breakfast. All bedrooms have heating, ceiling fans and electric blankets. There is also a guest barbeque area. Extended stay & group booking specials.

Narooma - Tilba   *Farmstay B & B*   *8 km W of Narooma*

Pub Hill Farm   AAATourism ★★★★☆
Micki & Ian Thomlinson
Box 227, Narooma, NSW 2546

Tel: (02) 4476 3177 Fax: (02) 4476 3177 Mobile: 0407 502 566
pubhill@austarnet.com.au
www.pubhillfarm.com

Double $85-$105 Single $70-$80 (Full Breakfast) Pet on property Pets welcome
3 Queen 2 Single (4 bdrm)
4 Ensuite

Pub Hill Farm is a small farm running beef cattle. It is situated high on a hill on the original site of the old Wagonga Hotel, overlooking the beautiful Wagonga Inlet with views over Mt. Dromedary to the South. Pub Hill has over one and a half kilometres of absolute water frontage onto the Inlet and also Punkallah Creek. The delightful seaside town of Narooma is just ten minutes away. The Wagonga Inlet enters the sea at Narooma and the magnificent turquoise colour of the water is a stunning sight to greet guests as they arrive by car. Narooma's 18 hole golf course is renowned throughout Australia; the first nine holes hugging the spectacular cliff tops, the second nine being tree lined and parklike. The heritage villages of Central Tilba and Tilba Tilba are just 11 kms from Pub Hill. Here you can browse in interesting shops, visit the beautiful Foxglove Spires open garden and enjoy a great cup of coffee or a wonderful light lunch at Love at First Bite Cafe. The popular whale watch tours to Montague Island depart daily in Spring. You can also view the fur seal and Little Penguin colonies on the island.

cont. next page

The birdlife at Pub Hill is both abundant and varied with native parrots, honey eaters, raptors and many wetland birds to be observed. Over 100 different birds have been sighted and listed at Pub Hill and the extreme quiet makes it an ideal place to bird watch. Small mobs of Eastern Grey kangaroos and Swamp wallabies also live on the property and can usually be seen at dusk. This is also a fisherman's paradise. Those keen to fish can do so in the estuary (named as one of the ten best fishing estuaries in Australia) in a hire boat available from various outlets in Narooma, or they may simply throw a line in while sitting on the bank of our creek which runs through the farm. Likely catches include mullet, bream, flathead and many other varieties. Cook the catch for dinner on one of our barbecues! Bushwalking in the quiet forests surrounding the farm is an ideal way to walk off the hearty breakfast.

Our aim is to make guests feel at home and to relax and enjoy our large gardens. All four rooms have water views and each has a private sitting-out area and private entrance. All rooms have ensuite bathrooms, microwaves and fridges, colour TV and tea and coffee making equipment. We welcome guests' pets if they are well behaved and our large garden is fully fenced. Pub Hill is a non-smoking household but guests may, of course, smoke whilst sitting outside enjoying the views.

We provide breakfast only but will happily recommend any of Narooma's excellent restaurants, all of which serve wonderful fresh fish, among other dishes. We have travelled extensively and have lived abroad in both U K and North and East Africa for many years. We love sharing our beautiful property, as we have been doing happily for 13 years, with guests from Australia and overseas, and enjoy swapping travellers' tales with our new friends.

Because of Narooma's very pleasant and mild winter climate we have no real "low season" at Pub Hill Farm and it is recommended that you make advance bookings to avoid disappointment.

"Quite the best B and B we have ever stayed at, anywhere. Superb hospitality." J and P J, Woodham, Surrey, England.

"Am speechless - loved every minute - your hospitality was warm and wonderful." Mary and Bill R, Los Osos, California USA.

"Just as relaxing 6th time around - thank you." Trish and Phil R and David N, East Ryde, Sydney.

"A home away from home but in the country - what more could you want? We love it and always want to return. Thank you Micki and Ian." Ann B, Petersham, Sydney.

Narrabri   *Self Contained Homestay Cottage*   *3 km S of Narrabri*

Como   AAATourism ★★★★
Pam & Hugh Barrett
26 Fraser Street, Narrabri, NSW 2390

Tel: (02) 6792 3193 Fax: (02) 6792 6066
Mobile: 0427 923 193   como@turboweb.net.au
www.bbbook.com.au/como.html
Double $95-$100 Single $75-$80 (Full Breakfast)
Child $15 Pets welcome
1 Queen 1 Double 2 Single (2 bdrm)
1 Ensuite 1 Private

Get away from it all in charming 'Como' Cottage located in the garden of 'Como' homestead (circa 1914). The cottage has been tastefully renovated with ensuite and sunroom. Guests are encouraged to enjoy the spacious garden, the shady mature trees, the in-ground swimming pool in summer and log fires in winter. 'Como' is located on 10 acres only two blocks from the Newell Highway and three minutes drive from Narrabri shopping centre. Children and pets (outside) are welcome. Laundry facilities are available.

Narrabri   *Homestay B & B*   *6km S of Narrabri*

Benbruik
Ellen & Rob Wallace
Forest Drive, Narrabri, NSW 2390

Tel: (02) 6792 1820 Fax: (02) 6792 5505
Mobile: 0427 003 339
ewallace@turboweb.net.au
www.webeffectint.com.au/benbruik
Double $85-$120 Single $65-$75 (Full Breakfast)
Child $25 Dinner $20 - $35 Pet on property
2 Queen 1 Double 1 Twin (4 bdrm)   2 Share

"Benbruik" is just off the Gunnedah Road, set in very pleasant gardens with swimming pool, has a wonderful view of Nandewar Range, and has lots of peace and quiet. An excellent breakfast is presented, and air-conditioning and central heating add to your comfort. Dinner is available and a country style afternoon tea, a sitting area, TV/books, and walks in the Pilliga Scrub nearby. "Benbruik" is central to all the local points of interest - Australia Telescope, Mount Kaputar, cotton and wheat research institutes, etc. "Warm hospitality - We felt 'looked after'!"

Narromine   *Self Contained Farmstay Homestay B & B*   *6 km W of Narromine*

Camerons Farmstay   AAATourism ★★★☆
Ian and Kerry Cameron, "Nundoone Park",
213 Ceres Road, Narromine, NSW 2821

Tel: (02) 6889 2978 Fax: (02) 6889 5229
www.bbbook.com.au/cameronsfarmstay.html
Double $90-$120 Single $65-$70
(Continental & Full Breakfast) Child $30
Dinner B/A S/C Cottage $100 Pet on property
2 Queen 1 Double 2 Single (4 bdrm)
1 Ensuite 1 Share

Our home, 30 minutes west of Dubbo, is modern and spacious with reverse cycle air-conditioning with each bedroom having a fan/heater; guest lounge has television, video, books, tea/coffee making facilities, fridge etc. It is surrounded by large gardens, all weather tennis court, and pool. Ian and Kerry run a successful Border Leicester Sheep stud - see lambs, shearing, haymaking, cotton growing and harvesting (seasonal), tour cotton gin. Visit: Rose Nursery, Iris Farm, Aviation Museum and Gliding Centre. " Excellent, comfortable accommodation and great hospitality. So good to come back." P&G, Belgium.

Newcastle   *B & B   Self Contained   Newcastle Central*

Newcomen B & B   AAATourism ★★★★
Rosemary Bunker
70 Newcomen Street, Newcastle, NSW 2300

Tel: (02) 4929 7313 Fax: (02) 4929 7645
Mobile: 0412 145 104
newcomen_bb@hotmail.com
www.newcomen-bb.com.au

Double $120 Single $90 (Full Breakfast)
Child $15 Credit Cards accepted
1 Queen 1 Single (1 bdrm)
1 Private

Discover the pleasures of this vibrant city with a country feel on the blue water coast. The garden studio in the heritage area looks over the sea and is close to beaches, restaurants and galleries. It has a private entrance and courtyard, swimming pool and garage. A stylish interior features Art Deco pieces and exciting contemporary art works along with every comfort, including the delights of Rosemary's leisurely breakfast treats.

Newcastle - East End   *B & B   Self Contained   800m SE of Newcastle*

Anne's B & B at Ismebury
Anne Creevey
3 Stevenson Place, Newcastle East, NSW 2300

Tel: (02) 4929 5376 Fax: (02) 4927 8404
Mobile: 0416 285 376   anne.creevey@hunterlink.net.au
users.hunterlink.net.au/~ddbpc/

Double $115-$200 Single $99-$132
(Continental Breakfast) Child $44
Suite (2 beds) $220 - $330 Credit Cards accepted
1 King/Twin 2 Double 1 Single (3 bdrm)
1 Ensuite 1 Private 1 Share

A large 1911, terrace house in the historic East End village. Fully restored with Edwardian ambience. Relax by the open fire, on a private balcony, or lay back in the spa and watch the clouds. Experience an historic train ride or a boat trip on the harbour only walking distance away. Stroll our magnificent beaches or foreshore and indulge at excellent cafes and restaurants. Longer stay and corporate rates available. Associate Member of the Australian B & B Council.

Newcastle - Hamilton   *B & B   6 km Newcastle*

Hamilton Heritage Laraine & Colin Bunt
178 Denison Street, Hamilton, NSW 2303

Tel: (02) 4961 1242 Fax: (02) 4969 4758
Mobile: 0414 717 688   colaine@iprimus.com.au
www.bbbook.com.au/hamiltonheritage.html

Double $95-$120 Single $80-$95
(Continental Breakfast) Dinner $20 - $60
Credit Cards accepted Pet on property Pets welcome
2 Queen (2 bdrm) 2 Ensuite

Hamilton Heritage B & B, "Old World Charm", situated on Historic Cameron Hill. Conveniently located to: Broadmeadow Race Course, Broadmeadow Station, Newcastle Entertainment Centre, Marathon Stadium, Newcastle Show Ground, Newcastle Harness Racing, International Hockey Venue, Beaumont Street the Cosmopolitan Heart of Newcastle. Close proximity to Newcastle Business District, Foreshore and Beaches. Rooms feature, Queen size beds, fridges, televisions, tea and coffee making, irons, hairdryers, fans. Continental Smorgasbord served in the Breakfast Room from 7 am. Enjoy coffee or tea in the garden. Laundry facilities available. Fax and e-mail access.

Newcastle - Lake Macquarie   *B & B   Self Contained   15 km S of Newcastle*

Grey Gums Guesthouse
Michael & Dianne Cootes
166 Pacific Highway,
Belmont North, NSW 2280

Tel: (02) 4947 4992
Mobile: 0409 224 240
mick.cootes@au.abb.com
www.bbbook.com.au/greygums.html
Double $100 Single $25 Child free
1 Queen 2 Single (2 bdrm)
1 Private

Grey Gums Guesthouse is a self-contained cottage set on 3 acres of beautiful gardens, tall grey gums and paddocks where goats, ducks and chooks roam freely.   Conveniently located 2 hours North of Sydney on the Pacific Highway 20mins Sth. of Newcastle and 5mins to either the beach,lake or shopping. The Hunter Valley vineyards are a comfortable 30min drive.   The cottage includes all the comforts of home and contains laundry facilities and a full kitchenette and is ideal for a weekend or short stay.

Newcastle - Merewether   *B & B   5 km S of Newcastle PO*

Merewether Beach B & B
Jane & Alf Scott
60 Hickson Street, Merewether, NSW 2291

Tel: (02) 4963 3526 Fax: (02) 4963 7926
Mobile: 0407 921 670
janescott@bigpond.com
www.australiatravel.au.com/merewether_beach/
Double $130 Single $100 (Full Breakfast)
Child by arrangement Credit Cards accepted
1 Double 2 Single (1 bdrm)   1 Ensuite

Wake up to this view! Go to sleep with only the sound of waves breaking on shore. Three minutes stroll to beach, 5 km from CBD, 1000 km from care. Featured on "Getaway" , air-conditioned, self-contained studio with kitchenette, glassed-in verandah, private entrance and garden. Children welcome. Not suitable for pets. Alf's ceramics and paintings lovingly adorn the rooms. With Jane's passion for cooking, expect a breakfast extravaganza. You are our only guests. Let us spoil you! "The view is as rare as the B & B itself. Superb cooking by Jane and like living in an Art Gallery thanks to Alf." L&DF, Bowral.

Nowra   *B & B   4 km N of Nowra*

Azalea House   AAATourism ★★★★
Margaret & Gerry Deighton
69 Meroo Road, Bomaderry, NSW 2541

Tel: (02) 4423 0498 Fax: (02) 4423 0498
Mobile: 0409 843 724
azalea@shoalhaven.net.au
www.bbbook.com.au/azaleahouse.html
Double $100 Single $70
(Full Breakfast) Credit Cards accepted
1 King/Twin 1 Queen (2 bdrm)
2 Ensuite

Azalea House is a Colonial style home, verandahs front and rear, a garden with seating for guests to relax in a quiet bush setting. Two hours drive from Sydney and 2 kms off the Princes Highway and clearly signposted, it is central to Kangaroo Valley and the historic township of Berry and Jervis Bay Marine National Park. Guests can relax with game of pool, chess, cards, and in-house video or read a book from the library. Eric, a toy poodle, is our family pet - no children.

Nowra *B & B   Self Contained   12km W of Nowra*

Jungara B & B
June & Graeme Hurst
120 Paringa Road, Nowra, NSW 2541

Tel: (02) 4423 5389 Fax: (02) 4423 5389
Mobile: 0412 398 955
jungara@shoal.net.au
www.shoal.net.au/~jungara
Double $100-$160 (Full Breakfast)
1 Queen (1 bdrm)
1 Ensuite

Comfortable self-contained accommodation amidst 60 acres of Australian bushland overlooking the beautiful Shoalhaven River. Two hours from Sydney on the magnificent south coast of NSW, Jungara features queen bed, ensuite, electric blanket, heating, ceiling fans, bathrobes, toiletries, separate sitting room/kitchenette, equipped for preparing light meals. Heated swimming pool, tennis court/games room, BBQ areas. Enjoy country hospitality in totally unique setting. We have a friendly dog. Facilities not suitable for children, smoking not permitted indoors.

Nowra *Self Contained Separate/Suite   12 km W of Nowra*

Shoalhaven Lodge   AAATourism ★★★★☆
Bob & Rae Logan
480 Longreach Road, Logan, NSW 2541

Tel: (02) 4422 6686 Fax: (02) 4422 6686
Mobile: 0412 151 582   shoallodge@shoal.net.au
www.shoal.net.au/~shoallodge
Double $110-$215 Single $110-$215
(Special Breakfast) Credit Cards accepted
4 King/Twin 4 King 3 Queen (9 bdrm) 8 Ensuite

Secluded waterfront self-contained accommodation in two-storey luxury chalet style air-conditioned lodges with superb water and bushland views, on the banks of the Shoalhaven River. Quality furnishings, linen and toiletries add to the romance and indulgence we offer. Sunny decks, gas barbecues and outdoor settings overlook the river for alfresco dining. Private beach, bushwalks, wildlife, swimming, fishing, canoe hire and private boat ramp. Only 12km from Nowra. Breakfast and picnic baskets available. Brochure on request. "Idyllic setting, perfect accommodation, easy rest, wonderful hosts . . . we'll be back!" PN Cooma

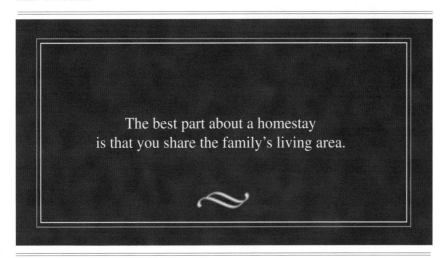

Nundle *B & B* *Nundle*

Jenkins Street Guest House B & B
Judy Howarth
85 Jenkins Street, Nundle, NSW 2340

Tel: (02) 6769 3239 Fax: (02) 9769 3222 ghnundle@northnet.com.au
www.nundle.info

Double $110-$160 Single $90 (Continental Breakfast) (Full Breakfast) Child $20 - $40
Dinner $20 - $60 Credit Cards accepted
7 Queen (7 bdrm)
4 Ensuite 2 Private 1 Share

Nundle is a tiny historic mining village of just 150 people nested in the foot hills of the Great Dividing Range.

Jenkins Street Guest House is a superbly renovated Bank building with sitting room, library and verandahs overlooking extensive gardens. Open fire places, damask linen and antiques surround you.

Fully licensed restaurant - Cha Cha Cha - open 7 days.

Horse riding, bush walks, farm tours, craft and antique shops and woollen mill nearby golf and tennis.

Nyngan   *Homestay B & B   5 km SW of Nyngan*

Burnside on the Bogan
Mary Lamph
Temple's Lane, Nyngan, NSW 2825

Tel: (02) 6832 1827 Fax: (02) 6832 1076
Mobile: 0427 200 885
www.nyngan.com/burnside.htm
Double $70-$80 Single $50-$55
Dinner $15 - $20 Pet on property
1 King/Twin (1 bdrm)
1 Ensuite

Burnside is set on 10 acres beside the Bogan river with fishing, boat ramp and ski club nearby. The home is surrounded by spacious elevated verandahs overlooking extensive lawns, gardens and rural scenery. There is just one suite for guests and they can be assured of true western hospitality. Top facilities provided for a comfortable stay with private entrance and undercover parking. Dinner by arrangement. Smoking outdoors and pets will be considered. Booking essential. "The hospitality was - as usual - top shelf!"

Orange   *Self Contained B & B   2 km W of Orange*

Acacia Grove AAATourism ★★★☆
Margaret Johnson & Alan Turner
33 Neal's Lane, off Cargo Road, Orange, NSW 2800

Tel: (02) 6365 3336 Fax: (02) 6365 3000
Mobile: 0419 653 336   www.acaciagrove.com.au
acaciagrove@ozemail.com.au
Double $95-$130 Single $80-$100 (Full Breakfast)
Child B/A Dinner $25 Credit Cards accepted
Self-contained: first nt. double $105, reductions 2nd nt
1 King 2 Queen 1 Twin (3 bdrm) 1 Ensuite 2 Private

ACACIA GROVE, is a traditional B & B where we welcome you to share our home. There is plenty of space for you to be as private or involved as you wish. Idyllic surroundings, glorious views and sumptuous breakfasts engender feelings of wellbeing . Children are welcome - at Acacia Grove B&B and Ridley Park our self contained cottage in town. Home grown and local produce used when available. "A wave of contentment overcomes one." IJ, Lane Cove. "I would like to take this B&B home." MN, Potts Point.

Orange   *Homestay   10 km W of Orange*

Killarney Homestead
Beth & Colin Magick
Darley Road, Nashdale, NSW 2800

Tel: (02) 6365 3419 Fax: (02) 6365 3419
Mobile: 0417 283 762   killarney@cww.octec.org.au
cww.octec.org.au/killarney
Double $90-$100 Single $65 (Full Breakfast)
Child $20 under 12 yrs Dinner $25 B/A
Credit Cards accepted
1 Queen 1 Double 2 Single (3 bdrm)
1 Ensuite 1 Share

Relax in a restored Federation homestead set amongst rambling gardens and orchards on slopes of Mt Canobolas. Only minutes from great bushwalking and Orange's parks, historic buildings galleries, gardens and golf courses. An ideal spot to use as a base when visiting Orange, the Central West or just passing through. Enjoy top hospitality and great cooking with friendly hosts who have an interest in antiques and a good knowledge of local attractions and places of interest. Log fire. No pets. No smoking.

Orange   *Homestay B & B   Orange Central*

Cleveland   AAATourism ★★★☆
Sue & Neil Skinner
9 Crinoline Street, Orange, NSW 2800

Tel: (02) 6362 5729 Fax: (02) 6361 2679
Mobile: 0408 306 349
clevebb@netwit.net.au
www.octec.org.au/Cleveland

Double $85-$90 Single $50-$55 (Full Breakfast)
Child by age Dinner $20 Credit Cards accepted
3 Queen 7 Single (4 bdrm)
2 Ensuite 1 Share

Our guest book is full of praise for our comfortable beds. We are ex farmers so that means good old country hospitality with a warm welcome & a hot cuppa on arrival. The House is heated throughout, the beds have electric blankets for that little extra warmth. We have evaporative cooling for the summer but summers are very pleasant. Two rooms have ensuites & two share a bathroom with a spa. We are 3 minutes from the CBD and can pick you up from the airport, station or V.I.C.

Parkes   *B & B   1.5 km E of Parkes CBD*

Kadina B & B   AAATourism ★★★★☆
Helen and Malcolm Westcott
22 Mengarvie Road, Parkes, NSW 2870

Tel: (02) 6862 3995 Fax: (02) 6862 6451
Mobile: 0412 444 452   Kadina@westserv.net.au
www.kadina.wis.net.au

Double $100 Single $70 (Full Breakfast)
Dinner B/A Credit Cards accepted
2 Queen 1 Single (2 bdrm)
2 Ensuite

Come and enjoy the tranquillity, ambience and quietness of this lovely modern spacious home with views off to the east. Watch TV, listen to music, play piano, read or just soak in the views. Dine in our traditionally furnished dining room, patio or secluded back garden. Mal is involved in a cereal growing and merino sheep enterprise 30 minutes form Parkes and guests may visit when convenient. Helen does embroidery and is happy to tutor. Come and see "The Dish". Relax in our luxurious therapeutic Hot Tub after the days travel.

Picton surrounding area   *Homestay B & B   10 km SW of Picton*

Coorumbene B & B @ Thirlmere Lakes
Toni & Wayne Johnstone
27 East Parade, Couridjah, NSW 2571

Tel: (02) 4681 0360 Fax: (02) 4683 0465
crmbene@ispdr.net.au
www.bbbook.com.au/coorumbene.html

Double $105-$120 Single $75-$85 (Full Breakfast)
Dinner $15-$20 Family stay 2A2C $140-$150
2 Double 1 Twin (3 bdrm)
1 Private 1 Share

Coorumbene B&B @ Thirlmere Lakes is a unique Australian Retreat, a great escape for couples, groups and families, offering warm caring hospitality. Featuring a Continental Buffet/Hot Breakfast, billiards/ games room, comp cycles, guest BBQ facilities and for those cold nights a cosy fire awaits you. Come and enjoy the beautiful landscapes and surrounding Gum Trees. We are situated minutes from Picton and Bowral. Each room offers a TV, CD/radio, bar fridge, bathrobes, elec. blankets and Doonas. Your stay will be a surprise!

Port Macquarie - Lighthouse Beach
Homestay B & B   6 km S of Port Macquarie
Belrina B & B   AAATourism ★★★★☆
Richard & Joy McHugh - Abel, 22 Burrawong Drive, Port Macquarie, NSW 2444

Tel: (02) 6582 2967 Fax: (02) 6582 2967 Mobile: 0409 076 719
belrina@midcoast.com.au   www.bbbook.com.au/belrinabb.html

Double $110-$120 Single $90 (Full Breakfast) Dinner $35pp
B/A Campervans $15 - $20
Credit Cards accepted   2 Queen 1 Twin (3 bdrm) 3 Ensuite

In sight of the Mountains and Sounds of the Sea. Belrina has been specifically designed for Bed & Breakfast accommodation for 'touring Australia' visitors, weekend away guests or those looking for a very comfortable relaxing overnight place to stay.

The ensuited bedrooms are beautifully appointed with private entrances from the balcony with views of the coastal panorama. A sitting room for guests provides TV and video entertainment, tea and coffee making facilities, refrigeration, a terraced BBQ and saltwater pool.

Dinner is by arrangement and includes Hastings Valley wines.

"Brilliant! We felt so welcome and 'at home'. Will tell all our friends to come!!" J&R, Gold Coast.

Port Macquarie - Bonny Hills
B & B   23 km S of Port Macquarie

Kookaburras.com.au Bed and Breakfast
AAAT★★★★☆   Annette and James Hunt
1121 Ocean Drive, Bonny Hills, NSW 2445

Tel: (02) 6585 5841 Fax: (02) 6586 3586
Mobile: 0427 452 006
bandb@kookaburras.com.au
www.kookaburras.com.au

Double $120-$150 Single $90-$120
(Continental Breakfast) Credit Cards accepted
2 Queen (2 bdrm)
2 Ensuite

Set on a leafy half acre close to the beach, this contemporary B & B, comprises two deluxe A/C queen bedrooms, each with en-suite bathroom, TV, DVD and private entrance. The comfy guests' lounge/ dining room has a kitchenette with 'fridge, microwave and tea making facilities. We are just a couple of minutes from beaches, shops and tavern. The area boasts wineries, golf courses, restaurants, galleries and national parks. We have no facilities for children or pets and are a non-smoking establishment.

Port Macquarie - Lighthouse Beach
7 km S of Port Macquarie
Homestay B &B Separate/Suite Self Contained

Lighthouse Beach B & B Homestay   AAAT★★★★☆
Kevin & Sue McDonald
91 Matthew Flinders Drive, Port Macquarie, NSW 2444

Tel: (02) 6582 5149 Fax: 02) 6582 6168
Mobile: 0409 784 986   lighthouseb_b@optusnet.com.au
www.bbbook.com.au/lighthousebeachb_b.html

Double $90-$140 Single $70-$110 (Special Breakfast)
Self-contained $120 - $145 Credit Cards accepted
1 King/Twin 1 Queen 1 Double 1 Twin 1 Single (3 bdrm)
3 Ensuite 3 Private

For a peaceful vacation welcome to Port's "closest to the beach" accommodation. Choose one of our poolside rooms or the added luxury of our romantic suite. After a hearty cooked breakfast enjoy the comfortable guest lounge or stroll to the lighthouse. Features: All ensuites - private access - TV - tea/ coffee facility - spa and pool - gas BBQ - smoke free environment. Independent wheelchair available downstairs. Only metres from Magnificent 14 km lighthouse beach relax to the sounds of the surf.

All our B&Bs are non-smoking
unless stated otherwise in the text.

New South
Wales

Benbellen
Country
Retreat

Fall in love with the green valleys, wooded hills, streams and the roller-coasting country lanes of Hannam Vale.
Be captivated by the large open plan homestead with its solar passive design and quietly stated elegance.
Feed the alpacas and wander the high fields among our Friesian heifers.
Fish for bass or warm-water rainbow trout.
Stroll along country lanes or bush walk past rock pools, streams and waterfalls.

Visit the many beaches, golf courses and other attractions of the Hastings and Manning Valleys.
Or simply relax and enjoy the peace, quiet and spectacular views from the balconies.
Choose between luxury ensuite rooms or our large two-bedroom cottage.
Locally grown produce, fresh (to die for) eggs from the farm, home-baked breads and homemade jams.

Port Macquarie - Taree - Hannam Vale
Farmstay B & B - Self-contained Family Cottage
20 km S of Laurieton
Benbellen Country Retreat   AAATourism ★★★★☆
Hosts: Peter & Sherry Wildblood/Stumm
Cherry Tree Lane, Hannam Vale, NSW 2443

Cost: Guest Rooms: 3 Queen all ensuite
Family Cottage: 1 Queen, 1 Double, 2 Single
Double $135 - $175, Single $110 - $135
- All Credit Cards, Dinner $35 per person
Tel: (02) 6556 7788   Fax: (02) 6556 7778
Freecall: 1800 187 888
info@bbfarmstay.com.au
www.bbfarmstay.com.au

Port Macquarie's Hinterland - Wauchope
500m W of Wauchope PO

B & B

Auntie Ann's Bed & Breakfast
AAATourism ★★★☆
Ann Pereira
19 Bruxner Avenue, Wauchope, NSW 2446

Tel: (02) 6586 4420
www.bbbook.com.au/auntieann'sbed&breakfast.html
Double $70 Single $50 (Full Breakfast)
Credit Cards accepted
1 Double 4 Twin (3 bdrm) 1 Share

Wauchope is the gateway to Port Macquarie's Hinterland. Within easy driving are several national parks, nature reserves and vineyards as well as the largest single drop waterfall in the Southern Hemisphere. Overlooking the golf course, Auntie Ann's is close to clubs, restaurants and shops. Visit Timbertown Heritage Park, art, pottery and furniture galleries or just relax by the pool with some locally made fudge. Also available: Air-conditioning, TV room, BBQ, tea/coffee making facilities, heaters and/or fans each room.

Port Stephens - Lemon Tree Passage
20 km E of Raymond Terrace

Homestay B & B

Larkwood of Lemon Tree **AAATourism ★★★★**
Anne & Alan Parker
1 Oyster Farm Road, Lemon Tree Passage, NSW 2319

Tel: (02) 4982 4656 Fax: (02) 4982 4656
Mobile: 0427 501 959   contactus@larkwood.net
www.larkwood.net

Double $110 Single $85 (Full Breakfast)
Child $20 Dinner $30 B/A Credit Cards accepted
3 Queen 1 Single (3 bdrm) 3 Ensuite

Lemon Tree Passage is located on the shores of beautiful Port Stephens, just two hours north of Sydney or twenty minutes form Raymond Terrace and the Pacific Highway. The area is renowned for its Koala Colony, abundant birdlife and wildflowers. Larkwood has three guest rooms with queen beds and ensuites, and the tariff includes a full cooked breakfast. Special diets catered for. We have a pool set in half acre of private garden, or there's a cosy fireplace for winter. We have one dog but no children. Finalists in Hunter Excellence in Tourism Awards for 1999.

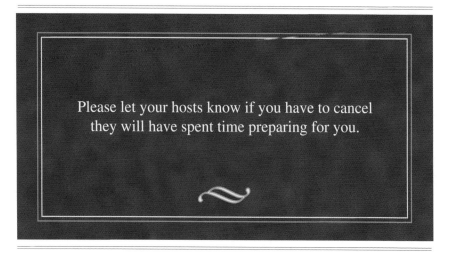

Please let your hosts know if you have to cancel
they will have spent time preparing for you.

Port Stephens - Nelson Bay
Homestay B & B   *4 km S of Nelson Bay*

Croft Haven B&B   **AAATourism ★★★★**
Dian & Dean Cox
202 Salamander Way, Nelson Bay, NSW 2317

Tel: (02) 4984 1799 Fax: (02) 4984 1799
Mobile: 0404 460 099   crofthav@nelsonbay.com
www.crofthaven.nelsonbay.com

Double $100-$130 Single $80-$100 (Full Breakfast)
Child $50 Credit Cards accepted
1 King/Twin 1 Queen 1 Double 1 Twin (3 bdrm)
2 Ensuite 1 Private

Relax, sit back and be pampered. Our bushland retreat is close to all activities and beaches, but so far from the hustle & bustle of city life. Beautifully appointed guest rooms, with in-house massage services. Sumptuous buffet with specialty breakfasts served at your leisure. With open fireplaces for winter comfort and barbecue area for summer sizzles, let the stress of everyday life drift away. Ask about our 'Indulgence Packages' to experience the ultimate in rest, relaxation & rejuvenation. RELAX - REFLECT - REJUVENATE.

Raymond Terrace
Homestay B & B   *5 km NW of Raymond Terrace*

Bloomfields B & B   **AAATourism ★★★☆**
Shirley & Peter Bloomfield
17 Ralston Road, Raymond Terrace, NSW 2324

Tel: (02) 4983 1839 Fax: (02) 4967 5481
Mobile: 0404 465 434
Shirlbb@bigpond.com
www.bbbook.com.au/bloomfieldsbb.html

Double $85 Single $50
(Full Breakfast) Dinner $17.50
1 Queen 2 Single (2 bdrm)
1 Private 1 Share

Join us in a tranquil rural setting on an 18 acre bush block. Spacious air conditioned rooms open onto wide verandahs with tables and chairs. We have large organic vegetable gardens, an orchard and extensive native plantings. We are centrally placed for visits to local attractions at Port Stephens, Morpeth and the vineyards. Children are welcome but we feel pets are a problem for our resident wildlife - we have geese and kangaroos/king parrots and other bird species are frequent visitors.

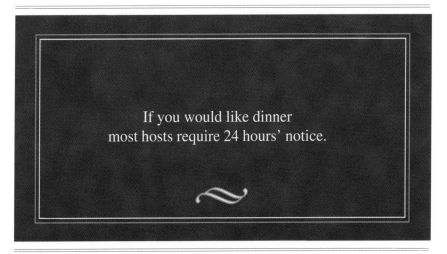

If you would like dinner
most hosts require 24 hours' notice.

Scone - Hunter Valley *Farmstay B & B Self Contained* *10 km NW of Scone*

Dartbrook Farm B & B

Athene & Michael Lambley, Upper Dartbrook Road, via Scone, NSW 2337

Tel: (02) 6545 1440 Fax: (02) 6545 1352 info@dartbrookfarm.com.au www.dartbrookfarm.com.au

Double $130-$150 (Continental Breakfast) (Full Breakfast) Dinner $20- $35

Credit Cards accepted Pets welcome

1 Queen (1 bdrm)

1 Private

The Perfect Place to Escape - Maximum privacy, far from hustle and stress. Peace and tranquillity - Do it all or do nothing! Exhausted business people, outdoor adventurers and romantic honeymooners all welcome. Perhaps that special anniversary - or for no reason at all.

Dartbrook Farm, just 10 minutes from Scone, surrounded by beautiful scenery is that Special destination" Set in a large garden, your own one bedroom, self contained cottage with private kitchen, dining, lounge and bathroom, caters to any requirements for a perfect relaxing holiday. After a leisurely breakfast guests can linger and read in front of the log fire in winter, take a walk along the Dart Brook checking on the abundant birdlife, the farm animals or the spectacular hills and rocky outcrops. A private bbq is available for your use or you may wish to have dinner, by prior arrangement, with us.

Dartbrook Farm is an ideal base to explore the many attractions of the Upper Hunter Valley - horse stud, winery, coal mine, and homestead tours can be arranged and other great destinations i.e. Glenbawn Dam, Towarri National Park, lunches at wineries, Burning Mountain and numerous other activities are all within a 2 hour drive.

Ask about our mid-week escape packages or gift certificates. We are a smoke free property catering expressly for adults. Pets by arrangement only. Tariffs: Saturday Night $150.00 Fri/Sat or Sat/Sun $130.00 per night Discounts available for long stay or multiple midweeks

Just as we have a variety of B&Bs
you will also be offered a variety of breakfasts,
and they will always be generous

New South
Wales

Snowy Mountains - Khancoban   *7 km N of Khancoban*
Farmstay Homestay B & B

Cossettini B & B   AAATourism ★★★☆
Joe & Kate Cossettini
Alpine Way, Khancoban, NSW 2642

Tel: (02) 6076 9332 Fax: (02) 6076 9332
cossettini@telstra.com.au
www.bbbook.com.au/cossettini.html
Double $70-$100 Single $50-$60
(Full Breakfast) Child $20
2 King/Twin 2 Queen (2 bdrm)
1 Ensuite 1 Private

Escape to peace and tranquillity in delightful Khancoban, with spectacular views of the Snowy Mountains, half way between Sydney and Melbourne. Enjoy warmth and hospitality in this centrally heated home. Relax in your private spa, sleep in crisp white linen and wake to the delicious aroma of freshly made cappuccino and a generous gourmet country breakfast. Access to a wide range of activities including fishing, golf, bush-walking, horse-riding, rock-climbing, white water rafting, skiing.

Southern Highlands - Burradoo - Bowral   *2 km S of Bowral*
Self Contained

Hartnoll Park
Julie & Bill Flemming
8 Ranelagh Road, Burradoo, NSW 2576

Tel: (02) 4861 7282 Fax: (02) 4861 7252
Mobile: 0429 001 042
stay@hartnollpark.com.au
www.hartnollpark.com.au
Double $150-$200 (Full Breakfast)
$350 2 night Weekend Package Credit Cards accepted
2 Queen (2 bdrm) 1 Private

Indulge yourself in our tranquil self-contained 2 bedroom cottage nestled in the old part of Burradoo. Plan your romantic escape to this inviting country cottage that features queen size beds, comfortable lounge, full kitchen, bathroom, separate laundry and private garden. Quality linen, TV/video, gas log heating, electric blankets and all those little luxuries for a relaxing break in the Southern Highlands. Only 75 minutes from Sydney - we look forward to welcoming you.

Southern Highlands - Bundanoon   *Self Contained*   *0.5 km Bundanoon*

Morvern Valley Guesthouse
Julie Summers, 22 The Gullies Road, Bundanoon, NSW 2578

Tel: (02) 4883 6801 Fax: (02) 4883 7453
morvern@bigpond.com www.bbbook.com.au/morvern.html
(Full Breakfast) Whole house $400 midweek 4 nts
Whole house $400 weekends 2 nts Credit Cards accepted
1 Queen 1 Double 1 Single (3 bdrm)
1 Private

Bundanoon in the Southern Highlands of New South Wales is a mere two hours from Sydney and Canberra. This 25 acre country retreat is situated within walking distance to the quiet village of Bundanoon with its shops, restaurants and cafes.

Morvern Valley guesthouse was one of the original guesthouses in Bundanoon in the 1930's and is not home to your host - indeed this tastefully restored cottage is exclusively yours for the duration of your stay.

Decorated with old world romance in mind the house has two open fireplaces with alternate heating in the other rooms, feather doonas and electric blankets, to ensure your stay is cheerful and enjoyable. Unwind and play in the Spa Bath by candlelight, relax in squashy sofas by the roaring open fire. Three individually decorated bedrooms, with authentic four poster beds.

Collect farm fresh eggs and cook them up in the wonderful old fully facilitated kitchen - a breakfast basket full of local produce is included in your tariff at no extra charge. Enjoy a stroll along our creek and check out the bird life, go in search of Wallabies, Lyre Birds, Platypus and echidnas. Say hello to Jack and the other ponies grazing in our paddocks. Feed colourful Crimson Rosellas and King parrots, the resident possum or maybe Harry the wombat. Bikes are provided at no extra charge, so perhaps on an excursion into the spectacular Morton national park located just metres from your front door is in order.

Bundanoon's spectacular waterfalls are a must see attraction. All plunge from sheer sandstone cliffs into deep rainforest gorges. There are 14 designated walks, from the gentle stroll along ' The Lovers Walk', or a challenging bushwalk to 'Fairy Bower Falls'. For an extra special memory why not take one of our Horse and Carriage gourmet picnics into the park, where you can find enchanting secluded spots next to a waterfall or in a rainforest, proving very popular, so bookings are essential.

A short distance away, are the Southern Highland towns of Berrima, Moss Vale, and Bowral. Country markets are held every Sunday. Eat at the many cafes, browse for antiques and collectables, visit wineries for cellar door sales, or play a round of golf at one of the many excellent golf courses. Experience the wonderful Southern Highlands hospitality from Morvern and remember - you can be there in just 2 hours.

Southern Highlands - Goulburn   *3 km S of Goulburn PO*

Farmstay Homestay B & B

South Hill Homestead
Elizabeth & Ian Lipscomb
Garroorigang Road, Goulburn, NSW 2580

Tel: (02) 4821 9591 Fax: (02) 4821 9591
www.bbbook.com.au/southhill.html

Double $110 Single $66 (Full Breakfast)
Child $33 Credit Cards accepted Pet on property
4 Double 6 Single (5 bdrm)
1 Ensuite 1 Private 1 Share

Enjoy views, space, walk the paddocks and experience a large Victorian country house with wood fires and third hand furniture. South Hill is great for a group gathering with large dining room (seats 24) and large comfortable sitting room. Small conferences are possible. Goulburn CBD has many excellent restaurants. Make South Hill a base for touring working farms. We have sheep dogs and peacocks on our small farm. Stay Tuesday night and attend a sheep sale on Wednesday. 2 hours from Sydney, 1 hour from Canberra makes it an ideal touring centre.

Southern Highlands - Goulburn   *located in CBD*

Boutique Bed & Breakfast

Mandelson's of Goulburn   AAATourism ★★★★
Renate Johnson-Barrett
160 Sloane Street, Goulburn

Tel: (02) 4821 0707 Fax: (02) 4821 0225
Mobile: 0414 813 601   mandelsons@bigpond.com
www.mandelsons.com.au

Double $150-$205 (Full Breakfast)
Credit Cards accepted
8 Queen (8 bdrm)   8 Ensuite

A splendid example of colonial architecture, Noel and Renate have passionately restored and refurbished Mandelson's into an elegant and luxurious yet homely boutique style B&B. A complementary decanter of port and chocolates, superior bedding, central heating, bathrobes and more are signs of the world class, warm and friendly hospitality all guests will receive. Your hosts are happy to recommend a number of restaurants within easy walking distance and a delicious full breakfast with homemade jam is served in the Dining Room.

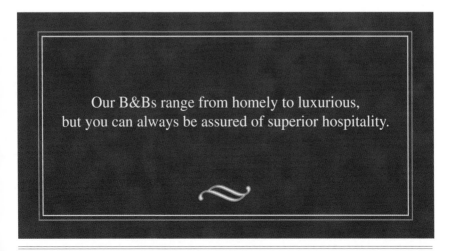

Our B&Bs range from homely to luxurious,
but you can always be assured of superior hospitality.

Southern Highlands - Moss Vale

Homestay B & B   1 km N of Moss Vale

Heronswood House   AAATourism ★★★★
Brian & Tina Davis
165 Argyle Street, Moss Vale, NSW 2577

Tel: (02) 4869 1477 Fax: (02) 4869 4079
heron@acenet.com.au
www.acenet.com.au/~heron

Double $115.5-$181.5 (Full Breakfast)
Single (mid-week) $71.50 Credit Cards accepted
2 King/Twin 3 Queen 1 Single (5 bdrm)
4 Ensuite 1 Private

This beautiful 19th century home, on the North side of town, in the heart of the Highlands, offers you friendly, comfortable accommodation. The five bedrooms are tastefully decorated with one adapted for the physically disabled. The lounge, sunroom and kitchenette are available to guests. Greeted with afternoon tea on arrival. Breakfast each morning is varied and generous, ranging from traditional to house specials eg "Herons Nest". The wide verandahs and one acre of grounds encourage you to relax and enjoy the delights of the Highlands. "Arrive as a visitor, leave as a friend".

Southern Highlands - Mt Murray - Robertson

B & B   8 km E of Robertson

Rose Ella B & B   AAATourism ★★★☆
Helen & Ron NonnenMacher
McGuinness Drive,
Mt Murray via Robertson, NSW 2577

Tel: (02) 4885 1401 Fax: (02) 4885 1717
Mobile: 0414 851 101   roseellabb@bigpond.com.au
www.highlandsnsw.com.au/roseella

Double $130-$150 Single $90-$130 (Full Breakfast)
Dinner $30pp Credit Cards accepted
2 Queen (2 bdrm) 2 Ensuite

Set on five acres with views of coast and escarpment Rose Ella is central to all Illawarra, South Coast and Southern Highlands activities. Suites are tastefully furnished with TV, clock/radio, electric blankets, heater, fans. Relax in the guest lounge with cosy open fire, or in the sunroom with complementary afternoon tea. Full country breakfast is included in the tariff. Dinner is served in the beautifully furnished dining room by prior arrangement. Smokers are invited to enjoy the veranda and gardens. Children by arrangement.

Southern Highlands - Sutton Forest

7 km S of Moss Vale

Homestay B & B Self Contained

Sutton Downs
Jeni & Charles Davies - Scourfield
Golden Vale Road, Sutton Forest, NSW 2577

Tel: (02) 4868 3126 Fax: (02) 4868 3802
suttonbb@hinet.net.au
www.highlandsnsw.com.au/suttondowns

Double $155-$185 (Full Breakfast)
Self-Contained Suite from $145 Credit Cards accepted
1 King/Twin 2 Queen (3 bdrm) 1 Ensuite 2 Private

For six years Sutton Downs has been one of the most highly praised B&Bs by guests and media writers. Enjoy peace, comfort and hospitality in this magnificent country house on 100 acres of beautiful countryside with views all round, just minutes from Moss Vale and Berrima. Accommodation is in King, Queen or Twin format, all with private bathrooms. The guest sitting room has a log fire. No children in the house but we now offer a self contained suite which can take two adults and two children.

Sydney   *Homestay B & B   Sydney Central*

139 Commonwealth Street Sydney Central
Julie Stevenson
139 Commonwealth Street
Surry Hills, Sydney, NSW 2010

Tel: (02) 9211 9920
Fax: (02) 9212 2450
Mobile: 0419 202 779
jas@bedandbreakfastsydney.com.au
www.bedandbreakfastsydney.com.au

(Continental Breakfast) $120 - $150
2 King/Twin 1 Queen (3 bdrm)
2 Private 1 Share

New South
Wales

An elegant Terrace house set in the heart of the best Sydney has to offer. Just a short walk to Hyde Park, Law Courts, Centrepoint Tower, Queen Victoria Building, Darling Harbour, Chinatown & Oxford Street.

Only ten minutes drive to Fox Studios, the Sydney Cricket Ground, Universities, race courses, Centennial Park and beaches. Walk to the Rocks, Circular Quay, the Opera House, the exciting harbour BridgeClimb. Board ferry to Manly, The Zoo and North Shore, relax in terrace garden.

Two resident cats. Non smoking. Not suitable for young children. KST Sydney Airporter to the door.

Sydney   *B & B*   *Sydney Harbour*

Bed & Breakfast Sydney Harbour   **AAATourism ★★★★**
John & Jan McLaughlin, 140 -142 Cumberland Street, The Rocks, NSW 2000

Tel: (02) 9247 1130 Fax: (02) 9247 1148 stay@bbsydneyharbour.com.au
www.bbsydneyharbour.com.au

Double $155-$249 Single $140-$199 (Continental Breakfast) (Full Breakfast) Child Welcome
Extra person $27.50 Credit Cards accepted
9 Queen 2 Twin (9 bdrm)
1 Ensuite 4 Private 4 Share

Bed & Breakfast Sydney Harbour offers visitors the unique opportunity of experiencing genuine Bed & Breakfast accommodation, right in the heart of the Rocks, Australia's birthplace.

The Rocks is the corner stone of Australia's history and Sydney's colourful past. Beautifully restored buildings, famous historic hotels, numerous restaurants, waterfront restaurants, outdoor eating and Sydney's largest selection of specialty shops along with the famous Rocks Markets make the Rocks a shopping delight. Stroll along Sydney Harbour, the world's most beautiful harbour from the Opera House to the Bridge. Take in a show at the Opera House or one of the famous theatres on the waterfront. For excitement the Rocks has it all. Stay at the Rocks, you are where the action is.

Bed & Breakfast Sydney Harbour offers guests the opportunity of staying in fully restored heritage buildings, providing superbly comfortable accommodation. We have a guest's sitting room, a delightful courtyard, which provides a quiet oasis for guests to relax after exploring the City, harbour or shopping. All rooms have remote control colour television.

"Dinki-di hospitality and down-to-earth, this Rocks B&B has it all - comfy beds, Opera House views and Sydney attractions right on the doorstep" - Anthony Dennis, Sydney Morning Herald, feature writer.

"Undoubtedly one of the best finds I've made on my travels. A jewel in Sydney's crown and now my top recommendation for Brits travelling south, best of luck I look forward to giving you a rave review" - Matt Rudd, Assistant Editor, Wanderlust Publications Ltd, Windsor UK.

Arrive as guests depart as friends.

Sydney - Annandale *B & B*   *4 km SW of Sydney CBD*

Aronui
Pamela Bond
72A Johnston Street, Annandale, NSW 2038

Tel: (02) 9564 1992 Fax: (02) 9560 5156
Mobile: 0403 283 568   pamela@aronui.com
www.aronui.com

Double $100-$130 Single $75-$110
(Special Breakfast) Seld Contained $130
1 Queen 2 Double 1 Twin (3 bdrm)
1 Ensuite 1 Private 1 Share

Built in 1895, Aronui is a superb example of Australian Victorian architecture, with high ceilings, ornate plasterwork, leadlight windows and marble fireplaces. The house is surrounded by lush rain forest gardens and has a solar saltwater swimming pool, barbeque area and delightful Koi fish pond. Located in inner-west Annandale, Aronui is close to restaurants, shops and all amenities including Sydney University, RPA Hospital, Italian Forum. Historical walking tours available on request, also evening meals and picnic lunches.

Sydney - Arcadia *B & B*   *8 km Castle Hill*

Lauders Loft
Allison & Jim Lauder
14 Blacks Road, Arcadia, NSW 2159

Tel: (02) 9653 2422 Mobile: 0438 086 474
laudersloft@yahoo.com
www.geocities.com/laudersloft

Double $125 Single $100
(Full Breakfast) Child $90
1 Queen 1 Double 1 Single (2 bdrm)
1 Private

Lauders Loft is a quaint country retreat less than (1) hour from Sydney. Self contained accommodation allows for complete privacy for a couple or family. Pristine waterways, parks and village shops are minutes away and historic Windsor provides for a good day out. A full country breakfast is available and local restaurants make dining out a pleasure. Pet Kennels are close by.

Sydney - Balmain *Homestay B & B*   *3 km W of Sydney Central*

Claremont Bed & Breakfast
Pauline Insley
12 Claremont Street,
Balmain, NSW 2041

Tel: (02) 9810 8358
Fax: (02) 9810 8358
pauline@insley.bu.aust.com
www.bu.aust.com/insley/claremont

Double $165-$185 Single $130-$135
(Special Breakfast) Credit Cards accepted
2 Queen (2 bdrm)
2 Ensuite

A boutique style B&B, centrally located in historic and cosmopolitan Balmain. A great place to stay to explore the Balmain Peninsula restaurants, cafes, pubs, boutiques and weekend markets. Only minutes to CBD Sydney. The century old, lovingly restored, timber terrace house offers spacious private guest suites, heating, air conditioned, refrigerator, tea/coffee making facilities and TV. Smoking outdoors.

Sydney - Balmain   *Self Contained B & B*   *2.5 km W of Sydney Central*

Balmain Village B & B Accommodation
E. Howerd & M. McGrane
45 Cove Street, Birchgrove, NSW 2041

Tel: (02) 9818 4587 Fax: (02) 9818 4587
info@balmainvillagebandb.com.au
www.balmainvillagebandb.com.au

Double $139-$170 Single $109-$135
(Continental Breakfast) Credit Cards accepted
1 Queen (1 bdrm)
1 Private

Ten minutes from Sydney centre by bus/ferry, our 116-year old cottage is in a charming, tree-lined street. Easy stroll to Balmain Village to explore restaurants, shops, cafes, boutiques and historic pubs. Guests enjoy a self-contained studio separated from the house by a courtyard with street entrance. Features own kitchen/dining area (microwave, refrigerator, crockery etc), bathroom, aircon./heating, ceiling fan, electric blanket, TV/VCR. Minimum two nights. No smoking, thank you. "Friendly, stylish and a haven to return to at the end of the day." AC, Michigan, USA.

Sydney - Bardwell Park   *Self Contained B & B*   *10 km S of Sydney*

Ambleside
Pamela & William Clifford
2 Pile Street North, Bardwell Park, NSW 2207

Tel: (02) 9556 2556 Fax: (02) 9556 2117
Mobile: 0412 130 847   pamela.clifford@bigpond.com
www.users.bigpond.com/pamela.clifford

Double $120-$135 Single $100-$115
(Continental Breakfast) Self cater from $700 per week
(shorter stays B/A) Pet on property
1 Queen 1 Twin (2 bdrm)   1 Private

Bed & Breakfast (generous continental) or self-catering at Ambleside, a charming 2-storey house, circa 1917, surrounded by trees in a quiet garden suburb. Accommodation is a large self-contained 1st floor apartment with attractively furnished bedrooms, open plan lounge/dining and separate, fully equipped kitchen. Hosts live on ground floor. For stays of 4 days or more, guests receive complimentary breakfast on 1st morning, afternoon tea on arrival and a bottle of Australian wine. Direct train to Sydney CBD; direct rail to International / Domestic Airport. Resident outside dog Jessie.

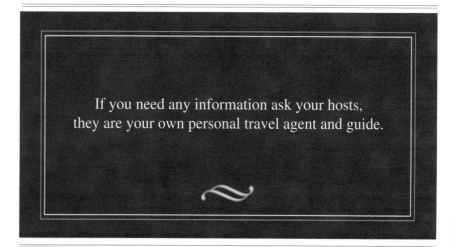

If you need any information ask your hosts,
they are your own personal travel agent and guide.

Sydney - Brooklyn - Hawkesbury River

B & B   45km N of city centre

Above the Hawkesbury: Brooklyn Luxury Bed & Breakfast

AAATourism ★★★★☆

Eva & Carl Southern

6 Bridge Street, Brooklyn, NSW 2083

Tel: (02) 9985 8584 Fax: (02) 9985 8577 Mobile: 0414 327 545

book@brooklynbb.com

www.brooklynbb.com

Double $150-$195 Single $120-$150 (Special Breakfast) Child $35 Dinner $35 - $55

Aromatherapy or Remedial Massage available on request Credit Cards accepted

1 King/Twin 1 Queen (2 bdrm)

2 Ensuite

Take a short break in Brooklyn, one of Sydney's last remaining fishing villages and be pleasantly surprised by a hidden gem . . . just a few minutes off the F3 freeway you will find 'Above the Hawkesbury' offering deluxe B & B accommodation, comfortable beds and great breakfasts.

Your accommodation is stylishly furnished and decorated. Television, video and refreshments are available in the dining/lounge room. Your rooms are well equipped and include CD players. Choose the River suite with ensuite bathroom and views from your bed over Brooklyn Village to Sandbrook Inlet and Long Island. Or relax in the Spa Suite and watch the day go by from your spa. Take breakfast in the dining room or on your private deck.

Eva and Carl offer unassuming service with an emphasis on relaxation and enjoyment. Privacy is assured with your accommodation on a separate level with a private entrance. You may also relax in your room taking an aromatherapy massage.

Brooklyn is only 50 minutes north of the city with direct rail and road access from the airport or city. You are no more than 5 minutes walk to restaurants, cafes, the pub, craft and curio shops or the marina. Walking tracks are nearby or take a ferry trip to beautiful Dangar Island.

"Thank you Carl & Eva for a perfect weekend." Anne & Phil.

"We have had a wonderful stay and the breakfast was magnificent." K & D Bathurst.

". . .the room, the view, the ambience, the breakfast, the massage - exceeded my expectations." ES, Kirribilli.

Sydney - Caringbah   *Homestay B & B*   *22 km S of Sydney*

Lilli Pilli B & B
Ray & Carol Cook
608 Port Hacking Road, Caringbah, NSW 2229

Tel: (02) 9525 5447 Fax: (02) 9525 5447
Mobile: 0439 952 554   raycook@bigpond.com
www.bbbook.com.au/lillipillibb.html

Double $95 Single $75 (Full Breakfast)
Dinner $20 Credit Cards accepted
2 Queen (2 bdrm)
2 Ensuite

In quiet, leafy Lilli Pilli, 30 minutes from the airport. Convenient to the city by train or car. Relax to the sound of native birds in the garden, surf Cronulla beaches, or golf on the nearby courses. Port Hacking and beautiful Royal National Park are close by. We specialise in delicious breakfasts and can arrange basket lunches or dinners. We are happy to discuss special dietary requirements. Complementary tea, coffee and snacks available.   Facilities include T.V. in rooms, air conditioning, hairdryers, laundry facilities and off-street parking. Discounts for longer stays.

Sydney - Castle Hill   *B & B*   *3 km E of Castle Hill*

Glenhope Bed & Breakfast
Cheryl & John Cooper
113 Castle Hill Road,
West Pennant Hills, NSW 2125

Tel: (02) 9634 2508 Fax: (02) 9659 1674
admin@glenhope-bnb.com.au
www.glenhope-bnb.com.au

Double $143-$192.5 Single $104.5-$154
(Continental & Full Breakfast) Credit Cards accepted
3 Queen 1 Double (4 bdrm)   4 Ensuite

Glenhope is a heritage listed former farmhouse set on the ridge at Castle Hill offering warm hospitality and personal attention in a comfortable, old world setting. There are 4 bedrooms upstairs, each with ensuite, full air conditioning, tv, phone. One bedroom even has a tower. Downstairs is the drawing room and formal dining room where we serve a wide range of breakfast fare. Evening dining available by arrangement. Set in more than an acre of gardens, Glenhope is conveniently located about 30 km NW of Sydney CBD in the attractive Hills area.

Sydney - Clovelly   *B & B*   *6 km SE of Sydney*

Clovelly   AAATourism ★★★★
Tony & Shirley Murray
2 Pacific Street, Clovelly, NSW 2031

Tel: (02) 9665 0009 Mobile: 0419 609 276
clovellybandb@yahoo.com
www.bbbook.com.au/clovelly.html

Double $105-$130 Single $95-$120
(Full Breakfast) Credit Cards accepted
1 Queen 1 Double 2 Twin (3 bdrm)   1 Private 1 Share

Clovelly, Coogee and Bronte beaches and cafes/restaurants are within walking distance. We are close to transport to many attractions - Airport, Sydney CBD, cricket ground, Centennial Park, University of NSW, Randwick Races, Football Stadium, Bondi Beach. Afternoon tea will be served on arrival. Tea and coffee available all day. Breakfast includes fresh fruit and juices, home made bread, and a hot dish. Bedrooms are located upstairs and each has a television, hairdryer and bathrobes. Guests have a separate sitting room. Unable to accommodate pets. "Immaculately clean, tastefully decorated accommodation. . .hosts attentive to our needs." RC, Qld.

Sydney - Clovelly *B & B   6 km SE of Sydney City Centre*

Nestle Brae Bed & Breakfast
Lynelle & Michael O'Connor
23 Arden Street, Clovelly, NSW 2031

Tel: (02) 9665 8030 Mobile: 0402 041 581
nestlebrae@hotmail.com
www.nestlebraebandb.com.au
Double $120 Single $85 (Full Breakfast)
1 Queen 1 Double (2 bdrm)
1 Share

Nestle Brae B & B, by the sea at beautiful Clovelly. Your smoke-free home away from home is tastefully restored 1910 cottage with original floorboards and fireplace with a modern guest bathroom including a deluxe corner spa bath. Both double bedrooms are situated on the ground floor and include tea/coffee making facilities, fridge, TV and guest bathrobes. We have an outside dog, inside cat and children aged 8 and 7. A full breakfast is served with a choice of two hot dishes, fresh seasonal fruit salad, juice and tea/coffee. Many attractions nearby including SCG and SFS, Fox Studios, Centennial Park & beaches. If there is anything you need just ask!

Sydney - Cronulla *Homestay Separate/Suite B & B   28 km S of Sydney*

Homestay Cronulla B & B
Betsy Eardley
10 Rose Street, Cronulla, NSW 2230

Tel: (02) 9523 1577 Fax: (02) 9501 5290
Mobile: 0413 414 440
gbe.cronulla@bigpond.com.au
www.bbbook.com.au/homestaycronulla.html
Double $100 Single $70 (Special Breakfast)
1 Double 2 Single (2 bdrm)
1 Private

Quiet seaside home, convenient to the airport. We meet guests at the airport/train/coach. Comfortable ground floor guest rooms. Delicious breakfasts. Tea/coffee making facilities, microwave, TV, fridge, etc. Laundry available. Cronulla's Mall has restaurants, fast-foods, clubs, banks, cinemas, etc. Excellent train service to Sydney's CBD and tourist attractions. Off-street parking. Delightful seaside walks, safe swimming, relax in the fresh air. Brochures on request. Our interests include travel, music, art, theatre, steam engines, Beta Sigma Phi and Rotary.

Sydney - Cronulla *Self Contained   0.75km W of Cronulla*

Bayview Apartment
Beverley and Alan Currie
Cronulla, NSW 2230

Tel: (07) 3203 4701 Fax: (07) 3203 4701
Mobile: 0418 403 671 bviewbb@ozemail.com.au
www.bbbook.com.au/bayviewcronulla.html
Double $176 extra person $12
Credit Cards accepted
1 Queen 2 Single (2 bdrm)
1 Private

Ground floor. Sleeps 6, sofa bed. Delightful,spotlessly clean, sunny, spacious open-plan lounge, dining,kitchen area. Large front balcony, sit and relax. Internal laundry, washer, dryer. Fully equipped kitchen. TV/Video. All linen provided. Security block, lock-up garage. Small balcony off main bedroom. Short walk to local and interstate bus service, ferry, shops, beaches (surf and swimming), cinemas, all within 10 minutes. Close to Tram Museum, Symbio Koala park. Gunamatta Bay 150 metres stroll. Ferry to Royal National Park. Train to Sydney CBD 48 minutes.

Sydney - Cronulla   *Homestay B & B   28 km S of Sydney*

Cronulla Seabreeze B & B
Maria & Richard Morey
6 Boronia Street, Cronulla, NSW 2230

Tel: (02) 9523 4908 Fax: (02) 9501 5950
Mobile: 0407 774 426
seabreezebnb@optusnet.com.au
www.seabreezebnb.com.au

Double $100-$120 Single $78-$88 (Full Breakfast)
Child B/A Extra person $30
1 King/Twin 1 Queen (2 bdrm)   2 Ensuite

A warm welcome awaits you at "Seabreeze" on picturesque Cronulla Peninsula. Guests enjoy private use of the upper level of our home, offering inviting bedrooms, guest lounge with delightful ocean outlook, fridge, TV/VCR/CD. Stroll to beaches, ocean pools, tranquil bayside parks and restaurants. District features include historic Kurnell, Symbio Koala Park, excellent golf courses and ferry to Royal National Park. Excellent train service to Central Sydney & Airport. Friendly pointer dog. We also speak German. No smoking indoors please.

Sydney - Curl Curl - Northern Beaches   *Self Contained   4 km N of Manly*

Beach House B&B
Joanna & John Jankaus
28 Surf Road, North Curl Curl, NSW 2099

Tel: (02) 9905 0219 Fax: (02) 9905 0219
Mobile: 0414 989 599
www.bbbook.com.au/beachhousebb.html

(Special Breakfast)
Breakfast Provisions supplied. Full Breakfast on request.
Daily rate on application $600-$800 per week
1 King/Twin 1 Queen (2 bdrm)   1 Private

Fully self contained 2 bedroom beachside accommodation opening May 2002. This sunny, brand new unit features private balcony overlooking reserve and Curl Curl beach, kitchenette & laundry facilities. Conveniently located in cul-de-sac with absolute reserve/beach frontage, on bus route to Manly. Reasonable weekly & monthly rates, enquiries please contact your hosts Joanna & John. About Manly: Popular surf beach located Sydney's Northern Beaches. 15 min Jetcat ride to Sydney City or 30 min by Ferry. Features many alfresco cafes, bars & restaurants. Year round tourist attraction.

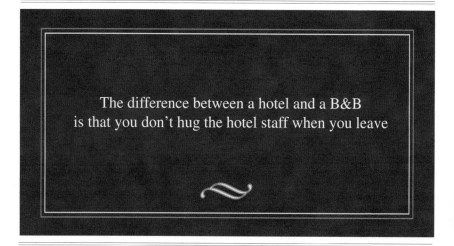

The difference between a hotel and a B&B
is that you don't hug the hotel staff when you leave

Sydney - Drummoyne   *Homestay B & B*   *5 km W of Sydney*

Eboracum
Jeannette & Michael York
18A Drummoyne Avenue, Drummoyne, NSW 2047

Tel: (02) 9181 3541 Mobile: 0414 920 975
mjyork@bigpond.com
www.bbook.com.au/eboracum.html

Double $120 Single $95 (Full Breakfast)
Dinner B/A Pet on property
1 Double 1 Twin (2 bdrm)
1 Private 1 Share

Charming water frontage home by the Parramatta River, amid beautiful trees, with glorious views. Boatshed and wharf at waters edge. Handy to transport, Water Taxi at the door, short stroll to the bus or Rivercat ferry wharf, off street under cover parking. Ideal central location for business or pleasure, close to city CBD, Darling Harbour, Opera House, museums theatres and sporting venues. Many restaurants and clubs, nearby... Enjoy, the hospitality of Jeannette and Michael, with their two cats and the ambience of their comfortable home.

Sydney - Dural - Hills Rural District   *10 km N of Castle Hill*

B & B   Self Contained

Hilltop Cottage
Dianne Marshall
16 Bangor Road, Middle Dural, NSW 2158

Tel: (02) 9652 1482 Fax: (02) 9652 0462
Mobile: 0414 223 331
www.bbook.com.au/hilltopcottage.html

Double $130 Single $90 (Full Breakfast)
Dinner by arrangement
1 Double (1 bdrm) 1 Private

In rural Sydney, Hilltop is the ideal retreat for honeymoons or a romantic hideaway. Situated on five peaceful and secluded acres, well away from the main house on the property, the cottage has all necessities to make your stay extremely comfortable, including fully equipped kitchen, freshwater pool, tennis court, television and CD system, crisp white linen,thick white towels and bathrobes. Full breakfast is served in the privacy of the cottage. Gourmet dinners are available by arrangement. Enjoy your time away from the every day.

Sydney - Dural - Hills Rural District   *15 km NE of Castle Hill*

Homestay B & B

Rosella Lodge
Brian & Jenny Fallon
15 Rosella Street, Dural, NSW 2158

Tel: (02) 9651 5197 Fax: (02) 9651 4393
Mobile: 0407 156 836   jfallon@optusnet.com.au
www.bbook.com.au/rosellalodge.html

Double $110-$130 Single $100 (Full Breakfast)
Dinner $25 - $30 Credit Cards accepted
2 Queen 1 Double (3 bdrm) 2 Ensuite 1 Private

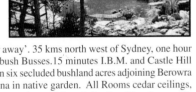

"ROSELLA LODGE" 'Away from it all, yet not too far away'. 35 kms north west of Sydney, one hour from Airport, 10 minutes from Express City and Homebush Busses.15 minutes I.B.M. and Castle Hill Shopping Complex, Cinemas etc. off street parking. Set in six secluded bushland acres adjoining Berowra Valley Bushland Park. Extensive wildlife, flora and fauna in native garden. All Rooms cedar ceilings, heaters, elec. blankets, ceiling fans, lounge and dining areas air conditioned plus Log Fire. Large salt-water pool. Accredited Tourist Operator ACC 17405. Transfers and Day Tours available.

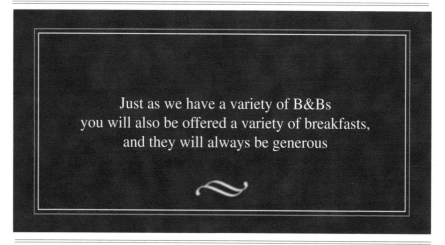

Just as we have a variety of B&Bs
you will also be offered a variety of breakfasts,
and they will always be generous

Sydney - Engadine   *28 km S of Sydney*   *Homestay B & B S/C Apartment*

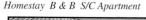

Engadine Bed & Breakfast   Pamela Pearse
33 Jerrara Street, Engadine, NSW 2233

Tel: (02) 9520 7009 Fax: (02) 9520 7009
Mobile: 0412 950 606   www.engadinebnb.com
engadinebnb@bigpond.com.au

Double $105-$140 Single $80 (Special Breakfast)
Child $25 Dinner B/A S/C Apartment $135p/c p/n
2 Queen 2 Double 2 Twin 2 Single (3 bdrm)
1 Ensuite 2 Private

Nestled amidst trees in leafy Sutherland Shire, Engadine, surrounded by The Royal & Heathcote National Parks, beaches, walking tracks, & restaurants, Stay awhile at Jerrara House & Gardens, Blending Antiques & modern conveniences in air-conditioned comfort, with separate entrances & sunny wide verandahs, an ideal stopover. Three luxury suites; Queen & Double, private romantic escapes for couples. Self contained Garden apartment, suitable for family & small groups, Business, Corporate. Gazebo & Gardens, small Weddings & Occasions, Relax, Revive, & Rejuvenate. AussieHost Accredited. Children by arrangement. Smoking outdoors. Sorry, No Pets. U/C Parking.

Sydney - Frenchs Forest - Northern Beaches   *15 km N of Sydney*
B & B

Bluegum Corner   Jan Cooke & Peter Butler
35 Bluegum Crescent, Frenchs Forest, NSW 2086

Tel: (02) 9452 2093 Fax: (02) 9452 1782
Mobile: 0412 769 351
info@bluegumcorner.com.au
www.bluegumcorner.com.au

Double $100-$120 Single $80-$90 (Full Breakfast)
Credit Cards accepted Pet on property
1 Queen 2 Double (3 bdrm)   1 Ensuite 1 Share

A light, spacious home among the gum trees in the leafy suburb of Frenchs Forest. Close to public transport, 20 minutes Sydney CBD, 10 minutes Warringah Mall and scenic Northern Beaches Peninsula (Manly to Palm Beach), cafes, restaurants, galleries galore! Garrigal and Ku-ring-ai Chase National Parks, beautiful beaches, sparkling Pittwater and Sydney Harbour. Whether visiting Sydney for business or pleasure - Jan, Peter & Kristo dog offer a warm welcome, comfortable beds, guest dining/TV lounge, tea/coffee facilities, BBQ courtyard, luxury spa, saltwater pool. Not suitable for children or pets.

Sydney - Glebe   *Homestay   3 km SW of Sydney*

Cathie Lesslie Bed & Breakfast
Cathie Lesslie
18 Boyce Street,
Glebe, NSW 2037

Tel: (02) 9692 0548
cathielesslie@excite.com
www.bbbook.com.au/lesslie.html
Double $90-$95 Single $70
(Full Breakfast)
Child $15
3 Double 2 Single (4 bdrm)
2 Share

Quiet leafy inner city, close to transport, cafes, cinemas, universities and Darling Harbour. Large comfortable room with cable TV, fridge and tea and coffee facilities. Hot "bacon and eggs" breakfast, your choice including fruit, juiced oranges and freshly baked croissants. We want you to feel welcome and at ease. Please phone first for bookings.

Sydney - Glebe   *Homestay   3 km W of Sydney Central*

Bellevue Terrace
Mrs Lisa Manchur
19 Bellevue Street,
Glebe, NSW 2037

Tel: (02) 9660 6096 Fax: (02) 9660 6096
bellevuebnb@pocketmail.com.au
www.bbbook.com.au/bellevueterrace.html
Double $95 Single $75
(Full Breakfast)
1 Queen 1 Double 2 Single (3 bdrm)
2 Share

My spacious, elegant townhouse is situated on a quiet residential street in the inner city suburb of Glebe, where you will find a great variety of restaurants, boutiques, galleries, pubs, and the Sydney University campus. Walk to Darling Harbour, Chinatown, Paddy's Market and the Powerhouse Museum, or take a bus to the City centre, just 3 kms away. We are happy to supply maps, brochures and lots of ideas for things to see and do in Sydney.

Sydney - Glebe   *Homestay   3 km W of Sydney Central*

Harolden
Leonie Dawes
Please Phone,

Tel: (02) 9660 5881 Mobile: 0414 481 881
harolden@mail.com
www.bbbook.com.au/harolden.html
Double $90 Single $65 (Full Breakfast)
Dinner $25 by arrangement
1 Double 1 Single (2 bdrm)
1 Share

Built in 1895 "Harolden" a comfortable and gracious Victorian home in historic Glebe, minutes from the restaurants of cosmopolitan Glebe Point Road. Public transport outside the door to Universities of Sydney and NSW, major hospitals and City Centre and a comfortable walk to the Fish Market, Darling Harbour and Light Rail. Your host, a descendant from the First Fleet to arrive at Sydney Cove in 1788 is well travelled and knowledgeable about Sydney. Unwind to warmth of log fires or breakfast in the garden. Tea and coffee available.

Sydney - Glebe

B & B Guest House, Garden Apartment   *2.5 km W of Sydney Central*

Tricketts   **AAATourism ★★★★☆**
Elizabeth Trickett
270 Glebe Point Road, Glebe, NSW 2037

Tel: (02) 9552 1141 Fax: (02) 9692 9462 trickettsbandb@hotmail.com
www.tricketts.com.au

Double $176-$198 Single $150 (Continental Breakfast) S.C Apartment for 2 people from $198
Credit Cards accepted Pet on property
1 Superking 6 Queen 1 Twin (7 bdrm)
7 Ensuite

Tricketts is a lovely Victorian mansion whose magnificent ballroom was once used as the Children's Court. Today this historic building has been fully restored to its original splendour. Large bedrooms with high ceilings, all beautifully decorated, all with ensuite, have top range Sealy beds.

Breakfast is served in the conservatory and in summer out on the secluded deck overlooking the garden with bottle brush trees providing a wonderful splash of colour. The tranquillity makes one forget the city is a short 431 bus ride away and Darling Harbour, Fish Markets, Power House Museum, the Chinese Temple and Sydney University are close by.

Glebe is an historic suburb full of interesting old homes that have been lovingly restored; and old fashioned gardens giving strong overtones of a bygone era. We are at the quieter "waterend" of Glebe Point Road, and a little further up lies the restaurant heart of Glebe, well known all over Sydney. Off street parking is available. We enjoy providing a luxury homestay for travellers and business people.

Also at Tricketts, the resident cat is Bandit, who ignores us all. Children over 12 in B&B. Tricketts is fully centrally heated and air-conditioned. All ages accepted in comfortable self-contained one bedroom garden apartment which sleeps four. We ask guests to smoke outside on verandahs.

Sydney - Greenwich *5 km N of Sydney*

Greenwich B&B
Jeanette & David Lloyd
15 Hinkler Street,
Greenwich, NSW 2065

Tel: (02) 9438 1204 Fax: (02) 9438 1484
Mobile: 041 140 9716
leafyglen@ozemail.com.au
www.greenwichbandb.com.au
Double $95-$125 Single $80-$105
1 King 1 Queen 1 Double 1 Twin (3 bdrm)
1 Ensuite 1 Share

New South Wales

"Leafyglen" this large delightful federation home is only 5km North of the CBD . Ample off street parking.Gore Creek Bushland reserve nearby. Minutes drive to Crows nest for large variety of restaurants. Close to public transport for trains, buses and ferry to the City, Manly, Bondi Junction and Chatswood. Pick up and delivery to St Leonards railway station can be arranged. Airport shuttle bus also available. Here you are sure of a warm and friendly welcome in Sydney's leafy lower North Shore.

Sydney - Hills Rural District - Windsor *B & B* *7 km SE of Windsor*

English Reflections
Linda Murphy
15 Blind Road, Nelson, NSW 2765

Tel: (02) 9679 0295 Fax: (02) 9679 0495
Mobile: 0411 882 530
englishreflections@bigpond.com
www.bbbook.com.au/englishreflections.html
Double $145 (Full Breakfast) Credit Cards accepted
2 Queen (2 bdrm)
1 Ensuite 1 Private

English Reflections is a spacious home with an English theme, set on 5 acres of gardens and woodlands. The guest accommodation has an elegant lounge room filled with memorabilia and the "Raffles" room has TV, videos and board games. We also have a pool and tennis court. Each themed bedroom has its own private bathroom: Sherlock Holmes, the great English detective and Shakespeare the infamous playwright.   English Reflections is only minutes from Rouse Hill and Windsor. Nearby are antique shops, beautiful garden nurseries, cafes, restaurants and markets.

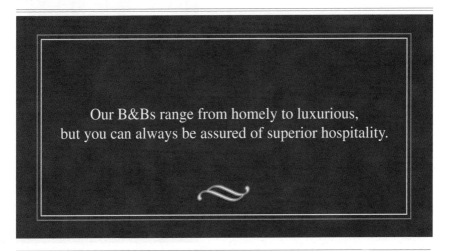

Our B&Bs range from homely to luxurious,
but you can always be assured of superior hospitality.

Sydney - Hunters Hill *Homestay B & B*   *7 km NW of Sydney*

Magnolia House Bed and Breakfast   AAATourism ★★★★☆
Fofie Lau
20 John Street, Hunters Hill, NSW 2110

Tel: (02) 9879 7078 Fax: (02) 9817 3705 Mobile: 0418 999 553
fofie@magnoliahouse.com.au
www.magnoliahouse.com.au

Double $143-$190 Single $110-$132 (Full Breakfast) Credit Cards accepted Pet on property
1 King/Twin 1 Queen (2 bdrm)
2 Ensuite

Set in the quiet and leafy surrounds of Sydney's historic Hunters Hill, Magnolia House offers traditional homestay bed and breakfast accommodation. Our Federation style family home is fully air conditioned and features elegant decor, antique furnishings and fine art pieces. A guest foyer and sitting room with lounge, writing desk and television are provided for guests. Telephone and computer access is available. Guest bedrooms also have their own televisions.

The spacious and airy Rustica Room with king or twin beds is richly furnished with an old world charm and opens onto a private balcony with outdoor furniture setting. The balcony overlooks the front garden and the quiet, leafy street. Private ensuite bathroom facilities with a double shower feature. The Verdi Room is elegantly furnished and offers a queen size bed with ensuite bathroom and looks through a large bay window to the front garden.

Guests are welcome to share the dining and living rooms with your hosts. All the rooms are beautifully furnished with many antiques. The dining room opens onto a comfortable rear deck overlooking the huge backyard. Coffee and tea making facilities are available for guests in the kitchen.

Magnolia House is conveniently located only 7 km from the heart of Sydney and is placed within easy reach of transport that takes you directly to the city centre. Bus or ferry transport is close by. Sydney Airport, The Sydney Opera House, Sydney Harbour and The Harbour Bridge, the CBD, galleries, museums, are all within easy reach. Taking the ferry to Sydney Harbour and The Opera House is a memorable trip.

Hunters Hill is one of Australia's oldest residential areas. Located on a peninsula between the Lane Cove and Parramatta Rivers, much of the suburb enjoys spectacular views over Sydney Harbour.   Transfers from the airport can be easily arranged.

Aqua Villa
At Historic Hunters Hill
Serene Village
Atmosphere in
The Heart of Sydney

COMPLIMENTARY " MEET and GREET " from City or Airport for longer stays. JOYCE and KAZ WELCOME YOU to their home, and INVITE YOU TO ENJOY, ALL YEAR ROUND the WARM ELEVEN METRE IONIZED INDOOR POOL HEATED TO 32 degrees C in cooler months.

RELAX in the SPA or SAUNA and try a gentle work out in the GYM AREA. THE SUN DECK on the roof has 360 degree RIVER, CITY SKYLINE and sublime DISTRICT VIEWS, and a HERB GARDEN.

BUS AT THE DOOR, HARBOUR FERRY to the CITY, easy access to several major shopping areas; to Lane Cove, North Ryde and Macquarie Park BUSINESS CENTRES; to UNIVERSITIES, SCHOOLS and many CHURCHES. There is OFF STREET PARKING available.

CHAUFFEURED ROLLS-ROYCE OR MINIBUS for guided or misguided tours and other transport, by arrangement. " Fifteen minutes from (almost) anywhere, and a million miles from care. " Fresh clean air, birdsong, water views and a charming village atmosphere in the heart of a bustling Metropolis, beautiful SYDNEY.

No wonder the early BRITISH, FRENCH and ITALIAN settlers chose this spot to establish SYDNEY'S FIRST GARDEN RESIDENTIAL AREA, and many wonderful Heritage Houses built from SYDNEY'S famous sandstone, including our neighbours, stand proudly today. Historic buildings and walks all around, Restaurants and cafes abound - for work or play, come and stay, you won't want to go away. GRAND PIANO, TWO SITTING ROOMS, CONFERENCE ROOM FOR SMALL GROUPS, Home movie centre with big screen TV, Foxtel cable TV channels, VCR, DVD, CD etc.

IN ALL BEDROOMS you have YOUR OWN TV and PRIVATE TELEPHONE LINE and NUMBER, for local calls and Internet access, and fans and oil heaters. Evening meals by arrangement.

BREAKFAST in the Conservatory, as you like it:- We give a CONTINENTAL - or choose HOT or SPECIAL dishes to YOUR taste. Coffee, Tea and Juice.

DAILY, WEEKLY AND LONGER TERM RATES. ALL CREDIT CARDS ACCEPTED : AMEX, JCB, BANKCARD, VISA, MASTERCARD, DINERS.

" AQUA VILLA " - ON THE HILL   MyHomeAwayFromHome.com.au

Sydney - Hunters Hill
B & B Self Contained Separate/Suite   8 km NW of Sydney
Aqua Villa
Joyce & Kaz Nagy
19a Alexandra Street, Hunters Hill, NSW 2110

Tel: (02) 9816 1258 Fax: (02) 9816 1913 Mobile: 0416 080 082
AquaVilla_BandB_HuntersHill@bigpond.com
www.bbbook.com.au/aquavilla.html

Double $150-$220 Single $110-$160 (Continental Breakfast) (Full Breakfast)
Child $60 or extra person Dinner $20 - $50 B/A 2 roomed suite $240 - $440, 3 roomed apartment $360
Credit Cards accepted Pet on property Pets welcome
3 King/Twin 1 Queen 3 Double (7 bdrm)
2 Ensuite 1 Private 3 Share

Sydney - Lane Cove *Homestay B & B*   *7 km N of Sydney*

Lane Cove Bed & Breakfast
AAATourism ★★★★☆
Christine and Terry Fitzgerald
58 Richardson Street West, Lane Cove, NSW 2066

Tel: (02) 9427 4846 Fax: (02) 9427 9019
Mobile: 0419 262 224   info@lanecovebb.com.au
www.lanecovebb.com.au

Double $125-$150 Single $110-$135
(Full Breakfast) Credit Cards accepted
2 Queen 2 Single (3 bdrm)   2 Ensuite 1 Private

Framed by two magnificent Jacaranda trees, our comfortable home offers deluxe accommodation with traditional "home away from home" hospitality including complimentary full breakfast. Three elegantly decorated air-conditioned bedrooms each have an ensuite or private bathroom, comfortable Queen or single beds and a private sitting area. Conveniently positioned in beautiful Lane Cove, our home is a few steps from a city bus and a short stroll from Lane Cove village. Christine and Terry offer friendly personal attention to ensure your stay is enjoyable.

Sydney - Manly *Homestay B & B*   *1km E of Manly*

Francois AAATourism ★★★☆
Ann Marvell
2/39 Quinton Road, Manly, NSW 2095

Tel: (02) 9977 6196 Mobile: 0414 776 196
www.bbbook.com.au/francois.html

Double $95-$110 Single $65-$75 (Full Breakfast)
1 King/Twin (1 bdrm)
1 Private

Located in a quiet area, a 10/15 minute walk to the ferry or jet cat to transport you to the CBD (or alternatively catch the bus). Manly offers beaches, scenic walks, scuba diving, restaurants, an aquarium, art gallery, historic quarantine station and bus services to the northern beaches. Golf clubs, bowling club and tennis courts nearby. Your hostess will meet you at the ferry, provide tea or coffee, offers use of sun room lounge with TV or an outdoor deck and information on trips available. No children. No smoking.

Sydney - Manly *B & B*   *1 km W of Manly*

Cecil Street B & B
Linda Hart
18 Cecil Street, Fairlight, NSW 2094

Tel: (02) 9977 8036 Fax: (02) 9977 4701
Mobile: 0415 359 388
www.bbbook.com.au/cecilstreet.html

Double $90-$130 Single $70-$90
(Continental Breakfast) Child 12yrs and under $35
1 Queen 2 Single (2 bdrm)
1 Share

Delightful Federation residence nestled in quiet, secluded cul-de-sac, 10 minute walk from the thriving beachside suburb Manly. Local attractions include beautiful beaches, bush and harbourside walks, Manly Aquarium, art gallery and historic Quarantine Station. Close to Manly Wharf and 15 minute Jetcat ride to Sydney City. Cosy breakfast/sitting room with TV, video, tea/coffee making, fridge and toaster. Delicious continental breakfast including fresh seasonal fruits. Linda will transport guests to and from Manly Wharf. Children welcome.

Sydney - Manly   *B & B   0.5 km E of Manly*

101 Addison Road B & B   AAATourism ★★★★
Jill Caskey
101 Addison Road, Manly, NSW 2095

Tel: (02) 9977 6216 Fax: (02) 9976 6352
Mobile: 0401 018 989   jillcaskey@bb-manly.com
www.bb-manly.com

Double $120-$140 Single $80-$100
(Special Breakfast) Child $50
Dinner N/A Credit Cards accepted
1 Queen 1 Double (2 bdrm)   1 Private

Charming Victorian cottage, just a stroll to several beaches, cafes, cinema and ferry to city centre. Spacious bedrooms; french doors to verandah (a second bedroom should you have friends or family with you). Children over 9 welcome. Tea/coffee facility, guest refrigerator. Enjoy music TV/video games, books and grand piano (private lounge room with open fire on winter nights). Friendly cat. Delicious breakfast with quality teas and freshly brewed coffee (special needs considered). Relaxing and Romantic! "A most beautiful end to a beautiful holiday. Thanks." A&S, London.

Sydney - Manly   *Manly*

B & B Boutique Hotel Self Contained Separate/Suite

Manly Lodge Guest House - Boutique Hotel
Miklos Power
22 Victoria Parade, Manly, NSW 2095

Tel: (02) 9977 8655 Fax: (02) 9976 2090
enquiries@manlylodge.com.au
www.manlylodge.com.au

Double $110-$350 (Continental Breakfast)
Child $20 Credit Cards accepted
6 Queen 17 Double 12 Twin (26 bdrm)   26 Ensuite

Manly Lodge is centrally located in the heart of beautiful Manly. Easy access to the famous Manly beach is literally a 30 second walk away, with Sydney harbour just a 1 minute walk. Shops, Restaurants, Cafes, local attractions and transport are all minutes walk away. The city centre is just 15 minutes by Jetcat or 30 minutes by Ferry. Victoria Parade is positioned two streets south of the Corso making it more quiet yet still conveniently located. Please visit our web site for more details or give us a call. Enquiries welcome.

Sydney - Manly - Balgowlah Heights   *Self Contained   3 km W of Manly*

LillyPilly Cottage   AAATourism ★★★★
Hans & Tricia Oechslin
72 Woodland Street, Balgowlah Heights, NSW 2093

Tel: (02) 9949 7090 Fax: (02) 9949 4094
Mobile: 0411 591 968   lillypillycot@ozemail.com.au
www.lillypillycottage.com.au

Double $110-$125 Single $110-$125
(Continental Breakfast) Pet on property
1 Queen (1 bdrm)   1 Ensuite

Balgowlah adjoins Manly, and its attractions, yet offers the peace and quiet of a garden suburb. Your quality, comfortable retreat is a self-contained garden studio featuring: Queen bed, ensuite bathroom, kitchenette, TV/Video, secluded patio area and more. Just minutes away from Manly, and 15 minutes by Jet Cat from the City. Shops, restaurants and beautiful Harbour walkways nearby. Continental breakfast hamper provided or self-catering option available. Tricia and Hans will ensure your visit is enjoyable. Sebastian is our cat and Barclay our yellow Labrador. "Location:10/10, Facilities 10/10, Hospitality:12/10! Well done!" K.D.Johannesburg

Sydney - Manly, Balgowlah   B & B   4 km W of Manly

Birdsong B & B   AAATourism ★★★☆
Margaret Broome
46 Woolgoola Street, North Balgowlah, NSW 2093

Tel: (02) 9907 9028 Fax: (02) 9400 4399
birdsongbandb@optushome.com.au
www.bbbook.com.au/birdsongbb.html

Double $85-$95 Single $45-$55 (Special Breakfast)
Weelky (double) $350 - $400
2 Queen 1 Twin (3 bdrm) 1 Ensuite 1 Share

In this Northern Beaches Australian home you will find large, open, private rooms. The rooms have a fridge, tea making facilities, TV, hairdryer, heating and cooling and electric blankets. Be at home with the solar pool, snooker room and use of a kitchen and facilities. A quality breakfast is provided. There are bush walks, golf and tennis within easy reach. Transport to the city, Manly and shopping. Come and enjoy the temperate beach climate in Margaret's friendly spacious home. "We have thoroughly enjoyed our week at your home and your hospitality to all that were here when we were is unique and inspiring." C&R, Mt. Waverley, Vic.

Sydney - Mona Vale - Northern Beaches   29km N of Sydney

Self Contained B & B
Pindara of Pittwater
Robyn & Phillip Muller
47 Rednal Street, Mona Vale, NSW 2103

Tel: (02) 9997 6483 Fax: (02) 9979 4085
pindara@netspace.net.au
www.bbbook.com.au/pindara.html

Double $120 (Continental Breakfast)
Longer stays by negotiation
1 Queen (1 bdrm) 1 Private

Our home is situated in a quiet waterfront street at the southern end of Pittwater. Mona Vale is one of the most spectacular areas of the Northern Beaches and is approximately 45 minutes travelling from Sydney. Accommodation is fully self contained and consists of a queensize bedroom, lounge/dining, TV, video, phone, bathroom and kitchen. A cot or sofa bed are available if required. A continental breakfast hamper is supplied which you can enjoy in the sitting room, on the verandah or by the pool.

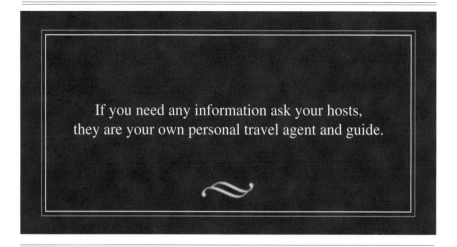

If you need any information ask your hosts,
they are your own personal travel agent and guide.

Sydney - Mosman   *Homestay   3 km N of Sydney Centre*

Lethe
Mrs S. Manthey
73 Cabramatta Road,
Mosman Sydney, NSW 2088

Tel: 02 9908 3630 Fax: 02 9908 3630
lethe@bigpond.net.au
www.bbbook.com.au/lethe.html
Double $100 Single $70 (Full Breakfast)
1 Queen 2 Single (2 bdrm)
1 Share

Lethe- a beautifully restored Federation home offering all the charm of a bygone era with hosts Soo and Merv offering friendly Bed and Breakfast accommodation. A few minutes from the city by bus or ferry in one of the city's most prestigious suburbs our home has two bedrooms for guests, one with queen sized bed, the other with twin beds, and guest bathroom. TV and video available in the lounge. (No children, one ginger cat). Fully cooked English breakfast with fresh fruit and cereals provided.

Sydney - Newport - Northern Beaches   *30 km N of Sydney Centre*
B & B Penthouse Self Contained

Bluewaters Penthouses B & B   AAAT★★★★★
Valerie & John Hans
56 Prince Alfred Parade, Newport, NSW 2106

Tel: (02) 9999 1245 Fax: (02) 9999 4530
vhans@bluewaters-oz.com   www.bluewaters-oz.com
Double $154-$187 Single $143
(Continental & Full Breakfast) Child $33
Penthouses $385 - $440 Credit Cards accepted
1 King 3 Queen 1 Twin (5 bdrm)
2 Ensuite 2 Private 1 Share

Overlooking beautiful Pittwater on Sydney's Northern Beaches, and boasting AAA 5 stars for the luxury Penthouse Suites, we invite guests to experience the unsurpassed ambience and tranquillity of our lovely retreat and this beautiful area. Featured in the June 2001 House & Garden magazine they were called 'A Perfect Retreat'. Regular priced B&B and SC suites are also available. All have private entrances. Famous surfing beaches are close by, also top restaurants, and Yacht Clubs. AAA 5 stars for the luxury Penthouse Suites.

Sydney - Newtown   *B & B Guest House   5 km W of Sydney Central*

Sydney Federation House
Maureen Bailey
46 Station Street,
Newtown, NSW 2042

Tel: (02) 9519 2208
www.bbbook.com.au/federationhouse.html
Double $90-$105 Single $80-$90
(Full Breakfast)
2 Double 2 Twin (4 bdrm)
2 Share

Large beautifully restored Victorian residence. Original features include timber polished floors, high ornate ceilings, marble fire places. Accommodation includes four large bedrooms, two bathrooms, enormous lounge and dining room, large country kitchen. With its vast proportions, light filled interiors this delightful Terrace is filled with antique furnishings. Situated on bus/train route minutes to Sydney Centre. One minute stroll to Newtown's famous King Street cafe strip. Hostess Maureen has now relocated to Sydney from Perth where her four star B&B was a Finalist in 1994 Tourism Awards.

Sydney - Newtown   *Self Contained B & B   4 km S of Sydney Central*

Jay's Place
Jay Novak
217 Wilson Street, Newtown, Sydney, NSW 2042

Tel: (02) 9550 5947 Fax: (02) 9557 3514
Mobile: 0410 341 899   jaynovak@bigpond.net.au
www.jaysbnb.com
Double $110 Single $85 (Full Breakfast)
S/C garden apartment $130 - $160
Credit Cards accepted
1 King/Twin 1 Double (2 bdrm)   2 Private

Jay's Place (circa 1890) is situated in a tree lined street just 10 minutes from Central Station and 4kms from Mascot Airport. Enjoy a well-appointed twin or kingsize bedroom with private bathroom or relax in the self-contained garden apartment which can accommodate 4-5 guests. Close by is Sydney University and King Street where guests can enjoy a multitude of dining experiences to suit every budget. Your host is a screen printer and tassel maker with a great love of the textile arts and looks forward to welcoming you.

Sydney - Paddington   *Homestay B & B   3 km E of Sydney Centre*

Rose Ash
Sally Southcombe
11 Queen Road,
Paddington, NSW 2021

Tel: (02) 9331 4970 Fax: (02) 9331 4970
www.bbbook.com.au/roseash.html
Double $95 Single $75
(Continental Breakfast)
1 Queen 2 Single (3 bdrm)
1 Share

My 110 year old terrace house is near Oxford Street where public transport to Circular Quay, Central Station (for airport train) and Bondi Beach are located, as are cafes, pubs, boutiques and the Saturday market. Fox studios, cricket and football grounds are a 15 minute walk away. I have lived in Paddington for 30 years and worked for an airline and the NZ Consulate. I am interested in travel, Clarice Cliff china and my tiny courtyard garden. Queen Road is one way off Paddington Street.

All our B&Bs are non-smoking
unless stated otherwise in the text.

Sydney - Paddington *Homestay* *2.8 km E of Sydney Central*

Harts
Katherine Hart
91 Stewart Street, nearest cross street - Gordon., Paddington 2021, NSW 2021

Tel: (02) 9380 5516 Fax: (02) 9332 2860 paddington91@bigpond.com
www.atn.com.au/harts

Double $110-$150 Single $70-$110 (Continental Breakfast) (Full Breakfast) (Special Breakfast)
Child B/A
1 Queen 2 Twin 1 Single (4 bdrm)
1 Ensuite 1 Private 1 Share

Tastefully decorated 19th Century Cottage in Sydney's Historic Paddington, courtyard garden, two minutes from Oxford Street and the bus service to the CBD, Sydney Harbour, Circular Quay, The Rocks, The Opera House, Botannical Gardens, Sydney Casino, Chinatown, and Bondi Beach. Nearby Centennial Park, Fox Studios, Aussie Stadium, Sydney Cricket Ground, Art Galleries, Antique Shops, Pubs, Restaurants, Fashion Boutiques, Cinemas, Paddington Markets.

All rooms with T.V, clock radios, electric blankets and feather quilts. Ironing facilities, varied breakfasts, fruit platters, special requests catered for, complimentary teas and coffee. Two resident cats.

"Dear Katherine, I remember you with a great pleasure. You are so kind and your breakfasts so good. My stay in your home was a great happiness." Michel, France.

"I'm missing your magnificent breakfasts which will stand out in my memory. Thank you for all your care of us." Jeanne, UK.

Sydney - Paddington   *Homestay B & B*   *2.5 km E of Sydney City*

Marshalls of Paddington   AAATourism ★★★★
David & Donna Marshall
73 Goodhope Street,
Paddington, NSW 2021

Tel: (02) 9361 6217 Fax: (02) 9361 6986
dmarsh@zipworld.com.au
www.marshallsbnb.net

Double $150 (Continental & Full Breakfast)
$60 Additional person Credit Cards accepted
1 Queen 1 Single (2 bdrm)
1 Ensuite

This historic terrace offers exclusive use of two levels including master bedroom with ensuite and balcony with city skyline views. As part of Fiveways, a local landmark, we are within an easy walk of cosmopolitan Oxford Street, art galleries, boutiques, restaurants and pubs. Centennial Park, Paddington Markets, Fox Studios, SCG, CYC and Double Bay provide a cross section of local places of interest. Watsons Bay, Bondi Beach, The Rocks, Darling Harbour, Sydney Opera House and the CBD are a short bus trip away.

Sydney - Paddington   *Homestay B & B*   *3 km E of Sydney Central*

Paddington B & B
Mary J de Merindol
7 Stewart Place, Paddington, NSW 2021

Tel: (02) 9331 5777 Fax: (02) 9331 7312
stay@paddingtonbandb.com.au
www.paddingtonbandb.com.au

Double $90 Single $63 (Full Breakfast)
Less 10% for 5 nights or 15% for 9 nights
Credit Cards accepted
1 Double 1 Twin 1 Single (3 bdrm) 2 Share

Your hosts, originally from England, are recent "empty nesters" who have travelled widely. The comfortable 5 bedroom family home dating from 1880 is furnished in traditional style and located in a tranquil cul-de-sac. It is 20 minutes from the Airport and a few minutes walk to the Football Stadium and Cricket Ground and to frequent bus services to the City Centre, Opera House, harbour ferries and Bondi Beach. Paddington is a residential area of heritage architecture enlivened by many galleries, boutiques, restaurants and cafes.

Sydney - Paddington   *B & B*   *2 km E of Sydney City*

Glenview B & B
Jan Davies
19 Glenview Street, Paddington, NSW 2021

Tel: (02) 9380 4412 Mobile: 0438 380 441
jandavies@bigpond.com
www.bbbook.com.au/glenviewbb.html

Double $100-$140 Single $85-$110 (Full Breakfast)
Studio $120 - $140
1 King/Twin 2 Queen (3 bdrm)
1 Ensuite 1 Share

Amazing location - stylish and bright Paddington Terrace tucked away in a quiet leafy street, yet just 5 minutes walk from Oxford Street shopping and cinemas, five ways cafes, and the restaurants of Darlinghurst and East Sydney. A short bus ride will take you to the city, Opera House and beach. Enjoy the luxury of sleeping in beautiful antique beds followed by a gourmet breakfast on the sunny deck or dining room.

Sydney - Palm Beach - Northern Beaches   *5 km N of Avalon Beach*
Homestay B & B

Palm Beach Bed & Breakfast
AAATourism ★★★★☆   Chris & Rudi Annus
122 Pacific Road, Palm Beach, NSW 2108

Tel: (02) 9974 1608 Fax: (02) 9974 4602
Mobile: 0409 000 013   bandb@palmbeachsydney.com
www.palmbeachbandb.com.au
Double $125-$250 Single $90-$110
(Continental Breakfast)
2 King/Twin 2 Queen 4 Single (4 bdrm)
3 Ensuite 1 Private 1 Share

New South
Wales

Palm Beach, the jewel of Sydney's Northern Beaches is renowned for its ambience and casual affluence. Our simple philosophy: "A traditional style B&B that's not a business, but a way of life"...says it all. AAA 4 1/2 star. Well travelled hosts enjoy a casual, laid back lifestyle, reflected in a relaxed, friendly atmosphere. Tastefully decorated, comfortable, not over indulgent. Tranquil bush setting, easy walking distance to everything Palm Beach has to offer. ALL rooms have water views, balconies AND off street parking.

Sydney - Parramatta   *B & B Guest House*   *2 km S of Parramatta*

Harborne Bed & Breakfast   AAAT★★★★
Josephine Assaf
21 Boundary Street, Parramatta, NSW 2150

Tel: (02) 9687 6626 Fax: (02) 9687 6626
stay@harborne.com.au
www.harborne.com.au
Double $105-$140 Single $95-$130
(Continental & Full Breakfast) Dinner from $20
Credit Cards accepted
7 Queen 1 Single (8 bdrm)
3 Ensuite 1 Private 1 Share

Harborne is a magnificent 1858 Georgian sandstone mansion. Harborne has recently been restored as a charming 8 room B&B. The beautiful home and the lush gardens have been classified by the National Trust, A glazed breakfast atrium with Tea & coffee facilities is available. Harborne is ideal for a relaxed stay or business or team stay Harborne, Your Home Away From Home.

Sydney - Penrith Valley   *Self Contained B & B*   *10 km S of Penrith*

Sojourners Rest Bed and Breakfast
Yvonne Reitsma, 60 Farm Road, Mulgoa,
Penrith Valley, Sydney Greater West, NSW 2745

Tel: (02) 4773 8709 Fax: (02) 4773 8641
Mobile: 0416 054 194   yvonne@sojournersrest.com.au
www.sojournersrest.com.au
Double $110-$140 Single $95 (Full Breakfast)
Child $30 Corporate rates on application
BBQ packs $20 Pets welcome
2 Queen 1 Twin (3 bdrm)   1 Ensuite 1 Private

Business or pleasure.......YOU are invited.. Your convenient base on rural acreage, quality two bedroom cottage or traditional authentic B&B experience with cooked breakfast in Historic valley at the foot of World Heritage Blue Mountains. Breakfast hamper with local fresh produce in season, free range chooks, a dog and two cats to stroke and the complimentary qualified services of a Tour guide who understands travellers needs/wants ..... Nice to come home to ... Airport 1 hour, Senior Card discount. Yours hosts, Yvonne, David and Dirk Reitsma.

Sydney - Petersham *B & B*   *5 km W of Sydney*

Brooklyn B & B   AAAT★★★   Angela Finnigan
25 Railway Street, Petersham, NSW 2049

Tel: (02) 9564 2312 Mobile: 0414 684 447
brooklynbb@iprimus.com.au
www.bbbook.com.au/brooklynbb.html

Double $80 Single $60-$70 (Continental Breakfast)
Triple $90 Credit Cards accepted
1 Queen 5 Double 4 Twin 5 Single (5 bdrm)
2 Private

Brooklyn is an elegantly furnished Victorian residence, which featured on "Getaway" and was the setting for the ABC Drama "GP". We are the oldest B&B in Sydney (est.1988),located 10 minutes from the city by public transport, 15 minutes to the airport and yet peaceful and quiet. We are a 5 minute walk to the Italian area of Sydney consisting of a huge piazza with shops, cafes, bookstores, cinemas and a myriad of restaurants. The location, spacious rooms (some with private balconies, the friendly advice and assistance, plus as much as you can eat of a hearty breakfast makes Brooklyn a wonderful choice for all types of travellers.

Sydney - Potts Point   *Guest House*   *2 km E of Sydney City*

Simpsons of Potts Point Boutique Hotel
Keith Wherry
8 Challis Avenue, Potts Point Sydney, NSW 2011

Tel: (02) 9356 2199 Fax: (02) 9356 4476
Mobile: 0408 282 802
hotel@simpsonspottspoint.com.au
www.simpsonspottspoint.com.au

Double $165-$215 Single $145-$195
(Continental Breakfast) Credit Cards accepted
14 Queen 3 Single (14 bdrm) 14 Ensuite

An historic 1892 mansion, the 14 bedrooms have private bathrooms, air-conditioning and all modern conveniences. The building itself has high ceilings, spacious rooms, stained glass windows and grand hallways. Located in quiet, exclusive Potts Point, less than one mile (leisurely 15min. stroll along the water) from the heart of Sydney or through the beautiful Botanical Gardens to The Opera House, Circular Quay Harbour Ferries or the historic Rocks area. It's within walking distance of some of the city's finest restaurants as well as the Oxford Street bars, clubs and night life.

Please let us know how you enjoyed your B&B experience.
Ask your host for a comment form,
or leave a comment on www.bbbook.com.au

Victoria Court
HOTEL–SYDNEY

Sydney - Potts Point

B & B Historic Boutique Hotel   within Sydney

Victoria Court Sydney
122 Victoria Street,
Sydney, Potts Point,
NSW 2011

Tel: (02) 9357 3200
Fax: (02) 9357 7606
Freecall: 1800 63 05 05
info@VictoriaCourt.com.au
www.VictoriaCourt.com.au

Double $99-$250 Single $60-$250
(Full Breakfast) Credit Cards accepted
22 King/Twin 3 Single (25 bdrm)
25 Ensuite

Victoria Court, whose charming terrace house dates from
1881, is centrally located on quiet, leafy Victoria Street
in Sydney's elegant Potts Point; the ideal base from which
to explore Sydney.

It is within minutes of the Opera House, the Central
Business District and Beaches. Friendly and personalised
service is offered in an informal atmosphere and amidst
Victorian charm.

No two rooms are alike; most have marble fireplaces,
some have four-poster beds and others feature balconies
with views over National Trust classified Victoria Street.
All rooms have en-suite bathrooms, hairdryers, air-
conditioning, colour television, a safe, radio-clock,
coffee/tea making facilities and direct dial telephones.

In the immediate vicinity are some of Sydney's most
renowned restaurants and countless cafés with menus
priced to suit all budgets. Public transport, car rental,
travel agencies and banks are nearby. An airport shuttle
bus operates to and from Victoria Court and security
parking is available.

Sydney - Rose Bay   *Homestay   6 km E of Sydney*

Syl's Sydney Homestay   AAAT★★★
Sylvia & Paul Ure
75 Beresford Road, Rose Bay, NSW 2029

Tel: (02) 9327 7079 Fax: (02) 9362 9292 Mobile: 0411 350 010
homestay@infolearn.com.au
www.sylssydneyhomestay.com.au

Double $120-$145 Single $85-$95 (Continental Breakfast) S/C Apartment $160 Double, extra person $40 Credit Cards accepted Pet on property
2 Queen 2 Double 3 Twin 4 Single (3 bdrm)
1 Ensuite 1 Private 1 Share

Rose Bay is one of Sydney's most beautiful harbourside suburbs and hospitality and friendliness are the essence of our modern, spacious family B & B with bush and harbour views, pet dogs and that real home away from home atmosphere.

We are just a short stroll from cafes, restaurants, tennis, golf, sailing and the most beautiful harbour in the world and on excellent bus and ferry routes to the City and Opera House, Bondi Beach, train stations and shopping centres.

Our B&B was featured on British TV in 1991 and we were one of Sydney's first B & Bs operating since 1980.

Syl and Paul are well travelled and always ready to share their local knowledge and hospitality in a relaxed informal setting to help travellers enjoy our wonderful city. So if formality is what you seek, then Syl's is not for you!

All rooms have TV and the self contained garden apartment is ideal for families. Guests are requested not to smoke inside the house.

Sydney - Woollahra - Bondi Junction   *4 km E of Sydney city*

Homestay B & B

Mayfield
John Ernst & Selma Maynard
7 Magney Street, Woollahra, NSW 2025

Tel: (02) 9369 2611 Fax: (02) 9369 2611
Mobile: 0409 660 455   maynards@zeta.org.au
www.bbbook.com.au/mayfield.html

Double $90-$100 Single $70-$80 (Special Breakfast)
Child B/A Dinner $20 - $30 B/A Pet on property
1 Double 2 Single (3 bdrm)   1 Ensuite 1 Share

Perfect Position - a heritage cottage, in quiet cul-de-sac, five minutes walk to Bondi Junction's Bus/ Rail Interchange's fast frequent transport - 10 minutes to City and sporting venues, 20 minutes to Opera House, Harbour and beaches. An Airport bus runs directly to this station. French,German spoken;offstreet parking;Abyssinian cat. Retired engineer and homemaker wife's interests include art, reading, politics, good food.Well travelled,experienced,we aim to ensure you a comfortable stay. "Very friendly with a wealth of knowledge" K.R. Middlesex.

Tamworth   *Self Contained Farmstay B & B*   *26 km N of Tamworth*

Laramee Country Home
Julie & Ross Harvey
Limbri Road, Kootingal, NSW 2352

Tel: (02) 6764 4246 Fax: (02) 6764 4209
Mobile: 0427 915 568   laramee@northnet.com.au
www.bbbook.com.au/laramee.html

Double $108 Single $54 (Full Breakfast)
Child $27 Dinner $26
1 Queen 2 Double 2 Twin 2 Single (7 bdrm)
1 Ensuite 2 Share

Traditional country home, vine shaded verandahs, large rambling garden, first class tennis court. House warm and welcoming with antiques and country furniture. Julie serves delicious meals - intimate dinners, by the fire in winter, and memorable breakfasts in timber lined kitchen. 3600 acre property of beautiful hills and valleys running beef cattle and cashmere goats. Exhausted business people, outdoor adventurers and romantic honeymooners all welcome. Experience the real country Australia. Horse riding including mustering by arrangement. Children and pets welcome. Eight minutes from New England Highway.

Tamworth   *B & B*   *500m E of Tamworth*

Jacaranda Cottage Bed and Breakfast
Elizabeth Maclean and Charles Cox
105 Carthage Street, Tamworth, NSW 2340

Tel: (02) 6766 4281 or (02) 6766 9996
Mobile: 0412 297 472
lizzymcharlesc@optusnet.com.au
www.bbbook.com.au/jacaranda.html

Double $110-$225 Single $95-$125 (Full Breakfast)
Dinner by arrangement Credit Cards accepted
4 Queen 2 Single (4 bdrm)   1 Ensuite 1 Share

Welcome to Jacaranda Cottage, formerly Graheasha Court, our beautifully restored federation home with four large comfortable bedrooms and a cosy log fire in the guests lounge. For the romantic at heart we have a private studio loft at the bottom of our cottage garden. Ideal for newly weds, a peaceful, relaxing getaway or a toe tapping music festival. Leafy verandahs and cosy nooks for afternoon tea, drinks, or a scrumptious home cooked breakfast. Dinner by request. Corporate rates available. Only 5 minutes walk to restaurants, clubs and CBD.

Tamworth   *Homestay B & B   20 km S of Tamworth*

Lalla Rookh Country House
Tony & Karen Ridley
Lalla Rookh, Werris Creek Road, Duri, NSW 2344

Tel: (02) 6768 0216 Fax: (02) 6768 0330
Mobile: 0427 634 753
larookh@bigpond.com
www.bbbook.com.au/lallarookh.html

Double $105 Single $75 (Full Breakfast)
2 Queen 2 Single (3 bdrm)
1 Ensuite 1 Share

Be captivated with views surrounding Lalla Rookh of Mountains and rolling hills. The peace and tranquillity will truly amaze the weary traveller as you enjoy a relaxing drink on the terrace, watching the birds or wandering through the garden. Lalla Rookh is a quiet place to relax between Sydney and Queensland being just 20kms from Tamworth and makes for a restful night sleep with comfortable beds, heating, cooling, large fluffy towels and a hearty breakfast that will suffice for the next day travel.

Taree   *Self Contained B & B   1 km E of Tinonee*

Deans Creek Lodge
Brian & Pauline Carney
2 Deans Creek Road, Tinonee, NSW 2430

Tel: (02) 6553 1187 Fax: (02) 6553 1187
deansck@midcoast.com.au
www.midcoast.com.au/~deansck/welcome.html

Double $95 Single $75 (Full Breakfast) Child POA
Dinner B/A Cottage $120 Credit Cards accepted
Pet on property Pets welcome
2 Queen 4 Single (4 bdrm)
1 Private 1 Share

Come and join us and our Jack Russell "Meg" on our ten acres of paradise. The secluded, well established gardens attract a wide variety of birdlife and the inground salt water pool overlooks the adjacent forest. Kingfisher Cottage allows you to self cater in air conditioned comfort. Watch the cows graze from the shady verandah or enjoy a BBQ under the trees. Well behaved pets are also welcome. The Manning Valley with its rainforests, beaches, rivers and plateaus is sure to surprise you.

Taree   *Self Contained Farmstay B & B   8 km NW of Wingham*

Tallowood Ridge   Ron & Shirley Smith
79 Mooral Creek Road,
Cedar Party via Wingham, NSW 2429

Tel: (02) 6557 0438 Fax: (02) 6557 0438
Mobile: 0411 035 945   twr@turboweb.net.au.
www.bbbook.com.au/tallowoodridge.html

Double $80-$90 Single $50-$60
(Continental Breakfast) Child $20
Campervans $20 Pet on property
2 Double 4 Single (3 bdrm) 1 Ensuite 1 Private

Come and share our country lifestyle. Enjoy the comforts of our modern home set on 33 hectares of undulating hills, magnificent views, colourful birds, friendly cows and Jessie the dog. We also have a fully equipped s/c cabin acc. 4. No smoking inside please. Relax by the pool or visit the many attractions in the area, historic buildings, a museum of past history, picturesque rainforest area alongside the Manning river or visit Ellenborough Falls. Clubs, pubs and restaurants in town. "Very hospitable - scenery fantastic - so peaceful - could stay longer." M&NC, Nthn Ireland.

Tea Gardens - Hawks Nest

Farmstay B & B   15 km W of Tea Gardens

Lavender Grove Farm   AAATourism ★★★★☆
Chris Townsley & Tony Irvine
55 Viney Creek Road, Tea Gardens, NSW 2324

Tel: (02) 4997 1411 Fax: (02) 4997 2001
Mobile: 0414 461 101   chris@sisters.com.au
www.bbbook.com.au/lavendergrovefarm.html
Double $70-$154 Single $45-$99 (Full Breakfast)
Child $20 - $45 Dinner $16.50-$50+ B/A
Credit Cards accepted Pet on property
1 Queen 2 Double 2 Single (2 bdrm)
2 Ensuite

Our B & B is on a 30 acre hobby farm only 2 hours north of Sydney. The Family Suite sleeps up to 6 & has a 3 way bathroom with spa bath. The Queen Room has a private verandah with a 2 person spa. Guests have own lounge room with log fire, tv & stereo. Laze on the large balcony, watch magical sunsets while kangaroos emerge, or relax in the solar heated salt water pool. Kids love to feed the animals. We aim to pamper our guests.

Tea Gardens - Hawks Nest

300m E of Tea Gardens

B & B   Separate/Suite

The Bellbuoy Bed & Breakfast Studios
AAAT★★★★   Jenny and Ian Wiseman
117 Marine Drive, Tea Gardens, NSW 2324

Tel: (02) 4997 1688 Fax: (02) 4997 1679
Mobile: 0417 023 342   bellbuoy@ceinternet.com.au
www.bellbuoy.com.au
Double $100-$143 Single $85-$115 (Full Breakfast)
Child $20 Credit Cards accepted
2 Queen 1 Single (3 bdrm)   1 Ensuite 2 Private

Private 4 star luxury studios located by the waterfront at picturesque Tea Gardens - on the northern shores of Port Stephens. Stylish, relaxing decor. Imagine enjoying our gourmet breakfast on the front verandah, overlooking the tranquil Myall River, watching dolphins & pelicans frolic in the glistening waters. A short stroll to superb restaurants featuring local seafood and alfresco dining. Walk to ferry that departs daily to Nelson Bay, explore the National Park, or relax on one of our magnificent white sandy beaches - all this and more just 2 hours north of Sydney.

Terrigal *B & B   1.5 km N of Terrigal*

Terrigal Lagoon Bed & Breakfast   AAAT★★★★☆
Roz Fuller & Bruce Fitzpatrick
58A Willoughby Road, Terrigal, NSW 2260

Tel: (02) 4384 7393 Fax: (02) 4385 9763
enquiries@terrigalbnb.com.au
www.terrigalbnb.com.au
Double $120-$170 Single $100-$150
(Continental & Full Breakfast) Credit Cards accepted
3 Queen (3 bdrm)
3 Ensuite

The comfortable, private facilities of this modern B&B provide the perfect base for exploring the magnificent beaches, lakes and National Parks of the Central Coast, or Sydney, Newcastle, and the Hunter Valley Wineries. The cosmopolitan seaside resort of Terrigal offers an extensive range of restaurants, speciality shops, galleries and entertainment in a picturesque setting. Queen rooms, ensuites, fans, TV, A/C. Separate guest entry and sitting room. Pool. Smoking outside only. No pets. Facilities not suitable for children. Parking. Public transport. Delicious breakfasts. Warm, friendly hospitality.

Tilba Central - Narooma *B & B*

The Two Story B & B
Ken & Linda Jamieson, Bate Street, Central Tilba, NSW 2546

Tel: (02) 4473 7290 Fax: (02) 4473 7290 Freecall: 1800 355 850
twostory@sci.net.au   www.babs.com.au/twostory

Double $95-$105 Single $85-95 (Full Breakfast) Credit Cards accepted
2 Queen 1 Double 1 Single (3 bdrm)   1 Ensuite 1 Share

A warm welcome awaits you from Aussie hosts Ken and Linda Jamieson and family at the Two Story
B&B. Nestled in foothills of Mt Dromedary situated in National Trust Village of Central Tilba. Our
building is 107 years old built 1894 and was originally the Post Office and residence, it has great
character and views overlook a superb valley of rolling hills and lush greenness, enjoy atmosphere and
warmth, a glass of Tilba Port in front of our log fire.

Our weather is temperate and beaches are close by. Situated 300km south of Sydney.

The Craft Village of Central Tilba is extensive, businesses include: leather shop, tea rooms, alpaca shop,
cheese factory, woodturning gallery and more. A short scenic drive takes you to a local winery, short
drives to Bermagui and Cobargo, bushwalking, fishing and swimming.

We offer our guests a choice of continental and full cooked breakfasts with tea/coffee facilities, off
street parking, in a total relaxed atmosphere in pleasant old world charm and non smoking environment.
Enquire about our package: 2 nights at The Two Story B & B and 3 nights at Bateman's Bay.

Tilba Tilba - Central Tilba   *Homestay B & B   Central Tilba*

Wirrina
Kay Esman-Ewin
Central Tilba, Blacksmiths Lane, NSW 2546

Tel: (02) 4473 7279 Fax: (02) 4473 7279
goodnite@acr.net.au

Double $105 Single $80 (Full Breakfast)
Dinner $30 Credit Cards accepted
1 Queen 1 Double 2 Single (3 bdrm)
1 Ensuite 1 Share

Central Tilba is a delightful small historic village in an unusual volcanic landscape, an ideal 4-5 hours from Sydney, 3 hours from Canberra. We pride ourselves on comfy beds and a great breakfast. You are also close to beaches and mountain; golf, horse riding and bushwalking available. "Wonderful weekend, delicious breakfasts, lovely atmosphere, THANKS" L & P K. "Two big smiles with legs walking out of the door - can't say too many thank-you's." DW and RJ. Children by arrangement. No indoor pets. Good weekly rate available.

www.bbbook.com.au/naturecoast-tourism.com.au/goodnite.html

Tumbarumba   *Farmstay   26 km NE of Tumbarumba*

The Lazy Dog B&B
Peter & Margeret McDermott
Moody's Hill Road,
Tumbarumba, NSW 2653

Tel: (02) 6948 3664 Fax: (02) 6948 3664
www.bbbook.com.au/thelazydogbb.html

Double $70-$80 Single $35-$40 (Full Breakfast)
Dinner $15 B/A Credit Cards accepted
1 Queen 1 Twin (2 bdrm)
2 Ensuite

The Lazy Dog Bed & Breakfast is built on 890 acres and is surrounded by an abundance of wildlife (Red Neck Wallabies, Black Wallabies, Kangaroos, Wombats and wild Brumbies. Also there are Emus, Kookaburras Parrots, Black Cockatoos and Eagles.) For a day trip you can drive to Mount Selwyn snowfields go fishing at Sue City or the Murray River tour the Snowy Mountains Hydro-electricity Scheme, visit Australia's Scheme, visit Australia's highest town at Cabramurra or take in the majestic beauty of Mount Kosciuzsko.

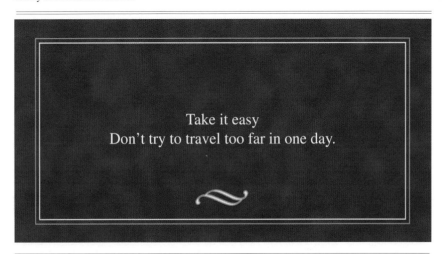

Take it easy
Don't try to travel too far in one day.

Ulladulla   *B & B   Guest House   Self Contained*   *100m Ulladulla*

Ulladulla Guest House   AAATourism ★★★★★
Andrew & Elizabeth Nowosad
39 Burrill Street, Ulladulla, NSW 2539

Tel: (02) 4455 1796 Fax: (02) 4454 4880 Freecall: 1800 700 905
ugh@guesthouse.com.au
www.guesthouse.com.au

Double $180-$278 Single $100-$248 (Full Breakfast) Child $50 Dinner $40 - $90
Credit Cards accepted
3 King/Twin 6 Queen 1 Double 3 Single (10 bdrm)
10 Ensuite

Ulladulla Guest House consists of 5 star (AAAT) accommodation, Elizans French Restaurant and Art Gallery and is located within minutes to town centre and picturesque harbour of Ulladulla.

Accommodation - All rooms are spacious and well-equipped with custom-designed furniture, warm carpeting and original artwork. Executive suites have marble bathrooms with private spas and king size beds. Two self-contained units have private entrances from the garden and cooking facilities.

Restaurant - Our executive chef Brendon Knight presents French cuisine utilizing local fresh produce, including seafood straight from fishing harbour 100 metres away, local cheeses and world famous Milton beef.

Art Gallery - The Gallery has permanent exhibiting artists including Judy Trick, David Benson, Giovanni and Maro Tozzetti and Dianne Gee. The current exhibitions are by Tracey Creighton and Peter Robinson - paintings, Lee Casey - pottery and Eddie Young woodwork.

Surrounded by lush sub-tropical gardens, the Guest House caters to any requirement for a perfect relaxing holiday. After a leisurely gourmet breakfast, guests have the choice of lingering in the lounges surrounded by African artwork: ambling outside with a book to browse in a secluded nook; plunging into the heated pool or one of the spas; or enjoying a sauna after a work out in the gym.

Ulladulla Guest House won 2002, 01, 00, 99, 98, 97 Tourism Awards for Excellence and is recommended by number of reputable guides Frommers (US), Rough (UK), Time-Out (London), Johansens.

Urunga   *Separate/Suite B & B   3 km NW of Urunga*

Newry Island Retreat   AAAT★★★★
Dianne & Graham Parmenter
29 The Grove, Newry Island, NSW 2455

Tel: (02) 6655 6050 Fax: (02) 6655 6050
Mobile: 0417 422 854
graham.parmenter@bigpond.com
www.bellingen.com/newryisland

Double $105-$110 Single $75-$80
(Continental Breakfast) Credit Cards accepted
1 Queen 1 Double (1 bdrm)   1 Ensuite

Private guest accommodation with verandah separated from main residence by covered barbecue & spa area, overlooks gardens and native birdlife, with backdrop of heritage listed Dorrigo National Park mountain ranges. Suite has table, chairs, refrigerator, coffee/tea and iron, TV/video, CD/tape. Pick up from local transport. Local attractions include beaches, white water rafting, Go Karts, horse riding, scenic drives. "So glad we found you, it's best B&B yet after 4 weeks in Australia & we have stayed in some lovely homes." (I.A. England).

Wagga Wagga   *Self Contained B & B   4 km NE of Wagga*

Wagga Wagga Country Cottages   AAAT★★★★
Lyn Burgmann
PO Box 933, Wagga Wagga, NSW 2650

Tel: (02) 6921 1539 Fax: (02) 6921 1503
Mobile: 0417 216 697
www.bbbook.com.au/waggacottages.html

Double $112 Single $93 (Continental Breakfast)
Child $22 Credit Cards accepted
1 Queen 2 Single (2 bdrm)
1 Private

Lynn and Graeme welcome you to share their little piece of heaven. 4 Minutes out of town on the north side. Enjoy elevated rural views and relax in the privacy of self contained cottages. Why not have space of a whole little cottage rather than just one room. Decorated in a by-gone era and all cottages have a spa for total relaxation. Children welcome but we are not set up for animals. Guests are invited to smoke on the verandah. Old world charm in a country setting.

Wagga Wagga   *Homestay B & B   1 km S of Wagga CBD*

Mowbray Cottage
Margaret McMaster
11 Charleville Road, Wagga Wagga, NSW 2650

Tel: (02) 6925 7135 Mobile: 0427 257 135
margaretmcmaster@bigpond.com
www.bbbook.com.au/mowbraycottage.html

Double $105 Single $85
(Full Breakfast) Pets welcome
1 Queen 1 Double (2 bdrm)
2 Share

Be pampered with genuine five star service on a B&B budget in the original character and charm of this graciously restored Edwardian home - truly one of Wagga's best kept secrets. Do as little or as much you like - sleep in, then enjoy a hearty country breakfast, read a book from the extensive library or sit on the leafy verandahs watching the birds or simply just relax in the study and watch TV. Quiet location close to main facilities including the Botanic gardens. We aim to make you feel comfortable and at ease - arrive as a guest and leave as a friend.

Wagga Wagga *Self Contained Homestay B & B*   *3 km S of Wagga Wagga*

Brae View Accommodation
Lyn McKay
3 Spokes Street, Wagga Wagga, NSW 2650

Tel: (02) 6926 2396 Fax: (02) 6926 1266
Mobile: 0438 262 396
braeview@optusnet.com.au
www.geocities.com/braeviewau

Double $105 Single $85
(Continental & Full Breakfast) Credit Cards accepted
2 Queen 2 Single (2 bdrm)
1 Ensuite 1 Private

Come and enjoy our modern home, with large bedrooms and ensuites, separate guest dining and lounge area with access to the delightful fernery courtyard. Enjoy a delicious full cooked breakfast with home made bread and jams. Relax with morning or afternoon tea in the beautiful award winning gardens overlooking rolling hill views. We also offer a 2 bedroom self contained apartment ultra modern, central heating and cooling, garden courtyard, lock up garage. Children welcome.

Wagga Wagga *Self Contained B & B B&B or Self Contained 3 km W of town centre*

Milsand B & B AAATourism ★★★☆
Milton & Sandra Wilson
46 Mimosa Drive,
Wagga Wagga, NSW 2650

Tel: (02) 6925 4134 Fax: (02) 6925 4134
Mobile: 0419 287 090   milsand@tpg.com.au
www.bbbook.com.au/milsand.html

Double $100 Single $85 (Continental Breakfast)
Credit Cards accepted
1 Double (1 bdrm)   1 Private

Milsand .....Wagga Wagga is the biggest inland city in NSW, part of the Riverina's (beautiful country) between Melbourne and Sydney. ... Milton is a Qualified Masseuse, we offer a Healthly Continental Breakfast and filtered water, Tranquil Surroundings, Adjacent to Botanic Gardens, 3 mins from main street...Milton has a gift with Wood carving - Sandra enjoys craft and gardening. Both enjoy bush walking, dancing, family and friends as well as a healthy lifestyle. We are now enjoying being grandparents for the first time. Spotlessly clean and safe, we have no pets. Suitable for Travellers and Romantic Stay.

Walcha *Separate/Suite B & B*   *4 km W of Walcha*

Country Mood B & B AAATourism ★★★☆
Louise & Alec Gill
PO Box 51, Walcha, NSW 2354

Tel: (02) 6777 2877 Fax: (02) 6777 2877
Mobile: 0413 905 391   algill@northnet.com.au
www.bbbook.com.au/countrymoodbb.html

Double $85 Single $70 (Full Breakfast) Child $15
Dinner $18 B/A Pet on property Pets welcome
1 Queen 1 Double 1 Single (1 bdrm)
1 Private

Perfect place to escape in quiet country garden - minutes from town, golf, National Parks, gorges, trout and kangaroos. We run mainly cattle offering views, tranquillity, style & warmth - own access for privacy. Tea/coffee, TV, CD, iron, flowers, comfortable Queen bed, under-cover parking, electric blankets. Delicious meals served. Perfect stopover, Sydney (5 hrs), a scenic drive via Gloucester - Brisbane (6 hrs) - or stay longer - only 1 hour Tamworth and 45 minutes Armidale.   "Beautiful environment, quiet, Great Hosts. An oasis on the mad tourist trail." C&D, Portland, Vic.

Wellington   *Homestay B & B   0.5km S of Wellington*

Carinya B&B   AAATourism ★★★☆
Miceal & Helen O'Brien
111 Arthur Street, Wellington, NSW 2820

Tel: (02) 6845 4320 Fax: (02) 6845 3089
Mobile: 0427 459 794   staywell@well-com.net.au
www.bbbook.com.au/carinyabb.html

Double $69-$89 Single $59-$79
(Continental & Full Breakfast) Child $12 - $18
Dinner $15 - $25 Credit Cards accepted
2 Queen 5 Single (3 bdrm)   2 Share

"Carinya" is a lovely Edwardian homestead, surrounded by an award-winning garden, pool and tennis court. Off street parking offers peace of mind. Easy to find on Mitchell Highway. Sydney side of Wellington. Family friendly. Billiard table is always popular. Minutes to attractions, Wellington Caves and Japanese Garden. Close to CBD. Walk on Mt Arthur or inspect the many significant historic buildings and acclaimed Cameron Park. Drives to Burrendong Dam and Arboretum make Wellington a pleasant stopover. Close to Dubbo Zoo, Mudgee and Parkes.

Wollongong - Mount Pleasant - South Coast

Self Contained B & B studio 5 km NW of Wollongong
Pleasant Heights Bed & Breakfast at Wollongong
John & Tracey Groeneveld, 77 New Mount Pleasant Road,
Mount Pleasant, NSW 2519

Tel: (02) 4283 3355 Fax: (02) 4283 3355
Mobile: 0415 428 950
pleasanthtsbnb@ozemail.com.au www.pleasanthtsbb.com

Double $140-$300 Single $110-$250 (Continental Breakfast)
(Full Breakfast)   Credit Cards accepted
1 King/Twin 2 Queen (3 bdrm) 3 Ensuite

PLEASANT HEIGHTS is a boutique style accommodation offering privacy and relaxation, in a luxurious coastal setting. Suites are self-contained in contemporary style with mountain & ocean views. The Pleasant Suite: has it's own private oriental courtyard, spa bath, balcony, and ocean views. King-size bed, kitchenette and waterfall ... Santa Fe Suite and Seascape Studio. Breakfast hamper provided. Only minutes from Wollongong CBD, University, Nan Tien Temple. Rhododendron Gardens and Balgownie village nearby. About 1hr drive from Sydney or Southern Highlands.

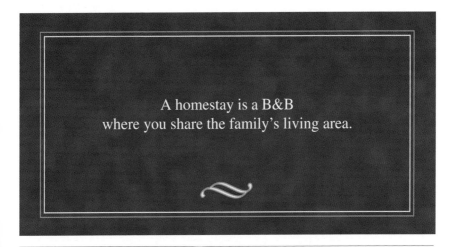

A homestay is a B&B
where you share the family's living area.

Yamba   *Homestay B & B   50 km N of Grafton*

Wynyabbie House
Greg & Kay Perry
Yamba Road, Palmers Island, NSW 2463

Tel: (02) 6646 0168 Fax: (02) 6646 0167
gregjp@tpg.com.au
www.bbbook.com.au/wynyabbiehouse.html

Double $90-$115 Single $60-$75
(Continental & Full Breakfast) Child $25
Stay 5 nights, 6th night free Credit Cards accepted
1 King 1 Double 2 Single (2 bdrm)   2 Private

Located just 10 minutes from Yamba with its magnificent beaches, Wynyabbie House (1890) sits tranquilly alongside the mighty Clarence River. Situated amidst peaceful gardens, we offer the ideal location for a Romantic Getaway. Watch the dolphins play, laze around the sparkling pool or dangle a line off the jetty, relax and enjoy the peaceful surrounds. Enjoy in-house flotation tank, followed by a stimulating body scrub, luxurious massage or soothing Reiki session by our qualified therapists. Wynyabbie House is perfect for Wedding Ceremonies and Photos, Baby Namings and Renewal of Vows.

Yass - Rye Park   *20 km SE of Boorowa   Separate/Suite B & B Country Inn*

The Old School   AAATourism ★★★★
Margaret Emery, Yass Street, Rye Park, NSW 2586

Tel: (02) 4845 1230 Fax: (02) 4845 1260
Mobile: 0418 483 613   oldschool@webone.com.au
www.theoldschool.com.au

Double $110-$140 Single $90-$100
(Full Breakfast) Child $20 Dinner $50
Extra person $40 Credit Cards accepted
1 King 2 Queen 1 Double 1 Twin 2 Single (6 bdrm)
2 Ensuite 1 Private 1 Share

Fine food, warm fires, good books and a piano make this retreat a return to life's simple pleasure. Set on three and a half acres amidst trees, roses, gardens and ponds an atmosphere is created that encourages relaxation. Margaret has built a reputation for her food and offers a seasonal menu, with influences from Belgium, the Mediterranean and Asia. The Old School won an Award of Distinction in the 2000 Capital Country Awards for Excellence in Tourism. Children and pets do not live at the School. Laundry available. Rye Park is half an hour north of Yass. AAA - 4 Stars.

Young - Cootamundra   *8 km W of Wallendbeen*
Homestay Farmstay Boutique Farm Holiday

Colleen & Old Sils Farmhouse Greg & Colleen Hines
Burley Griffin Way, Corang, Wallendbeen, NSW 2588

Tel: (02) 6943 2546 Fax: (02) 6943 2573
Mobile: 0429 432 546   colleenhines@bigpond.com
www.aussiefarmstay.com

Double $110-$150 Single $75-$95 (Full Breakfast)
Child B/A Dinner From $35 Guided Day Tours
pkd. lunch All meals available Credit Cards accepted
1 King/Twin 2 Double 1 Twin 5 Single (4 bdrm)
1 Ensuite 3 Private

Built in 1924, this 55 sq. farmhouse grew with our family, all now married and left! Spacious & luxurious-swimming, tennis & BBQ in landscaped gardens. Full catering if required. Explore this interesting Hilltops wine area. Private sitting room, deck with separate entrance. Tea/coffee facilities, TV, CD & Stereo. We are 1 1/2 hours from Canberra, 3-4 hours from Sydney and 6-7 hours drive from Melbourne. "If you are looking for city comfort in a beautiful country atmosphere, go to Colleen & Old Sil's Farmhouse." Dr. & Mrs Littman, Germany.

Young - Wallendbeen   *Farmstay Self Contained   3 km N of Wallendbeen*

Old Nubba Schoolhouse
Fred & Genine Clark
Wallendbeen, NSW 2588,

Tel: (02) 6943 2513 Fax: (02) 6943 2590
Mobile: 0438 432 513
nubba@dragnet.com.au
www.bbbook.com.au/oldnubba.html

Double $95 Single $75 (Full Breakfast)
Dinner $30 Pet on property Pets welcome
1 Queen 4 Double 8 Single (6 bdrm)
3 Private

Old Nubba is a sheep/grain farm midway
between Cootamumdra and Young, 3 1/2
hours SW of Sydney, 1 1/2 hours west of
Canberra.

The Schoolhouse, Killarney Cottage and
Peppertree Cottage are all fully self-contained
and have heating, cooling, electric blankets
and linen provided. They sleep 4-8.

Children will love the chickens, ducks, geese,
dogs and pet lambs and will be able to help
with farm activities.

Other farm attractions include peace and
quiet, bush walks, birdlife, bike riding, fishing
and olive picking (in season). Pets under
control are welcome.

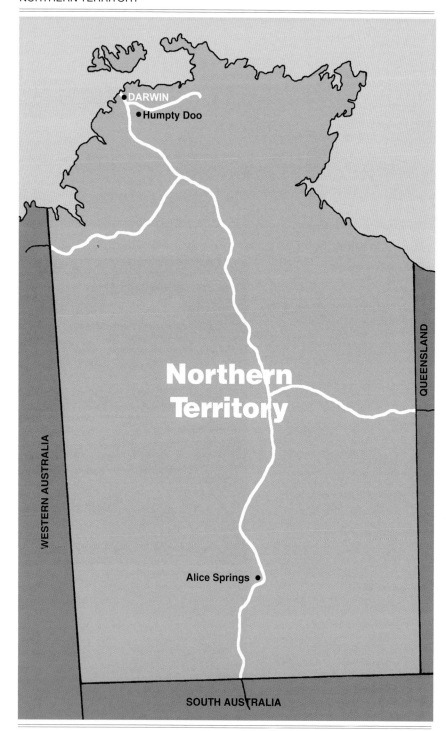

Alice Springs   *B & B   1 km E of Alice Springs town centre*

Orangewood, Alice Springs Bed & Breakfast
Lynne & Ross Peterkin
9 McMinn Street, Alice Springs, NT 0871

Tel: (08) 8952 4114 Fax: (08) 8952 4664
oranges@orangewood-bnb.au.com
www.orangewood-bnb.au.com

Double $187 Single $165 (Full Breakfast)
$220 Triple Credit Cards accepted
2 King/Twin 1 Queen 1 Double (4 bdrm)
3 Ensuite 1 Private

Orangewood offers quality accommodation in a comfortable home furnished with antiques, special family pieces and original art works. The guest sitting room and library has open fire, piano, music system, television, refrigerator and tea/coffee making facilities. The house is air-conditioned. Guest accommodation comprises three bedrooms in the house and the garden cottage. Breakfast is served in the breakfast room which overlooks the pool and orange grove and is supervised by Angus, the resident cat. Non-smoking establishment, not suitable for children.

Alice Springs   *Separate/Suite B & B   1 km Alice Springs*

Nthaba Cottage B & B
Anne & Will Cormack & Pets
83 Cromwell Drive, Alice Springs, NT 0870

Tel: (08) 8952 9003 Fax: (08) 8953 3295
Mobile: 0407 721 048
nthaba@nthabacottage.com.au
www.nthabacottage.com.au

Double $145 Single $120 (Full Breakfast)
Credit Cards accepted
1 King 2 Single (1 bdrm) 1 Private

Surrounded by the spectacular MacDonnell Ranges this quality cottage set in bird friendly gardens is a great base from which to explore the wonders of Central Australia. The bedroom has a kingsize bed or two single beds. The cosy sitting-room with T.V. has Edwardian chairs and other favourite pieces and opens onto a secluded patio with private garden. This cosy cottage is convenient to the new convention centre. Will, your host, is keen to share his local bird knowledge with you. Resident friendly cat and dog.

Alice Springs   *B & B   Self Contained   5 km Alice Springs*

Tmara Mara B & B
Tom & Vicky Engeham
PO Box 1084, Alice Springs, NT 0871

Tel: (08) 8952 7475 Fax: (08) 8952 7475
Mobile: 0417 855 598
colourtherapy@hotmail.com
www.bbbook.com.au/tmaramarabb.html

Double $130 Single $90 (Continental Breakfast)
1 Queen (1 bdrm)
1 Ensuite 1 Private

Relax at Tmara Mara B&B in an award winning rammed earth house and beautiful bush garden. A self contained two roomed unit featuring a romantic rose bedroom with lace canopy. A separate lounge and kitchen with all amenities, opening onto a private courtyard with BBQ. Indulge in a private two person spa with aromatherapy oils. Your host Vicki is a qualified aromatherapist offering massage after hours. Breakfast continental, Vicki spoils you with chocolates, towelling gowns, slippers and aromatherapy products.

Alice Springs   *Homestay B & B*

Hilltop Bed & Breakfast   AAATourism ★★★★☆
Roseanne & Robin Bullock
9 Zeil Street, Alice Springs, NT 0870

Tel: (08) 8955 0208 Fax: (08) 8955 0716
Mobile: 0409 550 208
hilltop@hilltopalicesprings.com
www.hilltopalicesprings.com

Double $140 Single $120 (Full Breakfast)
Dinner B/A Credit Cards accepted Pet on property
1 Queen (1 bdrm)   1 Ensuite

Located on a ridge overlooking the MacDonnell Ranges and Alice Springs Desert Park, Hilltop offers guests their choice of comfortable and finely furnished air-conditioned (smoke-free) rooms. The upstairs guest lounge also provides a wood-fire, tv/video, CD and tea/coffee quking facilities. Large plunge-spa and BBQ area. Bush walks are literally at your door, and mountain bikes are available. Extensive verandah overlooking the park and ranges offers a great place for meals, relaxing or bird watching. Two friendly dogs and Tigger the cat complete the welcoming party.

Alice Springs   *Homestay B & B*   *1 km E of Alice Springs*

Kathy's Place Bed & Breakfast
Kathy & Karl Fritz
4 Cassia Court, Alice Springs, NT 0870

Tel: (08) 8952 9791 Fax: (08) 8952 0052
Mobile: 0407 529 791   kathy@kathysplace.com.au
www.kathysplace.com.au

Double $130 Single $70
(Continental & Full Breakfast)
Credit Cards accepted Pet on property
2 Queen 1 Single (2 bdrm)   1 Share

Courtesy transfers available on request . You will be welcomed by a excitable but friendly husky called Neischka, and hosts Kathy and Karl who will help with tour booking and help you to enjoy your stay. Our guests rooms consist of: One Queen Room and one Queen and a single Bed in room. Our home (including the guestrooms) is air-conditioned. In the cooler months, a combustion heater provides a cosy atmosphere to read, chat or just watch TV. Enjoy a quiet day at Kathy's playing snooker, reading or just relaxing and enjoying a refreshing swim in our swimming pool and garden.

Alice Springs   *B & B*   *16km S of Alice Springs*

Bond Springs Outback Retreat
Janice Heaslip
Bond Springs Station, Alice Springs, NT 0871

Tel: (08) 8952 9888 Fax: (08) 8953 0963
Mobile: 0419 818 107
bondsprings@outbackretreat.com.au
www.outbackretreat.com.au

Double $231 (Full Breakfast) Child $45
Dinner B/A Credit Cards accepted
1 King/Twin 1 King 4 Queen
6 Twin 1 Single (12 bdrm)
12 Ensuite

An elegant retreat 16 km north of Alice Springs. Corkwood Cottage has 3 bedrooms, lounge, dining area. The Wurlie has 2 bedrooms, living area. Acacia Suite 1 king size, Witchetty Bush Suite 2 queen size bedrooms. Bush BBQ, cattle station tours can be arranged. Swimming pool. Jessica the dog loves to play. Children welcome.

Darwin *B & B   Self Contained*   *12 km SE of Darwin*

Red Lily Bed & Breakfast
Joy Williams
7 Phoenix Street, Nightcliff, NT 0814

Tel: (08) 8948 0984 Fax: (08) 8948 2490
Mobile: 0409 792 912
redlily@octa4.net.au
www.redlily.com.au
Double $100-$130 Single $80-$120 (Full Breakfast)
1 Queen 1 Double 4 Single (2 bdrm)
2 Ensuite

Guest room or apartment accommodation located opposite the popular Nightcliff Sunday Markets. Conveniently located near airport, beach, restaurants, shops and sporting facilities. Only 12km from the CBD on a regular bus route via Darwin Turf Club, Mindil Beach and the Casino. Accommodation units provide free off-street parking, private bathroom, air-conditioning and fans, refrigerator, tea/coffee making facilities, toaster and television. Guests are welcome to use the large inground pool, outdoor barbecue and entertaining area. Laundry service, secretarial service and airport transfers available with prior arrangement.

Northern Territory

Humpty Doo *Self Contained*   *45 km S of Darwin*

Humpty Doo Homestay AAATourism ★★★
Brian & Joyce Maden
45 Acacia Road, Humpty Doo, NT 0836

Tel: (08) 8988 1147 Fax: (08) 8988 1147
Mobile: 0407 767 413
bmadentopend@austarnet.com.au
Double $99 (Continental Breakfast) Extra person $10
Weekly $590 Credit Cards accepted Pet on property
1 Double 2 Single (2 bdrm)   1 Private

We are 5 minutes drive from Humpty Doo village and approx. 30 mins from Darwin City. The cottage has been described as "Bali in the bush". Furnished in early Australian antiques and with all mod cons, fully equipped kitchen, gas BBQ, private bathroom with washing machine, all set in large tropical garden, large inground swimming pool and children's play equipment. Non smoking indoors, wheelchair friendly. No pets allowed, 2 old friendly small dogs resident. We care for orphaned/injured local wildlife which run freely through the property.
www.bed-and-breakfast.au.com/humptydoohomestay.htm

Humpty Doo *B & B*   *38 km SE of Darwin*

Mango Meadows Homestay AAATourism ★★★☆
Nola & Ray Nendick
2759 Bridgemary Crescent, Humpty Doo, NT 0836

Tel: (08) 8988 4417 Fax: (08) 8988 2883
Mobile: 0409 036 168
nnendick@bigpond.com
www.bbbook.com.au/mangomeadows.html
Double $100 Single $85 (Continental Breakfast)
Dinner $15 $600 Weekly Credit Cards accepted
Pet on property
2 Queen (2 bdrm)   1 Share

Set in a lush tropical garden, alive with native birds and surrounded by 6 acres of Mango and Lime trees. Enjoy a large air conditioned lounge with television, video and stereo system with a self contained kitchen. Adjoining our games verandah is a large pool and spa. Why not try all the homemade Mango products. We are centrally located to both Litchfield and Kakadu National Park and many more tourist attractions. On arrival our dog will make you very welcome.

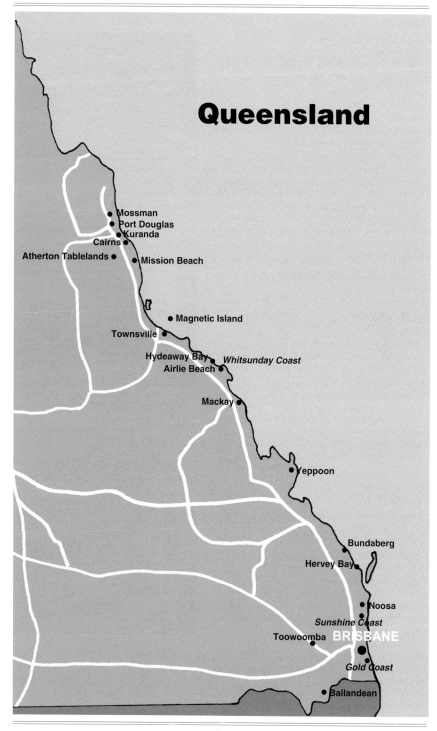

Queensland

- Mossman
- Port Douglas
- Kuranda
- Cairns
- Atherton Tablelands
- Mission Beach
- Magnetic Island
- Townsville
- Hydeaway Bay
- *Whitsunday Coast*
- Airlie Beach
- Mackay
- Yeppoon
- Bundaberg
- Hervey Bay
- Noosa
- *Sunshine Coast*
- Toowoomba
- BRISBANE
- *Gold Coast*
- Ballandean

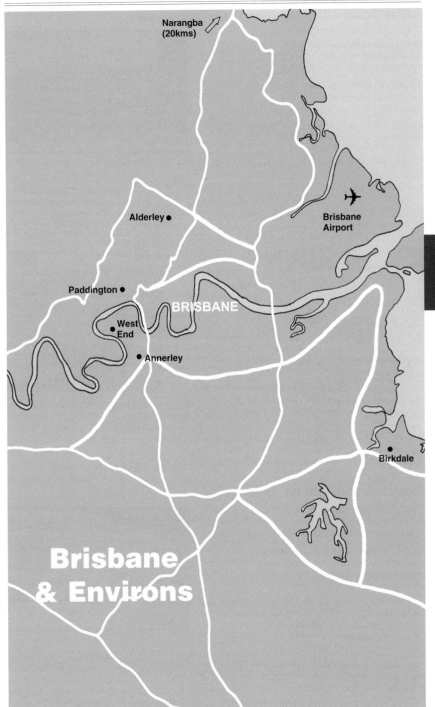

Narangba
(20kms)

Alderley ●

Brisbane
Airport

Paddington ●

BRISBANE

● West
End

● Annerley

● Birkdale

Brisbane
& Environs

Queensland

Airlie Beach - Whitsunday
300m SW of Airlie Beach

Homestay Studio Apartments
Whitsunday Moorings B&B
AAATourism ★★★★☆   Peter Brooks
37 Airlie Crescent, Airlie Beach, Qld 4802

Tel: (07) 4946 4692 Fax: (07) 4946 4692
info@whitsundaymooringsbb.com.au
www.whitsundaymooringsbb.com.au
Double $125 Single $115 (Full Breakfast)
extra person above 2 $25 Credit Cards accepted
1 Queen 1 Double (2 bdrm)   2 Private

Our studio apartments abut a garden terrace, poolside, with great views. Breakfast of fresh juice, tropical fruit in season, cereal, hot Australian homestyle entree, toast, homemade jams, tea or coffee. Each apartment features air-conditioning, ceiling fans, satellite TV, en suite with shower, hairdryer, refrigerator, microwave, equipped to prepare a light meal, alarm clock radio, laundry facilities, serviced daily. At the end of the day come home have a swim, relax with a cool drink as the sun sets, watch the boats return to the marina below.

Airlie Beach - Whitsunday
5 km W of Airlie Beach

Self Contained Queensland Heritage Cottage
Whitsunday Heritage Cane Cutters Cottage
Suzette Pelt
4 Braithwaite Court, Airlie Beach, Queensland 4802

Tel: (07) 4946 7400 Fax: (07) 4946 7698
Mobile: 0419 724 922   Freecall: 1800 075 013
pelt@whitsunday.net.au
www.bbbook.com.au/canecutterscottage.html
Double $110 Single $110 Credit Cards accepted
Extra Persons $15, max 4 total   1 Double   1 Private

The Cane Cutters Cottage is an historic, North Queensland workers cottage. Completely restored in 2001 and furnished with comfortable family antiques it offers an authentic Australian experience for visitors wishing to explore Airlie Beach, the Whitsunday Islands and Reef. Located only 5 minutes from town, in 6 acres country property, the Cottage is self contained with kitchen, laundry, one bedroom and cool verandah overlooking a dam and rainforest. Enjoy watching wallabies and birdlife from the verandah. The Owners live on the property and have two friendly family dogs.

Atherton Tablelands - Malanda
Country Lodge   8 km Malanda

Honeyflow Homestead   AAATourism ★★★★☆
Jim & Carmel Panther
Heidke Road (off Topaz Road), Malanda, Qld 4885

Tel: (07) 4096 8173 Fax: (07) 4096 8099
Mobile: 0438 315 665
info@honeyflow.com.au
www.honeyflow.com.au
Double $126-$137 Single $99-$110 (Full Breakfast)
Child P.O.A Dinner $35 B/A Credit Cards accepted
3 Queen 1 Double 3 Single (4 suites)
4 Ensuite 1 Share

Honeyflow is set amid a hectare of park-like gardens, surrounded by magnificent scenery. Your spacious suites are within the circa 1918 Homestead with private access from the verandah. The 'visiting friends' atmosphere is evident from the moment you arrive. Enjoy an excellent country-style hosted dinner. Breakfast is an extravagant affair served in the garden room. Stroll to see the Platypus, or enjoy the birds in the garden. Very central, peaceful and truly lovely! Enjoy your Tableland experience.

Ballandean   *Homestay B & B   20 km S of Stanthorpe*

Ballandean Lodge   AAATourism ★★★★
Dietmar & Dorothy Gogolka
Box 43, Ballandean - Stanthorpe, Qld 4382

Tel: (07) 4684 1320 Fax: (07) 4684 1340
ballandeanlodge@halenet.com.au
www.bbbook.com.au/ballandeanlodge.html
Double $115-$130 Single $70-$85 (Full Breakfast)
Dinner $30-$35pp Credit Cards accepted
Pet on property Pets welcome
1 Queen 1 Double 2 Single (3 bdrm)   3 Ensuite

Ballandean Lodge is a 100 year old Queenslander which nestles between the vineyards and stone fruit orchards of SE Queensland. 4 National Parks close by. Enjoy the privacy of your own comfortable room with ensuite and admire the magnificent views from all the verandahs. After a day in the wineries, sip your wine while watching the glorious sunset, before enjoying a home-cooked dinner in our dining room. Dietmar and Dorothy, together with their three beautiful pets, are waiting to make you welcome to the peace and tranquillity of their home.

Brisbane - Annerley   *B & B   4 km S of Brisbane city*

Annerley B&B - Ridge Haven
AAATourism ★★★★   Peter & Morna Cook
374 Annerley Road, Annerley, Qld 4103

Tel: (07) 3391 7702 Fax: (07) 3392 1786
ridgehaven@uq.net.au
www.uqconnect.net/ridgehaven
Double $99-$120 Single $85-$95 (Special Breakfast)
3rd person in dbl/sgl room $25 - $35.00
Credit Cards accepted
2 Queen 1 Double 1 Single (3 bdrm)   3 Ensuite

Traditional Queenslander (circa late 1800's) on Brisbane's southside, decorated to reflect the elegance and charm of a bye-gone era. Ensuites. Spacious bedrooms have mosquito nets, doonas and feather pillows while crisp white linen dress the comfortable beds. Breakfasts a speciality. Very accessible location. Under 10 mins to city. Public transport at door. Close to "Gabba" Cricket Ground & AFL venue. Southbank. Convention Centre. Weekend Markets. City Shopping & Casino. Fashion Warehouse Outlets. Freeway to Gold Coast & Toowoomba. Restaurants within walking distance. Award winning B&B 2000 & 2001.

Brisbane - Birkdale   *B & B   17 km E of Brisbane CBD*

Birkdale Bed & Breakfast   AAATourism ★★★★
Geoff & Margaret Finegan
3 Whitehall Avenue, Birkdale, Brisbane, Qld 4159

Tel: (07) 3207 4442 glentrace@bigpond.com
www.bbbook.com.au/birkdalebb.html
Double $80-$90 Single $55-$65
(Continental & Full Breakfast) Child $20
Dinner $15-30 Credit Cards accepted
2 Queen 1 Double 2 Single (3 bdrm)
2 Ensuite 1 Private

Only 20 minutes from Brisbane CBD and airport, but with a lovely country atmosphere. Set in half an acre of beautifully landscaped gardens, Birkdale B&B is a modern English style country home, with a new 4 Star motel style guest wing and separate entrance. All bedrooms have private facilities and reverse cycle air conditioning for your comfort. Minibar. Off street parking. Enjoy feeding the birds, go whale watching in nearby Moreton Bay or meet the local koalas. Qualified Aussie Hosts. Dual Tourism Award Winner.   Corporate and weekly rates.

Brisbane Central   *B & B*   *1 km S of Brisbane*

La Torretta Bed & Breakfast   AAATourism ★★★★
Charles and Dorothy Colman
8 Brereton Street, South Brisbane, Qld 4101

Tel: (07) 3846 0846 Fax: (07) 3846 0846
Mobile: 0414 465 387   colmanwilliams@bigpond.com
www.users.bigpond.com/colmanwilliams
Double $90-$95 Single $70-$75
(Continental Breakfast) Child half price
Credit Cards accepted Pet on property
1 King/Twin 1 Queen (2 bdrm)   2 Private

Ten minutes walk to the Convention Centre, Cultural Complex and beautiful Southbank Gardens, La Torretta is an elegant Queenslander with modern, comfortable, ground-floor guest accommodation and off-street parking. Our many return visitors come for the unfussy but meticulous service, homemade bread and jams, freshly ground Italian coffee, large friendly guest-lounge, with internet access, looking onto the leafy garden. The well-equipped kitchenette has coffee, teas and biscuits always available. West End's convivial cafés and new supermarket complex are just around the corner. "A great find - excellent and friendly service!" CT, UK

Brisbane - City   *B & B*   *Self Contained*   *1 km W of Brisbane*

Eton
Michelle Bugler
436 Upper Roma Street, Brisbane, Qld 4000

Tel: (07) 3236 0115   thornburyhouse@primus.com.au
Fax: (07) 3832 7756   www.bbbook.com.au/eton.html
Double $99-$110 Single $85-$95
(Continental Breakfast) Apartment $420/week
Credit Cards accepted
1 King 5 Queen 1 Double (6 bdrm)
4 Ensuite 2 Private

'Eton' (circa 1877) is a heritage listed restored colonial home within easy walking distance of the city, transit centre, south bank parklands, the cultural centre and the convention centre. We offer quality accommodation to the discerning traveller in a quiet location. Our air-conditioned rooms are traditionally furnished and have polished floors. A generous continental buffet breakfast is served in a tropical courtyard garden amongst the greenery of palms and ferns. The airport bus stops at our front door and we have ample off-street parking. Many fine restaurants and pubs are nearby.

Brisbane - Narangba   *B & B*   *4 km E of Narangba*

Richards B & B   AAATourism ★★★☆
Richard & Naomi Sieverts
341 Boundary Road, Narangba, Qld 4504

Tel: (07) 3888 3743 Fax: (07) 3888 3938
Mobile: 0417 071 188   Freecall: 1800 105 099
RichardsBnB@bigpond.com
www.bbbook.com.au/richardsbb.html
Double $76 Single $50 (Full Breakfast)
Child 1/2 price $150 Bridal Suite
Credit Cards accepted
3 Queen 2 Single (4 bdrm)   1 Ensuite 1 Share

"Richards' located 30km north of Brisbane 2 mins off Bruce Highway, one hour from Noosa, one hour Dreamworld, Gold Coast with all attractions in between. Our B&B is a large family home set in a tranquil 2 1/2 acre setting with wild birds and the odd koala. We have a pool room, bar etc, you have full use of all facilities. Also 20 mins to Morton Bay, Redcliff, fishing. We serve a full breakfast, late check out. Pick up from train 3 1/2km or airport 25km can be arranged. Two dogs live with us.

Brisbane - Paddington   *1.5 km NW of Brisbane Central*

Self Contained B & B   2 self contained apartments

Paddington B & B   AAATourism ★★★★
Annette Henry
5 Latrobe Terrace, Paddington, Qld 4064

Tel: (07) 3369 8973 Mobile: 0419 741 282
Fax: (07) 3876 6655   waverleypaddington@bigpond.com
www.bbbook.com.au/paddingtonbb.html

Double $110 Single $85 (Full Breakfast)
S/C Accom. $425 per week Credit Cards accepted
2 King 2 Queen 4 Single (4 bdrm)   4 Ensuite

Known locally as "Waverley" this romantic, 1888 Queensland colonial is deceptively spacious inside with polished timber floors and soaring ceilings. Situated in smart, leafy, cosmopolitan, inner - city Paddington, where interesting shops and cafes line the streets, it has the bonus of off - street parking and easy access to the city. There are two air - conditioned guest suites on the street level and two self-contained apartments with private entrances, fans and fully equipped kitchens on the lower level. Mango trees screen the decks on both levels. One resident cat: Felicity.

Brisbane - West End   *Homestay B & B   2 km SW of Brisbane*

Eskdale Bed & Breakfast   AAATourism ★★★☆
Paul Kennedy
141 Vulture Street,
West End, Qld 4101

Tel: (07) 3255 2519
eskdale_brisbane@yahoo.com.au
www.bbbook.com.au/eskdale.homestead.com.html

Double $90 Single $60 (Continental Breakfast)
Child 1/2 price Credit Cards accepted
1 King 1 Queen 1 Double 2 Single (4 bdrm)
2 Share

Eskdale Bed & Breakfast is a typical turn-of-the century Queensland house close to the restaurant district of West End. It's 2km to the city centre across the Victoria Bridge, and just 1km from the Southbank Parklands and the Brisbane Convention and Exhibition Centre, the Queensland Performing Arts Centre, Museum and Art Gallery. You'll be close to all the action and still be able to relax on the back deck and watch the birds feeding on the Australian native plants in the garden.

Bundaberg   *Homestay   2 km S of Bundaberg*

Whiston House   AAATourism ★★★☆
Sharron & Vic Sumner
9 Elliott Heads Road, Bundaberg, Qld 4670

Tel: (07) 4152 1447 Fax: (07) 4152 1447
Mobile: 0419 393 776   info@whistonhouse.com.au
www.whistonhouse.com.au

Double $75-$95 (Full Breakfast)
Credit Cards accepted
3 Queen 1 Twin (4 bdrm)
1 Ensuite 1 Share

Enjoy quality accommodation in an historic Queenslander nestled in one acre of tropical gardens, with shaded saltwater pool, undercover parking and lift. Tastefully appointed bedrooms with Queen beds, television, fridge, tea/coffee making facilities. Guests are very welcome to use the spacious lounge, verandahs and BBQ facilities. Complimentary transfers from bus, rail or airport. The famous Bundaberg Rum Distillery, Lady Musgrave and Lady Elliot Islands and Mon Repos Turtle Rookery are easily accessible from Whiston House.

Bundaberg   *B & B*   *2 km N of Bundaberg*

Waterview Estate B & B
Joy & John Wright
2 Gavin Street, North Bundaberg, Qld 4670

Tel: (07) 4154 4811 Fax: (07) 4154 4811
Mobile: 0418 444 111
waterviewestate@interworx.com.au
www.bbbook.com.au/waterviewestatebb.html

Double $85-$120 Single $80 (Full Breakfast)
Credit Cards accepted
2 Queen 1 Twin (3 bdrm) 2 Private

Waterview Estate B&B is a traditional Bed & Breakfast. Graciously furnished with elegance & sophistication of 19th century style blending effortlessly with 21st century convenience. This spacious home is set on 12 tranquil acres of rambling gardens & lawns to the river. Experience highest standard of hospitality, accommodation, comfort & service, with fine china, silverware, crisp linen & Devonshire teas. Enjoy open fires in cooler months or fresh breezes from the river on the many verandahs in summer. Waterview Estate is a place for all seasons…Easy to find…Hard to leave.

Bundaberg - Bargara Beach   *Homestay B & B*   *9 km E of Bundaberg*

Dunelm House B & B   AAATourism ★★★★☆
Rod & Maureen Hall
540 Bargara Road, Bargara Beach, Qld 4670

Tel: (07) 4159 0909 Fax: (07) 4159 0916
dunelm@austarnet.com.au
www.babs.com.au/dunelm

Double $75 Single $55 (Full Breakfast)
Child by arrangement Dinner $17.50
Credit Cards accepted
3 Queen 1 Twin (3 bdrm) 3 Ensuite

Maureen and Rod have restored a gentleman farmer's residence into a home away from home B&B with ensuite bathrooms, air conditioning, television lounge, heated saltwater pool/spa and sumptuous breakfasts. Dinner on request. Ideally located close to Bundaberg, Bargara Beach, Mon Repos Turtle Sanctuary and Lady Musgrave departure point. Golfers, bowlers and divers are well catered for. All your holiday tours can be arranged. A complimentary pick up service is available. Give us a ring, we are only a phone call away. Award winners.

Bundaberg - Gin Gin   *Farmstay B & B*   *18 km S of Gin Gin*

Walla Station
Bentley Briggs and Natalie Butcher
315 Walla Road, Gin Gin, Qld 4671

Tel: (07) 4157 6702 Fax: (07) 4157 6007
Mobile: 0409 613 195
info@wallastation.com.au
www.wallastation.com.au

Double $77-$88 Single $55-$66 (Full Breakfast)
Dinner $10 - $20
3 Queen 1 Twin (4 bdrm)
4 Ensuite

Walla Station is the oldest station on the Burnett River and has been in the same family since 1905. The timber homestead (c1860's) has impressive high ceilings and timber lined rooms. It has been restored and comfortably furnished in keeping with its heritage style. Stroll through the 4 acres of beautiful garden, take a bush walk to the ancient fig trees and spot bird and wildlife. Or simply relax under the deep shady verandahs. Horse stud on the property.

Cairns - Bayview Heights *B & B   8 km S of Cairns*

Bayview House Bed and Breakfast
Bill & Margaret Morgan
3 Vine Close, Bayview Heights, Cairns, Qld 4870

Tel: (07) 4033 6747 Fax: (07) 4033 7232
Mobile: 0411 898 218
margaret@cairnsluxurybandb.com.au
www.cairnsluxurybandb.com.au
Double $125 Single $80 (Full Breakfast)
King and Twin $135
1 King 2 Queen 1 Twin 3 Single (3 bdrm) 3 Ensuite

Nestled below world heritage rainforest overlooking Cairns and the Coral Sea Bayview House welcomes you. We are proud to offer a luxurious modern home with spacious air conditioned en-suite bedrooms, with ceiling fans, colour television and hairdryers. Guest lounge with tea/coffee making facilities. Extensive Breakfast Menu. Laundry/Ironing facilities. Tour booking service. Secure Parking. Relax on your patio with a complimentary glass of wine and snacks whilst overlooking our 9 meter swimming pool with ocean and city views. Cairns Golf Club, restaurants, public transport and shopping centres nearby. Smoking outside. Brochure available.

Cairns - Brinsmead   *Homestay B & B   10 km W of Cairns*

Jenny's Homestay
Jenny & Lex Macfarlane
12 Leon Close, Brinsmead, Qld 4870

Tel: (07) 4055 1639 Mobile: 0416 044 814
jennysbb@jennysbandb.com
www.jennysbandb.com
Double $80-$90 Single $60-$70
(Continental Breakfast) Queen with Ensuite $80-$90
1 Queen 2 Double 1 Twin (4 bdrm)
1 Ensuite 1 Private 1 Share

Jenny and Lex invite you to our home in Cairns. Wake to the sound of birds and a warm welcome from Misha our cat and Bella our poodle. A continental breakfast is served in the sunroom or around the pool. My husband and I are Photographers and enjoy outdoor activities. We are only a short distance from the tropical beaches, great restaurants, golf courses and the famous Kuranda Train and Skyrail. We are booking agents for all tours and rental cars. A complimentary pick up on arrival.

Cairns - Central   *Homestay B & B   3 km N of Cairns*

James Street Cottage
Terry & Dorothy Roos
25 James Street, Cairns, Qld 4870

Tel: (07) 4051 9114 Fax: (07) 4031 2078
Mobile: 0427 442 808
jamesstreet@bigpond.com
www.bbbook.com.au/jamesstreet.html
Double $77 Single $55 (Full Breakfast) Child $11
Credit Cards accepted Pet on property
2 Queen 1 Double 1 Single (3 bdrm)
1 Share

Charming Queenslander situated 3 km from the city centre. We offer a unique blend of tropical ambience with the convenience of a city location. Free Airport or Station transfer and would be happy to organise and book your tours. Flecker botanical Gardens and Centenary Lakes are an easy walk away. We serve a generous Aussie breakfast and the saltwater pool is always available. We have a very friendly dog who respects your required peace as much as your host.

Cairns - Crystal Cascades (via Redynch)   *14 km NW of Cairns*

Homestay B & B

Nutmeg Grove - Tropical Rainforest B&B
AAATourism ★★★★★   Ingrid & Terry Douglas
7 Woodridge Close, Crystal Cascades (via Redlynch)

Tel: (07) 4039 1226 Fax: (07) 4039 1226
Mobile: 0429 391 226   visit@nutmeggrove.com.au
www.nutmeggrove.com.au

Double $125-$165 (Special Breakfast)
Credit Cards accepted Pet on property
1 King/Twin 1 King 1 Queen (2 bdrm)   2 Private

Stunning 3 acre rainforest property - where you discover peace, privacy and breathtaking beauty of Nutmeg Grove. Elegant luxury living in one of the most awe-inspiring regions of the world. Nestled in the Freshwater Valley, at Crystal Cascades you are surrounded by forested mountain ranges. This ensures your tropical experience is complete. Private guest wing, a/c, fans, pool with waterfall and spa. Gourmet breakfasts and warm hospitality welcomes you. "Come as a Stranger and Leave as a Friend". Central to all tour destinations, Cairns, Beaches, Port Douglas, Island destinations and Daintree.

Cairns - Holloways Beach   *B & B*   *12 km N of Cairns*

Beaches
Josephine Hopkins
Cnr. Matthew & Marietta Streets,
Holloways Beach, Cairns, Qld 4878

Tel: (07) 4055 9972 Fax: (07) 4055 9886
bookings@beaches-at-holloways.com.au
www.beaches-at-holloways.com.au

Double $77-$99 Single $55-$66 (Full Breakfast)
Child B/A Extra person $25 Credit Cards accepted
2 Queen 1 Double 2 Single (3 bdrm)
2 Ensuite 1 Private

Our B&B offers you a warm welcome in a relaxed tropical home across the road from an unspoiled beach. Spacious guest sitting room, dining room and kitchen; wide shady verandah overlooking the Coral Sea. Handy public transport to the city and Jo will arrange your tours with pick-ups at the front gate. Good restaurants a five minute walk away or enjoy a poolside BBQ. Sam our beautiful labrador speaks all languages and will show you how to relax.

Cairns - Redlynch   *B & B*   *14 km NW of Cairns*

Zanzoo Retreat   AAAT★★★☆
Sharon & Marc Ryan
Lot 4 Mary Parker Drive, Redlynch, Qld 4870

Tel: (07) 4039 2842 Fax: (07) 4039 0450
Mobile: 0407 966 453
marc@zanzoo.com   www.zanzoo.com

Double $95-$132 Single $75-$110 (Full Breakfast)
Child $25 Dinner B/A Credit Cards accepted
5 Queen 1 Double (6 bdrm)
3 Ensuite 2 Share

Zanzoo Retreat located in the scenic Freshwater Valley, provides 14 acres (5.7 hectares) of lush tropical gardens, lawns and rainforest allowing you room to relax. Go for a swim and picnic on the banks of the rainforest fringed Freshwater Creek which flows the length of the property. Spacious accommodation in a historic two storey Queenslander homestead, includes air-conditioned rooms with share and private bathroom facilities. Enjoy a delicious full breakfast including the freshest tropical fruits. Close to restaurants and central to all tour destinations.

Cairns - Stratford   *B & B   8 km N of Cairns*

Lilybank   **AAAT**ourism ★★★★
Mike & Pat Woolford
75 Kamerunga Road, Stratford Cairns, Qld 4870

Tel: (07) 4055 1123 Fax: (07) 4058 1990 hosts@lilybank.com.au
www.lilybank.com.au

Double $88-$110 Single $77 (Full Breakfast) Child $20 Credit Cards accepted Pet on property
1 King/Twin 1 King 4 Queen 2 Twin 5 Single (5 bdrm)
5 Ensuite

"Lilybank" - a fine example of traditional "Queenslander" architecture. Selected as a "Frommers Favourite" since 1997, "Lilybank" owes its success to the happy blend of hospitality and privacy offered to our guests.

Bedrooms are air-conditioned, there's a guests' lounge with TV, video, salt-water pool, laundry, BBQ and off-street parking.

We'll serve a wonderful breakfast and help you choose and book tours which are right for you. Our excellent local restaurants are within walking distance.

Three poodles and a galah live in our part of house. There's a beautiful tropical garden and guests are welcome to pick their own fruit in season.

Cairns - Trinity Beach   *Homestay B & B   20 km N of Cairns*

Trinity Beach B & B
Elsa & Michael Lockwood
30 Petersen Street,
Trinity Beach, Qld 4879

Tel: (07) 4057 7990 Fax: (07) 4057 7509
micels@iprimus.com.au
home.iprimus.com.au/micels

Double $99 Single $55
(Full Breakfast) Child B/A
1 Queen 2 Single (2 bdrm)
2 Ensuite

Just a few minutes walk from one of Cairns' most beautiful beaches, Trinity Beach B&B also offers a palm-shaded pool, secluded hot tub and barbecue on site. A frequent bus service allows easy access to the city, beach-side restaurants and food outlets are a short walk away. Guests interested in Great Barrier Reef or tropical rainforest trips can avail themselves of the pickup services of tour operators. Our spacious rooms feature full ensuite facilities and TV. The occupants of the house include a dog and cat. A no smoking property.

Cairns - Trinty Beach   *B & B   15 km N of Cairns*

Trinity On the Esplanade   AAATourism ★★★★★
Elise Warring
21 Vasey Esplanade, Trinty Beach, Qld 4879

Tel: (07) 4057 6850 Fax: (07) 4057 8099
Mobile: 0417 750 480   Freecall: 1800 645 930
stay@trinityesplanade.com www.trinityesplanade.com

Double $175-$270 (Full Breakfast)
Credit Cards accepted
6 Queen (6 bdrm)   6 Private

Trinity "On the Esplanade" is situated on the beachfront at beautiful Trinity Beach. The ultimate in luxury accommodation featuring lime washed timber furniture, Persian rugs, and Australian Heritage linen, combined to create a romantic ambience perfect for any special occasion. Trinity "On the Esplanade" combines a first class destination with excellent personalised service. Here we respect your privacy and cater for your every need. A full breakfast is included. Trinity "On the Esplanade" is conveniently located to restaurants and all major tourist attractions, including the Great Barrier Reef, Skyrail, championship golf courses, Aboriginal dance & culture.

Cairns - Yorkeys Knob   *17km N of Cairns*

Homestay Self Contained Separate/Suite
A Villa Gail   Gail Simpson
36 Janett Street, Yorkeys Knob Cairns, Qld 4878

Tel: (07) 4055 8178 Fax: (07) 4055 8178
Mobile: 0417 079 575   gail@avillagail.com
www.avillagail.com

Double $100-$110 Single $65-$75 (Special Breakfast)
Guest Wing $110 - $120, S/C apartment $140
1 King 1 Queen 1 Double 1 Twin (4 bdrm)
1 Ensuite

"Villa Gail" on Millionaires Row was designed to make the most of our unique elevated location at Yorkey's Knob. Our cool Mediterranean-style house is set within lush tropical gardens overlooking the beach with breathtaking views across the Coral Sea. From the delightful in-ground swimming pool spacious guest's verandah or your own large room, you can relax and enjoy our tropical lifestyle. Villa Gail is only 15 minutes from Cairns. Tours to the World Heritage Wet Tropics Rainforest, the Outback and the Great Barrier Reef all pick up from our door.

Condamine   *Farmstay B & B Homestead*   *16 km W of Condamine*

Nelgai - Farmstay   AAATourism ★★★★
Priscilla & David Mundell
Nelgai, Condamine, Qld 4416

Tel: (07) 4627 7124 Fax: (07) 4627 7200
Mobile: 0427 958 018   nelgai@growzone.com.au
www.bbbook.com.au/mundell.html

Double $140 Single $70 (Full Breakfast) Child 50%
Dinner $30 Credit Cards accepted Pet on property
1 Queen 1 Twin (2 bdrm)
1 Ensuite 1 Private

Wake up in the Bush on a cattle property, en route to the outback. The large lagoon attracts abundant kangaroos, birds and other wildlife. Relax on the verandah of our comfortable air-conditioned homestead with a drink, before a country cooked dinner, watching the setting sun and starry sky. Spend the day with us on or off the property and/or go exploring on your own. Local attractions e.g. Miles Historical Village, Myall Park Botanic Gardens. Lunches and picnics available. "This was real Australia!" E.R. France

Gold Coast Hinterland   *B & B*   *6 km S of Nerang*

Gilston Retreat
Lois and Henk Van Der Vorst
53 Evanita Drive, Gilston, Nerang, Qld 4211

Tel: (07) 5533 2499 Fax: (07) 5533 2500
Mobile: 0403 366 777
hlvorst@technet2000.com.au
www.babs.com.au/gilston

Double $120-$140 Single $100-$110
(Full Breakfast) Dinner B/A Pet on property
3 Queen (3 bdrm) 2 Ensuite 1 Private

Come and enjoy the peace and tranquillity of our charming, colonial style Queenslander set on 7 1/2 acres. A superb breakfast can be served in either our large rustic country style kitchen or on our spacious deck overlooking natural bushland where native birdlife and the occasional kangaroo can be spotted. A variety of interesting activities can be had close by such as golf, horseback riding, hot air ballooning, fishing, canoeing as well as great shopping with Robina Town Centre and the Carrara Markets just 15 minutes away. We do have a friendly poodle x called Scruffy.

Gold Coast Hinterland - Guanaba   *18 km NW of Nerang*

B & B Self Contained

Jiana Park Lodge Bed & Breakfast
Diana & Jim Ingram
685 Guanaba Creek Road, Guanaba, Qld 4210

Tel: (07) 5533 7887 Fax: (07) 5533 7756
info@jianapark.com.au
www.jianapark.com.au

Double $120 Single $90 (Special Breakfast)
Child $55 1 child under 10 years free Pet on property
1 Queen 2 Single (1 bdrm) 1 Private

An enchanting 13 acres of creek frontage undulating into foothills. Great for walking or resting. We are tucked away in a secluded parkland valley with birdsong, the sound of the creek, wallabies, even fireflies and platypus. Only 15 minutes from Brisbane freeway, Movieworld and Dreamworld. Mt Tamborine restaurants and shops are 15 minutes drive, beaches and shopping 40 minutes. Your hosts absolutely spoil you with Champagne or Devonshire Tea on arrival, present you with your Breakfast Basket overflowing with food, then leave you to the privacy of your own Lodge and courtyard.

WOODLEIGH *Homestead*

BED & BREAKFAST

"The most beautiful B&B on the Mountain"

Mount Tamborine's Finest ★★★★☆

This would have to be Mt Tamborine's finest B&B, yet reasonably priced for families and couples alike. Set on 10 acres of lawns and gardens along with its grand entrance, Woodleigh offers stunning and sensational views. Stay in self contained rooms with kitchenette or private deluxe suites with spa and fireplace. Feed the Shetland Ponies and reindeer, have a leisurely swim in the pool or visit Lamington National Park just 45 minutes away, Movieworld & Dreamworld only 20 minutes. No wonder so many of our guests come back again and again . . . will you?

Full breakfast included!!

Cost:	Double $98	Suite $155
	Child $15	
	VISA/MC	
Beds:	6 Queen	2 Double
	(6 bdrm)	
Bath:	6 Ensuite	
Spa:	3	
Fireplace:	3	

SUPER MID WEEK SPECIAL

STUDIO ROOM
DBL / 4 Nights **$320**

DELUXE SUITE/SPA/FIREPLACE
DBL / 4 Nights **$440**

Your Hosts: Cynthia & Ian Portas
13 Munro Court, off Lahey Lookout Road Mt Tamborine Qld 4272
Tel: 07 5545 3121 • www.woodleigh.com
ONLY 20 MIN. TO DREAMWORLD & MOVIEWORLD

Gold Coast - Hinterland - Tamborine Mountain

Homestay B & B   10 km NE of Canungra

Sandiacre House B & B   AAATourism ★★★★☆
Margaret & David Carter
45-47 Licuala Drive, North Tamborine, Qld 4272

Tel: (07) 5545 3490 Fax: (07) 5545 0279
Mobile: 0407 453 490
www.tamborinemtncc.org.au/sandiacre.htm

Double $80-$130 Single $60-$130 (Full Breakfast)
2 Queen 2 Single (3 bdrm)
2 Ensuite 1 Share

Welcome to Sandiacre House Exquisite Bed & Breakfast on picturesque Tamborine Mountain; with Victorian decor, antique furnishings, log fire for that homely feeling in winter, tranquil gardens, chickens, ducks and bees. Our aim is to make your stay as relaxing and memorable as possible. Centrally located 2-10 minutes drive to all amenities, tourist attractions and craft shops. Weddings, anniversaries, special occasions and gift vouchers are our speciality. Award winning B & B. We have no facilities for children, pets.

Gold Coast Hinterland - Willow Vale   *30 min S of Brisbane*

Homestay Self Contained Cottage

Willow Vale Homestay
Brian and Jean Daly
48 Rosemount Drive,
Willow Vale, Qld 4218

Tel: (07) 5547 5606 Fax: (07) 5547 5606
www.bbbook.com.au/willowvale.html

Double $80-$90 Single $50-$55
(Continental & Full Breakfast)
2 Queen (2 bdrm)
1 Private

We live in a beautiful valley of Willow Vale. 35 minutes from the Gold Coast, 30 minutes from Brisbane - a rural Stay. 4 minutes from the M.1., quiet and peaceful. The cottage is fully self-contained situated in a park setting. Tour water, TV, private, children welcome, of course your well behaved dog. We are close to theme parks. Movie world, Water world, dream world, golf course and restaurants. Train service only 10 minutes away at Ormeau.

Gold Coast - Mermaid Beach - Surfers Paradise

B & B   8 km S of Surfers Paradise

Mermaid Beachside Bed & Breakfast
AAATourism ★★★★☆   Roz Green
115 Seagull Avenue, Mermaid Beach, Qld 4218

Tel: (07) 5572 9530 Fax: (07) 5572 9530
Mobile: 0412 513 355   rooms@mermaidbeachside.com
www.mermaidbeachside.com

Double $110-$150 Single $70-$90 (Full Breakfast)
Credit Cards accepted
1 King/Twin 1 King 3 Queen 1 Single (5 bdrm)
4 Ensuite

Relax in our Gold Coast 4 1/2 star Bed & Breakfast, 5 A/C luxury international themed rooms i.e. Australiana, Mediterranean, English, Oriental & Americana. 5 min Pacific Fair Shopping & Jupiters Casino. 8 km Surfers Paradise. We pride ourselves to provide that extra personal service that you don't receive from the high rises. Experience our delicious breakfasts. One street from beach in a quiet location, all you hear are the waves crashing. Cable TV, Secure parking. 3 bedroom self contained apartment available from $100 per night.

Hervey Bay   *B & B*   *500m S of Post Office*

Tara B & B
Kitty & Eddie O'Neill
7 Wright Way, Scarness, Qld 4655

Tel: (07) 4124 7072 Fax: (07) 4124 7072
Mobile: 0438 247 072   tarabb@itfusion.com.au
www.bbbook.com.au/tarabb.html

Double $90 Single $60 (Continental & Full Breakfast)
Child by age Pet on property Pets welcome
1 Queen 3 Double 2 Single (4 bdrm)
1 Ensuite 2 Private

Tara Bed and Breakfast can be found in the heart of the city of Hervey Bay, close to all amenities - Post Office, airport, bus terminal, and the magical Fraser Island. We can arrange all bookings - whale watching August to October, Lady Elliott Island, Great Barrier Reef, and Fraser Island. Breakfast can be served in dining room or the privacy of the verandahs. Continental or full breakfast served. Close to all beaches. Air conditioning in all rooms. Access from all rooms to verandahs, spa, pool table, fridge, tea making facilities. Privacy assured.

Hervey Bay   *B & B*   *Hervey Bay*

Lakeside Bed & Breakfast   AAATourism ★★★★☆
Pauline & Max Harriden
27 Lido Parade, Urangan, Hervey Bay, Qld 4655

Tel: (07) 4128 9448 Fax: (07) 4125 5060
Mobile: 0409 284122   lakesidebb@bigpond.com
www.herveybaybedandbreakfast.com

Double $80-$120 Single $70-$90
(Continental & Full Breakfast)
Dinner B/A Credit Cards accepted
1 Queen 1 Double (2 bdrm) 1 Ensuite 1 Private 1 Share

Hervey Bay - Gateway to Fraser Island with so much to do and see. Visit the natural wonders of Fraser Island and see whales close up as they migrate. Dine in or eat out, the choice is yours. Relax in your private garden spa. Enjoy a continental or full breakfast on the deck overlooking the lake while watching the bird life and turtles being hand fed. Lakeside Bed & Breakfast has it all. First class modern accommodation, friendly hosts, all in walking distance to restaurants and beaches. Complimentary pick up from airport and transit centre. Let us pamper you. What are you waiting for? Book now.

Hervey Bay   *B & B*   *38 km S of Maryborough*

Bay Bed & Breakfast
Brian & Susan Renew
180 Cypress Street, Urangan,
Hervey Bay, Qld 4655

Tel: (07) 4125 6919 Fax: (07) 4125 3658
baybednbreakfast@australis.aunz.com
www.herveybayqueensland.com/baybedandbreak.html

Double $80-$110 Single $55 (Full Breakfast)
4 King/Twin 2 Queen 1 Single (5 bdrm)
2 Ensuite 1 Share

Recommended by the Lonely Planet Qld. Quality accommodation in an idyllic tropical setting. Solar heated swimming pool, continental and cooked breakfast in our dining room or shady rear terrace. Quality bedrooms with ensuite/shared bathroom or suite with private lounge, bathroom and laundry for that extra touch of privacy. One street from the beach, close to shops, restaurants and clubs. Tours and transfers arranged free of charge. Courtesy pick up from Hervey Bay Airport or Coach Terminal. Pamper Package includes Picnic and Massage.

Hervey Bay - Howard *Self Contained B & B Country House* *30 km N of Maryborough*

Melvos Country House **AAATourism ★★★★**
Yvonne & Paul Melverton
Lot 84 Pacific Haven Circuit, Howard, Qld 4659

Tel: (07) 4129 0201 Fax: (07) 4129 0201
Mobile: 0428 290 201
www.bbbook.com.au/melvos.html

Double $66-$88 Single $55
(Full Breakfast) Bungalow $22 - $33
1 Queen 1 Double (2 bdrm) 1 Ensuite 2 Share

Central located between Maryborough - Hervey Bay - Childers on 44 acres in comfortable and affordable accommodation. Home cooked meals - BBQ facilities - BYO alcohol. Tropical gardens - inground pool/spa, TV/video. Two saltwater rivers, boat ramp, laundromat, golf course, tennis court nearby. Tours arranged - Frasers & Elliott Islands - whale watching - 4x4 hire, deep-sea fishing, camel rides. Complimentary tea/coffee anytime. Free pickup from Howard Tilt train or bus terminal. Dinner by arrangement. We have small well behaved dogs. Not suitable for children. Smoking outdoors. A warm welcome awaits you.

Ipswich *B & B* *2 km E of Ipswich*

Villiers B & B **AAATourism ★★★☆**
Joyce Ramsay
14 Cardew Street,
East Ipswich, Qld 4305

Tel: (07) 3281 7364 Mobile: 0407 572 398
www.bbbook.com.au/villiers.html

Double $69-$75 Single $39-$45
(Continental & Full Breakfast) Child 1/2 price
1 Double 1 Twin (2 bdrm)
1 Share

Traditional B&B, quiet and comfortable, air conditioned. See Ipswich's historic attractions plus Australian animals, Japanese Gardens and Gallery, The Workshops, Steam Train Rides, Cobb & Co, Wine Trails, day trips to surrounding countryside and Brisbane. Meet an Australian family. Reasonable tariff. 3 1/2 Stars. Suitable one night or one week. Member Qld B&B Assn. "Thanks, first timers - and now hooked for life!!!" M&K H, Uralla

Kuranda - Cairns *Farmstay B & B Self Contained* *40 km W of Cairns*

Koah Bed & Breakfast
Greg Taylor
Lot 4 Koah Road, MSI 1039 Kuranda, Qld 4872

Tel: (07) 4093 7074 Fax: (07) 4093 7074
koah@ozemail.com.au
www.kurandahomestay.com

Double $77 Single $55 (Continental Breakfast)
Child 50% (under 15) Dinner $12
Cabins (sleep 4) $95 Credit Cards accepted
2 Queen 2 Double 4 Twin 2 Single (2 bdrm)
1 Ensuite 1 Private

Comfortable country home on 10 acres 10 mins from the township in the Rainforest Kuranda and 30 mins from Cairns and Great Barrier Reef. Offering fully self contained cabins for families with balconies overlooking native bushland and large dam. Also in home accommodation of 2 double bedrooms with double opening doors onto verandah 1 guest bathroom (ensuite) fully insulated and screened with ceiling fans. Each bedroom can be fitted with single folding bed for children, pets also welcomed.

Mackay - Whitsunday District

Farmstay Homestay B & B Self Contained

Eagle Nest Farm   AAATourism ★★★★
Anne & Helmut Kley
M/S 895, Gormleys Road, Seaforth, Qld 4740

Tel: (07) 4959 0552 Fax: (07) 4959 0552
Mobile: 0418 747 751   foxcon@mrbean.net.au
www.bbbook.com.au/eaglenestfarm.html
Double $75 Single $59 (Full Breakfast)
Child $10 Dinner $19.50 Pets welcome
4 Queen 4 Single (4 bdrm)   4 Ensuite

Eagle Nest Farm is an idyllic cattle farm of 250 acres set amidst tropical bushland with sea and island views. We migrated from Germany in 1990 and built a comfortable homestead, which is designed to host guests from all over the world. Enjoy total tranquillity and discover close-by National Parks with rainforest walks, beaches and unique wildlife. The Whitsunday Islands and The Great Barrier Reef are also accessible. Dinners are served on request in our separately located "Private Retreat" or you are welcome to do your own cooking.

Magnetic Island   *Homestay   8 km NE of Townsville*

Marshalls B & B
Paul & Stella Marshall
3 Endeavour Road, Arcadia Bay,
Magnetic Island, Qld 4819

Tel: (07) 4778 5112 Mobile: 0407 150 665
www.bbbook.com.au/marshallsbb.html
Double $65 Single $45 (Continental Breakfast)
Child over 12 yrs Credit Cards accepted
2 Queen 1 Double 2 Twin 2 Single (4 bdrm)
2 Share

Magnetic Island is one of Australia's most famous Koala habitats and bird sanctuaries and is surrounded by the waters of the Great Barrier Reef. This magnificent National Park is also our home where we offer simple, home-style hospitality and old fashioned value for money. The island has 30 kms of walking tracks and 20 exquisite bays around its coastline. There's fishing, sailing, diving, kayaking and horse riding, or just relax in the warmth. Phone ahead. No smoking indoors. No children under 12 years. No pets.

Mission Beach   *B & B   210 km S of Cairns*

Bed and Beachfront   AAATourism ★★★★☆
Karen Bankin
92 Reid Road, Mission Beach, Qld 4852

Tel: (07) 4068 9990 Fax: (07) 4068 9990
Mobile: 0417 745 542
bedbeachfront@bigpond.com
www.oz-e.com.au/bbfront
(Continental Breakfast) $75 - $85
Credit Cards accepted
1 King/Twin 1 Queen (2 bdrm)   2 Ensuite

Award Winning Home located on Absolute Beachfront. Please visit and enjoy our peaceful, tropical surroundings on Queensland's best kept secret, Mission Beach. Our beach is only metres from your room and flows north or south as far as you can see. Each room has a fridge, t.v and airconditioner. Both our queen and twin rooms have an ensuite. Enjoy swimming in our beautiful tropical swimming pools or just relax on our sun deck with views to beautiful Dunk Island. Our accommodation is peaceful, private and affordable.

Mission Beach South   *Homestay B & B   Self Contained   120 km S of Cairns*

Leslie Lodge
Don
5 Leslie Lane,
Mission Beach South, Qld 4852

Tel: (07) 4068 8618 Fax: (07) 4068 9840
Mobile: 0417 784 965
lodge@znet.net.au
www.bbbook.com.au/leslielodge.html

Double $75 Single $45 (Full Breakfast)
Child $20 on sofa Dinner $20
S/C Double $60 Pets welcome
1 King/Twin (1 bdrm)
1 Private

Secure and private accommodation is offered in delightful property - manicured lawn and garden.   4 mins stroll to delightful sandy beach opposite Dunk Island accessible by water taxi or ferry - rainforest walks and fishing.

Mission Beach South   *Self Contained Separate/Suite   150 km S of Cairns*

Campbell Court
Allan & Linda Sellars
1 Leslie Lane, South Mission Beach, Qld 4852

Tel: (07) 4068 8311 or (07) 4068 8695
Fax: (07) 4068 8623
www.bbbook.com.au/campbellcourt.html

Double $65-$75 (Continental Breakfast)
Self Contained $90 - $120. Weekly rate available
Credit Cards accepted
2 Queen (2 bdrm)   2 Ensuite

Campbell Court is located in a peaceful street and only minutes from the beach and the Hull river. At Campbell Court, our guests have the choice of staying in our detached B & B unit which has its own entrance, ensuite, TV and fridge or stay in our fully self contained unit (sleeps 4). The unit has a fully equipped kitchen and laundry, perfect for those longer stays. A continental breakfast is delivered each day. Pool and barbecue facility available.

Mossman   *Homestay B & B   1 km W of Mossman*

Mossman Gorge Bed & Breakfast
Amanda Coxon
PO Box 1079,
Mossman, Qld 4873

Tel: (07) 4098 2497
www.bbbook.com.au/mossgorgebnb.html

Double $82-$104 Single $60-$82 (Full Breakfast)
Child $15 - $25 Dinner B/A Pet on property
1 Queen 2 Double (3 bdrm)
1 Ensuite 1 Share

Stunning views in tropical comfort - on the edge of the Mossman Valley. Experience tropical living in our modern timber tree-top home with a north Queensland family - children welcome. Listen for the sounds of green tree frogs, the barking of striped possums or the call of the lesser Sooty Owl. Birds and butterflies abound. Take a dip in our pool, or watch the sun go down over Daintree world heritage rainforest clad mountains. No pets or smokers indoors. Please phone for directions.

Queensland

Noosa - Sunshine Coast *Separate/Suite B & B   10 km N of Noosa*

Noosa Lakes B & B
Sigrid & Otto Simon
384 Lake Cooroibah Road, Tewantin, Qld 4565

Tel: (07) 5447 1263 Fax: (07) 5449 8000
Mobile: 0412 714 138   noosabnb@ottcom.net
www.ottcom.net/noosabnb

Double $79 Single $49 (Full Breakfast)
2 persons Separate Studio $89
Pets welcome Smoking area inside
1 Queen 1 Double (2 bdrm)   2 Private

German-born hosts have travelled the world and know that you love a natural environment away from it all but only 10 minutes from cosmopolitan Noosa, Australia's "St. Tropez"! Walk through our 10-acre, unspoilt bushland to the lake or the National Park, only watched by kangaroos & great birdlife. Enjoy our gourmet breakfast and your privacy. Get touring advice (we're living here 18 years), e.g. for Fraser Island and the hinterland or just relax on our great beaches. Bring your pet and do your e-mailing. We have a Labrador dog and welcome your pet. We guarantee a holiday you remember!

Noosa Hinterland - Cooroy   *B & B   5 km N of Cooroy*

Cudgerie Homestead B & B   AAAT★★★☆
David & Jenny Mathers
42 Cudgerie Drive, Cooroy, Qld 4563

Tel: (07) 5442 6681 cudgerie@hotmail.com
www.bbbook.com.au/cudgeriebb.html

Double $100-$125 Single $65-$75 (Full Breakfast)
Child discount Dinner $35 B/A
2 Queen 1 Double 1 Twin (4 bdrm)
3 Ensuite 1 Private

Conveniently located 20 mins from Noosa, 90 mins from Brisbane. Historic homestead lovingly converted to modern B&B. French doors lead from your comfortable bedroom to wide verandahs with magnificent views over tropical gardens, mountains and forests to the Noosa horizon. Relax over a sumptuous gourmet breakfast. Enjoy a romantic candlelit evening meal on the verandah in summer, or by the log fire in winter. Close to quality restaurants, local craft markets, galleries, bushwalking, beaches, fishing, golf course, horse-riding and more. Friendly and professional young hosts. Exceptional quality in a perfect location.

Noosa - Noosa Valley   *B & B   7 km W of Noosaville*

Noosa Country House B & B   AAAT ★★★★
Doreen & Bryan Constable
93 Duke Road, Noosa Valley, Qld 4562

Tel: (07) 5471 0121 Fax: (07) 5471 0941
www.bbbook.com.au/noosacountryhousebb.html

Double $135-$165 Single $90-$125
(Special Breakfast) Credit Cards accepted
4 Queen (4 bdrm)
4 Ensuite

On 12 acres in sub-tropical Noosa Valley. "Birdwatchers Paradise". Kangaroos. Heated spa. Woodfire in guest's sitting room. Port/chocolates. Air-cond. Bedrooms have fresh flowers, fruit/cheese platter, tea/coffee, fridge/C/fans. Each opening onto verandah, where we serve your private gourmet breakfast at a time to suit you. We have a genuine love of Noosa and provide a wealth of knowledge, maps, about things to do, where to eat. Fraser Island Tour pick up at front door. Not suitable for children. Discreet personal service. "Simply the best -total relaxation" Alan & Shirley.

Noosa - Noosa Valley   *B & B*   *10 km SW of Noosa*

Noosa Valley Manor Luxury B & B
AAAT ★★★★☆   Dianne Ray & Bruce Chapman
115 Wust Road, Doonan, Noosa Valley, Qld 4562

Tel: (07) 5471 0088 Mobile: 0408 034 080
Fax: (07) 5471 0066   www.noosavalleymanor.com.au
noosa_valley_manor@bigpond.com

Double $130-$145 (Full Breakfast)
Dinner In-House Meals Available
Stay 6 nights or longer only $120 per night
Credit Cards accepted
1 King/Twin 3 Queen (4 bdrm)   4 Ensuite

Weddings and Ceremonies. Award winning gardens. Personal service and comfort is assured. Rest on a magnificent covered terrace overlooking sub-tropical gardens and splendid landscaped rose gardens full of native birds. Relax around the heated pool and spa or fire and enjoy that enchanting feeling. Just the place to enjoy a pampered break, stay for a day or a week. An adults only retreat. Nature & Elegance Noosa Valley Manor the Perfect Mix. Our motto, "Arrive as guests leave as friends."

Noosa - Peregian   *B & B*   *Self Contained*   *14 km S of Noosa*

Lake Weyba Cottages   AAATourism ★★★★☆
Philip & Samantha Bown
79 Clarendon Road, Peregian Beach, Qld 4573

Tel: (07) 5448 2285 Fax: (07) 5448 1714
Mobile: 0404 863 504
info@lakeweybacottages.com
www.lakeweybacottages.com

Double $140-$220 (Full Breakfast)
Credit Cards accepted
1 King/Twin 4 Queen (5 bdrm)
5 Ensuite

Luxury self-contained cottages on the shores of Lake Weyba. Our cottages are designed for couples and feature double spas with soothing water views, a wood fire for winter and air-conditioning for summer. Each morning, a choice of 4 breakfasts is served to the verandah with a newspaper, perfect for relaxing and watching passing kangaroos and the abundant bird life. Only 5 minutes to Peregian Beach and just 15 minutes south of Noosa. Facilities include canoeing, cycling, swimming and fishing.

Stanthorpe   *Homestay*   *8 km S of Stanhorpe*

Jireh
Ken & Margaret Taylor
PO Box 64, Severnlea

Tel: (07) 4683 5298 ktaylor3@vtown.com.au
www.bbbook.com.au/jireh.html

Double $90-$110 Single $50 (Full Breakfast)
Child $25 Dinner $20 - $25 under 1 yrs half price
Pet on property Pets welcome
3 Double 1 Single (3 bdrm)
1 Ensuite 1 Share

A cosy farmhouse B&B in a quiet rural setting, close to the wineries and national parks of the Granite Belt. Antiques and country decor reflect family history and memorabilia, and includes many examples of Margaret's embroidery, patchwork, dolls and bears. Hearty home-grown country breakfasts are served and dinner (Traditional or Indian) is by arrangement. The combination of country home, personal attention, household pets, farm animals, and country rambles offers both a unique experience and value for money. " Wonderful friendly atmosphere and simply great food."

Sunshine Coast - Buderim   *3 km N of Buderim*
Self Contained B & B Cabins

Buderim Rainforest Cabins Bed and Breakfast
AAATourism ★★★★☆
Michael Sumner
27 Earlybird Drive, Buderim, Qld 4556

Tel: (07) 5445 4050
info@rainforestcabins.com.au
www.rainforestcabins.com.au
Double $130-$198 (Full Breakfast)
Credit Cards accepted
5 Queen (5 bdrm)   5 Ensuite

Do you want to know a Secret about a magical place in the rainforest? A place to escape for that perfect romantic getaway or a quiet honeymoon. Choose from in-house rooms or luxury 4 1/2 star cabins with double spa baths, log fires, verandah. Privacy assured yet only minutes to the fabulous beaches at Mooloolaba and Alexandra Headland. On site saltwater pool and all set on 7 acres of rainforest. Packages and gift certificates available. In-cabin massages, flowers, lunch hampers can be arranged. Bliss!!!

Sunshine Coast - Buderim   *500m E of Buderim   Bed and Breakfast*

Aquila House Luxury Accommodation
AAATourism ★★★★☆   Horst & Ophelia Rechlin
21 Box Street, Buderim, Qld 4556

Tel: (07) 5445 3681 Fax: (07) 5456 1140
Mobile: 0417 614 507   aquilaguest@bigpond.com
www.guesthousequeensland.com
Double $180-$250 Single $165-$235 (Full Breakfast)
Dinner on request 3 Nights mid-week special 25% off
Credit Cards accepted
7 Queen (7 bdrm)   7 Ensuite

Ask for our 3 Nights mid-week special! Experience the Magic of Eco-Architecture Where life is perfectly in tune with nature... Set on a hillside above the central Sunshine Coast, it is surrounded by it's own, lavishly landscaped, private gardens. 4 hectares of subtropical beauty where the contemporary architecture is in harmony with the environment. With seven spacious Queen rooms radiating from a central meeting place, a stay at Aquila House can be as social or as private as you like it to be. Winner of HMAA and AAAT Accommodation Industry Awards for Excellence 2002.

Sunshine Coast - Buderim - Tanawha   *5 km W of Buderim*
B & B Semi Self Contained

Main Creek Bower B & B   AAATourism ★★★★☆
Loretta Ford & Pam Fletcher
123 - 125 Main Creek Road, Tanawha, Qld 4556

Tel: (07) 5476 8327 Fax: (07) 5476 8327
Mobile: 0419 759 460   mcbower@bigpond.com
www.bbbook.com.au/maincreek.html
Double $132 Single $66 (Continental Breakfast)
Child $33 eftpos & Bank Card accepted
1 Double 2 Single (2 bdrm)   1 Private

One private cabin in 1930's Queensland style, originally a church hall, which is alongside our 1930's Queenslander. For exclusive use whether single, couple or family group. Away from the hype of the tourist strip. Between the sea and the hinterland nestled in rainforest. Kitchenette with microwave, lounge, television, CD, reverse cycle air-conditioning, barbecue and laundry. Child and small pet friendly. Our Jack Russells, Rupert and Godfrey will let us know when you have arrived. Cats, Claude and Amos you will hardly see. Smoking outside only.

Sunshine Coast - Eumundi *B & B   0.3 km N of Town*

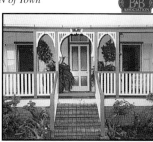

Eumundi Gridley Homestead   AAATourism ★★★★
John and Joyce Turnbull
Cnr Memorial and Sale Streets, Eumundi, Qld 4562

Tel: (07) 5442 7197 Fax: (07) 5442 7198
Mobile: 0419 218 347   info@gridley.com.au
www.bbbook.com.au/eumundigridley.html

Double $110 Single $90
(Continental & Full Breakfast) Dinner from $15
Credit Cards accepted
2 King/Twin 3 Double (4 bdrm)   4 Ensuite

Gridley Homestead is a 100 year old Queenslander beautifully restored and extended in a lovely garden setting on the site of the first white settler in Eumundi. Has beautiful mountain and river views: is 500m. from Eumundi's famous markets, its historic streetscape, its art galleries and a winery.   Fashionable Noosa and its beaches are 15 minutes away as are quaint little nearby towns. Your hosts provide a gourmet breakfast, help with tours and relaxation. Group packages, small conferences and weddings catered for.

Sunshine Coast Hinterland - Mapleton   *12 km W of Nambour*
B & B and Cottage

Eden Lodge B & B   AAATourism ★★★★
Kay and Russell Ezzy
97 Flaxton Drive, Mapleton, Qld 4560

Tel: (07) 5445 7678 Fax: (07) 5445 7653
Mobile: 0407 442 290   kay@edenlodge.com.au
www.edenlodge.com.au

Double $88-$110 Single $78-$88 (Full Breakfast)
S/C Cottage $120 - $140 Credit Cards accepted
1 King/Twin 4 Queen 1 Single (4 bdrm)
2 Ensuite 2 Private

Eden Lodge is situated at the northern Gateway to the Hinterland and welcomes you to a relaxing and refreshing stay on the range. A lovely, private Garden Cottage with fire place and four very comfortable rooms in the B&B give you a choice of accommodation. Fabulous views from coast to hinterland, plenty of native bird life, and delicious breakfast are all included in your affordable accommodation package.   Midweek and longer term rates available.

Sunshine Coast Hinterland - Montville *B & B   3 km N of Montville*

Tanderra House B & B   AAATourism ★★★★
Leah Sanders
11 Flaxton Mill Road, Flaxton, Qld 4560

Tel: (07) 5445 7179 Fax: (07) 5445 7120
Mobile: 0409 544 571   leah@tanderrahouse.com.au
www.tanderrahouse.com.au

Double $100-$175 Single $80-$150 (Full Breakfast)
Child $30 Credit Cards accepted
3 King/Twin 2 Queen 4 Twin 1 Single (5 bdrm)
3 Ensuite 2 Private

This beautiful historical homestead situated on 2 1/2 acres of stately gardens is now offering first class bed & breakfast in the heart of the Blackall Range. Only minutes to Montville's fine restaurants and shops and Kondalilla Falls National Park. Large private suites with own bathrooms and French doors opening onto wide verandahs. Start your day with home-baked croissants, plunger coffee, fresh fruit and a full cooked breakfast served on the verandah. Gift vouchers, Murder Mystery's, Christmas in July, Weddings and Conferences catered for.

Queensland

Sunshine Coast - Ninderry - Yandina - Coolum   *5 km E of Yandina*
B & B

Ninderry House
Mary Lambart
8 Karnu Drive, Ninderry, Qld 4561

Tel: (07) 5446 8556
www.bbbook.com.au/ninderryhouse.html
Double $130 Single $75 (Full Breakfast)
Dinner $20 - $25 Credit Cards accepted
1 King/Twin 1 Queen 2 Twin (3 bdrm)
3 Ensuite

Central Sunshine Coast location, views overlooking Mt Ninderry and Maroochy Valley to the Ocean. Close to beaches, native plant nurseries, ginger factory, art galleries, craft and produce markets of Eumundi and Yandina. First class restaurants nearby. Three ensuite guestrooms, comfortable sitting room with fire, deck for summer breezes or winter sun. Imaginative meals using fresh local produce. Special diets catered for. Dinner available if requested on booking. Full breakfast included in tariff. Children not catered for. Ph 07 5446 8556.

Thornton - Laidley   *50 km E of Toowoomba*
Farmstay B & B S/C Cottage

Denbigh Farm   AAATourism ★★★★
Warren & Judith Jefferys, 220 Mulgowie -Townson Rd,
Thornton via Laidley, Qld 4341

Tel: (07) 5466 7190 Fax: (07) 5466 7190
Mobile: 0418 290 612   visitus@denbighfarm.com
www.denbighfarm.com
Double $99-$143 Single $74-$91 (Full Breakfast)
Dinner $12-$25 per person Cottage $99-143
Credit Cards accepted Pet on property
3 Queen (3 bdrm)   1 Private 1 Share

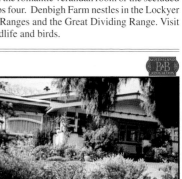

Denbigh Farm, the original Thornton State School was built in 1889. The original ceilings and walls boast a height of 15 feet. In the main house you may stay in the romantic verandah room or the secluded garden room. There is also a s/c garden cottage which sleeps four. Denbigh Farm nestles in the Lockyer Valley surrounded by magnificent views of the Liverpool Ranges and the Great Dividing Range. Visit us for a great getaway. Enjoy the farm animals, native wildlife and birds.

Toowoomba   *B & B*

Lauriston House B & B   AAATourism ★★★★☆
Greg & Yvonne Blakeney
67 Margaret Street, Toowoomba, Qld 4350

Tel: (07) 4632 4053 Fax: (07) 4639 5526
Mobile: 0417 630 807
lauristonhouse@bigpond.com
www.babs.com.au/lauriston
Double $140-$165 Single $95-$120
(Special Breakfast) Credit Cards accepted
1 King 1 Queen (2 bdrm)   2 Ensuite

Enjoy our heritage home & extensive gardens situated in the heart of Toowoomba. Minutes walk to Queens Park, restaurants, & antique galleries, Elegant King/Queen bedrooms with the finest linen, modern ensuite facilities, fresh flowers & R/C A/C. The spacious guest lounge with log fire exudes the atmosphere of a bygone era. Fine art and antiques which your hosts have collected from travels around the world decorate the house. Our fully cooked Gourmet breakfasts and country hospitality are special. Separate guest entrance, off street parking, fax and email facilities.

Toowoomba - Highfields *19 km N of Toowoomba*
Homestay B & B Self Contained

Oakleigh Country Cottage   AAATourism ★★★★☆
Lyn & Howard Postle
Lot 10 Bowtell Drive, Highfields, Qld 4352

Tel: (07) 4696 7021 Fax: (07) 4696 7284
Mobile: 0417 720 113   oakleighbnb@ozemail.com.au
www.bbbook.com.au/oakleighcottage.html

Double $120-$140 Single $75-$90 (Full Breakfast)
Child $20 Dinner B/A Credit Cards accepted
Pet on property Pets welcome
2 Queen 2 Single (2 bdrm)   1 Ensuite 1 Private

Experience the true meaning of 'getting away from it all' at Oakleigh where our beautiful rose gardens, country views and farmyard pets will refresh you. Relax in front of the cosy wood fire in the private, self-contained cottage where you can read a book, watch a video or listen to your favourite music and let the romantic country ambience envelope you. Alternatively you can stay in our beautiful homestead where we indulge you with our hearty country meals and warm and friendly hospitality.

Townsville *Homestay B & B Guest House*   *Townsville*

The Rocks Historic Guesthouse
Jennie Ginger and Joe Sproats
20 Cleveland Terrace, Townsville, Qld 4810

Tel: (07) 4771 5700 Fax: (07) 4771 5711
Mobile: 0416 044 409
therocks@therocksguesthouse.com
www.therocksguesthouse.com

Double $99-$119 Single $79-$99 (Special Breakfast)
Child $20 Credit Cards accepted Pet on property
1 Queen 5 Double 2 Twin (8 bdrm)   4 Ensuite 2 Share

Joe, Jennie and Sebastian live in one of Townsville most loved buildings, The Rock Guesthouse. Built in 1886 it boasts wide-open verandas overlooking Cleveland Bay and Magnetic Island. It also offers a billiard room, spa, And Victorian Drawing Room with piano and grandfather clock. Breakfast is served with collectible English china and silverware in the dining room/library, amongst eccentric collections. The multi award winning Rocks is centrally located making for an easy walk to the beach, restaurants, and city heart and nightlife areas.

Whitsunday Coast - Hydeaway Bay   *Homestay B & B*   *40 km NE of Proserpine*

Shenandoah
David & Maren Matthew
119 Gloucester Avenue,
Hydeaway Bay MS2248, Qld 4800

Tel: (07) 4945 7116 Fax: (07) 4945 7283
Mobile: 0414 904 970
marenm@tpg.com.au
www4.tpg.com.au/users/marenm

Double $90 Single $70 (Continental Breakfast)
Dinner $25 Pet on property
2 Queen (2 bdrm)   2 Ensuite 2 Private

Shenandoah is situated in one of the best kept secrets of the Whitsunday's. Our home is situated in a beautiful bushland setting 90 metres from the beach. Enjoy the wonders of the coral reef by walking or snorkelling in the aquamarine waters. Fishing, walking and observing the native wildlife are some of the pastimes. Each large well appointed room has a queen size bed ensemble, sitting area, air-conditioning, ceiling fans and your own en-suite bathroom. Not suitable for small children, no pets.

Yeppoon - Capricorn Coast   *B & B*   *2.4 km N of Yeppoon*

While Away B & B AAATourism ★★★★☆
Darryl Sloan
44 Todd Avenue, Yeppoon, Qld 4703

Tel: (07) 4939 5719 Fax: (07) 4939 5577
Mobile: 0421 074 064
whileaway@bigpond.com
www.bbbook.com.au/whileawaybb.html

Double $95-$105 Single $85 (Continental Breakfast)
Credit Cards accepted
1 King 3 Queen 2 Single (4 bdrm)
4 Ensuite

While Away B&B has been purpose built with the traveller in mind. We offer style, comfort and privacy in modern home less than 100 m to beach. All rooms have ensuites and are air-conditioned. We offer a generous tropical breakfast at a time to suit you - tea/coffee making facilities with cake/biscuits are available at all times. We are a much travelled couple who will do our best to ensure you enjoy your stay in this area.

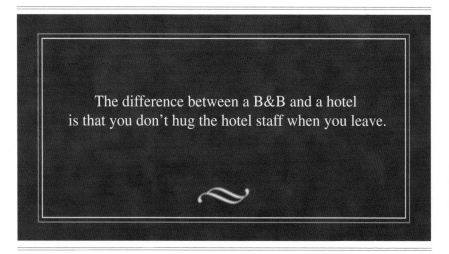

The difference between a B&B and a hotel
is that you don't hug the hotel staff when you leave.

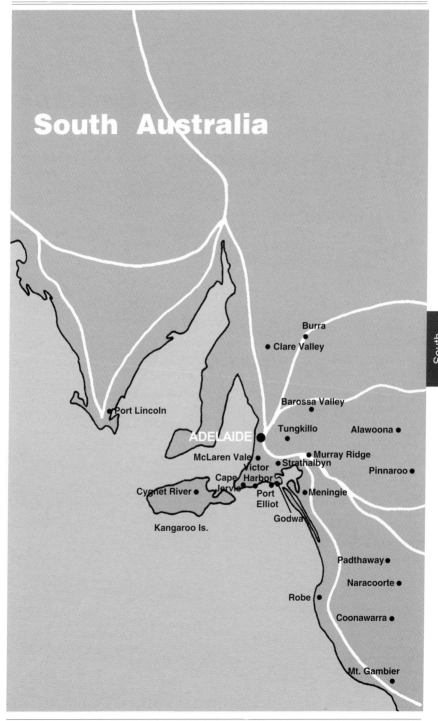

South Australia

Burra

Clare Valley

Barossa Valley

Port Lincoln

Tungkillo

Alawoona

ADELAIDE

McLaren Vale

Murray Ridge

Victor

Strathalbyn

Pinnaroo

Cape Harbor

Cygnet River

Jervie

Port Elliot

Meningie

Godwa

Kangaroo Is.

Padthaway

Naracoorte

Robe

Coonawarra

Mt. Gambier

South Australia

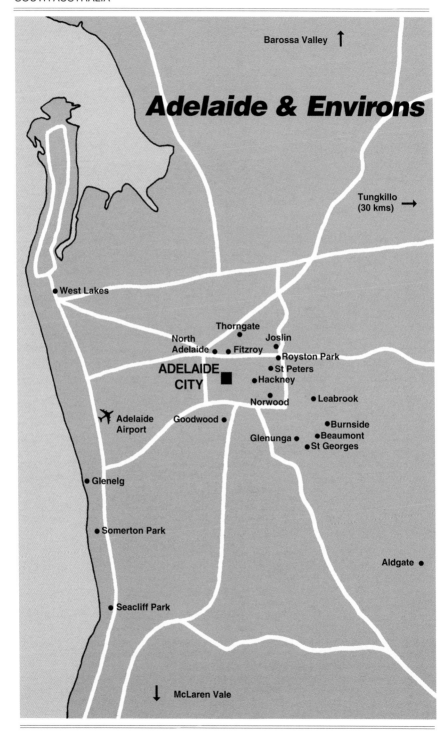

Adelaide - Burnside *B & B   Self Contained   6 km SE of Adelaide*

Petts Wood Lodge   AAATourism ★★★
Deborah Miller
542 Glynburn Road, Burnside, SA 5066

Tel: (08) 8331 9924 Fax: (08) 8332 5139
Mobile: 0408 829 666
pettswood@adelaide.on.net
www.users.on.net/pettswood

Double $105 Single $95 (Continental Breakfast)
Child $25 - $45 Credit Cards accepted
2 Queen 1 Single (2 bdrm)   2 Ensuite

Petts Wood Lodge is a charming two story English Tudor style residence nestled amongst a tranquil garden, by a willow-lined stream. The Garden and Attic Suites both adjoin the main residence, but have separate entrances. They feature ensuite bathrooms, kitchen facilities and a sofa bed in the lounge for a third person. Petts Wood is ideally located, a bus stop at the door, close to shops, the city centre, restaurants, parks and walking trails. Day Tours are easily accessible Member SAB&BT&C. No Pets. Cot and BBQ available. Air-conditioned

Adelaide - Burnside - St Georges *5 km SE of Adelaide*

B & B   Self Contained
Kirkendale   AAATourism ★★★★
Jenny & Steve Studer
16 Inverness Avenue, St. Georges, SA 5064

Tel: (08) 8338 2768 Fax: (08) 8338 2760
Mobile: 0413 414 140   kirken@internode.on.net
www.bbbook.com.au/kirkendale.html

Double $90-$110 (Continental Breakfast)
Child $15 - $20 Credit Cards accepted
1 Queen 2 Single (2 bdrm)   1 Private

South Australia

Idyllic "Country-style" 3 room suite, nestled in peaceful leafy garden, sun-dappled patio, French doors, terracotta floors, rose garden. A hint of the Provence. Fresh flowers, fruit basket, generous breakfasts, books, tourist information. Separate entrance, private bathroom, living room, kitchenette, sole occupancy. Quiet location. 5 km city, near restaurants, wineries, wildlife parks. Jenny and Steve are extremely well travelled, this is reflected by their gracious but unobtrusive hosting. Tours arranged. Smoking outdoors. "We loved our accommodation - our best yet in 6 weeks of travel." SS & DC, USA.

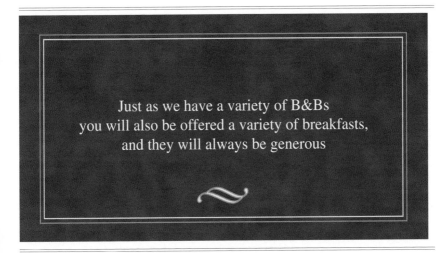

Just as we have a variety of B&Bs
you will also be offered a variety of breakfasts,
and they will always be generous

Adelaide - Central   *Self Contained B & B Cottages*   *Adelaide Central*

Adelaide Old Terraces   Ann Schioldann
26 QueenStreet, Adelaide, SA 5000
26 Blackburn Street, Adelaide, SA 5000

Tel: (08) 8364 5437 Mobile: 0416 150 655
Fax: (08) 8364 6961   stay@adelaideoldterraces.com.au
www.adelaideoldterraces.com.au

Double $140-$160 (Continental Breakfast) Child $20
Extra guest $40-$45   Credit Cards accepted
2 King 4 Queen 4 Double 1 Twin (4 Cottages)
6 Private

Relax in the privacy of one of our delightful historic cottages for your exclusive use. Situated in the inner-city, stroll to the colourful central markets, Festival Centre, Casino, CBD. Explore nearby parklands, gardens, restaurants and cafes. All four cottages are fully self contained, with courtyard gardens and a unique blend of Asian antique furnishings and accommodate 2 - 7 persons per cottage. Suitable for families, groups or romantic getaways. Airport bus to door. Danish, French and German spoken. Weekly rates. Concessions 4-6 sharing.

Adelaide - Fitzroy   *B & B   Self Contained   2.5 km N of Adelaide*

Whinham House
Julia Ann Jenkins
20 Whinham Street, Fitzroy, Adelaide, SA 5082

Tel: (08) 8269 3131 Fax: (08) 8269 3131
Mobile: 0439 727 895
info@whinhamhouse.com.au
www.whinhamhouse.com.au

Double $110-$130 (Full Breakfast)
3 Queen 2 Twin (3 bdrm)
3 Ensuite 1 Private

This charming bluestone villa, circa 1890, located in prestigious Fitzroy, adjacent to O'Connell Street, Adelaide's trendiest restaurant strip. Whinham House is the ideal choice for both corporate travellers, for location and home office facilities, and the holiday maker seeking the best of South Australia. Breakfast on the deck overlooking the tropical garden and listen to the waterfall. Enjoy the romance of the open fires, large spa bath, and complimentary champagne. Be thoroughly spoilt at Whinham House - The Discerning Choice.

Adelaide - Glenelg   *B & B   12km SW of Adelaide*

Angove Villa   AAATourism ★★★★
Margie & Rob White
14 Angove Road, Glenelg South, SA 5044

Tel: (08) 8376 6421 Fax: (08) 8376 9058
angovevilla@chariot.net.au
www.chariot.net.au/~angovevilla

Double $145 Single $135 (Full Breakfast)
Dinner B/A Seasonal concessions for longer stays
Credit Cards accepted
1 Queen (1 bdrm)   1 Ensuite

Close to Glenelg, South Australia's premier beachside tourist precinct, experience the luxurious ambience of this heritage style villa. With own entrance, this three roomed suite for your exclusive use includes private sitting room, ensuite bathroom, brass bed, air-conditioning, plunger coffee, quality teas, fresh fruit, port and truffles. Enjoy a sumptuous cooked breakfast including morning newspaper. Take a stroll along the sandy beach to historic, cosmopolitan Glenelg. Enjoy alfresco cafes, extensive shopping and cinemas. Within 20 minutes of wineries, golf courses, airport and City.

Adelaide - Glenunga *Homestay 5 km SE of Adelaide*

Bayree City Homestay
Doris & Cyril Kuehne
5 Rowell Avenue, Glenunga, SA 5064

Tel: (08) 8338 3707 Fax: (08) 8338 3701
Mobile: 0417 844 827   cdkuehne@chariot.net.au
www.chariot.net.au/~cdkuehne

Double $85-$100 Single $80
(Full Breakfast) Dinner B/A
1 Queen 1 Double (2 bdrm)
1 Private 1 Share

Bayree City Homestay, in leafy Glenunga, is the ideal base from which to explore Adelaide and surrounds. Some of Adelaide's most fashionable shops and restaurants are close at hand. Friendly and personalised service is offered amidst charming surrounds. The spacious guest area includes private bathroom, a/c gas fire, colour tv, tea and coffee making, laundry facilities. A 2 min walk to public transport, 30 mins to airport and 10 mins to CBD. Tours arranged. Your hosts have been entertaining guests since 1989.

Adelaide - Goodwood *Homestay B & B   2 km S of Adelaide*

Rose Villa
Doreen Petherick
29 Albert Street,
Goodwood, SA 5034

Tel: (08) 8271 2947 Fax: (08) 8271 2947
rosevilla@bigpond.com.au
www.picknowl.com.au/homepages/rosevilla

Double $105-$125 Single $95-$105
(Full Breakfast)
1 King 1 Queen (2 bdrm)
1 Ensuite 1 Private

Treat yourself to a romantic candle lit breakfast in my newly decorated Tea Rose salon. Rose Villa offers an elegant private suite (own entrance) overlooking the garden. Inside is an additional guest room with the use of the exquisite Blue-White-Russian Tea Cup bathroom. Stroll to trendy Hyde Park Road with its delightful cafes and coffee shops, boutiques and flower shops. Close by are buses and trams (to the Bay) and city. "Rose Villa" is roses, romance and caring hospitality. You are most welcome.

Adelaide - Hackney *1.5 km Adelaide*

Self Contained Separate/Suite

Fenners   AAATourism ★★★★☆
Wendy Alstergreen
7 Athelney Avenue, Hackney, SA 5069

Tel: (08) 8363 4436 Fax: (08) 8132 1057
studiosuite@fennersofadelaide.com
www.fennersofadelaide.com

Double $110-$140 (Continental Breakfast)
 Credit Cards accepted Pet on property
1 King (1 bdrm)
1 Ensuite

Treat yourself. Self contained large studio suite. Stylish, quiet and private. Easy walk to city, restaurants and gallery through the Botanic gardens. French doors open to vine covered courtyard. King size bed, video, tape and CD player. Daily breakfast provisions available from 3pm. Booking secured by credit card number. Parking by arrangement. "A wonderful place to stay tranquil and charming in every respect." CTN, Brisbane.

Adelaide Hills - Aldgate   *20 km SE of Adelaide*
Luxury Homestay   Separate/Suite   B & B

Arboury Manor
Roy and Julie Watson
11 Nation Ridge Road, Aldgate, SA 5154

Tel: (08) 8370 9119 Fax: (08) 8370 9484
arboury@bigpond.com   www.arbourymanor.com.au
Double $140 (Special Breakfast) Child $15 - $30
Dinner $15 - $45 Suites $170 - $210
Credit Cards accepted
3 Queen 1 Double 2 Twin (4 bdrm)   4 Private

This Grand Lady of the Hills sits in one of the most majestic settings only a short distance from Adelaide's CBD, Intl/Domestic airport and Hahndorf. Centrally located to the various tourist attractions, wineries and beaches Arboury Manor makes a great base while staying in Adelaide. The property features - Majestic entrance; large formal dining room; individually designed suites; stunning views; abundance of bird life; extensive formal gardens; magnificent grounds. Beautiful scenery and very friendly people make Arboury Manor an interesting and exciting destination.

Adelaide - Joslin - Royston Park   *5 km NE of Adelaide*
Homestay   B & B   Self Contained

Lambert House   AAATourism ★★★★
Jenny & Paul Gunson
31 Lambert Road, Joslin, Adelaide, SA 5070

Tel: (08) 8363 7222   users.senet.com.au/~lamberth
Fax: (08) 8362 7575   lamberthouse@senet.com.au
Double $130 Single $80-$90 (Special Breakfast)
Child $20 - $25 Dinner $25 - $35
Self-Contined Unit $80 - $130 Credit Cards accepted
1 King/Twin 1 Queen 1 Twin 1 Single (2 bdrm)
1 Ensuite 1 Private 1 Share

Lambert House is an early Australian bungalow built in 1922, a comfortable family home in quiet location offering air conditioning, floodlit tennis court, leafy gardens, guests sitting room, laundry facilities and bicycles, for use on near by Linear Park walking and cycling track. Base yourself in Adelaide, close to public transport and restaurants. Winery tours and farm visits can be arranged. Longer term rates available at our near by self contained garden apartment. Private car parking. We have a cat. Children welcome. We look forward to spoiling you.

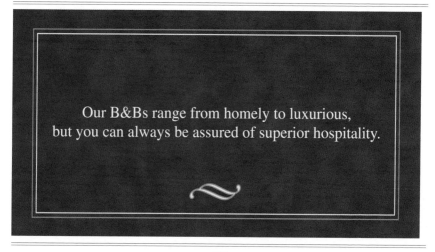

Adelaide - Leabrook   *Homestay B & B   5km E of Adelaide*

Leabrook Lodge   AAATourism ★★★☆
Barbara Carter, 314 Kensington Road, Leabrook, Adelaide, SA 5068

Tel: (08) 8331 7619 Fax: (08) 8364 4955 Mobile: 0411 665 144
barbara.carter@bigpond.com   www.bbbook.com.au/leabrooklodge.html

Double $85-$95 Single $60-$70 (Full Breakfast) Dinner $20 - $25 Credit Cards accepted
Pet on property   1 Queen 1 Twin 2 Single (4 bdrm)   2 Ensuite 1 Share

Leabrook Lodge is a traditional B&B ideally located in one of Adelaide's most prestigious suburbs (east of Adelaide and near the foothills). The charming stone bungalow, with its period decor, provides guests with quiet accommodation in a restful atmosphere where they can stay and enjoy their visit. It is convenient for business people or travellers alike. It's easy to find whether coming by plane, train or car.

All bedrooms have a garden view which includes huge gum trees that attract native birds; seating throughout the garden invites guests to locate a book from an extensive library and sit quietly outside. Breakfast is served in a courtyard when the weather is especially inviting, or there are log fires when the weather is chilly.

There are five excellent restaurants 200m away and Norwood Parade which has restaurants 'cheek by jowl' is 1 1/2 km distant. A free dinner is available with family and friends on Wednesday nights (organic ingredients are used whenever possible). Bushwalks are close to the hills or for the less active, it is pleasant to walk through the nearby parks and gardens. The property is adjacent to the local bus and the availability of the Day Pass makes it easy to manage without a car and yet negotiate the city and environs without difficulty.

Traditional B&B is for the guest who prefers to have their breakfast prepared and someone who wants information which is geared to their precise needs. Laundry facilities are here for those that need them. Two short-haired Dachshunds in residence.

Adelaide is the most centrally placed city, handy for Coober Pedy, Ayers Rock, Kangaroo Island as well as the Flinders Ranges. It is blessed with a Mediterranean climate, blue skies and lovely beaches.

COME TO ADELAIDE
COME TO LEABROOK LODGE B&B

Adelaide - Leabrook *Self Contained Apartment 5 km E of Adelaide Central*

City Fringe Apartment
Diana Hooper
15/15 Statenborough Street, Leabrook, SA 5068

Tel: (08) 8762 3038 Fax: (08) 8762 3394
Mobile: 0418 838 213   wongary@rbm.com.au
www.wongary.com.au

Double $85 Single $75 (Continental Breakfast)
Child $20 Credit Cards accepted
1 Queen 1 Double 1 Single (2 bdrm)   1 Private

Private, self-contained, tiny upstairs apartment. Beautifully appointed sitting room features peaceful balcony, reverse cycle air-conditioning, TV, video, CD, books, games and magazines. Fully equipped kitchen with good coffee. Stroll leafy streets to nearby parks offering summer swimming and spa, tennis courts, playgrounds and BBQ's. Minutes from Adelaide's theatres, restaurants, shops, bustling markets, Burnside Village and cosmopolitan Kensington and Norwood Parade. Enjoy day-trips to Barossa Wineries, McLaren Vale, Hills and Coast. Iron, ironing board and on-site coin-operated washing machine available plus free undercover parking.

Adelaide - North Adelaide *1 km N of Adelaide city centre*

B & B heritage accommodation

Adelaide Seek and Share   AAATourism ★★★★☆
Judy Fitzhardinge
112 Barnard Street, North Adelaide, SA 5006

Tel: (08) 8239 0155 Fax: (08) 8239 0125
Mobile: 0411 171 807   seekfitz@iweb.net.au
www.seekshare.com.au

Double $135-$195 Single $110-$150 (Full Breakfast)
Child $40 over age 2 years
Credit Cards accepted Pets welcome
3 Queen 1 Twin (4 bdrm)   3 Ensuite 1 Private

Adelaide Seek and Share is a heritage-listed property, 4 1/2 star AAAT rated, only 1 kilometre from Adelaide city, 500 metres from some of the best restaurants and cafes in Adelaide. The bluestone gentleman's residence has been sensitively renovated to include four lovely spacious bedrooms, two with large spa bathrooms and one with and an old style bathroom, a fourth bedroom is available on request. Seek and Share is magnificently decorated with Victorian antique furniture, leadlight and truly comfortable beds.

Adelaide - Norwood *Homestay B & B   3 km E of Adelaide CBD*

Laurel Villa
M L Crisp
101 Kensington Road, Norwood, SA 5067

Tel: (08) 8332 7388
Fax: (08) 8332 7388 or (08)8431 5902
www.bbbook.com.au/laurelvilla.html

Double $78 Single $52
(Special Breakfast) Child $35
1 Double 2 Twin (2 bdrm)
1 Share

Picture a 102-year-old State Heritage listed Victorian bluestone villa, with its original ceiling roses, chandeliers, fireplaces; thick stone walls affording complete privacy. Secure parking in private front courtyard; cozy patio in back garden. In historic Norwood on bus line 3 km from Adelaide CBD with its myriad museums, art galleries, parklands, bushwalks. Picture Norwood's 57 restaurants, cafes and colonial pubs offering ethnic and Australian cuisine at very modest prices.   Offering superb B & B for less since 1982. Please reply by telephone or fax. Payment by cash or cheque please.

Adelaide - Seacliff Park - Brighton   *Homestay B & B   2km S of Brighton*

Homestay Brighton
Ruth Humphrey & Tim Lorence
PO Box 319, Brighton, SA 5048

Tel: (08) 8298 6671 Fax: (08) 8298 6671
Mobile: 0417 800 755   timlorence@hotmail.com
www.bbbook.com.au/brighton.html

Double $60-$70 Single $40-$50
(Full Breakfast) Child B/A
1 Double 2 Single (2 bdrm)
1 Private 1 Share

Our spacious home and grounds are in a quiet suburb close to Brighton beach, bus and train routes to the city or day trips to the southern Fleurieu Peninsula. Guest rooms are upstairs including a TV-lounge area with heating and cooling. We can discuss your requirements for children, pets or to be met on arrival. Laundry and off-street parking available. Please phone, fax, write or e-mail. "Home from home" LJ, UK. "Top class in all respects" KB, Caloundra. "Like staying with friends" SC, Crookwell. "Loved staying here, will be back" GB, Melbourne.

Adelaide - Somerton Park   *Homestay B & B   2.5 km S of Glenelg*

Forstens Bed & Breakfast
John & Marilyn Forsten
19 King George Avenue,
Somerton Park, SA 5044

Tel: (08) 8298 3393
forstens_bandb@hotmail.com
www.bbbook.com.au/forstensbb.html

Double $65 Single $50 (Full Breakfast)
1 King/Twin 2 Single (1 bdrm)
1 Ensuite

Located in a residential area 600 metres from beautiful Somerton Beach, 2.5km south of the bustling seaside resort of Glenelg with its 'mile' of shopping and dining along Jetty Road. A city bus passes the house en route to Glenelg and Adelaide. Guests are accommodated in a lovely bedroom with a rear garden view, ensuite bath, TV, private entrance and off-street parking. Warm fresh bread is included in the cooked breakfast. Laundry facilities available. You are welcome to use our bicycles if you would like to pedal along the Esplanade! Many of our guests are repeat customers.

Adelaide - West Lakes   *13 km W of Adelaide*

Homestay B & B   Self Contained

Barb's Lakeview Bed and Breakfast
Barb and Ted Rix
29 Lakeview Avenue, West Lakes, SA 5021

Tel: (08) 8447 1420 Mobile: 0410 609 820
barb_rix@hotmail.com
www.bed-and-breakfast.net.au

Double $130 Single $110 (Special Breakfast)
Child $20 Extra person $35
1 Queen 1 Double (2 bdrm)
1 Private with Spa

Relax, enjoy & stay a while... nestled alongside shimmering waters of a lake in picturesque beachside suburb of West Lakes - an hour's drive from world famous Barossa Valley - Australia's leading Wine Region. Everything is close by... beaches, restaurants, sporting venues, airport. •Double spa bath •R/C air conditioning, kitchenette, TV/Video/CD/Radio, use of laundry •Gourmet cooked breakfasts •Bottle of wine, chocolates & flowers, tea, coffee & cookies, complimentary daily newspaper •Use of canoes.

SOUTH AUSTRALIA

Barossa Valley - Tanunda   *Luxury B & B*   *5 km SE of Tanunda*

The Hermitage of Marananga   AAAT★★★★★
Paul & Yin Knight
Cnr Seppeltsfield and Stonewell Roads,
Marananga, SA 5352

Tel: (08) 8562 2722 Fax: (08) 8562 3133
hosts@hermitageofmarananga.com.au
www.hermitageofmarananga.com.au
Double $220-$310 Single $195-$275 (Full Breakfast)
Child $50 Dinner $44 - $66 Credit Cards accepted
11 King (11 bdrm)   11 Ensuite

The Hermitage offers a unique combination of old world country house charm and modern hotel facilities. Spacious suites have amenities typical of the worlds best hotels as well as many added homely touches. Some have spa baths and wood fires . . .perfect for that winter escape. All romantic views through French doors of vineyards, olive groves and hills. Delicious gourmet breakfasts and dinners are served in our cosy dining room. World travellers are known to return every year for the speciality . . .Eggs Marananga. Our aim is to exceed all your expectations. As one American couple wrote after a one week stay. "Truly the essence of the Barossa."

Burra   *Self Contained*   *Burra Central*

Burra Heritage Cottages - Tivers Row
AAATourism ★★★☆
M & B Wright
1 Young Street, Burra, SA 5417

Tel: (08) 8892 2461 Fax: (08) 8892 2948
wright@capri.net.au
www.burraheritagecottages.com.au
Double $110-$140 Single $95 (Full Breakfast)
Child $30 Credit Cards accepted
5 Queen 5 Double 4 Twin (12 bdrm)   6 Private

Built in 1856 and meticulously restored by Barry and Maureen Wright, Tivers Row cottages provide unique accommodation with heritage listed authenticity. Fully self-contained, each with two bedrooms, the six separate cottages have cosy open fires but include extra comforts grandmother didn't have, like television and underfloor heating in the bathroom. A two day stay is recommended to explore the heritage township of Burra and Clare Valley wineries close by. No pets please. Tourism Council of Australia accreditation.

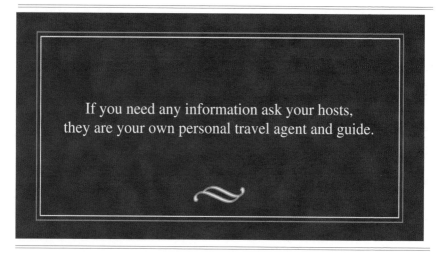

If you need any information ask your hosts,
they are your own personal travel agent and guide.

Clare   *B & B   Self Contained   3 km NE of Sevenhill*

Springfarm Heritage Accommodation Gardener's Retreat
Anne and Glen Kelly
Lot 3 Springfarm Road, Clare, SA 5453

Tel: (08) 8843 4261 Fax: (08) 8843 4261 Mobile: 0411 558 395
www.bbbook.com.au/springfarmretreat.html

Double $120-$140 Single $120-$135 (Special Breakfast)
Credit Cards accepted Pet on property
1 Double (1 bdrm) 1 Ensuite

This delightful two-storey stone retreat, which looks like it should be situated in Provence is privately nestled amid vineyards, historic farm buildings and cottage gardens. There is a romantic upstairs bedroom and a downstairs kitchenette/living/dining area, tastefully decorated in a rustic country style.

Package includes a bottle of Clare Valley wine for stays of 2 nights and provisions for self-catered breakfast.   Reduced tariff for third and subsequent nights.

South Australia

Clare   *B & B   Self Contained   3 km NE of Sevenhill*

Springfarm Heritage Accommodation Edwardian Suite
Anne and Glen Kelly
Lot 3 Springfarm Road, Clare, SA 5443

Tel: (08) 8843 4261 Fax: (08) 8843 4261 Mobile: 0411 558 395
www.bbbook.com.au/springfarmedwardian.html

Double $150-$160 Single $150-$155 Four people in Edwardian Suite $260 - 280
 Credit Cards accepted Pet on property
1 Queen 1 Double (2 bdrm)
1 Ensuite

Edwardian Suite   A touch of romantic elegance situated in the rolling vine-studded hills of the Clare Valley. The Edwardian suite commands picturesque views of glorious sunsets. This lovingly restored residence has beautiful turn-of-the-century appointments, along with the comforts of quality modern conveniences.

• Features include:
• Fully equipped kitchen
• 2 Bedrooms (ensuite attached to Master)
• Antiques
• Deep Claw Bath
• Gardens and Seclusion
• Bottle of Clare Valley wine for stays of 2 nights
• Supplies for self catered breakfasts
Reduced tariff for third and subsequent nights.

Clare Valley - Sevenhill   *Country House*   *6 km S of Clare*

Thorn Park Country House   AAATourism ★★★★☆
Michael Speers & David Hay
College Road, Sevenhill via Clare, SA 5453

Tel: (08) 8843 4304 Fax: (08) 8843 4296 Mobile: 0417 822 597
stay@thornpark.com.au
www.thornpark.com.au

Double $325-$350 Single $225-$250 (Full Breakfast) Child $125 Dinner $55 - $70
Credit Cards accepted
3 King/Twin 2 Queen 1 Double (6 bdrm)
6 Ensuite

In the heart of the Clare Valley lies Thorn Park Country House, a truly magnificent country home of traditional Australian style. Set in 60 acres of pastoral splendour it boasts tranquil vistas of undulating farmland studded with towering gums, grazing sheep and a dam; home to native ducks and other bird life.

The homestead was built in the 1850's from stone quarried on the site and was extensively restored in recent years to its original magnificence. The tranquil gardens feature hawthorn, elms and roses; a surround to the homestead in the traditional manner.

The house spreads itself to include six bedrooms, each with its own ensuite, with accommodation for 12 guests. The reception areas include a spacious drawing room, intimate library and magnificent art collection.

David and Michael are devoted to memorable dining, with food prepared utilising fresh, local produce. Meals are accompanied by the truly magnificent wines of the Clare Valley region.

For enquiries and reservations: Telephone (08) 8843 4304 Fax (08) 8843 4296
South Australian Tourism Award. Winner 1989, 1995, 1996, 1997.   Winner Jaguar Award for Excellence for Gastronomic Travel 2001.

Goolwa   B & B   *1.7 km N of Goolwa*

Birks of Goolwa
Pauline Bruce, 138A Liverpool Road, Goolwa, SA 5714

Tel: (08) 8555 5393 Fax: (08) 8555 5228   Mobile: 0417 150 245
birksofgoolwa@granite.net.au   www.bbbook.com.au/birksofgoolwa.html
Double $160 Single $140 (Full Breakfast)   Child $50 Credit Cards accepted
2 Queen 1 Double (2 bdrm)   2 Ensuite
Overlooking the river, historic Birks of Goolwa exudes character and charm in hosted Bed and Breakfast Accommodation. * Luxuriously appointed guest rooms, R/C air conditioning, queen beds, electric blankets, en suites and televisions. * Living room with log fires, magazines, library CDs and videos. * Guest entrance with refreshment facilities. * Sumptuous full breakfasts. * Wine and hors d'oeuvres on arrival. Relax in the tranquil garden with abundant bird life screened by majestic trees. Indulge in the ambience and privacy of this historic retreat   "Wonderful time, great host. Just fantastic." M.F.

Please let us know how you enjoyed your B&B experience.
Ask your host for a comment form,
or leave a comment on www.bbbook.com.au

McLaren Vale   *B & B*   *39 km S of Adelaide*

Ashcroft Country Accommodation at McLaren Vale   AAATourism ★★★★☆
Terry & Julie Jarvis
Johnston Road, McLaren Vale, SA 5171 **ourism**

Tel: (08) 8323 7700 Fax: (08) 8323 7711
welcome@ashcroftbnb.com.au
www.ashcroftbnb.com.au

Double $160 Single $160 (Continental Breakfast) (Full Breakfast) Child $30
Credit Cards accepted
Pet on property
4 Queen 1 Twin (5 bdrm)
5 Ensuite

Situated in the heart of the McLaren
Vale wine region, 'Ashcroft' is a three
acre country estate/vineyard with
uninterrupted views across to the
magical Willunga Hills.

Each of the five guest rooms in our
air-conditioned home contains an
ensuite bathroom with overhead
heaters, 'Hollywood' lighting, queen
and/or twin beds, television, clock
radio, coffee and tea-making
facilities, bar fridge, electric blanket,
hair-dryer, and its own intimate
private terrace complete with
umbrella, table and chairs. Log fires
in the guest Drawing Room complete
the picture.

Mount Gambier *Homestay   10 km E of Mount Gambier*

Worrolong B & B   AAATourism ★★★★☆
Bernard & Reet Lindner
Box 1309, Mount Gambier, SA 5290

Tel: (08) 8725 2256 Fax: (08) 8725 1074
Mobile: 0409 953 865
www.bbbook.com.au/worrolongbb.html
Double $99-$110 Single $70 (Full Breakfast)
Child $20 Dinner $20 Pet on property
1 Queen 1 Single (1 bdrm)
1 Ensuite

Our B&B is situated on a quiet and pleasant rural property. The spacious comfortable unit has ensuite
with two person spa, separate entrance, undercover parking. We offer country hospitality, with afternoon
tea on arrival, cooked breakfast served in the dining room of our home. We have a resident colourpoint
cat "Bronson". Mount Gambier is known as the Blue Lake City. Tourism facilities are located a short
drive away. These include limestone caves, sink holes and wineries of a world class standard. Smoke
free home.

Naracoorte *Guest House and Cottage   1 km W of Naracoorte*

Dartmoor Homestead
Jane Frost, 30 McLay Street, Naracoorte, SA 5271

Tel: (08) 8762 0487 Fax: (08) 8762 0481
Mobile: 0408 600 930   dartmoor@rbm.com.au
www.rbm.com.au/dartmoor
Double $195-$216 Single $127-$149
(Special Breakfast) Child $20 in Cottage
Dinner $49 - $51 B/A
Cottage $127 Credit Cards accepted
4 Queen 5 Single (3 bdrm) 1 Ensuite 1 Private 1 Share

Elegant country house and rustic settler's cottage, situated on 3 tranquil, town acres has now spanned
three centuries! Offering period furnishings, luxurious beds with fine linen and a warm relaxing ambience.
Some guest comments: "Lovely stay, fabulous dinner"; "Lovely spot, great hospitality"; "It was divine
- good food and wine". Sleeps up to 3 couples. Group discounts. The cottage offers living history with
its huge open fireplace and welcomes children and pets. What more can I say except treat yourself to
the same experience!

Naracoorte - Coonawarra *20 km SE of Naracoorte*
Self Contained B & B Cottages
Wongary Cottages AAATourism ★★★☆
Diana Hooper, Box 236, Naracoorte, SA 5271

Tel: (08) 8762 3038 Fax: (08) 8762 3394
Mobile: 0418 838 213   wongary@rbm.com.au
www.wongary.com.au
Double $120-$130 Single $90 (Continental Breakfast)
Child $20 Credit Cards accepted Pet on property
1 King/Twin 3 Queen 1 Double 6 Single
(2 bdrm & 3 bdrm cottages)   2 Ensuite 1 Private

Private self-contained multi Award Winning limestone cottages have wood fires and air conditioning,
kitchen, bath and bed linen plus electric blankets, lawn tennis, pond, farm animals, antiques, books, games,
TV, magazines and vine-covered BBQ patios. Ralph's Cottage also has a dishwasher, laundry and spa plus
free video movies. Surrounded by beautiful farmland and vineyards, Wongary is close to the World
Heritage Naracoorte Caves and Coonawarra's wineries and restaurants. Pets and children welcome. Also
availably are Wongary's self-contained, fully equipped service apartments in Adelaide and Penola. -

Padthaway *Homestay B & B   Self Contained   24km N of Padthaway*

Russells Camp   AAATourism ★★★☆
Annie Moorhouse
PMB 39, Naracoorte, SA 5271

Tel: (08) 8757 3061 Fax: (08) 8757 3060
www.bbbook.com.au/russellscamp.html
Double $170-$180 Single $90
(Continental Breakfast) S/C $100 - $120
3 King 2 Single (4 bdrm)
2 Private

Russells Camp, a quality year round country experience, is a rural property situated near the renowned wine producing area of Padthaway. The main Homestead surrounded by a wonderful garden with lovely views of the surrounding country side. Truly, an oasis in summer with a swimming pool, tennis court, and a private living area for guests. The Cottage nestled amongst mallee and yacca is a short distance from the Homestead. It is bright, comfortable and self-contained. Guests at the cottage and Homestead are all welcome to use and enjoy the garden.

Port Elliot   *Homestay B & B   Self Contained   4 km Victor Harbour*

Trafalgar House Accommodation   AAAT★★★☆
Romaine & Chris Dawson
25 The Strand, Port Elliot, SA 5212

Tel: (08) 8554 3888 Fax: (08) 8554 3888
Mobile: 0419 824 402   trafalga@granite.net.au
www.fleurieupeninsula.com.au
Double $110-$140 Single $95-$140
(Special Breakfast) Child $25-$35 Dinner $25-$35
5 Queen 2 Twin (7 bdrm)
2 Ensuite 3 Private 1 Share

Original 1890 Guest House. Faithfully restored, beautifully furnished, comfortable. Two minutes walk to beach, cliff walks, shops, cafes, tennis. Close to golf, wineries. Whale watch June - September. Heritage Accommodation 2002 winner Fleurieu Peninsula. Selected by Vogue Entertaining and Travel magazine 2001 for O/Night stopovers. Accommodation in Guest House; 4 room S/C suite, 2 bedroom maids' cottage, A/C and log fires. Peaceful private gardens; BBQ; Dinner by arrangement.

Port Lincoln   *B & B   2km E of Port Lincoln town centre*

Port Lincoln Bed & Breakfast   AAAT★★★★☆
Jenny & Graham Steele
2 Power Terrace, Port Lincoln, SA 5606

Tel: (08) 8682 3550 Fax: (08) 8682 1044
Mobile: 0419 811 200   plbb@ozemail.com.au
www.bbbook.com.au/plbb.html
Double $100-$140 Single $85-$100
(Continental & Full Breakfast) Child $25
1 Queen 1 Double (2 bdrm)
1 Ensuite

Port Lincoln Bed & Breakfast is situated in a quiet, peaceful setting overlooking Boston Bay and a minute walk to the beach and Parnkalla Walking Trail. The spacious upstairs suite with guests private entrance has reverse cycle air-conditioning, an ensuite bathroom with a 2 person spa, hair-dryer, tea/coffee making facilities, bar fridge, colour TV, cassette/CD player and a comfortable settee. Breakfast can be served on the patio or in guest suite, both with delightful sea views. "Top class accommodation, beautiful surroundings." MG, Vista, SA.

Robe   *Self Contained   Robe Central*

Criterion Cottages   AAATourism ★★★☆
Belinda Morgan
c/- 89 Stanley Street, North Adelaide, SA 5276

Tel: (08) 8768 2137 Fax: (08) 8768 2180
Mobile: 0417 829 190   criterion@seol.net.au
www.bbbook.com.au/criterioncottages.html

Double $110-$145
(Full Breakfast) Credit Cards accepted
Cottage 1: 1 Queen, 2 Twin
Cottage 2: 1 Queen, 4 Twin (5 bdrm)
2 Private

Two comfortable old cottages beautifully restored and private, yet in the centre of the old fishing port. Full kitchen facilities with generous supplies for a full cooked breakfast. The two bedroom cottage has a loft bedroom, sitting room with log fire and courtyard/sunroom. The three bedroom cottage has a sitting room with wood stove and an enclosed garden with sunroom. Both with washing machines. Close to beach, restaurants and shops. Wineries, National parks and golf nearby. Children welcome.

Strathalbyn - Fleurieu Peninsula   *B & B   55 km S of Adelaide*

Watervilla House
Helene Brooks
2 Mill Street, Strathalbyn, SA 5255

Tel: (08) 8536 4099 Fax: (08) 8536 4099
watervillahouse@triplei.net.au
www.bbbook.com.au/watervillahouse.html

Double $132 Single $110 (Full Breakfast)
Credit Cards accepted Pet on property Pets welcome
5 Queen 1 Twin (6 bdrm)
1 Ensuite 1 Private 1 Share

Watervilla House Bed & Breakfast - This charming 1840's homestead invites you to enjoy a unique and friendly experience, surrounded by 11/2 acres of tranquil gardens. The six bedrooms, guest lounge and dining room feature comfortable, elegant antique decor. Situated in the heart of historic Strathalbyn, centrally located within the Fleurieu Peninsula and close to The Southern Vales and Langhorne Creek wine Regions. One Sunday, 8 years ago Helene came to Strathalbyn for lunch and loved it so much she decided to stay. Watervilla House has been featured on The Great Outdoors and Discovery.

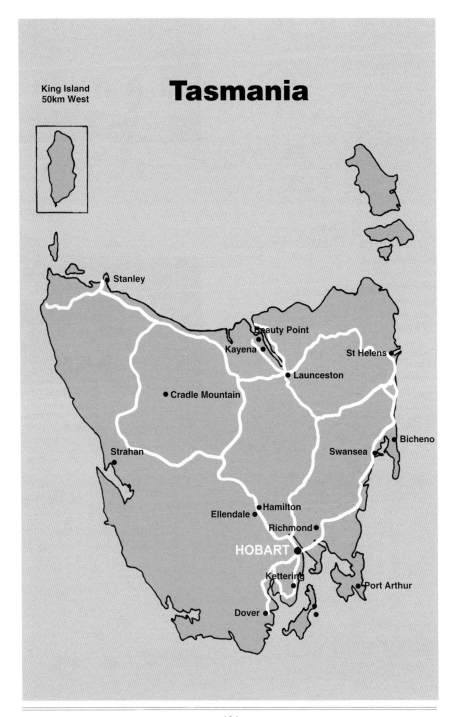

King Island
50km West

Tasmania

Stanley

Beauty Point

Kayena

St Helens

Launceston

Cradle Mountain

Strahan

Bicheno

Swansea

Ellendale

Hamilton

Richmond

HOBART

Kettering

Port Arthur

Dover

Beauty Point *B & B & Self Contained   40 km N of Launceston*

Pomona B&B & Cottages AAATourism ★★★★☆
Paula & Bruce Irvin
77 Flinders Street, Beauty Point, Tas 7270

Tel: (03) 6383 4073 Fax: (03) 6383 4074
Mobile: 0418 143 628   pomona.bp@tassie.net.au
www.pomonabandb.com.au

Double $120-$160 Single $90-$120 (Full Breakfast)
Credit Cards accepted
1 King/Twin 3 Queen 2 Single (4 bdrm)
4 Ensuite

Relax and enjoy a delicious breakfast, or evening drink on the Rotundas, overlooking spectacular views of the Tamar River/valley. Spoil yourself in the new spacious and sunny S/C Spa Cottages, or the beautiful Federation Homestead - guest lounge, open fire, central heating. Stroll in the gardens, through grape vines and along river to Restaurants, Seahorses. Explore the Tamar Valley Scenic Wine Route, National Parks, Penguins. Ferry & Airport- within 1 hour. Ideally located between Freycinet and Strahan.

Bicheno *B & B   10 km N of Bicheno*

Forest Ridge Country Retreat
Helen Preston
Denison River,
via Bicheno, Tas 7215

Tel: (03) 6375 1565 Fax: (03) 6375 1545
Mobile: 0419 338 141   helen.preston@tassie.net.au
www.bbbook.com.au/forestridge.html

Double $110-$132 Single $99 (Full Breakfast)
Child N/A Credit Cards accepted
2 Queen (2 bdrm)   2 Ensuite

'Retreat to peace and beauty between forest and sea. Forest Ridge, a mudbrick and timber home set on a high ridge against the Douglas Apsley National Park, offers country elegance, comfort and warmth. Glorious views from every room to the Denison beach, wild and beautiful, a few minutes below. Bicheno, a small fishing town 10kms south, offers fresh seafood, superb wines, fabulous granite coastline and white sand beaches. Penguin tours, charters. Nearby are Freycinet NP, waterfalls and coastal lagoons. Enjoy day trips to Maria Is NP, Ross and St Helens. Picnic basket/haversack provided A spacious suite with 'TV, Ph, microwave.'

Cradle Mountain & Lakes District   *17 km S of Sheffield*

Homestay B & B Guest House Self Contained
Cradle Vista   AAATourism ★★★★
June & Colin Hughes
978 Staverton Road, south of Sheffield, Tas 7306

Tel: (03) 6491 1129 Fax: (03) 6491 1930
Mobile: 0417 211 603   www.cradlevista.com.au
yourhosts@cradlevista.com.au

Double $130 Single $130 (Full Breakfast)
Dinner $30 B/A Self Contained $150   Credit Cards
3 Queen 3 Single (4 bdrm)   3 Ensuite 1 Private

On the scenic route from Sheffield to Cradle Mountain, Cradle Vista provides luxury (non-smoking) accommodation on a 50 acre farm property. Nestled under the triple peaks of local mountains with panoramic views from all windows. Imagine the vista from Cradle Mountain to Bass Strait. Explore the farm, admire mountain vistas, go horse riding, enjoy day trips to Cradle Mountain and local attractions. Relax in comfort by the open fire with pre dinner drinks talking to other guests before enjoying your delicious three course evening meal.

Cradle Mountain & Lakes District
8 km N of Sheffield

Farmstay B & B Guest House

Glencoe Farm Guest House AAATourism ★★★★
Jim & Trish Shipley
1468 Sheffield Main Road, Barrington, Tas 7306

Tel: (03) 6492 3267 Fax: (03) 6492 3267
Mobile: 0407 321 906   www.glencoefarm.com.au
glencoe_guest_house@bigpond.com.au

Double $120 Single $83 (Full Breakfast)
Child $25 Dinner $33 p.p. Credit Cards accepted
2 Queen 1 Double 3 Single (4 bdrm)   4 Ensuite

Glencoe Farm was originally built as a dairy property to federation style in 1890, over recent years it has been renovated and restored. Each of its four bedrooms features an individual ensuite, guests enjoy the comfort of warm comfortable lounge and dining room with warm fires in winter and cool high rooms in summer. Gourmet dinners extra to order. The house in 23 acres supports farm animals including sheep, chickens and cattle. Only 25 minutes from Devonport's "Spirit of Tasmania" and Airport. Accredited Tourist and Aussie Host Business.

Dover   *B & B   7 km S of Dover*

Riseley Cottage
Philip Emery & Greg Shelton
170 Narrows Road, Strathblane (Dover), Tas 7117

Tel: (03) 6298 1630 Fax: (03) 6298 1815
riseleycottage@hotmail.com   www.riseleycottage.com

Double $95-$105 Single $70-$75 (Full Breakfast)
Child $20 Dinner B/A Credit Cards accepted
Pet on property Pets welcome
2 Double 1 Twin (3 bdrm)   1 Ensuite 1 Share

Riseley Cottage's panoramic views to Esperance Bay and Hartz Mountain suggest an ideal location to explore the grandeur and rich natural history of the Far South. The quiet restful charm of cottage gardens (and bushland reserve), quality antiques and period furnishings make for a rewarding experience. Personalised - friendly service, cosy log fires, spacious guest lounge, balcony with a view, comfortable warm beds, delicious home cooked food are but a few of the treats you can expect. Book dinner in advance and enjoy fine regional cuisine served in our elegant dining room. Wine available. 'Country' hospitality at its very best! Children welcome.

Ellendale   *Self Contained   80km W of Hobart*

Hopfield Country Cottages
Anne & John Trigg
Hopfield Cottages, Ellendale, Tas 7140

Tel: (03) 6288 1223 Fax: (03) 6288 1207
Mobile: 0408 101 588
email hopfieldcots@trump.net.au
www.bbbook.com.au/hopfield.html

Double $99-$130 Single $90 (Full Breakfast)
Child $20 Credit Cards accepted
3 Queen 1 Double 6 Single (6 bdrm)   3 Private

Close to the famous Mt Field National Park you will find our delightfully restored cottages. They are cosy, comfortable, fully self-contained with log fires, fresh flowers, homemade bread and preserves. An ideal respite between Strahan and Hobart.   Enjoy bush walking, rain forest and alpine scenery, mystical Russell Falls, Southwest World Heritage, history and trout fishing. As night falls, spotlight for Tasmania's unique wildlife and be mesmerised by the glow worms' grotto. Ellendale is on the direct route for Lake Pedder, Mt Field National Park and Strahan.

Hamilton - Derwent Valley   *Farmstay Self Contained   3 km W of I*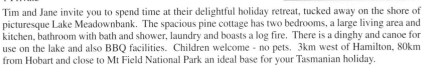

"Over the Back" Lakeside Holiday Accomodation
AAATourism ★★★★
Tim & Jane Parsons
Box 39, Hamilton, Tas 7140

Tel: (03) 6286 3332 Fax: (03) 6286 3350
Mobile: 0418 863 337   tparsons@bigpond.com
www.bbbook.com.au/overtheback.html

Double $145 Single $80-$90
(Full Breakfast) Child $20
1 Queen 3 Single (2 bdrm)
1 Private

Tim and Jane invite you to spend time at their delightful holiday retreat, tucked away on the shore of picturesque Lake Meadownbank. The spacious pine cottage has two bedrooms, a large living area and kitchen, bathroom with bath and shower, laundry and boasts a log fire. There is a dinghy and canoe for use on the lake and also BBQ facilities. Children welcome - no pets. 3km west of Hamilton, 80km from Hobart and close to Mt Field National Park an ideal base for your Tasmanian holiday.

Hobart - Battery Point   *B & B   1 km Hobart Central*

Colville Cottage AAATourism ★★★★☆
Carl Hankey & Louise Gerathy
32 Mona Street, Battery Point, Tas 7004

Tel: (03) 6223 6968 Fax: (03) 6224 0500
colvillecottage@bigpond.com
www.colvillecottage.com.au

Double $150-$170 Single $136-$140
(Full Breakfast) Child $35 Credit Cards accepted
6 Double 2 Twin (6 bdrm)
6 Ensuite

Elegance and ambience, rarely matched are yours to experience when you stay at Colville Cottage. Antique furniture and rugs, ornate fireplaces, stained glass windows and verandah lacework call up the gracious living of last century. Modern facilities provide every comfort and convenience, while the warmth of your welcome and the splendid cooked breakfast all combine to enhance your experience. Colville Cottage, built in 1877, is a large mid-Victorian home on a corner site. It is bordered on all sides by a beautiful cottage garden.

Hobart - Battery Point   *Self Contained   1 km S of Hobart*

Battery Point Boutique Accommodation
AAATourism ★★★★
Lynn
27-29 Hampden Road, Battery Point, Tas 7004

Tel: (03) 6224 2244 Fax: (03) 6224 2243
Mobile: 0417 366 540
batbou@alphalink.com.au
www.bbbook.com.au/batterypoint.html

Double $120-$155 Single $95-$125
(Continental Breakfast) Child $35
Credit Cards accepted
1 Queen 1 Single (2 bdrm) 1 Ensuite

Elegant fully self contained holiday and corporate serviced apartments in the heart of Battery Point. Just a short stroll to Salamanca, waterfront and the city. Stylish accommodation, featuring fully equipped kitchens, modern and comfortable sitting rooms with French doors opening to delightful bedrooms with ensuites. Every guest is assured a warm welcome and genuine hospitality. Off street parking.

Hobart - Battery Point *B & B   Separate/Suite   1 km E of Hobart*

Battery Point Manor   AAATourism ★★★★☆

Roz and John Lambert-Smith

13 - 15 Cromwell Street, Battery Point, Tas 7004

Tel: (03) 6224 0888 Fax: (03) 6224 2254

www.batterypointmanor.com.au

Double $95-$195 Single $75-$145
(Special Breakfast) Child $5 - $30
Credit Cards accepted
3 King/Twin 2 King 2 Queen 1 Double (10 bdrm)
10 Ensuite

We offer you fabulous harbour views, big comfortable beds, large comfortable en-suite rooms; spa studio apartment or 2 bedroom cottage, big yummy Tassie buffet breakfasts, fresh air, peaceful and happy surroundings, 5 mins exciting walk to Salamanca, lots to see and do with maps provided, the best café and restaurant info and complimentary refreshments anytime. 'Battery Point Manor', also known as 'Battery Point Harbour View Bed and Breakfast' is a substantial 'Georgian' home restored to our very comfortable 4∏ * B & B. We hope to meet you soon, with warm regards Roz and John Lambert-Smith.

Hobart - Lindisfarne *B & B   4 km E of Hobart*

Orana House   AAATourism ★★★★☆

Claire and Brian Marshall

20 Lowelly Road, Lindisfarne, Tas 7015

Tel: (03) 6243 0404 Fax: (03) 6243 9017
Mobile: 0402 344 964   Freecall: 1800 622 598
oranahouse@optusnet.com.au
www.oranahouse.com

Double $99-$150 Single $75-$95 (Full Breakfast)
Child $35 Credit Cards accepted
6 Queen 4 Double 4 Single (10 bdrm)   10 Ensuite

A large Federation home circa 1909 offers you warm hospitality for your stay in Hobart. Orana House is just 12 minutes from the airport and six minutes drive to Hobart city centre. It is a convenient base to explore southern Tasmania. Some of our many features for your enjoyment: superb breakfasts, great views from verandah and guest lounge, genuine antiques, log fire in lounge in winter, all rooms with ensuites, choice of standard, deluxe or spa rooms. Not suitable for young children. Superior Accommodations and Service With A Smile!

Hobart - Rose Bay *B & B   Self Contained   3.5 km NE of Hobart*

Roseneath B & B

Susan and Alain Pastre

20 Kaoota Road, Rose Bay, Tas 7015

Tel: (03) 6243 6530 Fax: (03) 6243 0518
Mobile: 0418 121 077   pastre@bigpond.com
www.roseneath.com

Double $95-$155 Single $85-$145
(Full Breakfast) Dinner $20 - $230BA
Winter discounts available Credit Cards accepted
2 Queen 2 Double 1 Twin (5 bdrm)   5 Ensuite

Stay with us at Roseneath and experience true Tasmanian hospitality and warmth with a French accent. With spectacular views of Mt Wellington, the Tasman Bridge and Derwent River, Roseneath is an ideal base for exploring southern Tasmania. We offer a self-catering suite (4 ∏ *) with a small kitchen (breakfast hamper provided), or in-house accommodation. Superb cooked breakfasts are served in the conservatory overlooking the pool and the spacious, secluded English-style gardens. Guest facilities include a lounge with log fire, the inground heated pool, BBQ's and private-undercover parking.

Hobart - Rosetta   *B & B   Guesthouse*   *10 min N of Hobart CBD*

Undine Colonial Accommodation   AAAT★★★★☆
Cyril and Jenny Clark
6 Dodson Street, Rosetta Hobart, Tas 7010

Tel: (03) 6273 3600 Fax: (03) 6273 3900
undine@ozemail.com.au
www.ozemail.com.au/~undine

Double $140 Single $105
(Full Breakfast) Child $35
Credit Cards accepted Pet on property
1 King/Twin 4 Queen 6 Single (5 bdrm)
5 Ensuite

Undine - circa 1820, is a splendid Georgian Colonial home set in a large cottage garden with luxurious rooms, log fires and complimentary chocolates, fruit and port. Relax and enjoy your stay. Swim in the heated, indoor pool, soak in the private spa, browse the extensive library by the fire with a coffee and a fresh, home baked treat. Indulge in a country style, cooked breakfast as you plan the day. Undine is located only 10 minutes form Hobart's CBD. Children welcome. Sorry no pets.

Kettering   *Self Contained Cottages*   *38 km S of Hobart*

Herons Rise Vineyard   AAATourism ★★★★
Gerry & Sue White
PO Box 271,
Kettering, Tas 7155

Tel: (03) 6267 4339 Fax: (03) 6267 4245
cwhite@vision.net.au
www.heronsrisevineyard.com.au

Double $110-$135 Single $90-$100 (Full Breakfast)
Child $30 Dinner $20 - $30
2 Queen 2 Twin 1 Single (3 bdrm)
2 Private

Enjoy the tranquillity of staying in four star cottages set in a private vineyard with beautiful water and rural views. Both cottages have full kitchens, baths, log fire heating and are attractively furnished. Herons Rise Vineyard is an ideal centre for experiencing Southern Tasmania. Within close proximity are Hobart, the Huon Valley, Hartz National Park and Bruny Island. At the end of the day spoil yourself with dinner and wine from the vineyard served in your cottage. Ideal for couples and families.

Launceston   *B & B   1 km E of Launceston CBD*

Kilmarnock House   AAATourism ★★★★
Bruce & Elizabeth Clark
66 Elphin Road, Launceston, Tas 7250

Tel: (03) 6334 1514 Fax: (03) 6334 4516
www.bbbook.com.au/kilmarnock.html

Double $95-$120 Single $80-$95 (Special Breakfast)
Child $15 under 14yrs 2 bedroom unit from $135
Credit Cards accepted
2 Queen 7 Double 2 Twin 3 Single (10 bdrm)
10 Ensuite

Situated on stately Elphin Road, ten minutes level walk from the city centre, via the City Park, "Kilmarnock House" is classified by the National Trust, Heritage listed and part of the National Estate. Extensive restoration and refurbishing throughout with antiques and period furniture reflect the charm and elegance of the Edwardian era. Our suites are fully self contained, with bay windows, private ensuite bathrooms, small concealed kitchen units, direct dial phones, dining facilities and comfortable chairs. Smoke free house. Off street parking and laundry facilities gor guests. All replies by fax please

Tasmania

Launceston   *B & B   1 km E of Launceston CBD*

Ashton Gate   AAATourism ★★★★
Tim & Marina Samoilov
32 High Street, Launceston, Tas 7250

Tel: (03) 6331 6180 Fax: (03) 6334 2232
info@ashtongate.com.au
www.ashtongate.com.au

Double $120-$150 Single $90-$110
(Continental Breakfast) Spa suite $150
Credit Cards accepted
3 Queen 4 Double 1 Twin (8 bdrm)   8 Ensuite

A charming Victorian home nestled into a rose filled cottage garden and just a short stroll to city centre. Enjoy modern comforts, the elegance of yesteryear and friendly personal service. The perfect place for you to relax and unwind. Spend the evening relaxing in the guest lounge by a log fire sipping port. Snuggle into a comfy bed under a feather doona for a restful slumber. Awake refreshed and enjoy a hearty breakfast in the cosy dining room overlooking a Village Green. No pets, no children.

Launceston - Campbell Town   *B & B   5 km S of Campbell Town*

Foxhunters Return
John King
132 High Street, Campbell Town, Tas 7250

Tel: (03) 6381 1602 Fax: (03) 6381 1545
www.bbbook.com.au/foxhuntersreturn.html

Double $132 Single $110 (Full Breakfast)
Child $25 Dinner $7 - $21 Credit Cards accepted
4 Queen 3 Double 6 Single (8 bdrm)
7 Ensuite 1 Private

Centrally located, Foxhunters Return is ideally placed for those touring Tasmania. Built with convict labour in the 1830's, today the hotel has retained its unique nostalgic ambience whilst providing all the expected comforts in eight beautifully appointed suites, including central heating and ensuites of exceptional quality. Enjoy pre dinner drinks in front of the open fire in the Chandelier Room whilst you ponder your selection from the a la carte menu. Meeting room available. "Brilliant atmosphere, great food, cosy rooms. Thanks! Simon & Joy, Sydney

All our B&Bs are non-smoking
unless stated otherwise in the text.

Launceston - Kayena *B & B   Self Contained   16 km NE of Exeter*

Tamar River Retreat   AAATourism ★★★★☆
Jeff & Pam Thorpe
123 Kayena Road, Kayena, Tas 7270

Tel: (03) 6394 7030 Fax: (03) 6394 7030
Mobile: 0418 871 685
info@tamarriverretreat.com.au
www.tamarriverretreat.com.au

Double $110-$125 Single $88 (Full Breakfast)
Dinner From $33 Credit Cards accepted
3 Queen 2 Single (4 bdrm)   4 Ensuite

What spectacular views from this waterfront rural retreat set on four acres of land and gardens high above the beautiful Tamar River! Enjoy pleasant riverside walks, Bonnie Beach at end of property. Fishing gear available to fish from jetty or simply sit by the water and feel yourself relax. Conveniently situated on wine route with four wineries close by. BBQ facilities available. Why not relax by the wood fire with complimentary pre-dinner drink followed by a home cooked dinner in the comfortable guest lounge!

Port Arthur - Koonya *B & B   Self Contained   5 km Taranna*

Cascades Colonial Accommodation   AAAT★★★★
Marcus Clark and Maria Stupka
533 Main Road, Koonya, Tas 7187

Tel: (03) 6250 3873 Fax: (03) 6250 3013
clark@cascadescolonial.com.au
www.bbbook.com.au/cascadescolonial.html

Double $110-$132 Single $100-$122
(Special Breakfast) Full Breakfast Provisions provided.
Additional persons $16.50-$22.00
Spa Cottage $160 - $200
1 Queen 4 Double 3 Single (5 bdrm)   6 Ensuite

Convicts on probation from Port Arthur built Cascades circa 1841. Explore a private family museum and convict remains that includes a cell block and a mess hall. Melt into your armchair in front of a crackling fire or enjoy a spa in your luxury cottage in the quiet dignity of colonial décor. Combine a relaxing waterfront walk to the site of the convict wharf or a temperate rainforest walk/horse ride which follows the convict trail to the mill and the quarry site. One day is never long enough . . .

Port Arthur - Taranna *B & B   10 km N of Port Arthur*

Norfolk Bay Convict Station   AAAT★★★★
Dot & Mike Evans
5862 Arthur Highway, Taranna, Tas 7180

Tel: (03) 6250 3487 Fax: (03) 6250 3487
evans@convictstation.com
www.convictstation.com

Double $120-$140 Single $80 (Full Breakfast)
Child $40 Credit Cards accepted
2 Queen 2 Double 1 Twin 3 Single (5 bdrm)
3 Ensuite 2 Private

Norfolk Bay Convict Station, built in 1838, was once an important part of Port Arthur convict settlement. Ships called here to transfer their passengers to the convict railway and you can still stroll or fish along the jetty in front of the house. We offer warm, comfortable rooms, a sitting room with a log fire and a wonderful breakfast. From here you can visit Port Arthur, drive the Convict Trail, walk in the Tasman National Park or, as we are licensed, relax on the front verandah with a glass of Tasmanian wine.

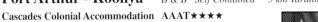

Richmond *Colonial B & B*   *7 km N of Richmond*

Campania House   AAATourism ★★★☆
Paddy Pearl
Estate Road, Campania, Tas 7026

Tel: (03) 6260 4281 Fax: (03) 6260 4493
www.bbbook.com.au/campaniahouse.html

Double $130 Single $80
(Full Breakfast) Child $25 Dinner $30
Credit Cards accepted Pets welcome
5 Double 3 Single (7 bdrm)
4 Share

"CAMPANIA HOUSE"

The construction of Campania House was begun in 1813 by George Weston Gunning shortly after his arrival in Van Diemen's land in 1810. It is listed on the National Estate Register and offers colonial accommodation on three storeys, bed and country breakfast in oak panelled kitchen or paved courtyard, heating and log fires in every room, elegant drawing room and large garden with views of the verdant Coal River valley. Campania is 7km from equally historic Richmond and half an hour from Hobart. Come and be restored. No smoking.

St Helens *B & B   Self Contained*   *3 km S of St Helens PO*

Warrawee   AAATourism ★★★★☆
E & B Lawson, Kirwans Beach,
Tasman Highway, St Helens, Tas 7216

Tel: (03) 6376 1987 Fax: (03) 6376 1012
Mobile: 0419 324 105   warrawee@vision.net.au
www.vision.net.au/~warrawee

Double $126-$186 Single $90
(Full Breakfast) S.C. Cottage $95 dbl.
Credit Cards accepted Pets welcome
5 Queen 2 Double 1 Single (7 bdrm) 7 Ensuite

Built in 1904 overlooking beautiful Georges Bay and the hills beyond, Warrawee first began operating in 1907, and continues today to offer 4 1/2 star comfort and style. Privately set on 3 1/2 hectares of paddocks and gardens, an ideal place to relax and unwind after a day of travelling. Browse through the eclectic collection of paintings, prints, petit point and old photographs. Warrawee has been tastefully refurbished to a high standard of elegance and comfort. * Ground floor accommodation * Non smoking * Serviced daily * 2 Deluxe rooms with double spa * Off street parking

Stanley *B & B*   *Stanley Central*

Hanlon House   AAATourism ★★★★☆
Maxine & Graham Wells
6 Marshall Street, Stanley, Tas 7331

Tel: (03) 6458 1149 Fax: (03) 6458 1257
Mobile: 0419 529 145   hanlon.house@tassie.net.au
www.tassie.net.au/hanlonhouse

Double $125-$165 Single $100-$120
(Full Breakfast) Child $35
Dinner $28 - $34 Credit Cards accepted
6 Queen 3 Single (5 bdrm) 5 Ensuite

Hanlon House offers excellent hospitality in a superbly renovated federation style home with magnificent sea views. Enjoy an excellent breakfast at your leisure whilst overlooking Godfrey's beach from the dining room. Take a walk up to the top of the 'Nut', a spectacular rocky headland rising from the ocean. Explore arts and craft galleries, coffee shops, restaurants and emporiums in this unique historic fishing village. Relax and be pampered with local hosts Maxine and Graham, in this award winning B&B. View penguins in the evening.

Strahan   *Self Contained B & B Cottages*   *800m N of Post Office*

McIntosh Cottages   AAATourism ★★★★
Wendy & Paul Helleman
18 Harvey Street, Strahan, Tas 7468

Tel: (03) 6471 7358 Fax: (03) 6471 7074
hellemanpaul@tassie.net.au
www.bbbook.com.au/mcintoshcottages.html

Double $140-$170 Single $120-$140
(Full Breakfast) Child $30 -35
Extra person $35
2 Queen 2 Single (3 bdrm)
2 Private

The original c1898 house has been carefully restored as two co-joined cottages. Both cottages have all those extras that will make your stay cosy and memorable: wood heating, fully equipped kitchen, off street parking, toys for children, fresh flowers, comfortable beds and complimentary port. The cottages are very popular as part of a honeymoon and for an anniversary surprise.

Swansea   *B & B Self Contained*   *18 km S of Bicheno*

Coombend Country Cottages
John & Jo Fenn-Smith
Coombend, Swansea, Tas 7190

Tel: (03) 6257 8881 Fax: (03) 6257 8484
coombend@bigpond.com   www.thr.com.au

Double $120-$144 Child $22
Dinner $22-30 per person
Credit Cards accepted
2 Queen 3 Twin (2 bdrm & 3 bdrm Cottages)
2 Private

Country and coast - you will have the best of both worlds at Coombend. Two self-contained cottages on a 4,000 acre working farm that has a vineyard and olive grove. Coombend Cottage has 2 Bedrooms and George's Cottage 3 bedrooms. Explore the bays, beaches, Freycinet and Apsley Douglas National Parks. Your hosts look after you themselves; the farms breakfasts alone will gladden your heart - eggs, ham, homemade jams, bread, orange juice and cereals - relax and enjoy dinner delivered to your cottage. "Real service involves giving, it is reflected everywhere at Coombend. Thank you." M&PT, Wahroonga, Sydney.

Tasmania

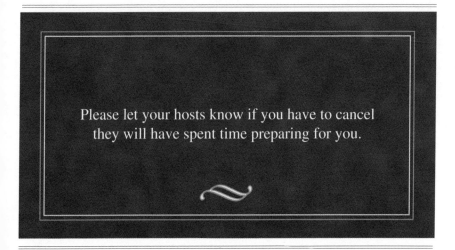

Please let your hosts know if you have to cancel
they will have spent time preparing for you.

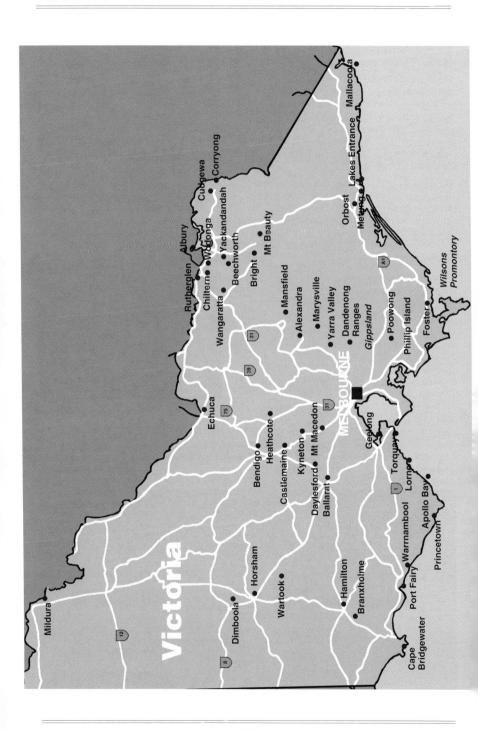

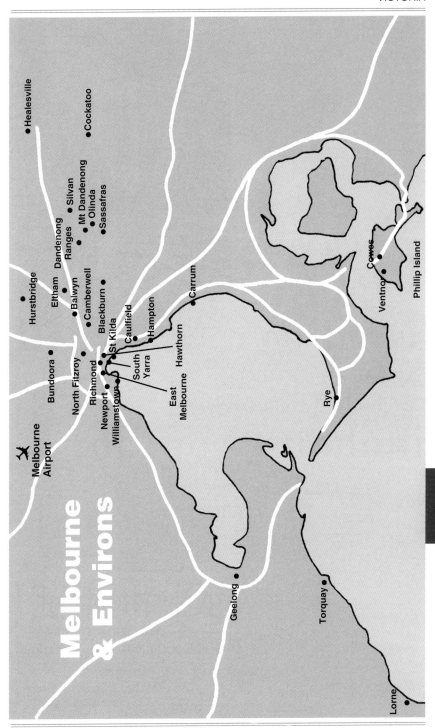

Alexandra   *Farmstay Self Contained Cottage*   *5 km Alexandra*

Idlewild Park Farm Accommodation   AAAT★★★★
Elizabeth & Don Deelen
RMB 1150, Alexandra, Vic 3714

Tel: (03) 5772 1178 idlewild@virtual.net.au
www.idlewild.com.au

Double $100 Single $80 (Full Breakfast) Child $15
Cottage $120 dbl Pet on property Pets welcome
1 King/Twin 2 Queen (3 bdrm)
1 Ensuite 1 Private

Enjoy this 3,000 acre grazing property 128 km NE of Melbourne. The beautiful district offers horse riding, fishing, water and snow sports, bush walking, golf & adventure activities. Stay in a fully equipped two bedroom cottage with double spa, wood heater, full kitchen and air conditioning. The location is superb with magnificent mountain views. There is tennis, gas BBQ and a beautiful garden. Property has sheep, cattle, horses and poultry (also kangaroos, koalas and native birds). Don and Elizabeth welcome you warmly to experience farm activities. They have four grown up children and two friendly Jack Russell dogs. Smoking outside. Homestead accommodation is also available

Apollo Bay   *Farmstay Homestay*   *10 km E of Apollo Bay*

Arcady Homestead   AAATourism ★★★☆
Marcia & Ross Dawson, 925 Barham River Road,
Apollo Bay - Great Ocean Road, Vic 3233

Tel: (03) 5237 6493 Fax: (03) 5237 6493
Mobile: 0408 376 493   arcadyhomestead@bigpond.com.au
www.bbbook.com.au/arcadyhomestead.html

Double $99-$120 Single $64.5-$75 (Full Breakfast)
Child 50% Dinner $25
1 Queen 2 Double 3 Single (4 bdrm) 1 Share

Set on sixty scenic acres, part farmland and part natural bush. Share breakfast with our Kookaburras, explore the Otway Forest trails, tree-fern and glow worm gullies and waterfalls, see some of the tallest trees in the world or visit or visit Port Campbell National Park, which embraces Australia's most spectacular coastline. Fishing (sea & river), surfing, swimming, golf & horse riding are all within easy reach & of course, the Otway Ranges are a bushwalkers paradise. Bird-watchers? We have identified around thirty species in the garden alone! Many visit our kitchen window! Our home has wood fires & spring water. Our beds are cosy, our meals country-style, and our atmosphere relaxed and friendly.

Apollo Bay   *B & B*   *7.5 km W of Apollo Bay*

Paradise Gardens   AAATourism ★★★★
Jo and Jock Williamson
715 Barham River Road, Apollo Bay, Vic 3233

Tel: (03) 5237 6939 Fax: (03) 5237 6105
Mobile: 0417 330 615
paradisegardens@bigpond.com.au
www.bbbook.com.au/paradisegardens.html

Double $115-$150 (Full Breakfast)
Credit Cards accepted
1 King (1 bdrm) 1 Ensuite 1 Private

Situated on 3 acres of landscaped gardens in a lush rainforest, we offer peace and tranquillity, 10 minutes from Apollo Bay. Our Unit is tastefully furnished and includes TV, VCR, CD player, dining setting with double spa and separate shower in ensuite. Private external entrance. Cafe on site. Complementary Devonshire tea. Enjoy nearby walks, abundant birdlife and glow-worms at night. Self-contained cottages to be built around our lake early 2003. "So idyllic, so peaceful." J&N, Houston, USA "Lovely room, beautiful setting." R&J, Wales, UK.

Victoria

Ballarat - Mt Helen   *Homestay*   *9 km S of Ballarat*

Woodside   AAATourism ★★★☆
Joan & David Goldsmith
120 Fisken Road, Mt Helen, Ballarat, Vic 3350

Tel: (03) 5341 3451 dgold@netconnect.com.au
www.bbbook.com.au/woodside.html

Double $90 Single $60 (Continental Breakfast)
1 Queen 2 Single (2 bdrm)
2 Private

Set in beautiful gardens, "Woodside" lies in the suburb of Mt Helen, close to Ballarat University and enjoys panoramic views of the surrounding countryside. On our ten acres, we run our mare Goldie, barn cat Chloe and several free-range hens. Our spacious guest lounge offers TV, stereo, library and cosy pot belly stove. "Woodside" is a peaceful place where you can relax and unwind. Do come and enjoy superior accommodation, lots of warmth and friendly service and delicious breakfasts.

Ballarat - Mt Helen   *Separate/Suite B & B*   *9 km S of Ballarat*

Ramble House
Elizabeth & Roger Trudgeon
130 Fisken Road, Mt Helen, Ballarat, Vic 3350

Tel: (03) 5341 2405 Fax: (03) 5341 2401
Mobile: 0409 356 759
trudgeon@netconnect.com.au
www.ballarat.com/ramblehouse.htm

Double $100 Single $80 (Continental Breakfast)
Credit Cards accepted
2 Queen (2 bdrm) 2 Ensuite

At Ramble House, a peaceful country interlude and a warm welcome await you. Relax in the private guest lounge or wander around the native garden of our five acre property. Spacious rooms have well-equipped ensuites, TV and electric blankets. A delicious healthy breakfast is served in the guest dining room overlooking the garden. We are ideally located, two minutes from Buninyong, close to the University and ten minutes from Ballarat. The Fine Art Gallery, Sovereign Hill, museums, theatres and superb dining are just minutes away.

Beechworth   *B & B*   *1 km Beechworth*

Apple Tree Cottage   AAATourism ★★★★☆
Joan Hilderbrand
16 Frederick Street,
Beechworth, Vic 3747

Tel: (03) 5728 1044 appletre@hotkey.net.au
www.bbbook.com.au/appletreecottage.html

Double $125 (Full Breakfast)
Credit Cards accepted
2 Queen (2 bdrm)
2 Ensuite

Apple Tree is simply a lovely place to stay. We offer you a quiet spot to rest and refresh yourselves in. Enjoy the ambience of old cedar furniture and fine china, relax in a comfortable chair in your own room or the guest lounge room. Select a book from the extensive library, listen to music or wander the garden. Wineries and history abound, we have been here since 1853. Pamper yourself, stay at Apple Tree it really is simply lovely; and our gourmet breakfasts are renowned.

Beechworth   *B & B   39 km S of Albury/Wodonga*

INN·HOUSE™

Kinross   AAATourism ★★★★☆
Bill & Christine Pearse
34 Loch Street, Beechworth, Vic 3747

Tel: (03) 5728 2351 Fax: (03) 5728 3333
kinross@dragnet.com.au
www.bbbook.com.au/kinross.html
Double $160 Single $130 (Full Breakfast)
Credit Cards accepted
2 King/Twin 3 Double (5 bdrm)
5 Ensuite

Bill and Christine Pearse invite you to experience their warm hospitality at Kinross which is situated within minutes walk of historic Beechworth. Kinross c 1858 has five large fully serviced guestrooms furnished with period pieces. In your room, experience the luxury of ensuites, open fireplaces, TV, comfortable chairs, tea and coffee making facilities. Sit with a book and a glass of wine on the front verandah and enjoy the beauty of the cottage garden. A delicious full breakfast is served.

Beechworth   *B & B Self Contained   1.4 Km W of Beechworth*

INN·HOUSE™

Country Charm Swiss Cottages   AAAT★★★★☆
Tony & Sarah Carter
22 Malakoff Road, Beechworth, Vic 3747

Tel: (03) 5728 2435 Fax: (03) 5728 2435/6
Mobile: 0438 282 436
info@swisscottages.com.au
www.swisscottages.com.au
Double $165-$225 Single $145-$210
(Full Breakfast) Child $35 Credit Cards accepted
5 Queen 4 Single (7 bdrm)
5 Ensuite

Five one and two bedroom self-contained B&B cottages built in the Swiss Chalet style on one and a half acres of beautifully landscaped gardens overlooking the Beechworth Gorge and Woolshed Valley. Queen beds, double spas, reverse cycle air-conditioning, open log fires in winter, (extra two single beds in the two bedroom cottage) and a living/dining area with kitchen. Breakfast provisions supplied. Four and a half star luxury hosted cottage B & B! Only a ten minute walk away from the town centre.

Victoria

Bendigo   *Homestay B & B   Separate/Suite   Self Contained   6 km S of Bendigo*

Whistle Inn B & B   AAAT★★★☆
Ken & Marian Craze
213 Allingham Street, Kangaroo Flat, Vic 3555

Tel: (03) 5447 8685 Fax: (03) 5447 8685
Mobile: 0407 844 821
whistlei@netcon.net.au
www.bbbook.com.au/whistleinnbb.html
Double $100 Single $65 (Full Breakfast) Child $10
1 Queen 1 Double 1 Twin 3 Single (4 bdrm)
2 Ensuite

Located in Kangaroo Flat within five minutes drive from Bendigo CBD. A private retreat set in spacious surroundings within a landscaped garden. Our two suites have beautifully appointed bathrooms each having a two person spa. Each suite is completely separate with private entrances. In "Platform 1" you can warm your toes by a cosy wood fire or stay cool in air conditioned comfort. Each suite has books, videos and music in a welcoming atmosphere. Enjoy our fully cooked breakfast from a variety of choices. Ideal for couples, families and singles.

Bendigo   *Self Contained B & B Cottage   8 km S of Bendigo*

Arbroath Lodge
Heather & Rod MacLeod
28 Clearing Court, Mandurang, Vic 3551

Tel: (03) 5439 3054 Fax: (03) 5439 3054
Mobile: 0407 349 733   rrhmacle@bigpond.net.au
www.bbbook.com.au/skyeglen.html
Double $100-$125 Single $70-$80
(Continental & Full Breakfast) Child $15 - $20
Additional adult $25
4 Queen 1 Twin 1 Single (6 bdrm) 3 Ensuite 1 Private

Idyllic stone retreat perfect for superb weekend getaways or longer stay. Tucked away in the beautiful Mandurang valley just a few minutes drive from Bendigo CBD, "Arbroath Lodge" offers exclusive 4 star accommodation consisting of two private suites. "The Highlander" a romantic retreat for two and "The Lodge" with stone fireplace, spacious bedrooms and ample room for 6 people. "Arbroath Lodge" has a Scottish theme that will intrigue you and a llama herd is of added interest. Traditional B&B also available in main house. So daily with the llamas and soak up the Scottish ambience and warm hospitality.

Bright *B & B* *4 km N of Porepunkah*

Sugar Maples Dinner & Doona®
Vivian Andersen & Chris Davey
133 Harris Lane, PO Box 61, Porepunkah, Vic 3740

Tel: (03) 5756 2919 Fax: (03) 5756 2920 Mobile: 0408 730 094
dndoona@dragnet.com.au
www.visitvictoria.com/sugarmaples

Double $120-$145 Single $90-$145 (Continental Breakfast) (Full Breakfast) (Special Breakfast)
Dinner from $40 Credit Cards accepted Pet on property
1 King/Twin 2 Queen (3 bdrm)
1 Ensuite 1 Private 1 Share

2002 Alpine Excellence Award Winner.   Boutique B&B - Sugar Maples Dinner & Doona®, offers you a romantic getaway in quiet, exclusive accommodation with great food and local cool climate wines. Located 10 min. from Bright - nestled in the foothills of Mt. Buffalo National Park in the heart of the High Country and set on 11 acres in the picturesque Buckland Valley with beautiful mountain views. Easy access on sealed road and only a short walk to river with waterfall swimming hole.

Activities: Skiing at the nearby resorts of Falls Creek, Mt. Hotham & Mt. Buffalo, wine tasting at local wineries, horse riding, scenic microlight flights, trout fishing, bicycle Rail Trail, mountain biking, golf, walking, gold panning, paragliding, photography, canoeing. Visit the Autumn & Spring festivals and admire the breathtaking scenery of the changing seasons (the Sugar Maple trees on our property are ablaze with magnificent shades of red, orange and yellow during autumn).

After a day exploring the surrounding areas, come home to enjoy a hot jacuzzi in the large spa room with wood heater and cosy seating area; then perhaps a drink in front of an open fire in the lounge and a gourmet dinner prepared by the Hilton trained chef and served in the candlelit dining room (individual tables) or on the terrace during the warm summer nights. In spring & summer, relax with a book on the terrace and watch the resident King Parrots and Crimson Rosellas feed or walk down to the waterfall swimming hole for a cooling dip or fish for trout.

The accommodation, which is separate to the host's, includes 3 tastefully decorated bedrooms (one with queen size bed, sofa bed, walk-in wardrobe and ensuite bathroom, 2nd also with queen size bed and 3rd with 2 single beds (or King size), 1 guest share bathroom & 1 private.

The tariff includes an excellent continental breakfast, but special breakfasts are available - e.g. berry pancakes with sugar maple syrup; smoked salmon scrambled eggs; full English breakfast etc.   We offer a set 3-course dinner menu, which changes on a daily basis. Our premises are fully licensed (not BYO with dinner) and we have a good selection of local wines plus beers & drinks available. We make our own muesli, lemon butter, jams, bread, cookies, cakes, paté etc.

Celebrate your birthday, honeymoon or anniversary here in a romantic atmosphere.

Children & dogs by arrangement only.   Gift vouchers available (valid for 1 year).   Danish & Spanish also spoken.   Animals on property: Horses, chooks, goat and "Sammi" the dog & heaps of wild parrots.   Booking advised.

Looking forward to pampering you at our gourmet Dinner & Doona® See you soon.

Cape Bridgewater   *Self Contained   Separate/Suite   B & B   20 km W of Portland*

Cape Bridgewater Seaview Lodge   AAAT★★★★
Jacqueline Carr, RMB 4370 Bridgewater Road,
Cape Bridgewater, Vic 3305

Tel: (03) 5526 7276 Fax: (03) 5526 7125
Mobile: 0418 525 191   seaviewlodge@hotkey.net.au
www.hotkey.net.au/seaviewlodge

Double $95-$130 (Full Breakfast) Child $12
Holiday house $130 per night minimum 2 nights
1 King/Twin 1 King 2 Queen 1 Double (5 bdrm)
5 Ensuite   Credit Cards accepted

Cape Bridgewater Sea View Lodge - on the beach at spectacular Bridgewater Bay - 20 km from Portland. Enjoy secluded beaches, rugged cliffs and coastal scenery of Cape Bridgewater. Spacious rooms with ensuites and stunning ocean views. Cosy lounges with wood fires. Guests' shared kitchenette. Perfect romantic getaway. Scenic attractions - blowholes, petrified forest, seal colony, Bridgewater lakes, giant sand dunes, limestone caves, secluded beaches. Laze away the hours or explore the area - fishing, surfing, snorkelling, canoeing, caving or bushwalking (Great South West Walk goes past our door).

Castlemaine   *Self Contained B & B   2 mins Castlemaine Central*   INN·HOUSE

Wisteria House   AAATourism ★★★★
Pam & Bob Gaunson
256 Barker Street, Castlemaine, Vic 3450

Tel: (03) 5470 6604 Mobile: 0438 706 604
wisteria@netcon.net.au
www.wisteriahouse.com.au

Double $120-$150 Single $100-$140 (Full Breakfast)
Child $20 Credit Cards accepted Pets welcome
4 Queen 1 Single (4 bdrm)
1 Ensuite 1 Private 1 Share

Wisteria House offers quality hospitality in a beautiful 1874 heritage home. Comfortable antique beds, private lounge room/dining room, music/library rooms for guests, hydronic heating/open fire, delicious silver service breakfasts, and attentive hosts. You can choose traditional B&B facilities or a self-contained cottage. Castlemaine is located in Australia's historic goldfields, with quality wineries, galleries, mineral springs and spas. One hour from Melbourne's airports, on major route from Sydney to Great Ocean Road, Wisteria House is your ideal stopover.

Castlemaine   *B & B   Castlemaine*

Clevedon Manor   AAATourism ★★★★
Stuart Ryan & Phil Page
260 Barker Street, Castlemaine, Vic 3450

Tel: (03) 5472 5212 Fax: (03) 5472 5212
Mobile: 0417 166 769
clevedon@netcon.net.au
www.bbbook.com.au/clevedon.html

Double $100-$120 Single $77 (Full Breakfast)
Dinner $35 Credit Cards accepted
5 Queen (5 bdrm)   3 Ensuite 2 Private

This beautifully restored 19th century home offers elegant living set in 1/2 acre 100 year old gardens. Clevedon offers guests a choice of spa room accommodation, ensuites and private facilities all with queen size beds. Private lounges and dining room with open fire, antique furnishings, central heating. Pool & BBQ. Clevedon is dedicated for guests only and is the perfect choice for either an intimate getaway or for groups wanting the complete package with meals. Clevedon is a 3 minute walk to historical central Castlemaine.

Chiltern *Farmstay B & B* *3 km E of Chiltern*

Forest View
Erika Hansen
Lancashine Gap Road, Vic 3683

Tel: (03) 5726 1337
Mobile: 0411 117 223
www.bbbook.com.au/forestview.html

Double $85 Single $70
(Full Breakfast) Dinner $25
1 Queen (1 bdrm)
1 Ensuite

Chiltern is very conveniently located between Albury/Wodonga and Wangaratta on the Hume Highway. It is close to Beechworth, Yackandanda and Rutherglen. Forest View is just 2 km from the highway and across the road from an extensive National Park renowned for its wildlife and flowers. A Winery Walkabout in June and a Jazz festival in November are just some of the other attractions in the area. The Murray River, Hume Weir and Snow fields are also within a short distance.

Corryong *Homestay B & B* *120 km E of Albury - Wodonga*

Mother Hubbards B & B   AAATourism ★★★★
Sandra & Richard Hubbard
57 Donaldson Street, Corryong, Vic 3707

Tel: (02) 6076 1570 Fax: (02) 6076 1570
Mobile: 0409 761 570
sandrich@corryongcec.net.au
www.bbbook.com.au/motherhubbardsbb.html

Double $80 Single $70 (Continental Breakfast)
2 Double (2 bdrm) 1 Ensuite 1 Private

Near the Murray River and the Snowy Mountain High Country, providing access to Khancoban Cudgwa, Koetong, Tintaldra, Walwa, Jingellic, and 5 National Parks, including the Burrowa-Pine Mountain and Alpine National Parks. Man from Snowy River's grave is here. Adventure tourism abounds, bush walking, hang gliding, 4WDriving, trout fishing, bird watching. The accommodation provides a comfortable lounge adjoining well-appointed bedrooms. A continental breakfast of fresh fruit, cereals and freshly baked breads are personally served in and elegant formal dining room, which is furnished with period furniture, silver and lace.

Cudgewa - Corryong *Self Contained* *120 km E of Albury - Wodonga*

Elmstead   AAATourism ★★★
Marja & Tony Jarvis
Ashstead Park Lane, Cudgewa, Vic 3705

Tel: (02) 6077 4324 Fax: (02) 6077 4324
Mobile: 0427 774 324
elmstead@corryongcec.net.au
www.bbbook.com.au/elmstead.html

Double $75 Single $55 (Continental Breakfast)
Child $7 Pet on property Pets welcome
1 Queen 2 Single (1 bdrm) 1 Ensuite

This lovely one-room cottage is set amongst magnificent old Elm trees on a working farm with panoramic views. Cudgewa (12 km from Corryong) is nestled in the foothills of the Snowy Mountains close to superb bushland and great fishing streams (fly fishing courses available). Tourist attractions include Burrowa-Pine Mountain National Park, Corryong with its Pioneer Museum and Jack Riley's grave (The Man from Snowy River). Thredbo and Mt Kosciusko are just over an hour away. Secluded 2 bedroom cottage also available. Preferably non-smokers. Children and pets welcome (we have both).

Victoria

Dandenong Ranges - Mount Dandenong   *500m N of Mount Dandenong*
B & B Self Contained Country House & Cottages

Penrith Country House Retreat   AAATourism ★★★★☆
Kaye & Graeme Bradtke-Stevenson
1411 Mount Dandenong Tourist Road,
Mount Dandenong, Vic 3767

Tel: (03) 9751 2447 Fax: (03) 9751 2391
penrithctyhse@bigpond.com
www.bbbook.com.au/penrithcountryhouseretreat.html
Double $110-$350 Single $100-$320
(Full Breakfast) Child $25 Credit Cards accepted
2 King/Twin 5 Queen (7 bdrm)   6 Ensuite 6 Private

"A Different World" - "The Ultimate Escape". A peaceful, private, retreat, nestled in the heart of the Dandenong Ranges amidst a 90 year old, 3 hectare, historical botanical wonderland with a spring fed stream. Meander through this tranquil world. Recapture the beauty of nature. Allow yourself to be renewed. Be indulged in "olde-worlde" luxurious, romantic spa-suites. Feast upon delicious breakfasts, curl up by the fire. Alternatively pamper yourself in our private, secretly located, luxurious, self-contained hermit House or Wishing Well Cottage..

Dandenong Ranges - Olinda   *Self Contained B & B   Olinda*

Britannia Boutique Bed & Breakfast
AAAT★★★★☆   Kathryn Hall & David Cooper
1558 Mount Dandenong Tourist Road, Olinda, Vic 3788

Tel: (03) 9751 2277 Fax: (03) 9751 2258
Mobile: 0419 555 900   info@britannia.com.au
www.britannia.com.au
Double $195-$295 Single $195-$295
(Continental Breakfast) Child $50
Dinner From $20 Credit Cards accepted
2 Queen (2 bdrm)   2 Ensuite

A rendezvous for romance awaits at your Tudor cottage set individually and uniquely in tranquil 1893 English acreage gardens. Each luxury cottage has a lovely deep double spa, sumptuous queen bed, flaming gas fire, A/C, CD player, TV & VCR, hair dryer, bathrobes, slippers, kitchenette, bar fridge, toaster, verandah and other special delights for your comfort. Stroll to restaurants, antiques, crafts and gardens. Drive to wineries, horse riding and golf courses. Sparkling wine, continental breakfast daily. "Perfect, Cosy, but most of all Romantic." JP, Melbourne

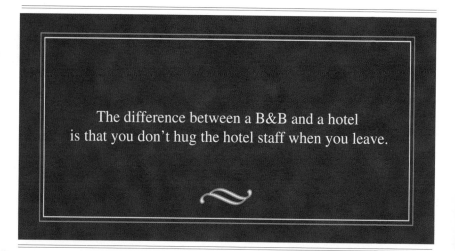

Dandenong Ranges - Sassafras   *B & B Self Contained*   *4 km S of Olinda*

Fleurbaix   AAATourism ★★★★
Maggie Murphy
286 Mt Dandenong Tourist Road,   Sassafras, Vic 3787

Tel: (03) 9755 1185 Fax: (03) 9755 1185 maggie@fleurbaix.com.au
www.fleurbaix.com.au

Double $140-$240 Single $100-$180 (Full Breakfast) Credit Cards accepted
2 Queen (2 bdrm)
2 Ensuite

Follow the brick path through the rhododendrons, camellias and azaleas to your relaxing getaway in the beautiful Dandenong Ranges. This charming house in the hills is less than an hours drive from Melbourne and well situated to explore all the treats the area has to offer.

Fleurbaix is only a short walk to Sherbrooke Forest with its towering mountain ash trees and fern gullies. Walk in the nearby forest, ride Puffing Billy, visit William Ricketts Sanctuary, or just browse through the many craft & speciality shops in the area. Nearby Sassafras and Olinda have many quaint tea rooms and first class restaurants. Superb gardens abound in the area and many are open to the public. Fleurbaix embodies the fine art of Bed & Breakfast, offering two styles of accommodation, the Traditional Suite and the Garden Cottage, with privacy a priority.

The Traditional Suite is a spacious separate wing of the 1930's home with private entrance for guests. The suite is elegantly furnished with antiques and has all the amenities for a memorable & relaxing stay, including a fire and spa. There is a kitchenette with some cooking facilities, but guests are treated to a beautifully cooked breakfast served discreetly to the door at your appointed time. The ensuite bathroom has an air-jet spa.

The Garden Cottage is self contained and very private. Breakfast provisions are supplied for guests to prepare themselves. There is a Coonara wood fire and the ensuite boasts an air spa.

Both rooms have TV, video CD player, fridge microwave, kettle, toaster and a warm and friendly welcome awaits you.

Dandenong Ranges - Silvan *Self Contained* *6 km Mt Evelyn*

Wandin Valley Cottage B & B **AAATourism ★★★**
Lynne & Robert Funston
30 Foch Road,
Silvan, Vic 3795

Tel: (03) 9737 9182 Mobile: 0418 558 307
www.bbbook.com.au/wandinvalleycottage.html
Double $100-$155 Single $70-$90 (Special Breakfast)
Child $10 - $15 Extra adult $30 - $40 Sleeps up to 6
1 Queen 1 Double (2 bdrm)
1 Share

Wandin Valley Cottage is nestled amongst towering 100 year old cypress trees, surrounded by rural countryside. Step inside and you'll think you are in another era. Period antique furniture and Australian paintings create an ambience that not only relaxes but also makes the pressure of city living disappear. Generous provisions for a hearty cooked breakfast. Central to all Dandenong Ranges and Yarra Valley attractions including over 50 wineries Wandin Valley Cottage is the perfect getaway, the place to enjoy full privacy, tranquillity and friendly service.

Dandenongs - Cockatoo *B & B Self Contained Separate/Suite* *8 km E of Emerald*

Whistle-Stopover **AAAT★★★★☆**
Robyn Buttifant
11 Doonaha Road, Cockatoo, Vic 3781

Tel: (03) 5968 8208 Fax: (03) 5968 8278
Mobile: 0418 865 889 www.whistlestopover.com.au
whistlestopover@iprimus.com.au

Double $150-$220 (Full Breakfast) Child $30 over 12
2 night package $250-$350 double Credit Cards
2 King/Twin 1 King 3 Queen 2 Single (4 bdrm)
2 Ensuite 1 Private

An enchanting cottage in a storybook setting. Experience the essential character of the Dandenongs, sounds of Kookaburras, the rustle of eucalypts, the lacy green ferns, Puffing Billy, Australia's favourite steam train passes property twice daily. Romantic self contained Federation cottage, three bedrooms, luxurious sunken spa. Full size kitchen, lounge, dining room. Couple, families, groups. Breakfast provisions provided. Whistle-Stopover also offers traditional B&B Spa Suite featuring queen size, lace draped four poster bed, luxury double spa. Full breakfast served to suite. Sleeps 11.   RELAXING, ROMANTIC GETAWAY

Daylesford - Hepburn Springs *B & B* *500m NW of Daylesford PO*

Pendower House **AAATourism ★★★★☆**
Renee Ludekens and Jacqueline Coates
10 Bridport Street, Daylesford, Victoria 3460

Tel: (03) 5348 1535 Fax: (03) 5348 1545
Mobile: 0438 103 460 pendower@netconnect.com.au
www.pendowerhouse.com.au
Double $150-$380 Single $105-$290
(Full Breakfast) Child B/A
Spa Suite $280-$460 Credit Cards accepted
3 Queen 1 Twin (4 bdrm) 4 Ensuite

Pendower House is a beautifully restored Victorian House situated in the heart of Australia's Spa Capital - Daylesford. Rated 4.5 stars Pendower House offers first class amenities: fine linens, antique furnishings, big brass beds, an open fire surrounded by beautiful cottage gardens. Tariff includes cooked delicious country breakfast, more like brunch than breakfast! Walking distance from restaurants, galleries, antique stores and Lake Daylesford. Our luxurious Spa Suite, with corner spa, TV/Video and private courtyard: ideal for total privacy, peace and pampering. Massages and Spa packages available.

Dimboola   *B & B*   *1km NE of Dimboola P.O.*

Wimmera Gums B & B
Rob & Lesley Schultz
8 School Street, Dimboola, Vic 3414

Tel: (03) 5389 1207 Fax: (03) 5389 1207
Mobile: 0418 347 256
www.bbbook.com.au/wimmeragumsbb.html

Double $105-$120 Single $75-$105 (Full Breakfast)
Dinner from $15pp
2 Double 2 Single (3 bdrm)
2 Ensuite 1 Private

Set amongst tall gums halfway between Melbourne and Adelaide, minutes form heritage Wimmera River/Little Desert National Park. Guests receive drinks, savouries, fresh fruit daily. Reading lounge, magazines, books, games; TV lounge with video library. Spectacular all season BBQ facilities. Evening meal by prior arrangement. Motorised bicycles for hire no licence required. Special bridal package - spa, champagne, chocolates.... Off street parking. Your host, a qualified therapist offers optional massage. "Our aim is to make your stay a memorable one".

Echuca   *B & B*   *Echuca*

River Gallery Inn   AAATourism ★★★★☆
Monica Gray
578 High Street,
Echuca, Vic 3564

Tel: (03) 5480 6902 Fax: (03) 5480 6902
inn@echuca.net.au   www.echuca.net.au/~inn

Double $155-$225 Single $130-$180
(Continental Breakfast)
Credit Cards accepted
8 Queen (8 bdrm) 8 Private

The award winning River Gallery Inn is located in Echuca's historic Port Precinct. Paddle steamers, wonderful restaurants, speciality shops and wine tasting are all within a 5 minute walk. The River Gallery Inn offers eight luxury suites, each a theme of a different country. Private facilities include double spa baths and open wood fires (May to October). A welcoming lounge, sunny balconies and courtyards are available to guests. A substantial continental breakfast is served in our cosy breakfast room. Midweek packages are available. "Thank you for the hospitality. Everything was perfect." P & R Ofer, Melbourne.

Echuca   *B & B*   *Echuca*

Murray House
Len Keeper and Doug Hall
55 Francis Street, Echuca, Vic 3564

Tel: (03) 5482 4944 Fax: (03) 5480 6432
keephall@mcmedia.com.au
www.innhouse.com.au/murrayhouse.html

Double $200 (Full Breakfast) S/C from $130
Dbl from $200, Sgl from $130,
Credit Cards accepted
1 King/Twin 4 Queen (5 bdrm)
5 Ensuite

Hidden behind a high brick wall is a 1930's home, which is a treasure trove of exquisitely furnished rooms filled with antiques and objects d'art. Here guests are entertained with an inimitable blend of pampering and personality. In house guests have a choice of five spacious ensuite bedrooms and may relax in the sitting room or by the fireside in the library where afternoon tea and pre dinner drinks are served. Breakfast in the sunny dining room is always a delight - a multi course repast that changes daily.

Victoria

Foster - Wilsons Promontory *Homestay B & B   3km SW of Foster*

Aruma Bed & Breakfast   AAATourism ★★★☆
Linda Robins & Michael Kellock
20 Maines Way, Foster, Vic 3960

Tel: (03) 5682 1715 Fax: (03) 5682 1716
Mobile: 0418 586 334   audax@tpg.com.au
www.promaccom.com.au/aruma
Double $110 Single $85 (Full Breakfast)
Child $40 Dinner $30 B/A Credit Cards accepted
Pet on property Pets welcome
1 Queen 1 Twin (2 bdrm)   1 Private

You will love Aruma B&B, our delightful country haven. Your upstairs, purpose-built suite is comfortably furnished, fully equipped and the balcony offers a superb view. Outside you can sit by the dam and watch the ducks at play, hand feed sheep and alpacas or wander through the extensive gardens. Our guests comment on the warmth and friendliness, the scrumptious breakfasts and eclectic conversation. Assisted by Hugo and Holly, the friendly papillons, we offer you a memorable sojourn. Arrive as strangers, depart as friends.

Foster - Wilsons Promontory *2.7 km SW of Foster*
Self Contained Homestay B & B

Larkrise   AAATourism ★★★★☆
Jon & Ros Wathen
395 Fish Creek/Foster Road, Foster, Vic 3960

Tel: (03) 5682 2953 Fax: (03) 5682 2953
jonandros@larkrise.com.au
www.larkrise.com.au
Double $130 Single $110 (Full Breakfast)
Credit Cards accepted
1 King/Twin 1 Queen (2 bdrm)   2 Ensuite

Larkrise Farm overlooks Corner Inlet and Wilson's Promontory, and offers easy access to the national parks, fishing villages, and pristine beaches for which this area is renowned. Quality accommodation offers a spacious guests' conservatory/living area, with stunning views of the Prom. and the night sky, where a full country breakfast is served, with home-baked bread and local produce. Features include wheelchair facilities, cosy wood heating, TV, tape/CD player, tea/coffee-making, walks over picturesque farmland with blackwood forest, fern gullies, native birds and animals.

Geelong *Homestay   10 km NW of Geelong*

INN·HOUSE™

Lilydale House   AAATourism ★★★★☆
George & Lit Belcher
100 Dog Rocks Road, Batesford, Vic 3221

Tel: (03) 5276 1302 Fax: (03) 5276 1026
Mobile: 0417 056 465   belcher@bigpond.com
www.innhouse.com.au/lilydale.html
Double $140-$150 Single $110-$130 (Full Breakfast)
Child B/A Dinner from $40 B/A
Credit Cards accepted
2 Queen 2 Single (3 bdrm)   3 Ensuite

Geelong's best kept accommodation secret offering peace and tranquillity in a unique 200 acre bush setting just 10 minutes from the centre of Geelong, 1 hour from Melbourne Airport, 80 minutes from most of Melbourne and with easy access to the Great Ocean Road. The gracious country style house is extensively furnished with antiques and dinner is available by prior arrangement. The house is extensively air conditioned with open fires in the sitting and dining rooms. Your hosts and two friendly dogs extend a warm welcome.

Gippsland - Dandenongs *5 km N of Princes Highway*
B & B   Self Contained

Serendipity Lavender Farm B & B   AAAT★★★★★
Jane & Rob Elliott
80 Croft Road, Nar Nar Goon North, Vic 3812

Tel: (03) 5942 9164 Fax: (03) 5942 9165
Mobile: 0419 549 536
www.serendipitylavenderfarm.com.au

Double $180 Single $120 (Full Breakfast)
Dinner $52 1 x Self-Contained unit $220
Credit Cards accepted
3 King/Twin 1 Double (4 bdrm)   3 Ensuite 1 Private

Our purpose built B&B is perched on top of a hill, with stunning views across to Westernport Bay. Every room has a view that is always changing, gentle pinks of sunrise in the breakfast conservatory, brilliant sunsets in the guests lounge. See the night lights whilst relaxing in the Spa (with a glass of wine, (we are fully licensed). The lavender fields below delight the eye. Winter days can be spent in fully air conditioned comfort, reading, watching TV, or trekking in the hills nearby.

Gippsland South - Poowong   *19 km NW of Korumburra*
Farmstay Homestay Separate/Suite B & B

Myrambeek B & B
Helen & Tim De Vere
56-62 Nyora Road, Poowong, Vic 3988

Tel: (03) 5659 2479 Mobile: 0429 004 270
Fax: (03) 5659 2411   myrambeekbandb@bigpond.com
www.bbbook.com.au/myrambeekbb.html

Double $145 Single $105 (Full Breakfast)
Child $35 under 3yrs free Dinner $35
1 Queen 1 Single (1 bdrm) 1 Ensuite

Nestled in rolling hills of South Gippsland, Myrambeek B & B is the ultimate romantic retreat for couples who want to escape from it all. This spacious homestead captures all the understated elegance and charm of yesteryear, whilst still providing the modern comforts that enhance your holiday experience. Whether you venture out to explore some of this land's most scenic countryside, partake in the local delicacies, or just relax beside the open fires in your private suite, you're sure to go home feeling rejuvenated. So isn't it time you spoilt yourself!

Victoria

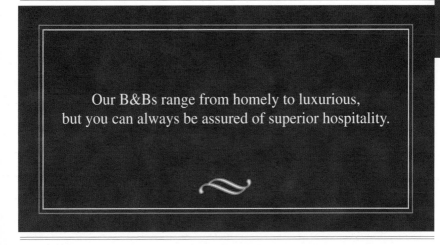

Our B&Bs range from homely to luxurious,
but you can always be assured of superior hospitality.

Grampians - Wartook   *Homestay B & B*   *29 km NW of Halls Gap*

Wartook Gardens   AAATourism ★★★★
Royce & Jeanne Raleigh
Mt Victory Road, Wartook, Vic 3401

Tel: (03) 5383 6200 Fax: (03) 5383 6240
bookings@wartookgardens.com.au
www.wartookgardens.com.au

Double $110-$145 Single $90 (Full Breakfast)
Dinner From $30 Credit Cards accepted
1 King/Twin 2 Queen (3 bdrm)
1 Ensuite 2 Private

Just minutes from the Grampians National Park, and set on 70 acres in the beautiful Wartook Valley famed for its mobs of kangaroos, Wartook Gardens offers elegant country living in a tranquil 5 acre garden of native and exotic plants and 110 bird species. Enjoy our delicious breakfast before visiting waterfalls, walks, wineries, lookouts, wildflower areas. Ceiling fans, air conditioning, saltwater pool, underfloor heating, woodheater, make your stay a very comfortable one - an all seasons destination. Enjoy friendly hospitality. Please phone.

Grampians - Wartook Valley   *B & B   Self Contained*   *55 km S of Horsham*

The Grelco Run   AAATourism ★★★
Graeme & Liz McDonald
Schmidt Road, Brimpaen, Vic 3401

Tel: (03) 5383 9221 Fax: (03) 5383 9222
grelco@grampians.net.au
www.grampians.net.au/grelco

Double $132 Single $66 (Full Breakfast)
Child $27.50 Dinner $60 Homestead Double $200
Credit Cards accepted
4 King/Twin 1 King 4 Queen 2 Twin 1 Single
(5 bdrm S/C 3 bdrm Homestead)   4 Ensuite 2 Share

The Grelco Run offers 2 s/c cottages set apart in natural bush, sleeping 6 in each, and a luxuriously appointed homestead with 3 guest bedrooms each with an ensuite. By prior arrangement we serve elegant hosted dinners in a convivial atmosphere. Our son Cameron operates the renowned Grampians Horse Riding Centre with escorted tours from the property. As we are adjacent to the National Park there are superb opportunities for bushwalking, 4WD driving, fishing, viewing abundant wildlife and wild flowers and visiting nearby wineries.

Just as we have a variety of B&Bs
you will also be offered a variety of breakfasts,
and they will always be generous.

Grampians - Wartook Valley *Homestay* *29 km NW of Halls Gap*

Carey Park
Peter & June Bruning
Northern Grampians Road,
Wartook, Vic 3401

Tel: (03) 5383 6334 Fax: (03) 5383 6334
www.bbbook.com.au/careypark.html
Double $115-$125 Single $80 (Full Breakfast)
Credit Cards accepted
1 King/Twin 1 Queen (2 bdrm)
2 Ensuite

Carey Park is forty acres of kangaroo country set against the mountainous backdrop of the majestic Grampians where the wildlife comes to you. Our large ranch style home has been especially designed as a B & B for your absolute comfort and delight. Each of the spaciously appointed guest rooms boasts a magnificent view, external entrance and internal access to the family home. This allows for interaction with your caring and friendly hosts, or privacy with a self-catering option. Minutes from National Park and popular attractions.

Hamilton - Branxholme *B & B Historic Homestead* *22 km SW of Hamilton*

Arrandoovong   AAAT★★★★
Jeanie & Bill Sharp
RMB 1285, Branxholme, Vic 3302

Tel: (03) 5578 6221 Fax: (03) 5578 6249
Mobile: 0408 528 228   arrandoovong@hotkey.net.au
www.bbbook.com.au/arrandoovong.html
Double $125-$154 Single $120
(Full Breakfast) Child by arrangement
Dinner $40 Credit Cards accepted
2 Queen 1 Twin (3 bdrm)   2 Private

Two storey bluestone homestead built in the 1850's with the historic gardens dominated by giant English oaks and a permanent stream shaded by poplars, elms and old pines, offering pleasant walks and relaxation. Spacious guest rooms offer queen size beds, with guest bathrooms upstairs. Spend time relaxing on the verandah or balcony, walking in the grounds or along the creek. Close to the Grampians, Great Ocean Road, Portland, Port Fairy and wineries. An ideal stopover Melbourne - Adelaide. Your stay at "Arrandoovong" will be something special. We look forward to your company.

Heathcote - Goldfields *B & B* *30 km Bendigo*

Emeu Inn Restaurant,
Bed & Breakfast and Wine Centre
AAAT★★★★☆   Fred & Leslye Thies
187 High Street, Heathcote, Vic 3523

Tel: (03) 5433 2668 Fax: (03) 5433 4022
info@emeuinn.com.au   www.emeuinn.com.au
Double $180 Single $130 (Full Breakfast)
Child $35 Dinner $17 - $26 Extra person $35
Credit Cards accepted Pet on property Pets welcome
5 Queen (5 bdrm)   5 Ensuite

Indulge yourself in luxury at the historic Emeu Inn where comfortable suites await you. Dine in The Age Good Food Guide recommended restaurant where international cuisine and great local wines are standard fare. This award-winning B&B has five spacious suites with queen-size beds, private ensuites with spas and all the extras gourmet travellers expect. Enjoy the homemade chocolates and sparkling wine. The lounge is a great gathering place with tea and coffee, nibbles and fresh fruit. Enjoy a game of golf, Lake Eppalock, the forests, the shops or the wine!

Victoria

Kyneton *Country House* *84 km NW of Melbourne*

Moorville at Kyneton AAATourism ★★★★
Fran & John Wigley
1 Powlett Street, Kyneton, Vic 3444

Tel: (03) 5422 6466 Fax: (03) 5422 6460
Mobile: 0411 208 448 moorville@bigpond.com
www.moorville.com.au

Double $130-$155 Single $100-$120 (Full Breakfast)
Dinner $45pp S.C. $160 Credit Cards accepted
2 Queen 1 Double 2 Single (4 bdrm)
2 Ensuite 1 Share

You will find Moorville a relaxing retreat in a quiet picturesque part of historic Kyneton. Experience and enjoy the lifestyle of the Edwardian era, surrounded by the comforts of one of the period's grandest local homes. Special breakfast with a view, featuring local and home made produce, evening meals by arrangement. Spacious living areas, library, veranda, indoor pool, tennis court, petanque. Close to River Walk and Botanic Gardens. Self-contained "cottage style" accommodation available at Pipers Retreat, secreted behind our bookshop. Enjoy Edwardian life style with today's comforts.

Lakes Entrance *B & B* *Self Contained* *Lakes Entrance Central*

Lou's AAATourism ★★★★☆
Mary-Lou Irwin
37 Esplanade, Lakes Entrance, Vic 3909

Tel: (03) 5155 2732 Fax: (03) 5155 2746
Mobile: 0419 183 932
marylou@net-tech.com.au
www.lakes-entrance.com/lous

Double $110-$135 Single $65-$105 (Full Breakfast)
Child POA Credit Cards accepted
Pet on property Pets welcome
1 King 1 Queen (2 bdrm) 2 Ensuite

"An oasis in a street of motels and caravan parks". A warm welcome, park in secure under cover parking. Settle in and enjoy the quiet comfort of well appointed rooms. A large breakfast is served in the sunny dining room looking over the pretty rear garden and BBQ area, with wild birds feeding (only a few metres away). Smoking retreats, front and rear gardens. Charlie, my friendly Lab, welcomes friendly dogs too. Stroll over the road along the foreshore pathway to shops, restaurants and cruises.

Lakes Entrance *B & B* *Boutique B & B*

Deja Vu AAATourism ★★★★☆
Beverly & Gerard Goris
Clara Street, Lakes Entrance, Vic 3909

Tel: (03) 5155 4330 Fax: (03) 5155 3718
Mobile: 0408 351 550 dejavu@dejavu.com.au
www.dejavu.com.au

Double $170-$240 Single $130 (Full Breakfast)
Dinner on request 2 bedroom waterfront villa
Credit Cards accepted
5 Queen 1 Single (5 bdrm) 5 Ensuite

Absolute private waterfront. 7 acres of wetland gully, temperate rainforest. Modern, innovative architecture, sculptured into the environment, 4 levels. Uniquely private suites capturing water views. in-room spas, balconies. Journey through some of Australia's most unspoilt country and Victoria's greatest lakes and national parks. 3.5 hrs east of Melbourne. 4.5hrs to Canberra. Facilities & Services: From the property, canoe to shops or picnic on the lake. Deja Vu "Happy Hour" cruise on our leisure boat. Wyanga Park Winery lunch or dinner cruise. Established: 1995

Leongatha - South Gippsland   *12 km S of Leongatha*

B & B Guest House

Lyre Bird Hill Winery & Guest House
AAAT★★★★☆
Owen & Robyn Schmidt
370 Inverloch Road, Koonwarra, Vic 3954

Tel: **(03) 5664 3204** Fax: (03) 5664 3206
rowen@lyrebirdhill.com.au
www.lyrebirdhill.com.au

Double $120-$150 Single $100-$110 (Full Breakfast)
Dinner $40 - 60 Credit Cards accepted Pet on property
3 Queen 2 Single (3 bdrm) 3 Ensuite

Family winery offering home-style hospitality in their modern homestead. Fine country cuisine with estate wines, especially Pinot Noir, may be enjoyed with other guests and the hosts. Two sitting rooms, a relaxing open fire and lovely rose gardens contribute to the serenity. Wine tasting and tours - golf nearby, walk the rail trail, beaches, Wilsons Prom and Phillip Island within easy reach. A three bedroom family cottage is also available. Ben the dog loves to welcome all guests in return for a scratch on the head.

Lorne - Aireys Inlet   *B & B   14 km E of Lorne*

Lorneview B & B   AAATourism ★★★★☆
Nola & Kevin Symes
677 Great Ocean Road, Eastern View, Vic 3231

Tel: **(03) 5289 6430** Fax: (03) 5289 6735
lorneview@primus.com.au
www.lorneview.com.au

Double $110-$150 Single $100-$140
(Continental Breakfast) Credit Cards accepted
2 Queen (2 bdrm)
2 Ensuite

Lorneview has two spacious guest rooms, separate from main house, one overlooking the ocean and the other overlooking the bush. Each room as QS bed, ensuite, TV, CD player, heating, air conditioning, refrigerator, iron, ironing board, tea and coffee facilities. Delicious breakfast of fresh fruit, homemade muesli, muffins and croissants is served in your room or on balcony overlooking beach. Dinner unavailable, but many excellent restaurants nearby. Barbecue and Games Room provided. Enjoy walks along the beach and go to sleep listening to the waves.

Lorne - Otway Ranges - Birregurra   *40 km N of Lorne*

B & B Heritage

Elliminook B & B   AAATourism ★★★★
Jill & Peter Falkiner
585 Warncoort Road, Birregurra, Vic 3242

Tel: **(03) 5236 2080** Fax: (03) 5236 2423
Mobile: 040 810 7021   enquiries@elliminook.com.au
www.elliminook.com.au

Double $145-$186 Single $120-$140
(Full Breakfast) Credit Cards accepted
2 Queen 2 Double 2 Single (4 bdrm)
3 Ensuite 1 Private

Elliminook c.1865 is a beautifully restored and decorated National Trust classified homestead featured in Country Style and House and Garden magazines. Guests will enjoy the historic garden, croquet boules and tennis, open fire places, liquor service, sumptuous cooked breakfast, fresh flowers in your room, and welcoming hospitality. From Elliminook you can explore the Great Ocean Road, Twelve Apostles, Shipwreck Coast and the walks, waterfalls and rain forest of the Otway Ranges. For a unique accommodation experience be our welcome guest.

Victoria

Macedon Ranges - Cherokee   *Self Contained B & B Retreat   12 km E of Woodend*

Craigielea Mountain Retreat   AAAT★★★★★
Simone Ivanyi & Richard Graham
109 Mountain Road, Cherokee, Vic. 3434

Tel: (03) 5427 0799 Fax: (03) 5427 0669
Mobile: 0411 444 449   info@craigielea.net
www.craigielea.net

Double $250-$325 Dinner from $50 pp
Credit Cards accepted Pet on property
3 King (3 bdrm)   3 Ensuite

FEATURED ON CHANNEL 7 WINTER SPECIAL 7.30PM TUESDAY 9 JULY 2002.   FEATURED AUG. 2002 EDITION OF BETTER HOMES & GARDENS MAGAZINE, ON SALE FROM 8 JULY 2002.   The hidden jewel of the Macedon Ranges, only 45 minutes from Melbourne. Brand new 5 star self-contained suites, within a stunning, historic 32 acre property. We are fully licensed and gourmet dinners can be served at the suite's own dining table by arrangement. All guests receive a complimentary bottle of champagne and an abundant selection of chocolates. This is a totally rejuvenating experience in stunning surroundings.

Mallacoota   *Homestay B & B   23 km SE of Genoa*

Mareeba Lodge   AAATourism ★★★☆
Anne & Wally Studd
59 Mirrabooka Road,
Mallacoota, Vic 3892

Tel: (03) 5158 0378 Fax: (03) 5158 0407
www.bbbook.com.au/mareebalodge.html

Double $65-$85 Single $50-$60
(Full Breakfast) Child B/A
1 Double 1 Twin 1 Single (3 bdrm)
1 Share

Anne and Wally offer personalised service in a clean comfortable, scenic location at Mareeba Lodge which is renowned for hospitality and friendly service. Modern shared facilities, electric blankets, lounge, TV, tea and coffee making facilities, fridge, barbecue. Rooms serviced daily. Off street parking. Meals are served upstairs with ocean, lake and mountain views. No pets, no children. Temperate climate, bird watch, fishing lakes and surf, bush walking. Golf with the kangaroos, tennis, bowls, boat hire, take a cruise, restaurants.

Mansfield   *B & B Self Contained   0.8 km N of Mansfield Centre*

Mary's Place Bed & Breakfast   AAAT★★★☆
Mary Luxton
32 Somerset Crescent,
Mansfield, Vic 3722

Tel: (03) 5775 1928 Fax: (03) 5775 1928
www.bbbook.com.au/marysplacebb.html

Double $90-$120
(Continental Breakfast)
Child $20 $30 Extra person
1 Queen 2 Single (2 bdrm)
1 Private

Mary's Place is a cosy, quiet SC unit in a beautiful garden with rural view towards Mt Buller yet close to town centre. Two bedrooms, one with QS bed and other with 2 singles. Car port, TV, linen, drying room and own bathroom. Provisions for a light breakfast and some cooking facilities. With mountains, rivers and lakes there is plenty to see and do. There are two welcoming small dogs to either spoil or ignore. Phone for availability and secure by sending deposit by cheque.

Marysville *B & B Country Guesthouse*

INN·HOUSE™

Kerami Guesthouse   AAATourism ★★★★☆
Grace & Terry Ross, 7 Kerami Crescent, Kerami, Vic 3779

Tel: (03) 5963 3260 Fax: (03) 5963 3525 Mobile: 0407 773 012
keramihouse@bigpond.com   www.innhouse.com.au/kerami.html

Double $130-$295 (Full Breakfast) Child B/A Weekend Package $380 - $440 Credit Cards accepted
4 Queen (4 bdrm)   4 Ensuite

An easy drive from Melbourne, through the stunning Black Spur road, the charming town of Marysville and the surrounding "Mystic Mountains' has attracted visitors for a hundred plus years. There does seem to be something in the air......... magical fern valleys, stunning waterfalls and the old world charm of Kerami House.

Nestled in a sumptuous glade of shade trees, let your hosts, Grace and Terry welcome you to Kerami House with afternoon tea to experience peace and tranquillity reminiscent of a more languid era, yet it is situated only moments from all the activities and beauty of sub-alpine Marysville.

Stretch those weary muscles, weary from exploration in front of a crackling open fire, or maybe enjoy a book on the verandah, shunning the exercise in favour of a well earned rest. At Kerami your time is your own.

Built in 1920, the country retreat of a millionaire. Fully restored 1920's charm and decor alongside modern comforts. Highlights include the 'Great Room' with billiard table and ten foot baronial style open fireplace, the smaller guest lounge for more secluded gatherings and the delightful dining room for romantic candlelit dining. Four ensuite rooms in-house (one with private balcony and spa) all located upstairs. Ideal atmosphere for a romantic weekend or a group to have fun.

"We thank you for a wonderful weekend, although the weather was dull, Kerami was bright, full of friendliness, laughter and warmth." (TJ Eltham)

Dining is a feature here - from the inclusive full breakfast to candlelit dinners for two. Most guests take advantage of the all inclusive weekend packages to savour quality meals, to relax and enjoy the views of the surrounding canopy gardens.

Victoria

Melbourne - Blackburn   *B & B   Self Contained   20 km E of Melbourne*

Bethbiri Brook B & B   AAATourism ★★★★
Lyn & Chris Russell
7 Jeffery Street, Blackburn, Vic 3130

Tel: (03) 9878 6142 Fax: (03) 9878 6600
Mobile: 0419 545 452   bethbiri@bigpond.com
www.bbbook.com.au/bethbiribrookbb.html

Double $95-$110 Single $90-$98
(Continental Breakfast)
Child $20+ Credit Cards accepted
1 Queen 1 Double (2 bdrm)   1 Private

Charming self-contained cottage in beautiful half-acre rustic garden. Bellbirds, kookaburras, and other wildlife are seen in the unique National Trust area. Short walk to bus and railway. 20 mins train journey to scenic Dandenong Ranges, 5 mins from major shopping complex, restaurants, theatres, swimming pool and sporting facilities. Airport bus close by. 20 km East of Melbourne city, cottage features main bedroom, separate lounge (2nd bedroom), ensuite, and fully equipped kitchen. Queen size bed (electric blanket), split-cycle air-conditioning/ heating, TV/Video in lounge, TV in bedroom, refrigerator, stove, microwave and guest parking.

Melbourne - Bundoora   *Homestay   12 km NE of Melbourne*

Bundoora Homestay
John & Cath Cantrill
6 Amber Court, Bundoora, Vic 3083

Tel: (03) 9467 1335
johncan@warrandyte.starway.net.au
www.bbbook.com.au/bundoora.html

Double $60 Single $40 (Continental Breakfast)
Child 50% Dinner $15
2 Double 1 Single (3 bdrm)
3 Share

Bundoora is an attractive suburb situated east of the Melbourne Airport and northeast from the city. Both can be reached by car in 20 minutes. The area is well served by public transport. The tram stop is only a few minutes away and the journey takes about 40-50 minutes. The area is also well served by bus and train. We have a comfortable two-storey dwelling, guests have their own bathroom which includes bath and shower. We are committed to offering warm and friendly hospitality.

Melbourne - Camberwell   *B & B   9km E of Melbourne*

Springfield's   AAATourism ★★★☆
Robyn & Phillip Jordan
4 Springfield Avenue,
Camberwell, Vic 3124

Tel: (03) 9809 1681 Fax: (03) 9889 3117
the.jordans@pacific.net.au
www.bbbook.com.au/springfields.html

Double $110 Single $75
(Full Breakfast)
1 King/Twin 1 Twin (2 bdrm)
1 Private

Welcome to "Springfield's" - our attractive and spacious family home situated in a quiet avenue in one of Melbourne's finest suburbs. As well as the two guest bedrooms and adjoining bathroom, guests can enjoy the peace and privacy of their own lounge - or join us in our family room. Two city tram routes and a city train (5 minutes) serve popular attractions and the city.   "Springfield's" is a non-smoking Homestay, where children are most welcome. Our home is your home when you next visit Melbourne.

Melbourne - Carrum   *B & B*   *Carrum Suburban*

B & B at Mac's - Carrum   AAATourism ★★★☆
Brian McKenzie
49 Valetta Street, Carrum, Vic 3197

Tel: (03) 9772 1435 Fax: (03) 9772 1435
bbMACS@Supportnet.com.au
www.bbbook.com.au/macscarrum.html

Double $75 Single $45 (Full Breakfast)
Child $20 Dinner $20pp, BBQ Pets welcome
1 Double 1 Twin (2 bdrm)
1 Share

I offer the amenities of a friendly home. This homely atmosphere includes two peaceful bedrooms with colour TV. Home-made bread, tea and coffee any time. Aussie BBQ on request $20 pp. It is a pleasant 5 minute walk to the beach. Carrum R/S is 4 minutes away. Mornington Peninsula 20 km away. Children welcome. Pets O.K. outside. A smoke-free home. "A lovely haven where graciousness, courtesy and exquisite service still exist . ." NB, Hamilton.

Melbourne - Caulfield   *B & B*   *11 km S of Melbourne*

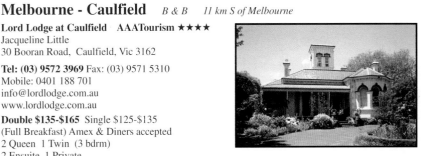

Lord Lodge at Caulfield   AAATourism ★★★★
Jacqueline Little
30 Booran Road, Caulfield, Vic 3162

Tel: (03) 9572 3969 Fax: (03) 9571 5310
Mobile: 0401 188 701
info@lordlodge.com.au
www.lordlodge.com.au

Double $135-$165 Single $125-$135
(Full Breakfast) Amex & Diners accepted
2 Queen 1 Twin (3 bdrm)
2 Ensuite 1 Private

Lord Lodge is a stately Victorian villa (circa 1880), located a short distance from downtown Melbourne. Listed as one of Australia's historic buildings it retains all of the features of this elegant era, with soaring 16 foot ceilings, elaborate hand painted cornices, open fires etc. Lord Lodge has won acclaim for its hospitality and service. You are assured of a warm friendly greeting and discreet unobtrusive service.

Melbourne - East Melbourne   *B & B*   *2 km E of Melbourne CBD*

La Paloma Rosa
Trudi McIntosh
33 Grey Street, East Melbourne, Vic 3002

Tel: (03) 9416 4770 Fax: (03) 9416 4770
Mobile: 0407 547852
trudim@ozemail.com.au
www.bbbook.com.au/lapalomarosa.html

Double $150-$195 Single $150-$175
(Continental & Full Breakfast) Credit Cards accepted
1 Double (1 bdrm)   1 Ensuite

We invite you to enjoy our lovely Italianate 1861 villa in historic East Melbourne village; only minutes by car to MCG, CBD, 15 minutes walk, trams 7 minutes via beautiful Fitzroy Gardens. Luxurious double room with ensuite overlooking leafy Darling Square. Relax in cosy, book-filled salon where afternoon tea is served or in secret garden. Breakfast includes only the best organic produce. Walk to Richmond's wonderful Bridge Road fashion shops/cafes or cosmopolitan Brunswick Street. Delicious hampers available for cricket/football/tennis season. Ample off-street parking.

Melbourne - Eltham   *B & B*   *20 km NE of Melbourne*

Cantala Bed and Breakfast
Bev and Peter Robertson
62 Henry Street, Eltham, Vic 3095

Tel: (03) 9431 3374 Fax: (03) 9431 3374
cantalabnb@bigpond.com
www.bbbook.com.au/cantalabnb.html
Double $110 Single $93.5 (Full Breakfast)
Credit Cards accepted
2 Queen (2 bdrm)
2 Ensuite

Rediscover the simple pleasures of life by indulging yourself at Cantala. Surrounded by shaded cottage gardens, this charming period home offers old world ambience and homely comforts. Two spacious and elegantly appointed bedrooms feature ensuites, cosy sitting areas, reverse cycle air conditioning or gas coal fireplace and private doors opening onto wide verandahs. Experience sensational food and wine tasting, browse in antique shops and open-air markets or simply take pleasure from magnificent scenery in the nearby Diamond and Yarra Valley regions. Be pampered at Cantala.

Melbourne - Hampton   *Homestay B & B*   *16 km S of Melbourne*

Peggy's Place
Peggy Hayton
19 Orlando Street,
Hampton, Vic 3188

Tel: (03) 9521 9187
bhayton@melbpc.org.au
www.bbbook.com.au/peggysplace.html
Double $120 Single $90
(Continental Breakfast) Pet on property
1 Queen 1 Single (2 bdrm)
1 Share

My 100 year old cottage with the sweetest garden is by the sea, furnished with antiques and is close to quick public transport, excellent shopping and loads of restaurants. You will share the house with me, Sissie the cat and a lovable dog Abigail. Your breakfast includes home made bread, fresh seasonal fruit, juice, homemade cereal, muesli and jams. Please ring (best time early morning or evening) or leave your name and phone number on my answering machine and I will ring you back as soon as possible.

Melbourne - Hawthorn   *B & B*   *4 km NE of Melbourne*

Honeyeater Lodge   AAATourism ★★★★☆
Judith & Patrick Farrelly
3 Xavier Avenue, Hawthorn, Vic 3122

Tel: (03) 9819 0772 Fax: (03) 9819 0873
Mobile: 0407 806 336
relax@honeyeaterlodge.com.au
www.honeyeaterlodge.com.au
Double $160-$240 Single $140-$160
(Full Breakfast) Credit Cards accepted
1 King/Twin 2 Queen (3 bdrm) 3 Ensuite

Honeyeater Lodge is an elegant 1920s home providing luxury accommodation in leafy Hawthorn, only 6km from Melbourne's CBD. Its polished timber floors, leadlight windows and high ceilings radiate a warm and welcoming ambience. Romantic bedrooms with ensuites (double spa bridal suite), tempting fireside breakfasts and generous hospitality together with a heated, saltwater pool set amongst palms and tree ferns offer the discerning guest a tranquil and memorable retreat close to Melbourne's many attractions. Accredited tourism business. Sorry, unsuitable for children or pets.

Melbourne - Hawthorn   *B & B*   *W of Hawthorn*

Daphne's at Hawthorn
Daphne Joyce Arthur
41 Mason Street, Hawthorn, Vic 3122

Tel: (03) 9818 5133 Fax: (03) 9818 7633
www.bbbook.com.au/daphnes.html

Double $120-$150 Single $100-$130
(Full Breakfast) Credit Cards accepted
1 King/Twin 1 Queen (2 bdrm)
2 Ensuite

Daphne's at Hawthorn offers superb accommodation and service in a delightful Edwardian home - away - from home. Public transport is only one minute's walk and Melbourne's CBD is only 3 kms away. Daphne's is situated in a heritage listed area with close proximity to Bridge Road shopping, and the famed Victoria Street restaurants, most sporting and entertainment venues and the Yarra River bicycle /walking tracks. Delicious breakfasts and other delights are served. King/twin or Queen or single bedrooms with ensuites, bar fridges, tea, coffee making facilities, televisions are beautifully decorated. There is a guest lounge and dining room, fax/email, and wheel chair access.

Melbourne - Hurstbridge   *25 km NE of Melbourne*

B & B Self-Contained Cottage

Bluehaven B & B   Helen & Malcolm Sterry
760-762 Heidelberg/Kinglake Road,
Hurstbridge, Vic 3099

Tel: (03) 9718 1811 Fax: (03) 9718 1811
Mobile: 0407 182 943   bluhaven@bigpond.com.au
www.bluehavenbandb.com.au

Double $110 Single $95 (Full Breakfast)
S.C Cottage ($165 double) Credit Cards accepted
1 King/Twin 3 Queen 2 Single (5 bdrm)
2 Ensuite 2 Private

Bluehaven is on the Yarra Valley Scenic Route and offers - a bluestone home with three bedrooms (own ensuite/ bathroom) and a 1920's two bedroom cottage (luxury bathroom). Open fires, ducted heating and air conditioning. Complimentary airport transfers."Bluehaven" is only a five minute walk to the Hurstbridge railway station allowing easy access to the centre of Melbourne. Tourist attractions include wineries, antiques, arts and goldfields. Restaurants and cafes a short walk or drive away. Quality, comfort and warm hospitality in a non-smoking environment.

Melbourne - Newport   *B & B*   *11km SW of Melbourne*

Brief Encounter B & B
Therese, Michael, Thomas (14) & Patrick (7) Slee
27 Laurie Street, Newport, Vic 3015

Tel: (03) 9391 2187
www.bbbook.com.au/briefencounter.html

Double $90-$100 Single $70-$90
(Full Breakfast)
Dinner $15 - $ 20 B/A
1 Double (1 bdrm)
1 Ensuite

With the emphasis on comfort and homemade - from the quilt on your antique double bed to the generous breakfast served to you in our dining room - we invite you to our charming 1920's home. Your accommodation includes a private sitting room where you can relax with a range of books, music and something special to have with tea or coffee. Located within a short drive to the historic seaport of Williamstown and the Westgate Freeway enables easy access to our local treasures, Melbourne's attractions and the major highways.

Victoria

Melbourne - North Balwyn   B & B   *13 km E of Melbourne*

Bellevue Bed & Breakfast   AAATourism ★★★☆
Di & Terry Lamb
32 Columba Street, North Balwyn, Vic 3104

Tel: (03) 9859 4492 Mobile: 0417 378 674
dtlamb@net2000.com.au
www.users.net2000.com.au/~dtlamb

Double $90 Single $75 (Continental Breakfast)
Child $10 - $20 Dinner N/A
1 King/Twin (1 bdrm)
1 Ensuite

At Bellevue we offer peace and tranquillity close to the city. A comfortable, air-conditioned bedroom with a spacious living area and kitchenette with widespread views is convenient and relaxing. Breakfast can be taken privately upstairs or formally downstairs amidst antique furniture. There are golf links, tennis courts, shops and restaurants within easy walking distance. Lygon Street shops, restaurants and theatres are 10 minutes via the Freeway. Bellevue is about a half-hour drive from the airport and is a good starting point for all Victoria's attractions.

Melbourne - North Fitzroy   *Self Contained*   *2 km N of Melbourne*

Slattery's North Fitzroy B & B   AAAT★★★★☆
Jacqui & Ron Slattery
41 Rae Street, North Fitzroy, Vic 3068

Tel: (03) 9489 1308
www.bbbook.com.au/slatterysnthfitzroybb.html

Double $110 Single $85 (Continental Breakfast)
Credit Cards accepted
1 Twin (1 bdrm)
1 Private

"Slattery's" offers superior self-contained accommodation in Melbourne's first suburb, 2 km from Melbourne's CBD. Air-conditioned, centrally heated accommodation comprises bedroom with twin beds, separate sitting room, bathroom, kitchenette and meals area. Tea & coffee facility, toaster, microwave, fridge, TV, video, hair-dryer, iron and ironing board, electric blankets, garage parking and roof garden with city views. Close to public transport, theatres, Edinburgh Gardens, Royal Exhibition Buildings and Brunswick Street cafes. Breakfast is your choice of juice, cereals, breads, and home-made jams and marmalades. Credit cards.

Melbourne - Richmond   *Self Contained B & B*   *1.5 km E of Melbourne Central*

Rotherwood
Flossie Sturzaker, 13 Rotherwood Street,
Richmond, Melbourne, Vic 3121

Tel: (03) 9428 6758 Fax: (03) 9428 6758
rotherwood@a1.com.au
www.bbbook.com.au/rotherwood.html

Double $130-$160 Single $110-$130
(Full Breakfast) Credit Cards accepted
1 Queen 1 Single (2 bdrm) 1 Private

"On the Hill" in Richmond, "Rotherwood" is at the heart of Melbourne's attractions. Walking distance of the MCG, Royal Botanic Gardens, National Tennis Centre, Royal Exhibition Centre, shops and restaurants. Only a 5 minute tram ride to City. Easy access to National Gallery, Concert Hall, Crown Casino, and Southbank. Private entrance to Victorian era apartment. Large sitting room with French doors leading to terrace overlooking garden. Bedroom (Q.S. Bed), private bathroom, and separate dining room with cooking facilities. Special French Breakfast provided. Extra fold-out bed. Airport transport available. Golfing excursions arranged. TV, Video. Suitable for short or long term stay.

Melbourne - Richmond   *B & B   3 km E of Melbourne CBD*

Villa Donati
Trevor Finlayson and Gayle Lamb
377 Church Street, Richmond, Vic 3121

Tel: (03) 9428 8104 Fax: (03) 9421 0956 Mobile: 0412 068 855
email@villadonati.com
www.villadonati.com

Double $160-$190 Single $130-$160 (Full Breakfast) Credit Cards accepted
3 Double (3 bdrm)
3 Ensuite

Villa Donati (Circa 1886) is an elegant Italianate villa restored to capture the essence of the European pensione. Originally built for one of Melbourne's best known architects and later home to the Anglican Archbishop, historic Villa Donati is now a stunning mixture of the contemporary and antique.

All bedrooms are luxuriously appointed with facilities including en-suites, TV, refrigerator, tea & coffee making, air-conditioning and hydronic heating. Each bedroom has its own unique style and furnishings ranging from a romantic, hand-forged, wrought iron, four poster bed to a classic art-deco look. Features include imported toiletries, fine bed linen, antiques and original art works.

Villa Donati is situated on the hill, amongst many fine churches, in the suburb of Richmond, one of Melbourne's most popular inner city areas. Only minutes away from the CBD and Melbourne's main entertainment, sporting and shopping precincts, Villa Donati is the perfect location for tourism and business.   From the Visitors' Book:Divine - everything!

Victoria

Melbourne - Richmond Hill   *B & B   Self Contained   3 km E of Melbourne City*

Richmond Hill Hotel   AAATourism★★★
Laurie Auer, 353 Church Street, Richmond, Vic 3121

Tel: (03) 9428 6501 Fax: (03) 9427 0128 Freecall: 1800 801 618
rhhotel@bigpond.net.au   www.richmondhillhotel.com.au

Double $85-$125 Single $75-$105 Child $12 Extra adult $28 Credit Cards accepted
8 King/Twin 22 Double 11 Twin 4 Single (45 bdrm)   27 Ensuite 7 Share

Richmond Hill Hotel is a boutique Bed & Breakfast centrally located in Cosmopolitan Richmond. Offering affordable prices and a range of accommodation options from single economy rooms to double or twin rooms with ensuites, large family rooms and self contained apartments.

Enjoy the spacious guest lounge with complimentary tea & coffee served all day, (open fire in winter). Our club bar is open every evening from 5pm. In warmer months, enjoy our front terrace or the quieter rear courtyard. We have free off-street parking for about 25 cars.

Richmond is only 3 km from the CBD (10 minutes by tram), the hotel is walking distance from MCG, Bridge Road Shops and cafes and Olympic Park and Tennis Stadiums. There is a host of restaurants offering a wide variety of cuisines nearby.

We have many letters from satisfied guests:

"The room was well presented, the staff ever helpful and the best breakfast in town" MT. Brisbane, Qld.

"We found the accommodation very comfortable and clean, great value, great location." JB. Bellbridge, Vic.

Please note there are tariff surcharges during AFL Grand Final, Melbourne Cup Carnival, Australian Tennis Open and Grand Prix.

Melbourne - South Yarra   *B & B*   *2 km SE of Melbourne*

Balmoral of Melbourne   AAATourism ★★★★
Lyn & Tory
783 Punt Road, South Yarra, Vic 3141

Tel: (03) 9866 4449 Fax: (03) 9866 4449
Mobile: 0417 366 540
balmoral@alphalink.com.au
www.bbbook.com.au/balmoralofmelbourne.html
Double $115-$145 Single $95-$125
(Continental Breakfast) Pet on property
1 Queen 1 Twin (2 bdrm)
1 Ensuite 1 Private

Elegant accommodation in the heart of South Yarra, Melbourne's most sophisticated and fashionable shopping area. Within walking distance to some of the city's best restaurants, Royal Botanic Gardens, St Kilda Business district, Victorian Arts Centre, Southbank, MCG, Tennis Centre, and much more. Balmoral offers guests an exclusive and vibrant location from which to explore and experience Melbourne for either business or pleasure We extend the highest standard of service and genuine hospitality. Guest parking.

Melbourne - St Kilda   *B & B*   *5 km S of Melbourne*

Fountain Terrace   AAATourism ★★★★☆
Heikki and Penny Minkkinen
28 Mary Street, St Kilda West, Vic 3182

Tel: (03) 9593 8123 Fax: (03) 9593 8696
Mobile: 0412 059 559   info@fountainterrace.com.au
www.fountainterrace.com.au
Double $165-$235 Single $130-$195 (Full Breakfast)
Child $25 Dinner $25 Credit Cards accepted
2 King 3 Queen (5 bdrm)   5 Ensuite

Fountain Terrace was originally built in 1880 as a gentleman's residence but had a more colourful and chequered history from the 1930's on. Heikki and Penny with the help of their aged foxie dog have undertaken major renovations returning the building back to its former glory and offer five guest rooms with reverse cycle air-conditioning, bar fridge and tea and coffee making facilities. St Kilda is one of the most vibrant and cosmopolitan places you can visit whilst in Melbourne and just minutes to the Grand Prix and Albert Park Lake, St Kilda Beach and Fitzroy Street. Light rail and tram are also less than five minutes walk from the house.

Melbourne - St Kilda   *B & B*   *5 km SE of Melbourne*

Alrae Bed & Breakfast   AAATourism ★★★☆
Vivienne Wheeler
7 Hughenden Road, St Kilda East, Vic 3183

Tel: (03) 9527 2033 Fax: (03) 9527 2044
Mobile: 0409 174 132   alrae2@bigpond.com
www.bbbook.com.au/alrae.html
Double $135-$165 Single $88-$110
(Special Breakfast) Child $20 - $55
Dinner $22 B/A Credit Cards accepted
1 Queen 1 Twin (2 bdrm)   1 Ensuite 1 Share

Alrae, formerly a private family home is now a certified tourism business, 5km from Melbourne CBD, handy public transport, beach, shops, sports venues, theatres etc. with on site parking. The queen bedroom has ensuite with bidet, fridge, air-conditioning, microwave, outdoor patio and private entrance. The twin bedroom has adjoining private bathroom with spa shower over bath tub. Both rooms have TV/VCR and access to laundry facilities. Specialty breakfasts, embracing dietary needs, are served in Edwardian dining room cum guests lounge. Corporate, senior, group enquiries invited.

Victoria

Melbourne - St Kilda   *B & B   4 km SE of Melbourne*

Annies Bed and Breakfast   AAATourism ★★★☆
Ann Briese
93 Park Street, St Kilda West, Vic 3182

Tel: (03) 8500 3755 Fax: (03) 9534 8705
Mobile: 0425 713 755
annies_StKilda@bigpond.com
www.anniesbedandbreakfast.com.au

Double $120 Single $100 (Full Breakfast)
Child $30 Dinner $30 Credit Cards accepted
3 Queen (3 bdrm)   2 Ensuite 1 Private

Annies is a restored and modernised 100 years old Edwardian cottage within walking distance of St Kilda's West Beach, world class restaurants, vibrant entertainment venues and Albert Park Lake (host to the Grand Prix). It is a 15 minute tram ride to Melbourne CBD. Breakfast is served in the spacious dining room and guests have access to a lounge and sitting room and backyard cottage garden. Hydronic heating and open fires in most rooms provide a warm winter retreat and we are airconditioned in summer.

Melbourne - St Kilda   *B & B   5 km S of Melbourne*

Boutique Hotel St Marine   AAATourism ★★★★
Pamela Allan
42 Marine Parade, St Kilda, Vic 3182

Tel: (03) 9534 1311 Fax: (03) 9534 1355
stmarine@iprimus.com.au   www.stmarine.com.au
Double $110-$165 Single $69-$121
(Continental Breakfast) Child $25
Credit Cards accepted Pets welcome
1 King 7 Queen 1 Twin 1 Single (10 bdrm)
1 Ensuite 2 Private 2 Share

St Marine Boutique Hotel is a charming Edwardian Home overlooking the St. Kilda Beach and Marina. Our beautifully appointed, spacious rooms allow guests to breakfast and relax in privacy. It is a short stroll to the buzz of Acland Street and its many fine restaurants, cafes and bars. A short Tram trip to the City Centre and the Casino. World famous Chappel Street is close by. We are 10 mins. from the Tasmanian Ferry.

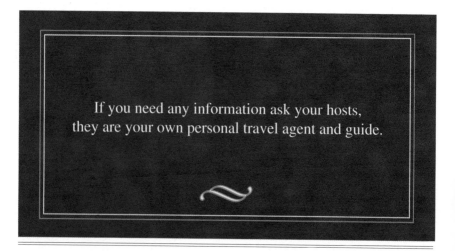

If you need any information ask your hosts,
they are your own personal travel agent and guide.

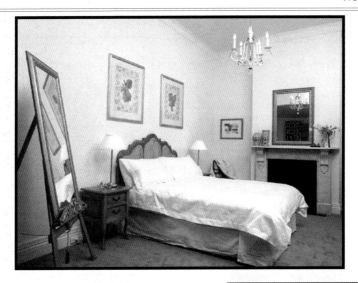

Melbourne - St Kilda West

Homestay B & B Self Contained   5 km S of Melbourne

Bishopsgate House   AAATourism ★★★★☆
Margaret Tudball and Ross Bishop
57 Mary Street, St Kilda West, Vic 3182

Tel: (03) 9525 4512 Fax: (03) 9525 3024
Mobile: 0402 057 351
marg@bishopsgate.com.au
www.bishopsgate.com.au

Double $165-$195 Single $145-$175 (Special Breakfast)
Dinner B/A Licensed property Credit Cards accepted
1 King/Twin 1 King 4 Queen 3 Single (5 bdrm)
2 Ensuite 1 Private 1 Share

Bishopsgate is a stunningly renovated two storey 1890's terrace
home furnished with antiques.   The three individually themed
guest rooms and   2 bedroomed apartment are luxuriously
appointed with quality fittings. Facilities include en-suites,
TV, tea and coffee making facilities, and individually controlled
heating and cooling.
Enjoy using Bishopsgate's own designer toiletries.
Bishopsgate is located in a grand, broad, tree-lined street. One
block from St Kilda's Fitzroy Street and just two blocks away
is the beach, rollerblading and bike riding.
Bishopsgate is the perfect accommodation for both tourism
and business.

 INN·HOUSE™

Melbourne - Surrey Hills   *B & B*   *12 km E of Melbourne*

Chestnut Cottage Bed & Breakfast   AAAT★★★★
Barbara and David Kitchen
15 Chestnut Street, Surrey Hills, Vic 3127

Tel: (03) 9808 6644 Fax: (03) 9808 6633
bandb@chestnutcottage.com.au
www.chestnutcottage.com.au
Double $110-$130 Single $75-$95
(Continental Breakfast) Credit Cards accepted
1 Queen (1 bdrm)
1 Private

Charming, modern cottage, separated from the main residence and situated in an attractive, tranquil garden. Generously sized bed-sitting room. Tea/coffee making facilities; refrigerator. Short stroll to local shops and city tram. Direct access by tram to Camberwell Junction, Tennis Centre, Melbourne Cricket Ground and central Melbourne. Easy access by car and/or tram to local restaurants. Convenient access to the city and Tullamarine Airport via the Eastern Freeway. A peaceful and comfortable retreat, providing excellent accommodation for tourists and business people.

Melbourne - Williamstown   *B & B*   *13 km SW of Melbourne*

Heathville House   AAATourism ★★★★
Philip Mawer & Stuart Absalom
171 Aitken Street, Williamstown, Vic 3016

Tel: (03) 9397 5959 Fax: (03) 9397 0030
Mobile: 0419 589 404   heath@jeack.com.au
www.melbournebest.com.au/heathville.html
Double $120-$140 Single $90-$110 (Full Breakfast)
Credit Cards accepted Pet on property
3 Queen 1 Twin (4 bdrm)
1 Ensuite 2 Private

Heathville House (c 1894) at Williamstown, Melbourne's first seaport, is the perfect base while visiting Melbourne. Accommodation with all the comforts of home includes four guest rooms, sitting room and sunny conservatory where breakfast using organic produce is served. The historic waterfront, cafes, restaurants, shops, galleries, heritage walks, swimming beach, Scienceworks, yacht clubs and wetlands are within walking distance or accessible by car. Melbourne's CBD is 15 minutes drive across Westgate Bridge and the M1 to the Great Ocean Road is 5 minutes away. Accredited Tourism Business.

Melbourne - Williamstown   *B & B*   *6km W of Melbourne*

North Haven By the Sea   AAATourism ★★★★
Margaret Weyl-Willett
69 Merrett Drive, Williamstown, Vic 3016

Tel: (03) 9399 8399 Fax: (03) 9397 8903
Mobile: 0417 564 676   mw2@bigpond.com.au
www.mraust.com
Double $100-$145 Single $70-$100 (Full Breakfast)
Child $50-$75 Dinner $25 pp
Credit Cards accepted Pets welcome
2 King/Twin 1 King 1 Queen 1 Double (3 bdrm)
1 Ensuite 1 Share

A modern home with sea and park views, close to restaurants and public transport. Three guest rooms with ensuite including spa or private bathroom. Private lounge with TV, VCR and Stereo. Outdoor covered patio, balcony to watch the sun set over the sea, outdoor heated spa and secure undercover parking. Walking, jogging and cycling track at front door. Dinner on request. Multiple night rates available. Children welcome with playground equipment in back yard. Pets welcome.

Melbourne - Wonga Park   *Self Contained B & B   5 km E of Warrandyte*

A Tudor Manor   AAATourism ★★★★☆
Inez & Keith Bowker
55 Jumping Creek Road, Wonga Park, Vic 3115

Tel: (03) 9722 2699 Mobile: 0418 510 413
inez@atudormanor.com
www.atudormanor.com

Double $99-$185 (Special Breakfast) Child $20
Dinner $20 - $65 double divan for 2 kids in SC
Credit Cards accepted
1 King/Twin 2 King 1 Double (4 bdrm)
3 Ensuite 1 Share

Not city, not quite country, gateway to the Yarra Valley. That's where you'll find A Tudor Manor. A place of elegance and superb hospitality. K/S beds, huge airy rooms and all the comforts of home. Need pampering? One spa bath ensuite, another a private sauna. Sunny courtyard with fountain & gazebo to relax . A game of billiards in the billiard room? Open log fire in guest lounge for cozy winter evenings and to top it all off a gourmet breakfast. Other meals by arrangement.

Metung   *B & B   250m E of Metung*

Clovelly of Metung B & B   AAATourism ★★★★☆
Bev and Ken Beecroft
5/7 Essington Close, Metung, Vic 3904

Tel: (03) 5156 2428 Fax: (03) 5156 2424
clovellybandb@datafast.net.au
www.clovellybedandbreakfast.com

Double $130-$165 Single $105-$132
(Special Breakfast) Credit Cards accepted
3 Queen (3 bdrm)
3 Ensuite

Clovelly means pampering, comfort & relaxation. Historic Clovelly sits on 1 1/3acres of peaceful gardens and overlooks Bancroft Bay and the Village of Metung. The Queen size guest rooms will delight you, they feature enormous ensuites with twin spas and fern filled atriums. Clovelly is just 250m from the village, with its gift shops, restaurants and waterfront hotel. It's just a short drive to galleries, wineries, rivers, lakes, bush walks or ocean beaches and mountain streams - It's all here waiting for you! Children - not suitable. No pet facilites.

Mildura   *Homestay B & B   15 km E of Mildura*

Mildura's Linsley House
Colin & Desley Rankin
PO Box 959, Mildura, Vic 3502

Tel: (03) 5024 8487 Fax: (03) 5024 8914
Mobile: 0417 593 483
www.bbbook.com.au/milduraslinsleyhouse.html

Double $99 Single $66 (Full Breakfast)
Credit Cards accepted
2 Queen 2 Single (3 bdrm)
2 Ensuite

Linsley House B & B has a magnificent river view. Colin and Desley Rankin take pleasure in welcoming you to their charming and tranquil home which is situated in a quiet rural setting and has panoramic views of the garden and Murray River from the bedrooms.   The large lounge/dining area includes: full kitchen facilities, TV, fridge, woodfire, air-conditioning and comfortable antiques. Mildura is renown for its oranges, dried fruits, wineries and Mediterranean weather.

Victoria

Mount Beauty
B & B and Self Contained   *1.5 km N of Mount Beauty*

Braeview B & B   **AAATourism ★★★★☆**
4 Stewarts Road,
Mt Beauty, Vic 3699

Tel: (03) 5754 4746
Fax: (03) 5754 4757
Mobile: 0418 572 834
info@braeview.com.au
www.braeview.com.au

Double $110-$200 Single $77-$95 (Full Breakfast)
Dinner B/A Credit Cards accepted Pet on property
1 King/Twin 3 Queen 1 Double (5 bdrm)
5 Ensuite

MULTI AWARD WINNING B&B - VICTORIA'S ALPINE HIGH COUNTRY with a landscape that inspires the imagination and a view to remember! Explore the High Country or simply relax.

HOW LONG HAS IT BEEN?? - since you INDULGED ALL your senses. Imagine the intimacy of a crackling log fire, romantic candlelight dinner wine a spa........ and an early night ....one of life's pleasures! **INDULGE** yourselves with ICE COLD CHAMPAGNE, FABULOUS FOOD, AMBIENCE - all of this and more awaits you at BRAEVIEW.

We offer a self contained studio apartment with spa and open fire place, In-House accommodation in en-suited spa rooms or a self contained rammed earth cottage with wood fire and a glassed spa looking into a cottage garden.

In-House guests enjoy a gourmet cooked breakfast -how does fruit pancake drizzled with maple syrup and topped with yoghurt, or freshly baked muffins hot from the oven with coffee sound ....HUNGRY??

Adults retreat where "Inspector Morse" our staffy will greet you at the front gate. Ask about our Weekend Indulgence Escape or Mid Week Escape

BOOK YOUR MAGICAL ESCAPE TODAY or check us out at: www.braeview.com.au - Accredited Tourism business.

Mt Beauty - Tawonga South   *B & B*   *3 km N of Mt Beauty*

Springfield Cottage
Sue Bennett
Lot 4 Simmonds Creek Road,
Tawonga South, Vic 3698

Tel: (03) 5754 1112 Fax: (03) 5754 1112
Mobile: 0418 992 327   springfield@netc.net.au
www.bbbook.com.au/springfieldcottage.html
Double $125 Single $90 (Full Breakfast)
Credit Cards accepted
1 Queen (1 bdrm) 1 Ensuite

"A Special Escape" This Japanese themed Bed & Breakfast overlooks Mt Bogong and Mt Beauty and provides a smoke free environment for two guests. Set in peaceful sun drenched gardens this stylish comfortable getaway offers country tranquillity, yet is only 3 km from Mt Beauty. Guests are served gourmet breakfasts, complimentary chocolates & port and, of course, at days end your very own relaxing spa. Springfield Cottage gives you all the comforts of home and none of the responsibilities and is an experience not to be missed.

Orbost   *Homestay B & B*   *2 km E of Orbost*

Riverview Rural Retreat AAATourism ★★★☆
Julie & Peter Young
PO Box 621,
Orbost, Vic 3888

Tel: (03) 5154 2411 Fax: (03) 5154 1949
Mobile: 0409 542 413   riverview@datafast.net.au
www.bbbook.com.au/riverview.html
Double $95 Single $65 (Full Breakfast)
Child $35 Credit Cards accepted
1 Double 2 Single (2 bdrm) 1 Share

The easy to find getaway. Close to National Parks, Ninety Mile Beach, famous Buchan Caves, Rain Forest Centre, golf, tennis, bowls and gaming club. Featuring all home comforts, peaceful country living, liquor licence, air con, fans, wood fire. Fantastic views of Snowy River Valley from lounge and verandahs. BBQ area, native bird feeding daily in spacious gardens. A place to be thoroughly pampered by experienced hosts of an accredited tourism business. Children welcome. No pets. Our motto - Your comfort is our concern.

Phillip Island - Cowes   *Self Contained*   *400m E of Cowes PO*

Abaleigh on Lovers Walk AAATourism ★★★★☆
Jenny & Robert Hudson
6 Roy Court, Phillip Island, Cowes, Vic 3922

Tel: (03) 5952 5649 Fax: (03) 5952 2549
abaleigh@nex.net.au
www.bbbook.com.au/abaleigh.html
Double $160 Single $150 (Full Breakfast)
Extra person $45 Apartment from $190 dble
Credit Cards accepted
2 King/Twin 1 King 2 Queen (5 bdrm) 5 Ensuite

Abaleigh's FSC direct beach frontage apartments and studios offer luxurious, homely accommodation. Featuring: spas, water views, Jetmaster log fires, double showers, breakfast-stocked kitchens, laundries, courtyards with barbecues for outdoor living, TV, video, stereo and more. Five minutes foreshore stroll to restaurants and central Cowes. Peaceful, private, ideal for small groups or couples. Winner Best New Business, Best Hosted Accommodation 2002 Regional Tourism Awards. AAA ★★★★+, "Our third time here, better than ever, we'll be back." D&M Toorak.

Victoria

Phillip Island - Cowes *B & B Boutique Hotel*   *Centre of town*

The Castle Villa by the Sea   AAATourism ★★★★☆
Jenni & Harley Boyle
7-9 Steele Street, Cowes, Phillip Island

Tel: (03) 5952 1228 Fax: (03) 5952 3926
Mobile: 0418 566 857   castle@nex.net.au
www.thecastle.com.au

Double $165-$350 Single $90-$225
(Special Breakfast) Child $15 - $60 Dinner $65pp
Credit Cards accepted Smoking area inside
1 King 4 Queen 3 Double 4 Single (6 bdrm) 7 Ensuite

Intimate and luxurious Mediterranean-style villa moments from the beachfront and the village shops. Exquisite accommodation for only a small number of guests. Indulgent cooked breakfasts, restaurant dining and superb wines. Bar, guest lounges, open fireplace, chesterfields, sundecks, private terraces, art gallery and gardens. Standard suites or luxury apartments: kitchenettes, private sunroom, libraries and games, laundry service. Double spas, Jacuzzi or garden spa. Log fires, air-conditioned, ceiling fans, individual heating. "Age Good Food Guide" recommendation. Member Johansen's Recommended Hotels and Lodges/Australia's Finest Gourmet Retreats.

Phillip Island - Cowes *B & B   400m E of Cowes*

Genesta House   AAATourism ★★★★☆
Sam & Jean Lanyon
18 Steele Street, Cowes, Vic 3922

Tel: (03) 5952 3616 Fax: (03) 5952 3616
Mobile: 0417 197 331
genesta@nex.net.au
www.genesta.com.au

Double $120-$140 Single $90-$125
(Full Breakfast) Credit Cards accepted
4 Queen (4 bdrm)
4 Ensuite

Genesta House is located within minutes walk of beach, restaurants and shops. 10 mins drive to penguins and seals. Beautifully restored 100 year old home, it has 4 tastefully decorated rooms with private ensuite and entrance, QS beds, individual heating and cooling with views and access to our peaceful gardens, sundeck and saltwater spa. To ensure your visit to Genesta House is relaxing and peaceful children are not catered for.

Phillip Island - Cowes *B & B   Self Contained   400m E of Cowes PO*

Rothsaye on Lovers Walk   AAATourism ★★★★☆
Jennifer Ridgeway
2 Roy Court, Cowes, Vic 3922

Tel: (03) 5952 2057 Fax: (03) 5952 2691
Mobile: 0414 433 320   rothsaye@nex.net.au
www.rothsaye.com

Double $120-$180 (Full Breakfast)
Credit Cards accepted
3 King/Twin 2 Queen (5 bdrm)
5 Ensuite

Directly on a superb swimming beach, multi award winning Rothsaye offers a charming self contained cottage and 4 suites with a private gate that leads directly to beautiful broad stretches of beach where one can fish, swim, walk or just relax. Each features: King or Queen size bed, ensuite, kitchen (stocked for breakfast), laundry, lounge/dining facilities, barbecue patio and more. Restaurants and shops within 5 minute stroll along a floodlit Lovers Walk. The perfect, peaceful, private getaway. Smoking outside only.   AAAT 4 1/2 star rating.

Phillip Island - Glen Forbes   *Self Contained B & B   21km N of San Remo*

Coorie Doon Country Retreat   AAAT★★★★☆
Judy & David Dewar
1205 Dalyston-Glen Forbes Road,
Glen Forbes, Vic 3990

Tel: (03) 5678 8451 Fax: (03) 5678 8791
cooriedoon@waterfront.net.au
www.bbbook.com.au/cooriedoon.html

Double $140 Single $100 (Full Breakfast)
Child from $25 Dinner from $35pp by arrangement
Credit Cards accepted Pets welcome
2 Queen 2 Single (3 bdrm)   2 Ensuite 1 Private

"Coorie Doon" an easy 90 min drive from Melbourne and only 15 mins to Phillip Island and Wonthaggi. Set on 5 acres, high in the hills with spectacular views to Venus Bay and Wilsons Promontory this is country living at its best. Your choice of S/C Spa Suite for a couple or S/C Bluestone 2 bedroom cottage for a couple or small family (max. 2 children). Queen beds, wood fires and peace and quiet. Judy's delicious home cooked dinner available by prior arrangement. Children and pets welcome in the cottage.**2170**

Phillip Island - Ventnor   *Farmstay B & B   7 km W of Cowes*

First Class B & B
Graeme Wells
Ventnor Road, Ventnor, Phillip Island

Tel: (03) 5956 8329 Fax: (03) 5956 8373
Mobile: 0408 389 284
gwells@waterfront.net.au
www.penguins.org.au

Double $80-$150 Single $60-$100 (Full Breakfast)
Credit Cards accepted Pets welcome
6 Queen 2 Single (6 bdrm)
6 Ensuite

Fine country accommodation with panoramic views of Westernport Bay and the Mornington Peninsula. A traditional B&B in a tranquil rural setting, a touch of paradise near to the Penguin Parade, Seal Rocks Sea Life Centre and the Nobbies boardwalks. Your friendly host will delight you from our country kitchen. Luxury Spa Rooms, Log Fire, Pool Table, Horse Riding available.

Port Fairy   *B & B   Port Fairy Central*

Boathouse on Moyne   AAATourism ★★★★
Denise & Gordon Harman
19 Gipps Street, Port Fairy, Vic 3284

Tel: (03) 5568 2608 Fax: (03) 5568 2740
Mobile: 0418 577 291
www.bbbook.com.au/boathouse.html

Double $100 Single $70 (Special Breakfast)
 Credit Cards accepted
1 Queen 1 Double 1 Twin 2 Single (2 bdrm)
1 Ensuite 1 Private

The "Boathouse on Moyne" is situated right on the historic Moyne River fishing port. If you wander out the front gate you are right on the jetty where the fishing trawlers bring in their catch. Easy walking distance to shopping centre, main beach and restaurants. Make yourself at home in this spacious bed & breakfast with guests' lounge, TV, kitchen, fridge and tea and coffee-making facilities. We prepare generous breakfasts which include freshly-baked croissants, fresh fruit, fruit juice and locally made jams.

Victoria

Port Fairy   B & B   *500m W of Port Fairy P.O*

Kingsley Bed & Breakfast   AAATourism ★★★★
Peter Strickland & Angela Beagley
71 Cox Street,
Port Fairy, Vic 3284

Tel: (03) 5568 1269 Fax: (03) 5568 2069
www.bbbook.com.au/kingsleybb.html
Double $90 Single $60 (Full Breakfast)
Credit Cards accepted
2 Queen (2 bdrm)
1 Ensuite 1 Private

Kingsley, a beautifully restored Federation house (c1913), is the ideal place to stay and enjoy Port Fairy's natural and historic attractions. Both our individually decorated guest rooms have open gas coal fireplaces. Our guests have exclusive use of the formal sitting room with original Art Nouveau mantelpiece and pressed metal ceiling and enjoy a leisurely breakfast served in the elegant dining room. You can always be sure of a warm welcome at Kingsley. Our two cats are discretely kept away from guest areas, unless you are happy with their company.

Port Fairy   *Self Contained B & B*   *100m S of Post Office*

Hanley House   AAATourism ★★★☆
Ann Parker
14 Sackville Street, Port Fairy, Vic 3284

Tel: (03) 5568 2709 Mobile: 0428 106 575
hanleyhouse@port-fairy.com
www.bbbook.com.au/hanleyhouse.html
Double $95-$105 Single $70-$85 (Special Breakfast)
Child $30 Self-Contained $150
2 Queen 2 Single (2 bdrm)
2 Private

Gracious home offers two large beautifully appointed bedrooms. Each has queen and single bed and own bathroom. Large sitting/music room with log fire. Breakfast room adjoining sheltered courtyard and garden. Guests warmly welcomed to a hosted stay or partly or fully self-contained accommodation. Hanley House has strong musical links with talented and well known musicians performing there. Archie Roach recorded his last CD in the music room. Central location offers a relaxing stay with easy walks to all the delights of Port Fairy. Off street parking. Children by arrangement. Pets outside only.

Port Fairy   *Self Contained B & B*   *Port Fairy Central*

Cherry Plum Cottage B & B   AAATourism ★★★★
Anne and John Ardlie
37 Albert Road,
Port Fairy, Vic 3284

Tel: (03) 5568 2433 Fax: (03) 5568 3006
cherryplum@bigpond.com
www.bbbook.com.au/cherryplumcottagebb.html
Double $100-$120 Single $90 (Full Breakfast)
1 Double (1 bdrm)
1 Ensuite

Situated on 4 acres in historic Port Fairy, Cherry Plum Cottage is a spacious, one roomed timber cottage, complete with period furnishings, kitchenette and BBQ. Set in a leafy garden amongst historic buildings we are well located to enjoy the old wharf, restaurants and beaches. We offer a traditional breakfast of local breads, home made preserves and farm eggs, cooked on a wood stove and served in your host's adjoining 1860's stone cottage or should you prefer, a "Pamper hamper" delivered to your cottage.

Portland   *B & B*   *Portland*

Burswood Homestead B & B
AAATourism ★★★★☆   Carol Frost & Ken Rogan
15 Cape Nelson Road, Portland, Vic 3305

Tel: (03) 5523 4686 Fax: (03) 5523 7141
burswood@ansonic.com.au
www.bbbook.com.au/burswood.html

Double $145-$220 Single $105-$135
(Special Breakfast) Child POA
Family rates POA Credit Cards accepted
6 Queen 1 Double 3 Twin 5 Single (7 bdrm)
5 Ensuite 2 Private

Be our special guest at Burswood Homestead (c1856), the bluestone mansion of Edward Henty, Victoria's founding settler offering the ultimate in luxurious heritage accommodation in the gracious 19th C style (with modern, private facilities) to which you could quite easily become accustomed. Nestled within 12 acres of historic gardens but still just a gentle 15 minute stroll from the town centre and restaurants, enjoy Devonshire tea on arrival in the grand drawing room, and relax over a full cooked breakfast in the sunroom overlooking the garden.

Princetown - Twelve Apostles   *6 km E of Princetown*

Homestay B & B

Arabella Country House   AAATourism ★★★★☆
Lynne & Neil Boxshall
7219 Great Ocean Road, Princetown, Vic 3269

Tel: (03) 5598 8169 Fax: (03) 5598 8186
arabella.ch@bigpond.com   www.greatoceanroad.au

Double $110-$120 Single $75 (Full Breakfast)
Child $25 Dinner $15 - $30
Credit Cards accepted Pet on property
3 Queen 1 Double 2 Single (4 bdrm)   4 Ensuite

Guests from Australia and overseas enjoy Arabella's quality accommodation while exploring 12 Apostles, Port Campbell National Park and Otway National Park. Lynne and Neil's modern Australian colonial design rural homestead has guest wing with private entry, spacious rooms, queen-size beds, TV, ensuite bathrooms, shared lounge, tea and coffee always available. All rooms have panoramic views. Our corgi and cats will help you to enjoy our cosy fire or sun filled verandah. Complemented by our sumptuous Australia country breakfast.

Rutherglen   *B & B*   *45 km W of Albury/Wodonga*

Holroyd Bed & Breakfast   AAAT★★★★
John Stevenson & Charles Dunn
28 Church Street, Rutherglen, Vic 3685

Tel: (02) 6032 8218 Fax: (02) 6032 8218
holroyd@net.net.au
www.holroyd.visitrutherglen.com.au

Double $135 Single $100 (Full Breakfast)
Dinner $45 Credit Cards accepted Pet on property
1 King 1 Queen (2 bdrm)
1 Ensuite 1 Private

Holroyd Bed & Breakfast offers superb accommodation surrounded by lush award winning gardens in the heart of town. Choose from our charming Muscat room with ensuite or Tokay with its own private bathroom. Relax and enjoy a hearty country style breakfast in the dining room, or on the verandah and enjoy the gardens. Dinner and picnic hampers can be arranged with 24 hour notice. Curl up with a book or talk to the cats whilst you relax and unwind. An easy drive to some of Australia's finest wineries.

Victoria

Rye   *Self Contained B & B*   *3 km S of Rye*

Hilltonia Homestead   AAATourism ★★★★☆
Jo-Anne Williamson
Lot B1 Browns Road, Rye, Vic 3941

Tel: (03) 5985 2654 Fax: (03) 5985 2684
sales@hilltonia.com.au
www.hilltonia.com.au

Double $145-$260 (Continental & Full Breakfast)
Credit Cards accepted
1 King/Twin 1 King 7 Queen (9 bdrm)
9 Private

Experience for yourself the pleasures of Hilltonia Homestead. Set amongst 40 picturesque acres on the Mornington Peninsula (1 hour form Melbourne). Select from five uniquely themed and totally private cottages marked around the property. Each with bayviews or dazzling sunset views over rolling sand dunes. Spa's, TV/Video/CD, Kitchen, Balcony with BBQ. Alternatively, select from four traditional B&B suites within the main homestead. Lagoon swimming pool & Tennis court. Minutes to Bay & Ocean beaches, fine wineries and superb golf courses.

Rye Beach - Mornington Peninsula   *2km S of Rye Beach*
Self Contained B & B

Acacia Rye   AAATourism ★★★★★
Pene & Des Moxey
32 Bethany Close, Rye Beach, Vic 3941

Tel: (03) 5985 8820 Fax: (03) 5985 1377
Mobile: 0417 099 044   acaciarye@pacific.net.au
home.pacific.net.au/~acaciarye

Double $225-$275 Single $210-$260
(Full Breakfast) Credit Cards accepted
3 Queen (3 bdrm)   3 Ensuite

Award winning five star romantic getaway. Luxurious Suites designed for elegance and charm have air-conditioning, TV, Video, CD. Ensuites offer large spa baths and double showers. The guest lounge, opening onto the floodlit swimming pool (solar) and outdoor hot spa, has rural views, separate entrance and gas log fireplace. Choose from in-house suites (silver service breakfast) or the self-contained Studio (breakfast provisions). Peninsula attractions and Sorrento ferries close by. "Enjoy every luxury of the modern day without compromising the ambience of yesteryear".

Torquay - Surf Coast   *Self Contained B & B*   *17 km S of Geelong*

Ocean Manor B & B   AAATourism ★★★★☆
Helen & Bob Bailey
3 Glengarry Drive, Torquay, Vic 3228

Tel: (03) 5261 3441 Fax: (03) 5261 9140
Mobile: 0407 597 100   oceanmanor@bigpond.com
www.bbbook.com.au/oceanmanorbb.html

Double $110-$130 Single $90-$100
(Continental Breakfast) Child $20
Family Suite $150 Credit Cards accepted
1 Queen 1 Twin (2 bdrm)   1 Ensuite 1 Share

The 2 bedroom suite is situated upstairs to ensure privacy and take maximum advantage of the ocean view. The master bedroom features a queen sized bed, en suite bathroom and walk in robe. Adjoining is a combined lounge and dining area which leads onto a decked balcony with sweeping ocean views. The air conditioned lounge has Foxtel, TV and video. The mini kitchen with fridge and microwave leads to a second bedroom with separate toilet facilities and 2 single beds. A generous continental breakfast is included.

Wangaratta   *B & B   6 km E of Wangaratta*

The Pelican   AAATourism ★★★☆
Margaret & Bernie Blackshaw
RMB 2975, Wangaratta, Vic 3678

Tel: (03) 5727 3240 Mobile: 0413 082 758
pelicanblackshaw@hotmail.com
www.bbbook.com.au/thepelican.html
Double $100 Single $65 (Full Breakfast) Child $35
Dinner $25 B/A Credit Cards accepted Pets welcome
1 Queen 1 Twin 2 Single (3 bdrm)
1 Private 1 Share

The Pelican is a charming historic homestead set in parklike surroundings. Cattle and horses are raised on the 400 acres and early risers can go "trackside" to watch the harness horses at work. Guest rooms are in an upstairs wing of the home and have lovely country views where peacocks and pelicans are often spotted. The main bedroom has its own private balcony overlooking a lagoon fringed with giant redgums. Hearty breakfasts feature homegrown produce and evening meals are available on request. We have pets.

Warrnambool   *Homestay B & B   Warrnambool*

Merton Manor Exclusive B & B   AAATourism ★★★★☆
Pamela & Ivan Beechey
62 Ardlie Street,
Warrnambool, Vic 3280

Tel: (03) 5562 0720 Fax: (03) 5561 1220
Mobile: 0417 314 364
merton@ansonic.com.au
members.datafast.net.au/merton
Double $150-$170 Single $130 (Full Breakfast)
Credit Cards accepted
1 King/Twin 5 Queen 2 Single (6 bdrm)
6 Ensuite

Merton Manor is a traditional B&B set within an historic Victorian villa. It features antiques, open fires, billiard and music rooms and grand dining room. All suites feature private entrances, climate control heating and air conditioning, private lounge rooms and ensuites with double spas. Merton Manor is situated close to the cultural attractions and restaurants of Warrnambool. AAAT 4 1/2 stars.

Warrnambool   *Self Contained B & B   Warrnambool*

Walsingham B & B
John & Kathy Moir
12 Henna Street, Warrnambool, Vic 3280

Tel: (03) 5561 7978 Fax: (03) 5561 2095
Mobile: 0427 617 978   Walsingham@bigpond.com
www.seasidecottages.net
Double $110-$150 Single $90-$130 (Full Breakfast)
Dinner B/A Cottage $150 Credit Cards accepted
5 Queen 1 Double 1 Twin 2 Single (7 bdrm)
6 Ensuite 1 Private

"Walsingham" Bed and Breakfast (circa 1881) gives you location, luxury and variety at reasonable prices. Relax in old world character and charm and enjoy living in a special place overlooking the cottage garden. Enjoy a tasteful specially prepared breakfast. Choose from: Self Contained Cottages 1 or 3 bedroom or the B&B 3 room suite with spa and open fire or 2 bedrooms (one Queen and one double) each with ensuite. Cool house in summer and warm in winter. Children welcome in cottages. No pets.

Victoria

Warrnambool   *Self Contained B & B*   *Warrnambool*

Wollaston B & B   AAATourism ★★★★
Geoff & Helen Smith
84 Wollaston Road, Warranambool, Vic 3280

Tel: (03) 5562 0050 Fax: (03) 5562 0385
Mobile: 0407 097 840
inquiry@wollaston.com.au
www.wollaston.com.au
Double $100-$140 Single $100-$110 (Full Breakfast)
Credit Cards accepted
1 King 1 Queen 1 Double (3 bdrm)
1 Ensuite 1 Private

History - Quality - Hospitality. Enjoy the peace and tranquillity of the elegant homestead (c 1854) or the private olde world Governor's Cottage. A quiet retreat only 4 minutes form CBD. Set on 4 acres with river frontage. Enjoy shaded gardens in summer and open fires in winter.. Highly commended by Warrnambool Business Achievement Awards, "The Age" Travelogue - "Wollaston is a delightful secluded retreat". Great starting point or finish to the Great Ocean Road and famous 12 Apostles.

Wilsons Promontory   *B & B Guest House*   *4 km S of Yanakie*

Vereker House   AAATourism ★★★★
Mary and John O'Shea
10 Iluka Close, Foley Road, Yanakie, Vic 3960

Tel: (03) 5687 1431 Fax: (03) 5687 1480
vereker@tpg.com.au
www.vereker.com
Double $140-$160 Single $110 (Full Breakfast)
Dinner $44 Credit Cards accepted
3 Queen 1 Twin (4 bdrm)
4 Ensuite

Our traditional guesthouse is located in native gardens with abundant birdlife and sweeping mountain and sea views to Wilsons Promontory. The massive timber posts, beams and adobe walls combine to produce an ambience and charm which will suit the discerning traveler who appreciates relaxation and comfort. Relax by the log fire in the great hall, dine in the conservatory overlooking the Vereker Mountains or browse through the library. Quality home cooked meals and an extensive range of boutique local wines are available to complement your stay.

Wodonga - Baranduda   *Farmstay Homestay B & B*   *13 km S of Wononga*

Baranduda Homestead B & B
Ken and Liz Fuchsen
RMB 1027 Kiewa Valley Highway,
Wodonga, Vic 3691

Tel: (02) 6020 8888 Fax: (02) 6020 8888
Mobile: 0409 998 118
bb@barandudahomestead.com.au
www.barandudahomestead.com.au
Double $110 Single $95 (Full Breakfast)
Dinner $25 Credit Cards accepted
1 Queen (1 bdrm) 1 Ensuite

Baranduda Homestead offers a peaceful, spacious retreat where the beautiful Yackandandah Creek and Kiewa River Valleys meet. Enjoy the hospitality offered by 4th generation owners Ken & Liz, their children and their dog Rockie. Take pleasure in a leisurely walk, open fire, private court yard, mountain views, wineries, nearby snowfields, historic gold mining towns, antiques, cosy country pubs, Lake Hume and Murray River water sports.

Yackandandah   *Self Contained Homestay B & B   30 km S of Wodonga*

Downham House   AAATourism ★★★☆
Diana Nicholls
Racecourse Road, Yackandandah, Vic 3749

Tel: (02) 6027 1690 Fax: (02) 6027 1690
www.bbbook.com.au/downham.html
Double $99-$125 Single $66-$90
(Continental & Full Breakfast)
Child $30 Pet on property
3 Queen (3 bdrm)
1 Ensuite 1 Private 2 Share

Comfort Beauty Views Service. Downham House is situated in a beautiful area on 8 acres in NE Victoria. Magnificent views of tree covered hills, mountains, undulation farmland, small lake, Bird life, breathtaking sunrises, sunsets, starlit skies viewed in comfort from guests rooms, underfloor heating giving warm comfy Queen beds in winter. Cooling in summer. Spacious living and dining area. Sumptuous or light breakfast. So much to see and do. Historic buildings, antiques, wineries, bush walking, golf, festivals, snow & water skiing. Friendly enjoyable. Wheelchair friendly.

Yarra Valley - Healesville   *B & B   6.5 km N of Healesville*

Brentwood   AAATourism ★★★☆
Anne Garner and George Nowara
506 Myers Creek Road, Healesville, Vic 3777

Tel: (03) 5962 5028 Fax: (03) 5962 4749
Mobile: 0417 326 193   brentwood@hotkey.net.au
www.brentwoodbandb.com.au
Double $110-$130 Single $75-$90 (Full Breakfast)
Credit Cards accepted
2 Queen 1 Twin (3 bdrm)
3 Ensuite

A warm welcome awaits you at 'Brentwood'. A tranquil oasis, situated amid towering gums and ferny gullies, adjacent to Yarra Ranges National Park with walking tracks from back door. A much loved 1920's property, modernised, offering comfortable ensuite accommodation. Separate entrances. Full vegetarian/vegan breakfast. Wake to the sound of Lyrebirds, breakfast with parrots. Be lulled to sleep by the creek, visited by wallabies, wombats and deer, yet only 10 minutes from town, wineries, restaurants and wildlife sanctuary. Children by arrangement. Sorry no pets.

Yarra Valley - Yarra Glen   *B & B   7 km N of Yarra Glen*

Amethyst Lodge   AAATourism ★★★★★
Marjorie & Mike Woollands
139 Wills Road, Dixons Creek, Yarra Glen, Vic 3775

Tel: (03) 5965 2559 Fax: (03) 5965 2559
Mobile: 0428 409 010
woollands@amethystlodge.com.au
www.amethystlodge.com.au
Double $154-$220 Single $143-$209 (Full Breakfast)
Dinner $33 - $37.50 Credit Cards accepted
4 King/Twin (4 bdrm)   4 Ensuite

Idyllic Five Star Retreat amid vineyards with Private Balconies, Spas, Gym, Games room, Dining room and Sitting room. Start your day with a wonderful breakfast here or a Balloon ride over 'The Valley', followed by visits to Wineries, Healesville Sanctuary, Galleries and Antique Shops or sampling wonderful local produce. Finish at one of our outstanding Restaurants. You can of course just relax at Amethyst Lodge with a glass of wine and a good book! "No etiquette book can do you justice! Superb small touches and attention to detail." KR.

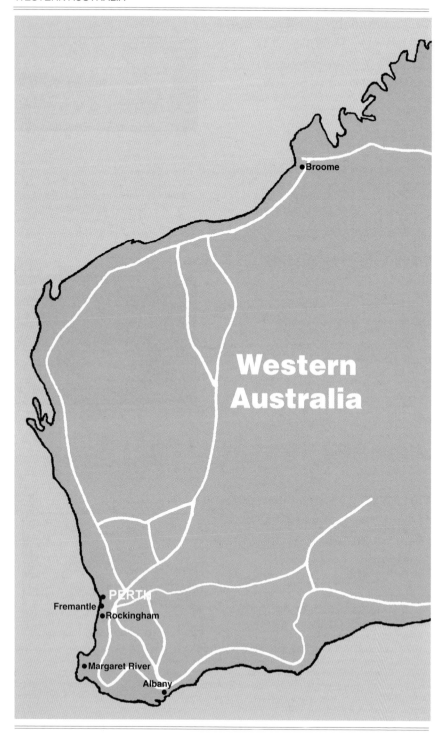

Western
Australia

Broome

PERTH
Fremantle
Rockingham
Margaret River
Albany

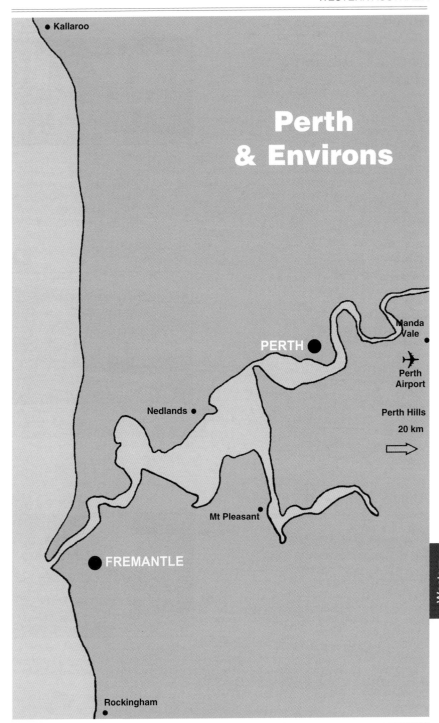

Albany *Homestay B & B   2 km E of Albany*

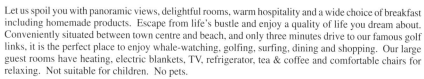

Clarence House
John & Beth Berridge
110 Hare Street, Albany, WA 6330

Tel: (08) 9841 5409 Fax: (08) 9841 5409
Mobile: 0418 945 940   clarence@albanyis.com.au
www.albanyis.com.au/~clarence
Double $95-$110 Single $90-$100 (Full Breakfast)
Third person sharing $37.50 Credit Cards accepted
2 Queen (2 bdrm)
2 Ensuite

Let us spoil you with panoramic views, delightful rooms, warm hospitality and a wide choice of breakfast including homemade products. Escape from life's bustle and enjoy a quality of life you dream about. Conveniently situated between town centre and beach, and only three minutes drive to our famous golf links, it is the perfect place to enjoy whale-watching, golfing, surfing, dining and shopping. Our large guest rooms have heating, electric blankets, TV, refrigerator, tea & coffee and comfortable chairs for relaxing. Not suitable for children. No pets.

Albany *Homestay B & B   5 km E of Albany*

B & B by the Sea   AAATourism ★★★★☆
Sue Buckingham and Les Jones
7 Griffiths Street, Albany, WA 6330

Tel: (08) 9844 1135 Fax: (08) 9844 1135
Mobile: 0417 990 673
holiday@bbythesea.com.au
www.bbythesea.com.au
Double $99-$110 (Full Breakfast)
Child $35 Credit Cards accepted
2 Queen 1 Double (3 bdrm) 3 Ensuite

Welcome to our home by the sea, ideally located close to the town centre, golf course, and walking trails. Imagine the sound of waves. Imagine panoramic views of the bay from your window. Imagine sumptuous breakfasts on a sunny balcony, or in a cosy dining room. Relax in our modern and spacious rooms, all with ensuites, TV, fridge, comfortable beds, and heating. Offering absolute comfort and privacy at an affordable price. Watch whales during the migration season (May to November) A memorable holiday by the sea.

Albany *Homestay B & B   0.5 km E of Albany*

Memories of Albany B & B   AAAT★★★★☆
Su and Bob Walton
118 Brunswick Road, Albany, WA 6330

Tel: (08) 9842 9787 Fax: (08) 9842 6516
Mobile: 0418 139 157   memoriesBandB@bigpond.com
memoriesofalbany.com.au
Double $95-$115 Single $80-$95 (Special Breakfast)
Extra person $40 - $50 Credit Cards accepted
2 Queen 2 Twin (4 bdrm)
3 Ensuite 1 Share

"Rekindle Old 'Memories' or give birth to new ones." Your hosts Bob and Sue Walton welcome you into our elegant old home (C 1889) to enjoy our English-style B & B. Share the friendly warm ambience of a bygone era. Luxury Queen and twin ensuite bedrooms with all those homely comforts and more to ensure your stay is one of 'Happy Memories'. Park surrounds, minutes walk to town cafes, restaurants, galleries, museums, beaches and eco tours. Just relax and enjoy the beautiful coastline and historical past.

Albany - Emu Point   *B & B*   *5 km S of Albany*

Kenryl House on Sea
Marjorie & Rodney Wright
4 Cunningham Street, Emu Point, Albany

Tel: (08) 9844 8585 Fax: (08) 9844 8787
Mobile: 0429 373 439
kenryl@westnet.com.au
www.bbbook.com.au/kenryl.html
Double $120 Single $95 (Full Breakfast)
1 Queen 1 Twin (2 bdrm)
1 Ensuite 1 Private

Kenryl House is situated on the beach at Emu Point with Water Views from both rooms. Guests share a sitting room with tv, games and books. Tea and coffee is available in the sitting room. Access to restaurant and cafe is a 2 minute walk. Kenryl is furnished in antiques and Blue & White china. Whale watching in season.

Broome   *B & B*   *1.5 km NE of China Town*

The Temple Tree B & B   AAATourism ★★★★
Helga & Terry Crisp
31 Anne Street, Broome, WA 6725

Tel: (08) 9193 5728 Fax: (08) 9193 5121
crisp@tpgi.com.au
www.bbbook.com.au/thetempletreebb.html
Double $89-$99 Single $75-$89 (Special Breakfast)
Dinner neg Credit Cards accepted
2 Double (2 bdrm)
2 Ensuite

The Temple Tree is located in old Broome within walking distance of Town Beach, shops and restaurants. Accommodation comprises two attractive double rooms each with ensuite and private entrance. Each has remote TV, fridge, clock radio, air-con/ceiling fans, tea and coffee. Each room has its own outside sitting area. Breakfast and dinner are served on the verandah which is screened from insects. To ensure the safety of wildlife in the garden we regret that we cannot accept pets. Phone for brochure.

Broome   *B & B*   *5 km N of Broome*

The Lounging Lizard B & B
Maureen and Mark
528 Broome Road, Broome, WA 6725

Tel: (08) 9193 7439 Fax: (08) 9193 7429
Mobile: 0417 536 508
lounging.lizard@bigpond.com
www.bbbook.com.au/lounginglizard.html
Double $120 Single $100 (Special Breakfast)
1 Queen 1 Double (2 bdrm)
2 Ensuite

Western Australia

The Lounging Lizard is a fully refurbished, rammed earth home set among established tropical gardens and includes a beautiful landscaped pool. Offering two bedrooms, each with huge private ensuites. One with spa/shower, the other with a double shower. Your hosts, Maureen and Mark are long term Kimberley residents and are eager to share their experiences and local knowledge with you. A peaceful, relaxing environment with Kimberley bush surrounds, but only 5 minutes drive from town or Cable Beach.

Fremantle   *Homestay   4 km E of Fremantle*

Homestay East Fremantle
Val & Ron Pyman
3 Munro Street,
East Fremantle, WA 6158

Tel: (08) 9339 4496 Fax: (08) 9339 4497
www.bbbook.com.au/homestayeastfremantle.html

Double $80 Single $50
(Continental Breakfast)
2 Single (1 bdrm)
1 Private

We live in a short quiet street, which ends in a panoramic view of Fremantle harbour, Swan River, Indian Ocean, magnificent at sunset. Within close proximity are excellent restaurants, yacht clubs, Rottnest Island ferries. Minutes away is wonderful cosmopolitan Fremantle, full of museums, cafes, shops, food, art, craft markets, fisherman's harbour, and fast rail service to Perth. Tea, coffee anytime, TV in room, patio smoking, no children or pets, bus 200 mtrs to Perth or Fremantle. Warm welcome assured by well travelled Aussies, Ron is a Rotarian.

Fremantle   *B & B   500m E of Fremantle*

Danum House   AAATourism ★★★★
Christine & Geoff Sherwin
6 Fothergill Street, Fremantle, WA 6160

Tel: (08) 9336 3735 Fax: (08) 9335 3414
danum@iinet.net.au
www.staywa.net.au/ads/danum

Double $100-$110 Single $90-$100 (Special Breakfast)
Credit Cards accepted Pet on property
2 Queen (2 bdrm)
1 Ensuite 1 Private

Danum House is a lovely Federation home situated close to Fremantle. Our accommodation offers elegantly furnished bedrooms, one ensuite and one with private facilities, each with its own TV. The comfortable sitting room has sound system, books, tea & coffee. Fremantle offers many tourist attractions including the famous markets, prison museum, galleries and historic buildings. Your hosts Christine and Geoff are travellers, enjoy bush walking, sport, music and reading and together with Brinnie the cat, will make your stay pleasant and relaxing in a smoke free haven for adults.

All our B&Bs are non-smoking
unless stated otherwise in the text.

Margaret River *Farmstay B & B* *16 km NW of Margaret River*

Valley Views B & B
Jan & Barry Walsh
Lot 2 Tindong-Treeton Road,
Margaret River, WA 6285

Tel: (08) 9757 4573 Fax: (08) 9757 8181
Mobile: 0429 11 62 78   valleyviews@westnet.com.au
www.hsnwa.com/valleyviews

Double $90 Single $60 (Full Breakfast)
Child $20 under 12yrs Dinner $20 - $35
2 Queen 2 Single (3 bdrm) 1 Share

Large colonial homestead on 108 acres with state forest on two sides. On the farm we have fine wools sheep, two cows, four horses, a friendly sheep dog and 4 boys and a girl at home sometimes. We grow wine grapes and olives. A great place to relax and enjoy country hospitality in a peaceful environment. Guests have large rooms, a comfortable lounge with log fire, library, fridge, tea facilities, microwave, TV, video, stereo and a barbecue outside. Children under school age not catered for. No pets or in-house smoking. Full cooked breakfast included.

Margaret River *B & B Guest House* *2 km W of Margaret River*

Kangaridge AAATourism ★★★★
Nikki and Barry Newton
cnr Walclffe & Devon,
Margaret River, WA 6285

Tel: (08) 9757 3939 Fax: (08) 9757 3939
Mobile: 0409 291 861   kanga@highway1.com.au
www.mronline.com.au/cape/accom/kanga

Double $120-$140 Single $100
(Continental Breakfast) Credit Cards accepted
4 Queen 2 Single (4 bdrm) 4 Ensuite

Adult Getaway. Unique 4 Star luxury accommodation set on 8 acres near Margaret River township, overlooking forest and prolific birdlife. Features indoor heated therapy pool and spa by the log fire. Only four suites so no crowds. All rooms queen sized with own ensuites, private decks, TV, video and tea making. Australian style homestead with rambling decks. Price is all inclusive with buffet continental breakfast(cooked breakfast is available), pitch & putt golf and mountain bikes. We offer a 10% discount card. Close to town beaches, wineries, and kangaroo colony. Massages and alternative healing available on request.

Margaret River *B & B Guest House* *10 km N of Margaret River*

The Noble Grape AAATourism ★★★★
Marlene, Brenton and Brittany Webb
Lot 18, Busell Highway, Cowaramup, WA 6284

Tel: (08) 9755 5538 Fax: (08) 9755 5538
Mobile: 0427 772 249   noblegrape@netserv.net.au
www.bbbook.com.au/thenoblegrape.html

Double $99 Single $82 (Continental Breakfast)
Child $12 6-12yrs Dinner B/A
Extra person $22 Credit Cards accepted
6 Queen 1 Double 4 Single (6 bdrm) 6 Ensuite

The Noble Grape is an intimate guesthouse in Margaret River Wine Region. Colonial style charm, antiques and English cottage gardens, with ensuites to all rooms. Within walking distance of galleries and the Regional Wine Centre, the vineyards and beaches are minutes away. Breakfasts are special in the sunny dining room overlooking the garden. Watch native birds enjoy the flower beds, come and have a grape holiday. Spacious rooms with ensuite, TV, radio, fridge, tea/coffee facilities, heating, ceiling fans. Catering for families and people with disabilities. Smoking outside. Hair dryers.

Western Australia

Margaret River *Farmstay B & B Self Contained   2.5 km W of Town*

Margaret House   AAATourism ★★★★
Bruce Darby
Cnr Wallcliffe Road and Devon Drive,
Margaret River

Tel: (08) 9757 2692 mhbb@starwon.com.au
www.margarethouse.starwon.com.au
Double $100-$120 Single $95-$120
(Continental Breakfast) Credit Cards accepted
Pets welcome
1 King/Twin 1 Queen 1 Twin (2 bdrm)
2 Ensuite

Nestled in a fragrant native garden that attracts an abundance of bird life, Margaret House is a charming stopover from which to base your Southwest adventure holiday. Situated on a picturesque 7 acre treed pasture property, each of our two units offer privacy and seclusion. Wake up to the sounds of the birds and watch the sheep and kangaroos grazing as you have breakfast on your private sundeck. Good walk trails are nearby and we have good access to the golf course, the beach, the wineries and many restaurants.

Margaret River *Self Contained   22 km S of Margaret River*

Boranup Forest Retreat
Sheila Penman
Cnr Caves & Sebbes Road, Margaret River, WA 6286

Tel: 08 9757 4111 or (08) 9757 7039
Fax: 08 97574111 Mobile: 0402 404 057
forestretreat@smartchat.net.au
www.bbbook.com.au/forestretreat.html
Double $110 (Special Breakfast) Child $15
Extra person $40 $250 per night (6 persons)
Credit Cards accepted
4 Queen 8 Single (4 bdrm) 1 Ensuite 1 Share

Magnificent Boranup Lodge allows self-catering luxury on 50 acres adjacent to Boranup Forest. Uniquely furnished from the on-site gallery, enjoy a glass of wine from well-known vineyards in front of the wood-burning stove or a game of snooker or table tennis. Visit nearby beaches or the breath-taking local caves. Relax observing kangaroos, emus or the wonderful bird-life that inhabit the property. Whether you are a couple, family or group Boranup caters for all your needs including cafe/restaurant on site. We can also arrange a chef-in-house.

Perth   *B & B   Separate/Suite 1 km NE of Perth*

Pension of Perth   AAATourism ★★★★
Andrew Martin
3 Throssell Street, Perth, WA 6000

Tel: (08) 9228 9049 Fax: (08) 9228 9290
Mobile: 0403 359 442   stay@pensionperth.com.au
www.pensionperth.com.au
Double $108 Single $80
(Continental & Full Breakfast)
Child $20 Credit Cards accepted
1 King/Twin 3 Queen 3 Double 2 Twin (7 bdrm)
7 Ensuite

The Pension of Perth is the perfect choice for couples looking for a special place to stay or business traveller wanting somewhere value for money sophisticated, homely and private. It has the amenities of a fine hotel. The luxurious refurbishment reflects the elegance and comfort of its origins in 1897. It overlooks Hyde Park. Within walking distance from the centre of Perth. Pamper package are available. Our A-la-carte breakfast menu will make your stay memorable.

Perth - Airport   *B & B   Self Contained   8 km E of Perth*

Airport Accommodation Perth   AAAT ★★★★
Wendy & Jamie Brindle
103 - 105 Central Avenue, Redcliffe, WA 6104

Tel: (08) 9478 2923 Fax: (08) 9478 2770
Freecall: 1800 447 000
wendy@accommodation-perthairport.com
www.accommodation-perthairport.com
Double $85 Single $65 (Continental Breakfast)
Self Contained from $450/wk Credit Cards accepted
4 Queen 1 Double 2 Twin (6 bdrm)
2 Ensuite 2 Private

Airport Accommodation Perth and Airport Bed & Breakfast offers in-house B&B as well as a self contained two bedroom/one bathroom cottage. Features include * Airport transfers * 10 minutes drive from central Perth * Five minutes walk to bus stop * 5 mins drive to Swan Valley and wineries * Easy access to Fremantle with courtesy drop off at local train station for extended stays. Your hosts have a 'wealth' of knowledge of WA. Restaurants within walking distance. "Come as guests and leave as friends."

Perth - Hills   *B & B Guest House   1 km N of Kalamunda*

Rosebridge House   AAATourism ★★★★☆
Peter & Rosemary Bridgement
86 Williams Street, Gooseberry Hill, WA 6076

Tel: (08) 9293 1741 Fax: (08) 9257 2778
peter@rosebridgehouse.com.au
www.rosebridgehouse.com.au
Double $125-$175 Single $100-$150
(Full Breakfast) Pet on property
3 Queen 2 Single (4 bdrm)   4 Ensuite

On the edge of Gooseberry Hill National Park, this charming Colonial home has four romantically furnished bedrooms, big brass beds, ensuites, two with spas, air-conditioning, refrigerator, television etc. Rooms have private access with French doors opening onto verandahs and surrounded by glorious gardens featuring a swimming pool. This romantic adult retreat is conveniently located just 1 km from the village of Kalamunda with its large variety of restaurants, Vineyards close by, 30 minutes from Perth City and 15 minutes form the Airport. Rosemary, Peter and their Golden Retrievers look forward to welcoming you.

Perth - Kallaroo   *B & B   22 km N of Perth*

Clareville House   AAATourism ★★★★☆
Michele and Stuart Ratcliffe
5 Clareville Crescent, Kallaroo, WA 6025

Tel: (08) 9401 9437 Fax: (08) 9401 9407
Mobile: 0404 876 370
ratcliffe.perth@onaustralia.com.au
www.clarevillehouse.com.au
Double $77-$99 Single $55-$71.5 (Full Breakfast)
Child $10 - $25 Credit Cards accepted
2 Double 1 Twin (3 bdrm) 1 Ensuite 1 Share

Luxurious a/c accommodation adjacent to pristine beaches on the Sunset Coast, in own wing with private entrance. Facilities consists of 3 double bedrooms, one with ensuite, the other two share a private bathroom. Downstairs lounge with fridge, tea/coffee making facilities, microwave, toaster, iron/ironing board. Upstairs games/lounge room with cable TV/VCR, stereo system and pool table. Balcony with ocean glimpses. Outside, heated swimming pool and BBQ area. Our border collie and two cats will make you very welcome.

Western Australia

Perth - Maida Vale   *Self Contained*   *3 km NW of Kalamunda*

Vale House   AAATourism ★★★☆
Dennis & Irene Thorburn
5 Casuarina Road, Maida Vale, WA 6057

Tel: (08) 9454 6462 Fax: (08) 9454 6233
Mobile: 0407 388 966
valehouse@ausconnect.net
www.bbbook.com.au/valehouse.html

Double $99 Single $66 (Continental Breakfast)
1 Queen 1 Double 2 Single (3 bdrm)
1 Family Share

Nestled in the foothills of Perth, amongst lush gardens and lots of trees; Vale House is the perfect place for a family getaway or for accommodation. We live next door and are available to help with directions and tourist information for the Perth area. A fully equipped kitchen and laundry, and all linen is supplied. Also a TV video, radio, bath, hair dryer, tile fire, ducted air. and under cover parking. Convenient to shopping centres, restaurants, sporting facilities, bush walks, bus stop and service station. "So comfortable, clean and tidy. Thanks Irene for your kindness." I&CD, NSW.

Perth - Nedlands   *Homestay B & B*   *5 km W of Perth Central City*

Caesia House Nedlands
Jane and David Tucker
32 Thomas Street, Nedlands, Perth, WA 6009

Tel: (08) 9389 8174 Fax: (08) 9389 8173
tuckers@iinet.net.au
www.caesiahouse.com

Double $95-$120 Single $85-$110 (Special Breakfast)
Child $20 Weekly rate   Credit Cards accepted
1 King/Twin 1 Queen (2 bdrm)
2 Ensuite

A quiet oasis in the city. Enjoy our executive home located only 7 minutes from city centre, near the Swan River, Kings Park(Views and Wildflowers) and UWA. A wonderful base for holiday or business with easy access to Airport. Off-street parking leads you to guest entrance and lounge with TV, library,desk,fridge, phone and internet. Enjoy breakfast, (including seasonal WA fruit and homemade jams) in our dining room, overlooking the pool or in the garden. Restaurants/cafes within strolling distance. Ask about our fine dining program. We look forward to welcoming you.

Rockingham   *B & B*   *2 km Rockingham*

Rockingham B & B   AAATourism ★★★★
Iain and Margaret Colquhoun
102 Penguin Road, Safety Bay, WA 6169

Tel: (08) 9527 6842   Mobile: 0419 832 177
Fax: (08) 9527 6842
rockinghambandb@bigpond.com
www.bbbook.com.au/rockinghambb.html

Double $85 Single $60 (Full Breakfast)
Child $25 Credit Cards accepted
1 Queen 2 Double 1 Twin 1 Single (4 bdrm)
2 Ensuite 1 Private

A warm friendly welcome awaits you at our spacious beach side accommodation only 45 minutes Perth Airport. Stroll to restaurants or shops. Take the ferry to Penguin Island or swim with the dolphins. Relax in the comfort of our lovely home which offers TV, video, fridge and tea/coffee making facilities. Air conditioned for your comfort in summer - cosy log fire in winter. Accommodation consists of large ensuite rooms, guest lounge & dining room. Enjoy a full hearty breakfast, a pre dinner drink on the balcony.

Index of B&B Names

Index

Index

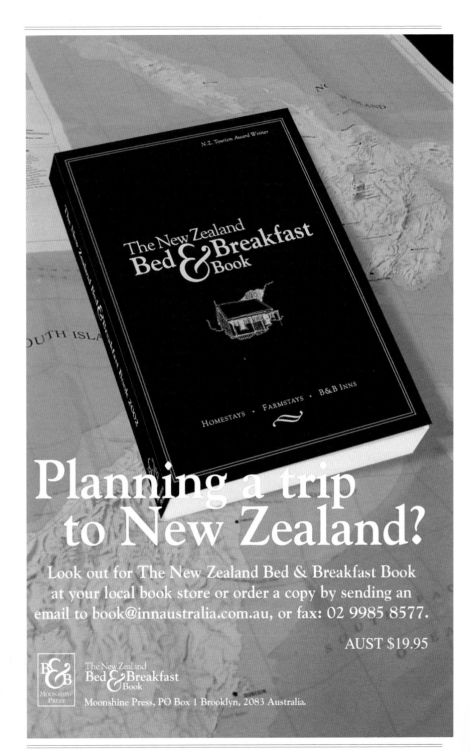

Index of Towns

Index

Notes